The Decline and Fall of the Roman Empire;

THE DECLINE AND FALL OF THE
ROMAN EMPIRE

VOL. XI

CONTENTS OF THE ELEVENTH VOLUME

CHAPTER LXI

Partition of the Empire by the French and Venetians — Five Latin Emperors of the Houses of Flanders and Courtenay — Their Wars against the Bulgarians and Greeks — Weakness and Poverty of the Latin Empire — Recovery of Constantinople by the Greeks — General Consequences of the Crusades

Digression on the Family of Courtenay

CONTENTS

CHAPTER LXII

The Greek Emperors of Nice and Constantinople — Elevation and Reign of Michael Palæologus — His false Union with the Pope and the Latin Church — Hostile Designs of Charles of Anjou — Revolt of Sicily — War of the Catalans in Asia and Greece — Revolutions and Present State of Athens

CHAPTER LXIII

Civil Wars, and Ruin of the Greek Empire — Reigns of Andronicus, the Elder and Younger, and John Palæologus — Regency, Revolt, Reign, and Abdication of John Cantacuzene — Establishment of a Genoese Colony at Pera or Galata — Their Wars with the Empire and City of Constantinople

CONTENTS

CHAPTER LXIV

Conquests of Zingis Khan and the Moguls from China to Poland — Escape of Constantinople and the Greeks — Origin of the Ottoman Turks in Bithynia — Reigns and Victories of Othman, Orchan, Amurath the First, and Bajazet the First — Foundation and Progress of the Turkish Monarchy in Asia and Europe — Danger of Constantinople and the Greek Empire

CHAPTER LXV

Elevation of Timour or Tamerlane to the Throne of Samarcand — His Conquests in Persia, Georgia, Tartary, Russia, India, Syria, and Anatolia — His Turkish War — Defeat and Captivity of Bajazet — Death of Timour — Civil War of the Sons of Bajazet — Restoration of the Turkish Monarchy by Mahomet the First — Siege of Constantinople by Amurath the Second

CONTENTS

CHAPTER LXVI

Application of the Eastern Emperors to the Popes — Visits to the West, of John the First, Manuel, and John the Second, Palæologus — Union of the Greek and Latin Churches, Promoted by the Council of Basil, and Concluded at Ferrara and Florence — State of Literature at Constantinople — Its Revival in Italy by the Greek Fugitives — Curiosity and Emulation of the Latins

CHAPTER LXVII

Schism of the Greeks and Latins — Reign and Character of Amurath the Second — Crusade of Ladislaus, King of Hungary — His Defeat and Death — John Huniades — Scanderbeg — Constantine Palæologus, last Emperor of the East

THE HISTORY OF THE DECLINE AND FALL OF THE ROMAN EMPIRE

CHAPTER LXI

*Partition of the Empire by the French and Venetians —
Five Latin Emperors of the Houses of Flanders and
Courtenay — Their Wars against the Bulgarians and
Greeks — Weakness and Poverty of the Latin Empire —
Recovery of Constantinople by the Greeks — General Con-
sequences of the Crusades*

AFTER the death of the lawful princes, the French and
Venetians, confident of justice and victory, agreed to divide
and regulate their future possessions.[1]   It was stipulated by
treaty, that twelve electors, six of either nation, should be
nominated; that a majority should choose the emperor of
the East; and that, if the votes were equal, the decision of
chance should ascertain the successful candidate.   To him,
with all the titles and prerogatives of the Byzantine throne,
they assigned the two palaces of Boucoleon and Blachernæ,
with a fourth part of the Greek monarchy.   It was defined
that the three remaining portions should be equally shared
between the republic of Venice and the barons of France,
that each feudatory, with an honourable exception for the

---

[1] See the original treaty of partition, in the Venetian Chronicle of Andrew
Dandolo, p 326–330 [Tafel und Thomas, Urkunden zur altern Handels-
und Staatsgeschichte der Republik Venedig, 1 454   The treaty was concluded and drawn up before the city was taken], and the subsequent election
in Villehardouin, No 136–140, with Ducange in his Observations, and the
1st book of his Histoire de Constantinople sous l'Empire des François.

doge, should acknowledge and perform the duties of homage and military service to the supreme head of the empire; that the nation which gave an emperor should resign to their brethren the choice of a patriarch; and that the pilgrims, whatever might be their impatience to visit the Holy Land, should devote another year to the conquest and defence of the Greek provinces. After the conquest of Constantinople by the Latins, the treaty was confirmed and executed, and the first and most important step was the creation of an emperor The six electors of the French nation were all ecclesiastics, the abbot of Loces, the archbishop elect of Acre in Palestine, and the bishops of Troyes, Soissons, Halberstadt, and Bethlehem, the last of whom exercised in the camp the office of pope's legate; their profession and knowledge were respectable; and, as *they* could not be the objects, they were best qualified to be authors, of the choice. The six Venetians were the principal servants of the state, and in this list the noble families of Querini and Contarini are still proud to discover their ancestors. The twelve assembled in the chapel of the palace, and, after the solemn invocation of the Holy Ghost, they proceeded to deliberate and vote. A just impulse of respect and gratitude prompted them to crown the virtues of the doge; his wisdom had inspired their enterprise; and the most youthful knights might envy and applaud the exploits of blindness and age. But the patriot Dandolo was devoid of all personal ambition, and fully satisfied that he had been judged worthy to reign. His nomination was overruled by the Venetians themselves; his countrymen, and perhaps his friends,[2] represented, with the eloquence of truth, the mischiefs that might arise to national freedom and the common cause from the union of two incompatible characters, of the first magistrate of a republic and the emperor of the

---

[2] After mentioning the nomination of the doge by a French elector, his kinsman Andrew Dandolo approves his exclusion, quidam Venetorum fidelis et nobilis senex, usus oratione satis probabili, &c, which has been embroidered by modern writers from Blondus to Le Beau.

East. The exclusion of the doge left room for the more
equal merits of Boniface and Baldwin, and at their names
all meaner candidates respectfully withdrew. The marquis
of Montferrat was recommended by his mature age and fair
reputation, by the choice of the adventurers and the wishes
of the Greeks; nor can I believe that Venice, the mistress of
the sea, could be seriously apprehensive of a petty lord at the
foot of the Alps.[3] But the count of Flanders was the chief of
a wealthy and warlike people; he was valiant, pious, and
chaste; in the prime of life, since he was only thirty-two
years of age; a descendant of Charlemagne, a cousin of the
king of France, and a compeer of the prelates and barons who
had yielded with reluctance to the command of a foreigner.
Without the chapel, these barons, with the doge and marquis
at their head, expected the decision of the twelve electors.
It was announced by the bishop of Soissons, in the name of his
colleagues "Ye have sworn to obey the prince whom we
should choose · by our unanimous suffrage, Baldwin, count
of Flanders and Hainault, is now your sovereign, and the
emperor of the East " He was saluted with loud applause,
and the proclamation was re-echoed throughout the city by
the joy of the Latins and the trembling adulation of the
Greeks. Boniface was the first to kiss the hand of his rival,
and to raise him on the buckler; and Baldwin was transported
to the cathedral and solemnly invested with the purple
buskins. At the end of three weeks he was crowned by the
legate, in the vacancy of a patriarch, but the Venetian clergy
soon filled the chapter of St Sophia, seated Thomas Morosini
on the ecclesiastical throne, and employed every art to
perpetuate, in their own nation, the honours and benefices
of the Greek church[4] Without delay, the successor of

---

[3] Nicetas (p 384), with the vain ignorance of a Greek, describes the marquis
of Montferrat as a *maritime* power Λαμπαρδίαν δὲ οἰκεῖσθαι παράλιον Was
he deceived by the Byzantine theme of Lombardy, which extended along the
coast of Calabria ?

[4] They exacted an oath from Thomas Morosini to appoint no canons of

Constantine instructed Palestine, France, and Rome of this
memorable revolution.   To Palestine he sent, as a trophy,
the gates of Constantinople and the chain of the harbour,[5]
and adopted from the Assise of Jerusalem the laws or customs
best adapted to a French colony and conquest in the East.[6]
In his epistles, the natives of France are encouraged to swell
that colony and to secure that conquest, to people a magnificent city and a fertile land, which will reward the labours
both of the priest and the soldier.   He congratulates the
Roman pontiff on the restoration of his authority in the
East; invites him to extinguish the Greek schism by his
presence in a general council, and implores his blessing and
forgiveness for the disobedient pilgrims.   Prudence and
dignity are blended in the answer of Innocent [7]   In the subversion of the Byzantine empire, he arraigns the vices of man
and adores the providence of God; the conquerors will be
absolved or condemned by their future conduct; the validity
of their treaty depends on the judgment of St. Peter; but he
inculcates their most sacred duty of establishing a just sub-
ordination of obedience and tribute, from the Greeks to the
Latins, from the magistrate to the clergy, and from the clergy
to the pope.

In the division of the Greek provinces,[8] the share of the

St Sophia, the lawful electors, except Venetians who had lived ten years at
Venice, &c   But the foreign clergy were envious, the pope disapproved this
national monopoly, and of the six Latin patriarchs of Constantinople only
the first and last were Venetians

[5] Nicetas, p 383

[6] [The Assises of Jerusalem, at least the Assise of the Haute Cour, was
probably not codified so early as 1204   But it had been introduced into the
Peloponnesus before 1275]

[7] The Epistles of Innocent III are a rich fund for the ecclesiastical and
civil institution of the Latin empire of Constantinople, and the most important of these epistles (of which the collection in 2 vols in folio is published by Stephen Baluze) are inserted in his Gesta, in Muratori, Script.
Rerum Italicarum, tom iii p i, c 94–105   [Migne, Patrol Lat , vols 214,
215, 216]

[8] In the treaty of partition, most of the names are corrupted by the scribes,
they might be restored, and a good map, suited to the last age of the Byzantine

Venetians was more ample than that of the Latin emperor.
No more than one fourth was appropriated to his domain; a
clear moiety of the remainder was reserved for Venice; and
the other moiety was distributed among the adventurers of
France and Lombardy.   The venerable Dandolo was proclaimed despot of Romania, and invested, after the Greek
fashion, with the purple buskins.   He ended, at Constantinople, his long and glorious life; and, if the prerogative was
personal, the title was used by his successors till the middle of
the fourteenth century, with the singular though true addition
of lords of one fourth and a half of the Roman empire.[9]
The doge, a slave of the state, was seldom permitted to
depart from the helm of the republic; but his place was
supplied by the *bail*, or regent, who exercised a supreme
jurisdiction over the colony of Venetians; they possessed
three of the eight quarters of the city, and his independent
tribunal was composed of six judges, four counsellors,
two chamberlains, two fiscal advocates, and a constable.
Their long experience of the Eastern trade enabled them to
select their portion with discernment; they had rashly accepted the dominion and defence of Hadrianople; but it was
the more reasonable aim of their policy to form a chain of
factories and cities and islands along the maritime coast,
from the neighbourhood of Ragusa to the Hellespont and the
Bosphorus.   The labour and cost of such extensive conquests
exhausted their treasury, they abandoned their maxims of
government, adopted a feudal system, and contented themselves with the homage of their nobles,[10] for the possessions

empire, would be an improvement of geography, but, alas! d'Anville is no
more!   [The act of partition annexed to the treaty with geographical notes
was edited by Tafel in his Symbolæ criticæ geographiam Byzantinam Spec-
tantes, part 2]

[9] Their style was Dominus quartæ partis et dimidiæ imperii Romani, till
Giovanni Dolfino, who was elected Doge in the year 1356 (Sanuto, p 530,
641).   For the government of Constantinople, see Ducange, Histoire de
C P p 37

[10] Ducange (Hist. de C. P. ii 6) has marked the conquests made by the

which these private vassals undertook to reduce and maintain.
And thus it was that the family of Sanut acquired the duchy
of Naxos, which involved the greatest part of the Archipelago.
For the price of ten thousand marks the republic purchased
of the marquis of Montferrat the fertile island of Crete, or
Candia, with the ruins of an hundred cities; [11] but its improvement was stinted by the proud and narrow spirit of an
aristocracy; [12] and the wisest senators would confess that the
sea, not the land, was the treasury of St Mark.   In the moiety
of the adventurers, the marquis Boniface might claim the
most liberal reward; and, besides the isle of Crete, his exclusion from the throne was compensated by the royal title and
the provinces beyond the Hellespont   But he prudently
exchanged that distant and difficult conquest for the kingdom
of Thessalonica, or Macedonia, twelve days' journey from
the capital, where he might be supported by the neighbouring
powers of his brother-in-law the king of Hungary [13]   His
progress was hailed by the voluntary or reluctant acclamations of the natives; and Greece, the proper and ancient

state or nobles of Venice of the islands of Candia, Corfu, Cephalonia, Zante,
Naxos, Paros, Melos, Andros, Myconè, Scyro, Cea, and Lemnos. [See
Appendix 3]
   [11] Boniface sold the isle of Candia, Aug 12, A D 1204. See the acts in
Sanuto, p 533, but I cannot understand how it could be his mother's portion,
or how she could be the daughter of an emperor Alexius. [Boniface's
Refutatio Cretis is printed in Tafel u Thomas, Urkunden, 512, and in Buchon,
Recherches et Matériaux, i 10   Crete had been formally promised him by
the young Alexius   He seems to have claimed Thessalonica on the ground
that his brother had been created king of Thessalonica by Manuel, see
vol x p 335   The erection of the kingdom of Thessalonica was by no
means agreeable to Baldwin, it threatened, weakened, and perhaps ruined
the Empire of Romania   It was nearly coming to war between Baldwin
and Boniface, but the Doge persuaded Baldwin to yield]
   [12] In the year 1212, the doge Peter Zani sent a colony to Candia, drawn
from every quarter of Venice   But, in their savage manners and frequent
rebellions, the Candiots may be compared to the Corsicans under the yoke
of Genoa, and, when I compare the accounts of Belon and Tournefort, I
cannot discern much difference between the Venetian and the Turkish
island
   [13] [He married Margaret, widow of Isaac Angelus]

Greece, again received a Latin conqueror,[14] who trod with indifference that classic ground. He viewed with a careless eye the beauties of the valley of Tempe, traversed with a cautious step the straits of Thermopylæ; occupied the unknown cities of Thebes, Athens, and Argos;[15] and assaulted the fortifications of Corinth and Napoli,[16] which resisted his arms. The lots of the Latin pilgrims were regulated by chance, or choice, or subsequent exchange; and they abused, with intemperate joy, the triumph over the lives and fortunes of a great people. After a minute survey of the provinces, they weighed in the scales of avarice the revenue of each district, the advantage of the situation, and the ample or scanty supplies for the maintenance of soldiers and horses.

[14] Villehardouin (No 159, 160, 173-177) and Nicetas (p 387-394) describe the expedition into Greece of the marquis Boniface   The Choniate might derive his information from his brother Michael, archbishop of Athens, whom he paints as an orator, a statesman, and a saint   His encomium of Athens, and the description of Tempe, should be published from the Bodleian MS. of Nicetas (Fabric Bibliot. Græc tom vi p 405), and would have deserved Mr Harris's inquiries   [The works of Michael Akominatos have been published in a full edition by S Lampros (1879-80, 2 vols)   The dirge on Athens had been already published by Boissonade in Anecdota Græca, 5, p 373 sqq (1833).   Gregorovius in his Gesch der Stadt Athen im Mittelalter (where he draws a most interesting sketch of Akominatos in caps 7 and 8) gives specimens of a German translation of the dirge, p 243-4]

[15] [Leo Sguros of Nauplia made himself master of Nauplia, Argos, Corinth, and Thebes.   He besieged Athens (see below, p 90, note 72), and the Acropolis, defended by the archbishop Akominatos, defied him   From Thebes he went to Thessaly, and meeting the Emperor Alexius at Larissa married his daughter and received from him the title of *Sebastohypertatos*   When Boniface and his knights approached, father-in-law and son-in-law retreated to Thermopylæ, but did not await the approach of the enemy   Bodonitza close to the pass was granted by Boniface as a fief to Guy Pallavicini   Before he proceeded against Thebes, Amphissa, which about this time assumes the name Salona (or Sula), was taken, and given with the neighbouring districts including Delphi and the port of Galaxidi to Thomas of Stromoncourt   For Thebes and Athens see below, p 90-1]

[16] Napoli di Romania, or Nauplia, the ancient sea-port of Argos, is still a place of strength and consideration, situate on a rocky peninsula, with a good harbour (Chandler's Travels into Greece, p 227) [It narrowly escaped becoming the capital of the modern kingdom of Greece.]

Their presumption claimed and divided the long-lost depend-
encies of the Roman sceptre; the Nile and Euphrates rolled
through their imaginary realms; and happy was the warrior
who drew for his prize the palace of the Turkish sultan of
Iconium.[17] I shall not descend to the pedigree of families
and the rent-rolls of estates, but I wish to specify that the
counts of Blois and St. Pol were invested with the duchy of
Nice and the lordship of Demotica; [18] the principal fiefs were
held by the service of constable, chamberlain, cup-bearer,
butler, and chief cook; and our historian, Jeffrey of Villehardouin, obtained a fair establishment on the banks of the
Hebrus, and united the double office of marshal of Champagne and Romania. At the head of his knights and archers
each baron mounted on horseback to secure the possession
of his share, and their first efforts were generally successful.
But the public force was weakened by their dispersion; and
a thousand quarrels must arise under a law, and among men,
whose sole umpire was the sword   Within three months after
the conquest of Constantinople, the emperor and the king of
Thessalonica drew their hostile followers into the field; they
were reconciled by the authority of the doge, the advice of
the marshal, and the firm freedom of their peers.[19]

Two fugitives, who had reigned at Constantinople, still
asserted the title of emperor; and the subjects of their fallen
throne might be moved to pity by the misfortunes of the elder

[17] I have softened the expression of Nicetas, who strives to expose the
presumption of the Franks. See de Rebus post C P. expugnatam, p 375–
384.

[18] A city surrounded by the river Hebrus, and six leagues to the south of
Hadrianople, received from its double wall the Greek name of Didymoteichos,
insensibly corrupted into Demotica and Dimot   I have preferred the more
convenient and modern appellation of Demotica   This place was the last
Turkish residence of Charles XII

[19] Their quarrel is told by Villehardouin (No. 146–158) with the spirit of
freedom   The merit and reputation of the marshal are acknowledged by
the Greek historian (p 387), μέγα παρὰ τοῖς Λατίνων δυναμένου στρατεύμασι.
unlike some modern heroes, whose exploits are only visible in their own
memoirs.

Alexius, or excited to revenge by the spirit of Mourzoufle.
A domestic alliance, a common interest, a similar guilt, and a
merit of extinguishing his enemies, a brother and a nephew,
induced the more recent usurper to unite with the former the
relics of his power. Mourzoufle was received with smiles
and honours in the camp of his father Alexius; but the
wicked can never love, and should rarely trust, their
fellow-criminals: he was seized in the bath, deprived of
his eyes, stripped of his troops and treasures, and turned
out to wander an object of horror and contempt to those
who with more propriety could hate, and with more justice
could punish, the assassin of the emperor Isaac and his son.
As the tyrant, pursued by fear or remorse, was stealing
over to Asia, he was seized by the Latins of Constantinople,
and condemned, after an open trial, to an ignominious death.
His judges debated the mode of his execution, the axe, the
wheel, or the stake; and it was resolved that Mourzoufle [20]
should ascend the Theodosian column, a pillar of white
marble of one hundred and forty-seven feet in height.[21]
From the summit he was cast down headlong, and dashed in
pieces on the pavement, in the presence of innumerable
spectators, who filled the forum of Taurus, and admired the
accomplishment of an old prediction, which was explained
by this singular event.[22] The fate of Alexius is less tragical:

[20] See the fate of Mourzoufle, in Nicetas (p 393), Villehardouin (No 141-
145, 163), and Guntherus (c 20, 21) Neither the marshal nor the monk
afford a grain of pity for a tyrant or rebel, whose punishment, however, was
more unexampled than his crime

[21] The column of Arcadius, which represents in basso-relievo his victories,
or those of his father Theodosius, is still extant at Constantinople It is
described and measured, Gyllius (Topograph iv 7), Banduri (ad l i
Antiquit C P p 507, &c), and Tournefort (Voyage du Levant, tom ii
lettre xii p 231) [Nothing of the column remains now except its base]

[22] The nonsense of Gunther and the modern Greeks concerning this
columna fatidica is unworthy of notice, but it is singular enough that, fifty
years before the Latin conquest, the poet Tzetzes (Chiliad, ix 277) relates
the dream of a matron, who saw an army in the forum, and a man sitting
on the column, clapping his hands and uttering a loud exclamation.

he was sent by the marquis a captive to Italy, and a gift to the king of the Romans; but he had not much to applaud his fortune, if the sentence of imprisonment and exile were changed from a fortress in the Alps to a monastery in Asia. But his daughter, before the national calamity, had been given in marriage to a young hero, who continued the succession, and restored the throne, of the Greek princes [23]   The valour of Theodore Lascaris was signalised in the two sieges of Constantinople   After the flight of Mourzoufle, when the Latins were already in the city, he offered himself as their emperor to the soldiers and people; and his ambition, which might be virtuous, was undoubtedly brave.   Could he have infused a soul into the multitude, they might have crushed the strangers under their feet, their abject despair refused his aid; and Theodore retired to breathe the air of freedom in Anatolia, beyond the immediate view and pursuit of the conquerors.   Under the title, at first of despot, and afterwards of emperor, he drew to his standard the bolder spirits, who were fortified against slavery by the contempt of life; and, as every means was lawful for the public safety, implored without scruple the alliance of the Turkish sultan.   Nice, where Theodore established his residence, Prusa and Philadelphia, Smyrna and Ephesus, opened their gates to their deliverer; he derived strength and reputation from his victories, and even from his defeats, and the successor of Constantine preserved a fragment of the empire from the banks of the Mæander to the suburbs of Nicomedia, and at length of Constantinople.   Another portion, distant and obscure, was possessed by the lineal heir of the Comneni, a son of the virtuous Manuel, a grandson of the tyrant Andronicus.   His name was Alexius; and the epithet of *great* was applied perhaps to his stature, rather than to his exploits.   By the

---

[23] The dynasties of Nice, Trebizond, and Epirus (of which Nicetas saw the origin without much pleasure or hope) are learnedly explored, and clearly represented, in the Familiæ Byzantinæ of Ducange

indulgence of the Angeli,[24] he was appointed governor or duke of Trebizond.[25] his birth gave him ambition, the revolution independence, and, without changing his title, he reigned in peace from Sinope to the Phasis, along the coast of the Black Sea. His nameless son and successor[26] is described as the vassal of the sultan, whom he served with two hundred lances; that Comnenian prince was no more than duke of

[24] [Rather, by the help of his aunt Queen Thamar of Iberia   On the death of Andronicus in 1185 his two grandsons, Alexius and David, escaped to Iberia   Their aunt helped Alexius to found the independent state of Trape-zus in 1204, and there he assumed the title of Grand-Komnenos   His brother David seized Paphlagonia   The Comneni never made common cause with the Emperors of Nicaea against the common enemies, either Turks or Latins   On the contrary, Theodore Lascaris defeated David and wrested his kingdom from him, leaving him only a small region about Sinope (1212), and in 1214 the Turks captured Sinope and David fell fight-ing.   On the other hand Alexius maintained himself at Trebizond, and the Empire of Trebizond survived the Turkish conquest of Constantinople by eight years]

[25] Except some facts in Pachymer and Nicephorus Gregoras, which will hereafter be used, the Byzantine writers disdain to speak of the empire of Trebizond, or principality of the *Lazi*, and among the Latins, it is conspicu-ous only in the romances of the xivth or xvth centuries.   Yet the indefatigable Ducange has dug out (Fam Byz p 192) two authentic passages in Vincent of Beauvais (l xxxi c 144), and the protonotary Ogerius (apud Wading, A D 1279, No 4)   [The short history of the Emperors of Trebizond from 1204–1426, by Michael Panaretos of Trebizond (lived in first half of 15th century) was published by Tafel at the end of his edition of Eustathius (p 362 *sqq*), 1833   It is translated in St Martin's ed of Lebeau's Hist du bas-empire, vol xx p 482 *sqq*   The first, who went thoroughly into the history of Trebizond, was Fallmerayer, and he published more material See the Abhandlungen des Bavarian Academy, 3cl, vol 3, 1843, and Geschichte des Kaiserthums von Trapezunt, 1827   The story is told at length by Finlay in History of Greece, vol iv p 307 *sqq*   But there is much more material, and A Papadopulos-Kerameus has recently (1897) issued vol i. of Fontes Historiæ Imperii Trapezuntini   And a new history of Trapezus, from the earliest times to the present day, has appeared in modern Greek Ἱστορία τῆς Τραπεζοῦντος (Odessa), 1898, by T E Evangelides]

[26] [His stepson Andronicus Gidos succeeded him in 1222, and was suc-ceeded in 1235 by John, the eldest son of Alexius, who reigned only three years   Then came Manuel, and then John, who assumed the title "Em-peror of the East, Iberia, and Peratea," avoiding the title of Roman Em-peror, in order to keep the peace with the Palaeologi of Constantinople. Peratea was a part of the Crimea which acknowledged his sway]

Trebizond, and the title of emperor was first assumed by the pride and envy of the grandson of Alexius. In the West, a third fragment was saved from the common shipwreck by Michael, a bastard of the house of Angeli,[27] who, before the revolution, had been known as an hostage, a soldier, and a rebel. His flight from the camp of the marquis Boniface secured his freedom, by his marriage with the governor's daughter he commanded the important place of Durazzo, assumed the title of despot, and founded a strong and conspicuous principality in Epirus, Ætolia, and Thessaly, which have ever been peopled by a warlike race. The Greeks, who had offered their service to their new sovereigns, were excluded by the haughty Latins[28] from all civil and military honours, as a nation born to tremble and obey. Their resentment prompted them to show that they might have been useful friends, since they could be dangerous enemies; their nerves were braced by adversity, whatever was learned or holy, whatever was noble or valiant, rolled away into the independent states of Trebizond, Epirus, and Nice; and a single patrician is marked by the ambiguous praise of attachment and loyalty to the Franks. The vulgar herd of the cities and the country would have gladly submitted to a mild and regular servitude; and the transient disorders of war would have been obliterated by some years of industry and peace But peace was banished, and industry was crushed, in the disorders of the feudal system. The *Roman* emperors of Constantinople, if they were endowed with abilities, were armed with power for the protection of their

----

[27] [Michael was natural son of Constantine Angelus, uncle of the Emperors Isaac and Alexius III He and his successors assumed the name *Comnenus Angelus Ducas* Michael was murdered in 1214 and succeeded by his brother Theodore]

[28] The portrait of the French Latins is drawn in Nicetas by the hand of prejudice and resentment οὐδὲν τῶν ἄλλων ἐθνῶν εἰς Ἄρεος ἔργα παρασυμβε-βλῆσθαι ἠνείχοντο, ἀλλ' οὐδέ τις τῶν χαρίτων ἢ τῶν μουσῶν παρὰ τοῖς βαρβά-ροις τούτοις ἐπεξενίζετο, καὶ παρὰ τοῦτο οἶμαι τὴν φύσιν ἦσαν ἀνήμεροι, καὶ τὸν χόλον εἶχον τοῦ λόγου προτρέχοντα.

subjects; their laws were wise and their administration was
simple. The Latin throne was filled by a titular prince, the
chief, and often the servant, of his licentious confederates:
the fiefs of the empire, from a kingdom to a castle, were held
and ruled by the sword of the barons; and their discord,
poverty, and ignorance extended their ramifications of
tyranny to the most sequestered villages. The Greeks were
oppressed by the double weight of the priest, who was invested with temporal power, and of the soldier, who was
inflamed by fanatic hatred: and the insuperable bar of
religion and language for ever separated the stranger and the
native   As long as the crusaders were united at Constantinople, the memory of their conquest and the terror of their
arms imposed silence on the captive land; their dispersion
betrayed the smallness of their numbers and the defects of
their discipline, and some failures and mischances revealed
the secret that they were not invincible. As the fear of the
Greeks abated, their hatred increased. They murmured;
they conspired; and, before a year of slavery had elapsed,
they implored or accepted the succour of a Barbarian, whose
power they had felt, and whose gratitude they trusted.[20]

The Latin conquerors had been saluted with a solemn and
early embassy from John, or Joannice, or Calo-John, the revolted chief of the Bulgarians and Walachians. He deemed
himself their brother, as the votary of the Roman pontiff,
from whom he had received the regal title and an holy banner; and in the subversion of the Greek monarchy he might
aspire to the name of their friend and accomplice. But Calo-
John was astonished to find that the count of Flanders had
assumed the pomp and pride of the successors of Constantine;
and his ambassadors were dismissed with an haughty message, that the rebel must deserve a pardon by touching with

[20] I here begin to use, with freedom and confidence, the eight books of the
Histoire de C P sous l'Empire des François, which Ducange has given as a
supplement to Villehardouin, and which, in a barbarous style, deserves the
praise of an original and classic work

his forehead the footstool of the Imperial throne. His resentment [30] would have exhaled in acts of violence and blood; his cooler policy watched the rising discontent of the Greeks; affected a tender concern for their sufferings; and promised that their first struggles for freedom should be supported by his person and kingdom. The conspiracy was propagated by national hatred, the firmest band of association and secrecy: the Greeks were impatient to sheathe their daggers in the breasts of the victorious strangers; but the execution was prudently delayed, till Henry, the emperor's brother, had transported the flower of his troops beyond the Hellespont. Most of the towns and villages of Thrace were true to the moment and the signal. and the Latins, without arms or suspicion, were slaughtered by the vile and merciless revenge of their slaves. From Demotica, the first scene of the massacre, the surviving vassals of the count of St. Pol escaped to Hadrianople; but the French and Venetians who occupied that city were slain or expelled by the furious multitude; the garrisons that could effect their retreat fell back on each other towards the metropolis; and the fortresses that separately stood against the rebels were ignorant of each other's and of their sovereign's fate. The voice of fame and fear announced the revolt of the Greeks and the rapid approach of their Bulgarian ally; and Calo-John, not depending on the forces of his own kingdom, had drawn from the Scythian wilderness a body of fourteen thousand Comans, who drank, as it was said, the blood of their captives, and sacrificed the Christians on the altars of their gods.[31]

[30] In Calo-John's answer to the Pope, we may find his claims and complaints (Gesta Innocent III c 108, 109), he was cherished at Rome as the prodigal son [The name *Kalo*-John was also used of John Vatatzes, and of the young John Lascaris, son of Theodore II , see Méliarakês, Ἱστορία τοῦ βασ τῆς Νικαίας, p 541, note]

[31] The Comans were a Tartar or Turkman horde, which encamped in the xiith and xiiith centuries on the verge of Moldavia The greater part were Pagans, but some were Mahometans, and the whole horde was converted to Christianity (A D 1370) by Lewis, king of Hungary [See vol x p 49, n 52, and p 165, n 36]

Alarmed by this sudden and growing danger, the emperor despatched a swift messenger to recall Count Henry and his troops; and, had Baldwin expected the return of his gallant brother, with a supply of twenty thousand Armenians, he might have encountered the invader with equal numbers and a decisive superiority of arms and discipline. But the spirit of chivalry could seldom discriminate caution from cowardice; and the emperor took the field with an hundred and forty knights, and their train of archers and serjeants. The marshal, who dissuaded and obeyed, led the vanguard in their march to Hadrianople; the main body was commanded by the count of Blois; the aged doge of Venice followed with the rear; and their scanty numbers were increased on all sides by the fugitive Latins. They undertook to besiege the rebels of Hadrianople, and such was the pious tendency of the crusades that they employed the holy week in pillaging the country for their subsistence, and in framing engines for the destruction of their fellow-Christians. But the Latins were soon interrupted and alarmed by the light cavalry of the Comans, who boldly skirmished to the edge of their imperfect lines, and a proclamation was issued by the marshal of Romania, that on the trumpet's sound the cavalry should mount and form, but that none, under pain of death, should abandon themselves to a desultory and dangerous pursuit. This wise injunction was first disobeyed by the count of Blois, who involved the emperor in his rashness and ruin. The Comans, of the Parthian or Tartar school, fled before their first charge; but, after a career of two leagues, when the knights and their horses were almost breathless, they suddenly turned, rallied, and encompassed the heavy squadrons of the Franks. The count was slain on the field; the emperor was made prisoner, and, if the one disdained to fly, if the other refused to yield, their personal bravery made a poor atonement for their ignorance or neglect of the duties of a general.[32]

---

[32] Nicetas, from ignorance or malice, imputes the defeat to the cowardice

Proud of his victory and his royal prize, the Bulgarian advanced to relieve Hadrianople and achieve the destruction of the Latins. They must inevitably have been destroyed, if the marshal of Romania had not displayed a cool courage and consummate skill, uncommon in all ages, but most uncommon in those times, when war was a passion rather than a science. His grief and fears were poured into the firm and faithful bosom of the doge, but in the camp he diffused an assurance of safety, which could only be realised by the general belief. All day he maintained his perilous station between the city and the Barbarians: Villehardouin decamped in silence at the dead of night; and his masterly retreat of three days would have deserved the praise of Xenophon and the ten thousand. In the rear the marshal supported the weight of the pursuit, in the front he moderated the impatience of the fugitives; and, wherever the Comans approached, they were repelled by a line of impenetrable spears. On the third day, the weary troops beheld the sea, the solitary town of Rodosto,[33] and their friends, who had landed from the Asiatic shore. They embraced, they wept, but they united their arms and counsels; and, in his brother's absence, Count Henry assumed the regency of the empire, at once in a state of childhood and caducity [34] If the Comans withdrew from the summer-heats, seven thousand Latins, in the hour of danger, deserted Constantinople, their brethren, and their vows. Some partial success was overbalanced by the loss

of Dandolo (p 383), but Villehardouin shares his own glory with his venerable friend, qui viels home ére et gote ne veoit, mais mult ére sages et preus et vigueros (No 193)

[33] The truth of geography and the original text of Villehardouin (No 194 [366]) place Rodosto [Rhædestus] three days' journey (trois jornées) from Hadrianople, but Vigenère, in his version, has most absurdly substituted trois heures, and this error, which is not corrected by Ducange, has entrapped several moderns, whose names I shall spare

[34] The reign and end of Baldwin are related by Villehardouin and Nicetas (p 386-416), and their omissions are supplied by Ducange, in his Observations, and to the end of his first book.

of one hundred and twenty knights in the field of Dusium; and of the Imperial domain no more was left than the capital, with two or three adjacent fortresses on the shores of Europe and Asia. The king of Bulgaria was resistless and inexorable; and Calo-John respectfully eluded the demands of the pope, who conjured his new proselyte to restore peace and the emperor to the afflicted Latins The deliverance of Baldwin was no longer, he said, in the power of man · that prince had died in prison; and the manner of his death is variously related by ignorance and credulity The lovers of a tragic legend will be pleased to hear that the royal captive was tempted by the amorous queen of the Bulgarians; that his chaste refusal exposed him to the falsehood of a woman and the jealousy of a savage; that his hands and feet were severed from his body, that his bleeding trunk was cast among the carcases of dogs and horses, and that he breathed three days before he was devoured by the birds of prey.[35] About twenty years afterwards, in a wood of the Netherlands, an hermit announced himself as the true Baldwin, the emperor of Constantinople, and the lawful sovereign of Flanders. He related the wonders of his escape, his adventures, and his penance, among a people prone to believe and to rebel: and, in the first transport, Flanders acknowledged her long-lost sovereign. A short examination before the French court detected the impostor, who was punished with an ignominious death, but the Flemings still adhered to the pleasing error, and the countess Jane is accused by the gravest historians of sacrificing to her ambition the life of an unfortunate father.[36]

In all civilised hostility a treaty is established for the

---

[35] After brushing away all doubtful and improbable circumstances, we may prove the death of Baldwin 1 By the firm belief of the French barons (Villehardouin, No 230) 2 By the declaration of Calo-John himself, who excuses his not releasing the captive emperor, quia debitum carnis exsolverat cum carcere teneretur (Gesta Innocent III, c 109)

[36] See the story of this impostor from the French and Flemish writers in Ducange, Hist de C P m 9, and the ridiculous fables that were believed by the monks of St Alban's in Matthew Paris, Hist Major, p 271, 272

exchange or ransom of prisoners; and, if their captivity be prolonged, their condition is known, and they are treated according to their rank with humanity or honour. But the savage Bulgarian was a stranger to the laws of war, his prisons were involved in darkness and silence, and above a year elapsed before the Latins could be assured of the death of Baldwin, before his brother, the regent Henry, would consent to assume the title of emperor. His moderation was applauded by the Greeks as an act of rare and inimitable virtue. Their light and perfidious ambition was eager to seize or anticipate the moment of a vacancy, while a law of succession, the guardian both of the prince and people, was gradually defined and confirmed in the hereditary monarchies of Europe. In the support of the Eastern empire Henry was gradually left without an associate, as the heroes of the crusade retired from the world or from the war. The doge of Venice, the venerable Dandolo, in the fulness of years and glory, sunk into the grave. The marquis of Montferrat was slowly recalled from the Peloponnesian war to the revenge of Baldwin and the defence of Thessalonica. Some nice disputes of feudal homage and service were reconciled in a personal interview between the emperor and the king, they were firmly united by mutual esteem and the common danger; and their alliance was sealed by the nuptial of Henry with the daughter of the Italian prince. He soon deplored the loss of his friend and father. At the persuasion of some faithful Greeks, Boniface made a bold and successful inroad among the hills of Rhodope. the Bulgarians fled on his approach; they assembled to harass his retreat. On the intelligence that his rear was attacked, without waiting for any defensive armour, he leaped on horseback, couched his lance, and drove the enemies before him; but in the rash pursuit he was pierced with a mortal wound; and the head of the king of Thessalonica was presented to Calo-John, who enjoyed the honours, without the merit, of victory. It is here, at this melancholy event, that the pen or the voice of Jeffrey of Villehardouin seems to drop or to expire;[37] and, if he still exercised his military office of marshal of Romania, his subsequent exploits are buried in oblivion.[38] The character of Henry was not unequal to his arduous situation in the siege of Constantinople, and beyond the Hellespont, he had deserved the fame of a valiant knight and a skilful commander; and his courage was tempered with a degree of prudence and mildness unknown to his impetuous brother. In the double war against the Greeks of Asia and the Bulgarians of Europe, he was ever the foremost on shipboard or on horseback, and, though he cautiously provided for the success of his arms, the drooping Latins were often roused by his example to save and to second their fearless emperor. But such efforts, and some supplies of men and money from France, were of less avail than the errors, the cruelty, and the death of their most formidable adversary. When the despair of the Greek subjects invited Calo-John as their deliverer, they hoped that he would protect their liberty and adopt their laws; they were soon taught to compare the degrees of national ferocity, and to execrate the savage conqueror, who no longer dissembled his intention of dispeopling Thrace, of demolishing the cities, and of transplanting the inhabitants beyond the Danube. Many towns and villages of Thrace were already evacuated; an heap of ruins marked the place of Philippopolis, and a similar calamity was expected at Demotica and Hadrianople by the first authors of the revolt. They raised a cry of grief and repent-

[37] Villehardouin, No. 257 I quote, with regret, this lamentable conclusion, where we lose at once the original history, and the rich illustrations of Ducange The last pages may derive some light from Henry's two epistles to Innocent III (Gesta, c 106, 107) [Villehardouin's story is poorly continued by Henry of Valenciennes, whose chronicle is printed along with Villehardouin in Wailly's edition (ed 3, 1882)]

[38] The marshal was alive in 1212, but he probably died soon afterwards, without returning to France (Ducange, Observations sur Villehardouin, p 238) His fief of Messinople, the gift of Boniface, was the ancient Maximianopolis, which flourished in the time of Ammianus Marcellinus, among the cities of Thrace (No 141). [Messinopolis is the Mosynopolis of Greek historians]

ance to the throne of Henry; the emperor alone had the magnanimity to forgive and trust them   No more than four hundred knights, with their serjeants and archers, could be assembled under his banner, and with this slender force he fought and repulsed the Bulgarian, who, besides his infantry, was at the head of forty thousand horse.   In this expedition, Henry felt the difference between an hostile and a friendly country; the remaining cities were preserved by his arms; and the savage, with shame and loss, was compelled to re-linquish his prey.   The siege of Thessalonica was the last of the evils which Calo-John inflicted or suffered; he was stabbed in the night in his tent; and the general, perhaps the assassin, who found him weltering in his blood, ascribed the blow, with general applause, to the lance of St. Demetrius.[39] After several victories the prudence of Henry concluded an honourable peace with the successor of the tyrant, and with the Greek princes of Nice and Epirus   If he ceded some doubtful limits, an ample kingdom was reserved for himself and his feudatories; and his reign, which lasted only ten years, afforded a short interval of prosperity and peace.   Far above the narrow policy of Baldwin and Boniface, he freely entrusted to the Greeks the most important offices of the state and army; and this liberality of sentiment and practice was the more seasonable, as the princes of Nice and Epirus had already learned to seduce and employ the mercenary valour of the Latins   It was the aim of Henry to unite and re-ward his deserving subjects of every nation and language; but he appeared less solicitous to accomplish the impracti-cable union of the two churches.   Pelagius, the pope's legate, who acted as the sovereign of Constantinople, had interdicted the worship of the Greeks, and sternly imposed the payment of tithes, the double procession of the Holy Ghost, and a blind

[39] The church of this patron of Thessalonica was served by the canons of the holy sepulchre, and contained a divine ointment which distilled daily and stupendous miracles (Ducange, Hist de C. P ii 4).

obedience to the Roman pontiff. As the weaker party, they pleaded the duties of conscience, and implored the rights of toleration: "Our bodies," they said, "are Cæsar's, but our souls belong only to God." The persecution was checked by the firmness of the emperor, [40] and, if we can believe that the same prince was poisoned by the Greeks themselves, we must entertain a contemptible idea of the sense and gratitude of mankind. His valour was a vulgar attribute which he shared with ten thousand knights; but Henry possessed the superior courage to oppose, in a superstitious age, the pride and avarice of the clergy. In the cathedral of St. Sophia, he presumed to place his throne on the right hand of the patriarch, and this presumption excited the sharpest censure of Pope Innocent the Third.[41] By a salutary edict, one of the first examples of the laws of mortmain, he prohibited the alienation of fiefs, many of the Latins, desirous of returning to Europe, resigned their estates to the church for a spiritual or temporal reward; these holy lands were immediately discharged from military service, and a colony of soldiers would have been gradually transformed into a college of priests.[42]

The virtuous Henry died at Thessalonica, in the defence of that kingdom, and of an infant, the son of his friend Boniface. In the two first emperors of Constantinople, the male line of the counts of Flanders was extinct. But their sister Yolande was the wife of a French prince, the mother of a numerous progeny, and one of her daughters had married Andrew, king of Hungary, a brave and pious champion of the cross. By

[40] Acropolita (c. 17) observes the persecution of the legate, and the toleration of Henry (῎Ερη [᾽Ερρῆ gen , ᾽Ερρῆς nom], as he calls him) ἀλυδῶνα κατεστόρεσε

[41] [The dispute with Innocent was compromised at a parliament which Henry held at Ravennika in northern Greece (near Zeituni?) on May 2, 1210]

[42] See the reign of HENRY, in Ducange (Hist de C P l ι c 35-41, l ii. c 1-22), who is much indebted to the Epistles of the Popes Le Beau (Hist du Bas Empire, tom xvi p 120-122) has found, perhaps in Doutreman, some laws of Henry, which determined the service of fiefs and the prerogatives of the emperor

seating him on the Byzantine throne, the barons of Romania would have acquired the forces of a neighbouring and warlike kingdom; but the prudent Andrew revered the laws of succession; and the princess Yolande, with her husband, Peter of Courtenay, count of Auxerre, was invited by the Latins to assume the empire of the East. The royal birth of his father, the noble origin of his mother, recommended to the barons of France the first-cousin of their king. His reputation was fair, his possessions were ample, and in the bloody crusade against the Albigeois the soldiers and the priests had been abundantly satisfied of his zeal and valour   Vanity might applaud the elevation of a French emperor of Constantinople; but prudence must pity, rather than envy, his treacherous and imaginary greatness. To assert and adorn his title, he was reduced to sell or mortgage the best of his patrimony. By these expedients, the liberality of his royal kinsman, Philip Augustus, and the national spirit of chivalry, he was enabled to pass the Alps at the head of one hundred and forty knights and five thousand five hundred serjeants and archers. After some hesitation, Pope Honorius the Third was persuaded to crown the successor of Constantine; but he performed the ceremony in a church without the walls, lest he should seem to imply, or to bestow, any right of sovereignty over the ancient capital of the empire. The Venetians had engaged to transport Peter and his forces beyond the Adriatic, and the empress, with her four children, to the Byzantine palace; but they required, as the price of their service, that he should recover Durazzo from the despot of Epirus. Michael Angelus, or Comnenus, the first of his dynasty, had bequeathed the succession of his power and ambition to Theodore, his legitimate brother, who already threatened and invaded the establishments of the Latins   After discharging his debt by a fruitless assault, the emperor raised the siege to prosecute a long and perilous journey over land from Durazzo to Thessalonica. He was soon lost in the mountains of Epirus; the passes were fortified; his provisions exhausted; he was delayed and deceived by a treacherous negotiation, and, after Peter of Courtenay and the Roman legate had been arrested in a banquet, the French troops, without leaders or hopes, were eager to exchange their arms for the delusive promise of mercy and bread. The Vatican thundered, and the impious Theodore was threatened with the vengeance of earth and heaven; but the captive emperor and his soldiers were forgotten, and the reproaches of the pope are confined to the imprisonment of his legate No sooner was he satisfied by the deliverance of the priest and a promise of spiritual obedience, than he pardoned and protected the despot of Epirus. His peremptory commands suspended the ardour of the Venetians and the king of Hungary; and it was only by a natural or untimely death [43] that Peter of Courtenay was released from his hopeless captivity [44]

The long ignorance of his fate, and the presence of the lawful sovereign, of Yolande, his wife or widow, delayed the proclamation of a new emperor. Before her death, and in the midst of her grief, she was delivered of a son, who was named Baldwin, the last and most unfortunate of the Latin princes of Constantinople. His birth endeared him to the barons of Romania; but his childhood would have prolonged the troubles of a minority, and his claims were superseded by the elder claims of his brethren. The first of these, Philip of Courtenay, who derived from his mother the inheritance of Namur, had the wisdom to prefer the substance of a marquisate to the shadow of an empire, and on his refusal, Robert, the second of the sons of Peter and Yolande, was called to the throne of Constantinople Warned by his

[43] Acropolita (c 14) affirms that Peter of Courtenay died by the sword (ἔργον μαχαίρας γενέσθαι), but from his dark expressions, I should conclude a previous capacity, ὡς πάντας ἄρδην δεσμώτας ποιῆσαι σὺν πᾶσι σκεύεσι The Chronicle of Auxerre delays the emperor's death till the year 1219, and Auxerre is in the neighbourhood of Courtenay

[44] See the reign and death of Peter of Courtenay in Ducange (Hist de C P l ii c 22-28), who feebly strives to excuse the neglect of the emperor by Honorius III

father's mischance, he pursued his slow and secure journey
through Germany and along the Danube; a passage was
opened by his sister's marriage with the king of Hungary; and
the emperor Robert was crowned by the patriarch in the
cathedral of St. Sophia. But his reign was an era of calamity
and disgrace, and the colony, as it was styled, of NEW FRANCE
yielded on all sides to the Greeks of Nice and Epirus. After
a victory, which he owed to his perfidy rather than his courage,
Theodore Angelus entered the kingdom of Thessalonica, expelled the feeble Demetrius, the son of the marquis Boniface,
erected his standard on the walls of Hadrianople, and added,
by his vanity, a third or fourth name to the list of rival emperors. The relics of the Asiatic province were swept away
by John Vataces, the son-in-law and successor of Theodore
Lascaris, and who, in a triumphant reign of thirty-three years,
displayed the virtues both of peace and war. Under his discipline, the swords of the French mercenaries were the most
effectual instrument of his conquests, and their desertion from
the service of their country was at once a symptom and a cause
of the rising ascendant of the Greeks. By the construction of
a fleet he obtained the command of the Hellespont, reduced
the islands of Lesbos and Rhodes,[45] attacked the Venetians
of Candia, and intercepted the rare and parsimonious succours of the West. Once, and once only, the Latin emperor
sent an army against Vataces; and, in the defeat of that army,
the veteran knights, the last of the original conquerors, were
left on the field of battle. But the success of a foreign enemy
was less painful to the pusillanimous Robert than the insolence of his Latin subjects, who confounded the weakness of
the emperor and of the empire. His personal misfortunes will
prove the anarchy of the government and the ferociousness of
the times. The amorous youth had neglected his Greek

[45] [When the empire was overthrown by the crusaders, Leo Gabalas made
himself master of Rhodes. In 1233 John Vatatzes compelled him to acknowledge his supremacy, but left him in possession   The island was
conquered by the knights of St John in 1310]

bride, the daughter of Vataces, to introduce into the palace a
beautiful maid, of a private, though noble, family of Artois,
and her mother had been tempted by the lustre of the purple
to forfeit her engagements with a gentleman of Burgundy.
His love was converted into rage; he assembled his friends,
forced the palace gates, threw the mother into the sea, and
inhumanly cut off the nose and lips of the wife or concubine of
the emperor. Instead of punishing the offender, the barons
avowed and applauded the savage deed,[46] which, as a prince
and as a man, it was impossible that Robert should forgive.
He escaped from the guilty city to implore the justice or compassion of the pope; the emperor was coolly exhorted to return
to his station; before he could obey, he sunk under the weight
of grief, shame, and impotent resentment.[47]

It was only in the age of chivalry that valour could ascend
from a private station to the thrones of Jerusalem and Constantinople. The titular kingdom of Jerusalem had devolved to Mary, the daughter of Isabella, and Conrad of
Montferrat, and the grand-daughter of Almeric or Amaury.
She was given to John of Brienne, of a noble family in Champagne, by the public voice, and the judgment of Philip
Augustus, who named him as the most worthy champion
of the Holy Land.[48] In the fifth crusade, he led an hundred
thousand Latins to the conquest of Egypt; by him the siege
of Damietta was achieved; and the subsequent failure was

---

[46] Marinus Sanutus (Secreta Fidelium Crucis, l. ii. p. 4, c. 18, p. 73) is so
much delighted with this bloody deed that he has transcribed it in his margin
as a bonum exemplum Yet he acknowledges the damsel for the lawful
wife of Robert

[47] See the reign of Robert in Ducange (Hist. de C. P. l. iii c. 1-12) [Fin-
lay thinks that Robert should have "seized the culprit immediately, and
hung him in his armour before the palace gates, with his shield round his
neck" (iv p 114)]

[48] Rex igitur Franciæ, deliberatione habitâ, respondit nuntiis, se daturum
hominem Syriæ partibus aptum, in armis probum (*preux*), in bellis securum,
in agendis providum, Johannem comitem Brennensem Sanut Secret
Fidelium, l. iii. p xi. c. 4, p 205 Matthew Paris, p. 159.

justly ascribed to the pride and avarice of the legate   After
the marriage of his daughter with Frederic the Second,[49]
he was provoked by the emperor's ingratitude to accept the
command of the army of the church, and, though advanced
in life, and despoiled of royalty, the sword and spirit of John
of Brienne were still ready for the service of Christendom.
In the seven years of his brother's reign Baldwin of Courtenay
had not emerged from a state of childhood, and the barons
of Romania felt the strong necessity of placing the sceptre
in the hands of a man and a hero.   The veteran king of
Jerusalem might have disdained the name and office of regent;
they agreed to invest him for his life with the title and prerogatives of emperor, on the sole condition that Baldwin
should marry his second daughter and succeed at a mature
age to the throne of Constantinople.[50]   The expectation,
both of the Greeks and Latins, was kindled by the renown,
the choice, and the presence of John of Brienne; and they
admired his martial aspect, his green and vigorous age of
more than fourscore years, and his size and stature, which
surpassed the common measure of mankind.[51]   But avarice
and the love of ease appear to have chilled the ardour of enterprise; his troops were disbanded, and two years rolled away
without action or honour, till he was awakened [52] by the dangerous alliance of Vataces, emperor of Nice, and of Azan,
king of Bulgaria.[53]   They besieged Constantinople by sea

[49] Giannone (Istoria Civile, tom. ii. l. xvi p 380–385) discusses the marriage of Frederic II with the daughter of John of Brienne, and the double
union of the crowns of Naples and Jerusalem

[50] [For the act see Buchon, Recherches et Matériaux, p 21–23]

[51] Acropolita, c 27   The historian was at that time a boy, and educated
at Constantinople   In 1233, when he was eleven years old, his father broke
the Latin chain, left a splendid fortune, and escaped to the Greek court of
Nice, where his son was raised to the highest honours

[52] [He did not arrive at Constantinople till 1231]

[53] [For this able and humane prince, see Jireček, Geschichte der Bulgaren,
chap. xvi   He defeated the forces of Thessalonica and Epirus in the battle
of Klokotnitza (near the Strymon), 1230, and extended his power over the
greater part of Thrace, Macedonia, and Albania   His empire touched three

and land, with an army of one hundred thousand men, and a
fleet of three hundred ships of war; while the entire force of
the Latin emperor was reduced to one hundred and sixty
knights and a small addition of serjeants and archers. I
tremble to relate that, instead of defending the city, the hero
made a sally at the head of his cavalry, and that, of forty-
eight squadrons of the enemy, no more than three escaped
from the edge of his invincible sword. Fired by his example,
the infantry and citizens boarded the vessels that anchored
close to the walls; and twenty-five were dragged in triumph
into the harbour of Constantinople At the summons of the
emperor, the vassals and allies armed in her defence; broke
through every obstacle that opposed their passage; and, in
the succeeding year, obtained a second victory over the same
enemies By the rude poets of the age, John of Brienne is
compared to Hector, Roland, and Judas Maccabæus,[54]

seas and included the cities of Belgrade and Hadrianople. An inscription
in the cathedral of Trnovo, which he built, records his deeds as follows
"In the year 6738 [= 1230] Indiction 3, I, Joannes Asēn, the Tsar, faithful
servant of God in Christ, sovereign of the Bulgarians, son of the old Asēn,
have built this magnificent church and adorned it with paintings, in honour
of the Forty Martyrs, with whose help, in the 12th year of my reign, when the
church was painted, I made an expedition to Romania and defeated the
Greek army and took the Tsar, Kyr Thodor Komnin, prisoner, with all his
bolyars I conquered all the countries from Odrin [Hadrianople] to Dratz
[Durazzo], — Greek, Albanian, and Servian The Franks have only retained the towns about Tzarigrad [Constantinople] and that city itself; but
even they submitted to my empire when they had no other Emperor but me,
and I permitted them to continue, as God so willed For without him neither
work nor word is accomplished. Glory to him for ever, Amen " (Jireček,
p 251-2)]

[54] Philip Mouskes, bishop of Tournay (A D 1274-1282), has composed a
poem, or rather a string of verses, in bad old Flemish French, on the Latin
emperors of Constantinople, which Ducange has published at the end of
Villehardouin [What Ducange published was an extract from the Chronique
rimée of Mouskès, which began with the Trojan war The whole work was
first published by De Reiffenberg in 1836 Gibbon identifies Mouskès with
Philip of Ghent, who became bishop of Tournay in 1274 This is an error.
Mouskès was a native of Tournay and died in 1244] See p 224, for the
prowess of John of Brienne

N'Aie, Lector, Roll' ne Ogiers

but their credit and his glory receives some abatement from the silence of the Greeks.[55] The empire was soon deprived of the last of her champions; and the dying monarch was ambitious to enter paradise in the habit of a Franciscan friar.[56]

In the double victory of John of Brienne, I cannot discover the name or exploits of his pupil Baldwin, who had attained the age of military service, and who succeeded to the Imperial dignity on the decease of his adopted father.[57] The royal youth was employed on a commission more suitable to his temper; he was sent to visit the Western courts, of the pope more especially, and of the king of France, to excite their pity by the view of his innocence and distress; and to obtain some supplies of men or money for the relief of the sinking empire He thrice repeated these mendicant visits, in which he seemed to prolong his stay and postpone his return, of the five-and-twenty years of his reign, a greater number were spent abroad than at home; and in no place did the emperor deem himself less free and secure than in his native country and his capital. On some public occasions, his vanity might be soothed by the title of Augustus and by the honours of the purple; and at the general council of Lyons, when Frederic the Second was excommunicated and deposed, his Oriental colleague was enthroned on the right hand of the pope But how often was the exile, the vagrant, the Imperial beggar humbled with scorn, insulted with pity, and degraded in his own eyes and

> Tant ne fit d'armes en estors
> Com fist li Rois Jehans cel jors,
> Et il defors et il dedans
> La paru sa force et ses sens
> Et li hardiment qu'il avoit

[55] [John Asēn, threatened by the approach of Zenghis Khan (see below, chap lxiv), gave up the war and made a separate peace and alliance with the Eastern Emperors But the alliance was soon abandoned, and Asēn returned to his friendship with Nicæa]

[56] See the reign of John de Brienne, in Ducange, Hist de C. P. l iii c 13–26

[57] See the reign of Baldwin II till his expulsion from Constantinople, in Ducange (Hist. de C P l iv c 1–34, the end l v c. 1–33).

those of the nations! In his first visit to England he was stopt at Dover by a severe reprimand that he should presume, without leave, to enter an independent kingdom. After some delay, Baldwin, however, was permitted to pursue his journey, was entertained with cold civility, and thankfully departed with a present of seven hundred marks.[58] From the avarice of Rome he could only obtain the proclamation of a crusade, and a treasure of indulgences : a coin whose currency was depreciated by too frequent and indiscriminate abuse. His birth and misfortunes recommended him to the generosity of his cousin, Lewis the Ninth ; but the martial zeal of the saint was diverted from Constantinople to Egypt and Palestine ; and the public and private poverty of Baldwin was alleviated, for a moment, by the alienation of the marquisate of Namur and the lordship of Courtenay, the last remains of his inheritance. [59] By such shameful or ruinous expedients he once more returned to Romania, with an army of thirty thousand soldiers, whose numbers were doubled in the apprehension of the Greeks His first despatches to France and England announced his victories and his hopes, he had reduced the country round the capital to the distance of three days' journey, and, if he succeeded against an important though nameless city (most probably Chiorli),[60] the frontier would be safe and the passage accessible. But these expectations (if Baldwin was sincere) quickly vanished like a dream ; the troops and treasures of France melted away in his un-

[58] Matthew Paris relates the two visits of Baldwin II to the English court, p 396, 637, his return to Greece armatâ manu, p. 407, his letters of his nomen formidabile, &c p 481 (a passage which had escaped Ducange), his expulsion, p 850

[59] Louis IX disapproved and stopped the alienation of Courtenay (Ducange, l iv c 23) It is now annexed to the royal demesne, but granted for a term (*engage*) to the family of Boulanvilliers Courtenay, in the election of Nemours in the Isle de France, is a town of 900 inhabitants, with the remains of a castle (Mélanges tirés d'une grande Bibliothèque, tom. xiv p 74-77)

[60] [Tzurulos]

skilful hands, and the throne of the Latin emperor was protected by a dishonourable alliance with the Turks and Comans   To secure the former, he consented to bestow his niece on the unbelieving sultan of Cogni, to please the latter, he complied with their Pagan rites. a dog was sacrificed between the two armies; and the contracting parties tasted each other's blood, as a pledge of their fidelity.[61]   In the palace or prison of Constantinople, the successor of Augustus demolished the vacant houses for winter-fuel, and stripped the lead from the churches for the daily expenses of his family. Some usurious loans were dealt with a scanty hand by the merchants of Italy; and Philip, his son and heir, was pawned at Venice as the security for a debt.[62]   Thirst, hunger, and nakedness are positive evils; but wealth is relative; and a prince, who would be rich in a private station, may be exposed by the increase of his wants to all the anxiety and bitterness of poverty.

But in this abject distress the emperor and empire were still possessed of an ideal treasure, which drew its fantastic value from the superstition of the Christian world.   The merit of the true cross was somewhat impaired by its frequent division; and a long captivity among the infidels might shed some suspicion on the fragments that were produced in the East and West   But another relic of the Passion was preserved in the Imperial chapel of Constantinople; and the crown of thorns, which had been placed on the head of Christ, was equally precious and authentic.   It had formerly been the practice of the Egyptian debtors to deposit, as a security, the mummies of their parents; and both their honour and religion were bound for the redemption of the pledge.   In the same manner, and in the absence of the emperor, the barons of Romania borrowed the sum of thirteen thousand one hundred and thirty-

[61] Joinville, p 104, édit du Louvre   A Coman prince, who died without baptism, was buried at the gates of Constantinople with a live retinue of slaves and horses

[62] Sanut. Secret Fidel Crucis, l ii p iv c 18, p 73

four pieces of gold,[63] on the credit of the holy crown; they failed in the performance of their contract, and a rich Venetian, Nicholas Querini, undertook to satisfy their impatient creditors, on condition that the relic should be lodged at Venice, to become his absolute property if it were not redeemed within a short and definite term. The barons apprised their sovereign of the hard treaty and impending loss; and, as the empire could not afford a ransom of seven thousand pounds sterling, Baldwin was anxious to snatch the prize from the Venetians, and to vest it with more honour and emolument in the hands of the most Christian king.[64] Yet the negotiation was attended with some delicacy In the purchase of relics, the saint would have started at the guilt of simony; but, if the mode of expression were changed, he might lawfully repay the debt, accept the gift, and acknowledge the obligation. His ambassadors, two Dominicans, were despatched to Venice, to redeem and receive the holy crown, which had escaped the dangers of the sea and the galleys of Vataces. On opening a wooden box, they recognised the seals of the doge and barons, which were applied on a shrine of silver; and within this shrine the monument of the Passion was enclosed in a golden vase. The reluctant Venetians yielded to justice and power; the emperor Frederic granted a free and honourable passage, the court of France advanced as far as Troyes in Champagne, to meet with devotion this inestimable relic, it was borne in triumph through Paris by the king himself, barefoot, and in his shirt; and a free gift of ten thousand marks of silver reconciled Baldwin to his loss. The success of this transaction tempted the Latin emperor to

[63] Under the words *Perparus, Perpera, Hyperperum*, Ducange is short and vague: Monetæ genus From a corrupt passage of Guntherus (Hist C P c 8, p 10), I guess that the Perpera was the nummus aureus, the fourth part of a mark of silver, or about ten shillings sterling in value. In lead it would be too contemptible

[64] For the translation of the holy crown, &c from Constantinople to Paris, see Ducange (Hist de C P l iv c 11-14, 24, 35), and Fleury (Hist Ecclés. tom. xvii p 201-204)

offer with the same generosity the remaining furniture of his chapel:[65] a large and authentic portion of the true cross; the baby-linen of the Son of God; the lance, the spunge, and the chain of his Passion; the rod of Moses, and part of the scull of St John the Baptist. For the reception of these spiritual treasures, twenty thousand marks were expended by St. Louis on a stately foundation, the holy chapel of Paris, on which the muse of Boileau has bestowed a comic immortality   The truth of such remote and ancient relics, which cannot be proved by any human testimony, must be admitted by those who believe in the miracles which they have performed   About the middle of the last age, an inveterate ulcer was touched and cured by an holy prickle of the holy crown .[66] the prodigy is attested by the most pious and enlightened Christians of France; nor will the fact be easily disproved, except by those who are armed with a general antidote against religious credulity.[67]

The Latins of Constantinople[68] were on all sides encompassed and pressed . their sole hope, the last delay of their ruin, was in the division of their Greek and Bulgarian enemies;

[65] Mélanges tirés d'une grande Bibliothèque, tom xliii p 201–205   The Lutrin of Boileau exhibits the inside, the soul and manners of the *Sainte Chapelle,* and many facts relative to the institution are collected and explained by his commentators, Brossette and de St Marc

[66] It was performed A D 1656, March 24, on the niece of Pascal; and that superior genius, with Arnauld, Nicole, &c were on the spot to believe and attest a miracle which confounded the Jesuits, and saved Port Royal (Oeuvres de Racine, tom vi p. 176–187, in his eloquent History of Port Royal)

[67] Voltaire (Siècle de Louis XIV c 37, Oeuvres, tom ix p 178, 179) strives to invalidate the fact, but Hume (Essays, vol ii p 483, 484), with more skill and success, seizes the battery, and turns the cannon against his enemies.

[68] The gradual losses of the Latins may be traced in the third, fourth, and fifth books of the compilation of Ducange, but of the Greek conquests he has dropped many circumstances, which may be recovered from the large history of George Acropolita, and the three first books of Nicephorus Gregoras, two writers of the Byzantine series, who have had the good fortune to meet with learned editors, Leo Allatius at Rome, and John Boivin in the Academy of Inscriptions of Paris.

and of this hope they were deprived by the superior arms and policy of Vataces, emperor of Nice. From the Propontis to the rocky coast of Pamphylia, Asia was peaceful and prosperous under his reign, and the events of every campaign extended his influence in Europe. The strong cities of the hills of Macedonia and Thrace were rescued from the Bulgarians; and their kingdom was circumscribed by its present and proper limits, along the southern banks of the Danube The sole emperor of the Romans could no longer brook that a lord of Epirus, a Comnenian prince of the West, should presume to dispute or share the honours of the purple, and the humble Demetrius changed the colour of his buskins, and accepted with gratitude the appellation of despot. His own subjects were exasperated by his baseness and incapacity: they implored the protection of their supreme lord. After some resistance, the kingdom of Thessalonica was united to the empire of Nice;[89] and Vataces reigned without a competitor from the Turkish borders to the Adriatic gulf. The princes of Europe revered his merit and power; and, had he subscribed an orthodox creed, it should seem that the pope would have abandoned without reluctance the Latin throne of Constantinople. But the death of Vataces, the short and busy reign of Theodore his son, and the helpless infancy of his grandson John suspended the restoration of the Greeks

[89] [The conquest of Thessalonica, from the young Demetrius, son of Boniface, by Theodore Angelus, despot of Epirus, and Theodore's assumption of the Imperial title A D 1222, have been briefly mentioned above, p 24 His brother Manuel, and then his son John, succeeded to the Empire of Salonica It was a matter of political importance for Vatatzes to bring this rival Empire into subjection, he marched against Thessalonica, but raised the siege (A D 1243) on condition that John should lay down the title of Emperor and assume that of despot John died in the following year and was succeeded by his brother Demetrius, but in 1246 Demetrius was removed by Vatatzes, and Thessalonica became definitely part of the empire of Nicæa Thus the Thessalonian empire lasted 1222–1243 Meanwhile Epirus had split off from the empire of Salonica, in 1236-7, under Michael II (a bastard son of Michael I), whose Despotate survived that Empire See below, note 71]

In the next chapter I shall explain their domestic revolutions; in this place it will be sufficient to observe that the young prince was oppressed by the ambition of his guardian and colleague, Michael Palæologus, who displayed the virtues and vices that belong to the founder of a new dynasty. The emperor Baldwin had flattered himself that he might recover some provinces or cities by an impotent negotiation His ambassadors were dismissed from Nice with mockery and contempt. At every place which they named, Palæologus alleged some special reason which rendered it dear and valuable in his eyes in the one he was born, in another he had been first promoted to military command, and in a third he had enjoyed, and hoped long to enjoy, the pleasures of the chase. "And what, then, do you propose to give us?" said the astonished deputies. "Nothing," replied the Greek, "not a foot of land If your master be desirous of peace, let him pay me, as an annual tribute, the sum which he receives from the trade and customs of Constantinople. On these terms I may allow him to reign. If he refuses, it is war. I am not ignorant of the art of war, and I trust the event to God and my sword."[70] An expedition against the despot of Epirus was the first prelude of his aims If a victory was followed by a defeat; if the race of the Comneni or Angeli survived in those mountains his efforts and his reign; the captivity of Villehardouin, prince of Achaia, deprived the Latins of the most active and powerful vassal of their expiring monarchy.[71]   The republics of Venice and Genoa disputed,

[70] George Acropolita, c lxxviii p 89, 90, edit Paris

[71] [This victory was won by John Palæologus, brother of Michael, in the plain of Pelagonia near Kastoria, in Macedonia The despot of Epirus, Michael II (bastard of Michael I), had extended his sway to the Vardar, and threatened Salonica He was supported by Manfred, king of Sicily, who sent four hundred knights to his aid, as well as William Villehardouin, prince of Achaia Finlay places the coronation of Michael Palæologus in Jan 1259 — *before* the battle of Pelagonia (iii 339), but it seems to have been subsequent, in Jan 1260, see Mēliarakēs, Ἱστορία τοῦ βασιλείου τῆς Νικαίας κ.τ λ. (1898), p 536-543]

in the first of their naval wars, the command of the sea and the commerce of the East. Pride and interest attached the Venetians to the defence of Constantinople   their rivals were tempted to promote the designs of her enemies, and the alliance of the Genoese with the schismatic conqueror provoked the indignation of the Latin church [72]

Intent on his great object, the emperor Michael visited in person and strengthened the troops and fortifications of Thrace   The remains of the Latins were driven from their last possessions; he assaulted without success the suburbs of Galata,[73] and corresponded with a perfidious baron,[74] who proved unwilling, or unable, to open the gates of the metropolis. The next spring,[75] his favourite general, Alexius Strategopulus, whom he had decorated with the title of Cæsar, passed the Hellespont with eight hundred horse and some infantry,[76] on a secret expedition. His instructions enjoined him to approach, to listen, to watch, but not to risk

[72] The Greeks, ashamed of any foreign aid, disguise the alliance and succour of the Genoese, but the fact is proved by the testimony of J Villani (Chron l vi c 71, in Muratori, Script Rerum Italicarum, tom viii p 202, 203) and William de Nangis (Annales de St Louis, p 248, in the Louvre Joinville), two impartial foreigners, and Urban IV. threatened to deprive Genoa of her archbishop. [For the treaty of Michael with Genoa in March, 1261, see Buchon, Recherches et matériaux, p 462 *sqq* (in French), or Zacharia v Lingenthal, Jus Græco-Rom , iii p 574 *sqq* (in Latin)   The Genoese undertook to furnish a fleet , but when these ships arrived Michael was already in possession of the city]

[73] [Spring, 1260.]

[74] [Anseau de Cayeux (if that is the name), who was married to a sister-in-law of John Vatatzes   Cp Méliarakês, *op cit* p 551-2]

[75] [Michael himself this spring passed and repassed repeatedly from Asia to Europe   He first took Selymbria, which was a valuable basis for further operations (Pachymeres, p 110)   Ecclesiastical business then recalled him to Asia; and having settled this he recrossed the Hellespont and for the second time besieged Galata (Pachymeres, p 118 *sqq*)   He raised the siege and returned to Nymphæum, where he concluded the treaty with the Genoese]

[76] Some precautions must be used in reconciling the discordant numbers, the 800 soldiers of Nicetas, the 25,000 of Spandugino (apud Ducange, l v c 24), the Greeks and Scythians of Acropolita, and the numerous army of Michael, in the Epistles of Pope Urban IV (1 129)

any doubtful or dangerous enterprise against the city. The adjacent territory between the Propontis and the Black Sea was cultivated by an hardy race of peasants and outlaws, exercised in arms, uncertain in their allegiance, but inclined by language, religion, and present advantage to the party of the Greeks. They were styled the *volunteers*,[77] and by their free service the army of Alexius, with the regulars of Thrace and the Coman auxiliaries,[78] was augmented to the number of five and twenty thousand men. By the ardour of the volunteers, and by his own ambition, the Cæsar was stimulated to disobey the precise orders of his master, in the just confidence that success would plead his pardon and reward. The weakness of Constantinople, and the distress and terror of the Latins, were familiar to the observation of the volunteers; and they represented the present moment as the most propitious to surprise and conquest. A rash youth, the new governor of the Venetian colony, had sailed away with thirty galleys and the best of the French knights, on a wild expedition to Daphnusia, a town on the Black Sea, at a distance of forty leagues;[79] and the remaining Latins were without strength or suspicion. They were informed that Alexius had passed the Hellespont; but their apprehensions were lulled by the smallness of his original numbers, and their imprudence had not watched the subsequent increase of his army. If he left his main body to second and support his operations, he might advance unperceived in the night with a chosen

---

[77] Θεληματάριοι   They are described and named by Pachymer (l ii c 14) [The chief of these, who was very active in the capture of the city, was named Kutritzakês]

[78] It is needless to seek these Comans in the deserts of Tartary, or even of Moldavia   A part of the horde had submitted to John Vataces and was probably settled as a nursery of soldiers on some waste lands of Thrace (Cantacuzen l i c 2).

[79] [Daphnusia, a town on a little island (now desert and named Kefken Adassi) off the coast of Bithynia, about 70 miles east of the mouth of the Bosphorus   Thynias was another name   Cp Ramsay, Hist Geography of Asia Minor, p 182]

detachment. While some applied scaling-ladders to the lowest part of the walls, they were secure of an old Greek, who would introduce their companions through a subterranean passage into his house; [80] they could soon on the inside break an entrance through the golden gate, which had been long obstructed, and the conqueror would be in the heart of the city, before the Latins were conscious of their danger. After some debate, the Cæsar resigned himself to the faith of the volunteers; they were trusty, bold, and successful; and in describing the plan I have already related the execution and success. [81] But no sooner had Alexius passed the threshold of the golden gate than he trembled at his own rashness, he paused, he deliberated, till the desperate volunteers urged him forwards by the assurance that in retreat lay the greatest and most inevitable danger. Whilst the Cæsar kept his regulars in firm array, the Comans dispersed themselves on all sides, an alarm was sounded, and the threats of fire and pillage compelled the citizens to a decisive resolution. The Greeks of Constantinople remembered their native sovereigns; the Genoese merchants, their recent alliance and Venetian foes; every quarter was in arms; and the air resounded with a general acclamation of "Long life and victory to Michael and John, the august emperors of the Romans!" Their rival Baldwin was awakened by the sound; but the most pressing danger could not prompt him to draw his sword in the defence of a city which he deserted, perhaps, with more pleasure than regret: he fled from the palace to the sea-shore, where he descried the welcome sails of the

[80] [Near the Gate of Selymbria or Pegæ (see above, vol iii, plan opp p 100), and it was through this gate that the entrance was to be broken]

[81] The loss of Constantinople is briefly told by the Latins, the conquest is described with more satisfaction by the Greeks by Acropolita (c 85), Pachymer (l ii c 26, 27), Nicephorus Gregoras (l iv c 1, 2). See Ducange, Hist de C P l v c 19–27 [It is also described by Phrantzes, p 17–20, ed Bonn., and in an anonymous poem on the Loss (1204) and Recovery (1261) of Constantinople, composed in A D 1392 (published by Buchon. Recherches historiques 2, p 335 *sqq*, 1845)]

fleet returning from the vain and fruitless attempt on Daphnusia. Constantinople was irrecoverably lost, but the Latin
emperor and the principal families embarked on board the
Venetian galleys, and steered for the isle of Euboea, and afterwards for Italy, where the royal fugitive was entertained by
the pope and Sicilian king with a mixture of contempt and
pity.   From the loss of Constantinople to his death, he consumed thirteen years, soliciting the Catholic powers to join
in his restoration   the lesson had been familiar to his youth;
nor was his last exile more indigent or shameful than his three
former pilgrimages to the courts of Europe. His son Philip
was the heir of an ideal empire; and the pretensions of *his*
daughter Catherine were transported by her marriage to
Charles of Valois, the brother of Philip the Fair, king of
France. The house of Courtenay was represented in the
female line by successive alliances, till the title of emperor
of Constantinople, too bulky and sonorous for a private
name, modestly expired in silence and oblivion.[82]

After this narrative of the expeditions of the Latins to
Palestine and Constantinople, I cannot dismiss the subject
without revolving the general consequences on the countries
that were the scene, and on the nations that were the actors,
of these memorable crusades.[83] As soon as the arms of the
Franks were withdrawn, the impression, though not the memory, was erased in the Mahometan realms of Egypt and Syria.
The faithful disciples of the prophet were never tempted by

[82] See the three last books (l v –viii), and the genealogical tables of
Ducange In the year 1382, the titular emperor of Constantinople was
James de Baux [titular Emperor, 1373–1383], duke of Andria in the kingdom of Naples, the son of Margaret, daughter of Catherine de Valois [mar-
ried to Philip of Tarentum], daughter of Catherine [married to Charles of
Valois], daughter of Philip, son of Baldwin II (Ducange, l viii c 37, 38)
It is uncertain whether he left any posterity
[83] Abulfeda, who saw the conclusion of the crusades, speaks of the kingdom
of the Franks, and those of the negroes, as equally unknown (Prolegom ad
Geograph) Had he not disdained the Latin language, how easily might
the Syrian prince have found books and interpreters!

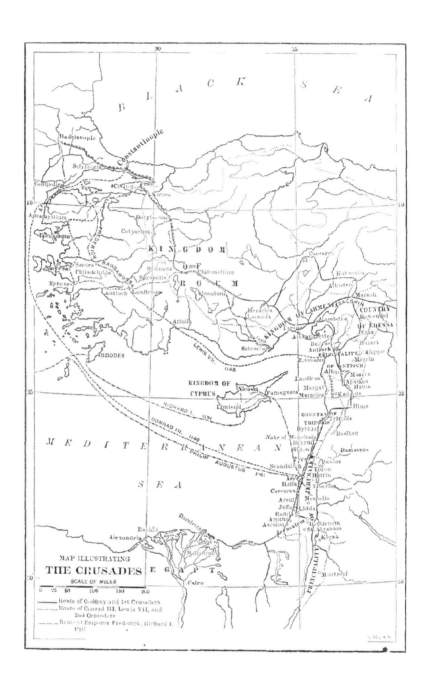

MAP ILLUSTRATING
THE CRUSADES
SCALE OF MILES
0   25   50   100   150   200

——— Route of Godfrey and 1st Crusaders
·········· Route of Conrad III, Lewis VII, and
           2nd Crusaders
-·-·-·- Route of Emperor Frederick, Richard I,
           Phil.

a profane desire to study the laws or language of the idolaters; nor did the simplicity of their primitive manners receive the slightest alteration from their intercourse in peace and war with the unknown strangers of the West. The Greeks, who thought themselves proud, but who were only vain, shewed a disposition somewhat less inflexible. In the efforts for the recovery of their empire they emulated the valour, discipline, and tactics of their antagonists The modern literature of the West they might justly despise; but its free spirit would instruct them in the rights of man, and some institutions of public and private life were adopted from the French The correspondence of Constantinople and Italy diffused the knowledge of the Latin tongue; and several of the fathers and classics were at length honoured with a Greek version.[84] But the national and religious prejudices of the Orientals were inflamed by persecution, and the reign of the Latins confirmed the separation of the two churches

If we compare, at the era of the crusades, the Latins of Europe with the Greeks and Arabians, their respective degrees of knowledge, industry, and art, our rude ancestors must be content with the third rank in the scale of nations. Their successive improvement and present superiority may be ascribed to a peculiar energy of character, to an active and imitative spirit, unknown to their more polished rivals, who at that time were in a stationary or retrograde state. With such a disposition, the Latins should have derived the most early and essential benefits from a series of events which

[84] A short and superficial account of these versions from Latin into Greek is given by Huet (de Interpretatione et de claris Interpretibus, p 131-135) Maximus Planudes, a monk of Constantinople (A D 1327-1353 [born c 1260, died 1310]), has translated Cæsar's Commentaries, the Somnium Scipionis, the Metamorphoses and Heroides of Ovid [the proverbial philosophy of the elder Cato, Boethius' De Consolatione], &c (Fabric Bib Græc tom x p 533 [ed Harl xi 682 sqq , Krumbacher, Gesch der byz Litt 543 sqq The Letters of Planudes have been edited by M Treu (1890), who has established the chronology of his life (Zur Gesch der Ueberlieferung von Plutarchs Moralia, 1877)])

opened to their eyes the prospect of the world, and introduced them to a long and frequent intercourse with the more cultivated regions of the East. The first and most obvious progress was in trade and manufactures, in the arts which are strongly prompted by the thirst of wealth, the calls of necessity, and the gratification of the sense or vanity. Among the crowd of unthinking fanatics, a captive or a pilgrim might sometimes observe the superior refinements of Cairo and Constantinople · the first importer of windmills [85] was the benefactor of nations; and, if such blessings are enjoyed without any grateful remembrance, history has condescended to notice the more apparent luxuries of silk and sugar, which were transported into Italy from Greece and Egypt. But the intellectual wants of the Latins were more slowly felt and supplied; the ardour of studious curiosity was awakened in Europe by different causes and more recent events; and, in the age of the crusades, they viewed with careless indifference the literature of the Greeks and Arabians   Some rudiments of mathematical and medicinal knowledge might be imparted in practice and in figures; necessity might produce some interpreters for the grosser business of merchants and soldiers; but the commerce of the Orientals had not diffused the study and knowledge of their languages in the schools of Europe.[86] If a similar principle of religion repulsed the idiom of the Koran, it should have excited their patience and curiosity to understand the original text of the gospel; and the same grammar would have unfolded the sense of Plato and the beauties of Homer. Yet in a reign of sixty years, the Latins of Constantinople disdained the speech and learning of their subjects; and the manuscripts were the only

[85] Windmills, first invented in the dry country of Asia Minor, were used in Normandy as early as the year 1105 (Vie privée des François, tom. 1. p 42, 43, Ducange, Gloss Latin tom iv p 474).

[86] See the complaints of Roger Bacon (Biographia Britannica, vol i p 418, Kippis's edition). If Bacon himself, or Gerbert, understood *some* Greek, they were prodigies, and owed nothing to the commerce of the East

treasures which the natives might enjoy without rapine or envy. Aristotle was indeed the oracle of the Western universities, but it was a Barbarous Aristotle; and, instead of ascending to the fountain-head, his Latin votaries humbly accepted a corrupt and remote version from the Jews and Moors of Andalusia. The principle of the crusades was a savage fanaticism; and the most important effects were analogous to the cause. Each pilgrim was ambitious to return with his sacred spoils, the relics of Greece and Palestine;[87] and each relic was preceded and followed by a train of miracles and visions. The belief of the Catholics was corrupted by new legends, their practice by new superstitions; and the establishment of the inquisition, the mendicant orders of monks and friars, the last abuse of indulgences, and the final progress of idolatry flowed from the baleful fountain of the holy war. The active spirit of the Latins preyed on the vitals of their reason and religion; and, if the ninth and tenth centuries were the times of darkness, the thirteenth and fourteenth were the age of absurdity and fable

In the profession of Christianity, in the cultivation of a fertile land, the Northern conquerors of the Roman empire insensibly mingled with the provincials and rekindled the embers of the arts of antiquity. Their settlements about the age of Charlemagne had acquired some degree of order and stability, when they were overwhelmed by new swarms of invaders, the Normans, Saracens,[88] and Hungarians, who replunged the Western countries of Europe into their former state of anarchy and barbarism. About the eleventh century,

[87] Such was the opinion of the great Leibnitz (Oeuvres de Fontenelle, tom v. p. 458), a master of the history of the middle ages I shall only instance the pedigree of the Carmelites, and the flight of the house of Loretto, which were both derived from Palestine

[88] If I rank the Saracens with the Barbarians, it is only relative to their wars, or rather inroads, in Italy and France, where their sole purpose was to plunder and destroy.

the second tempest had subsided by the expulsion or conversion of the enemies of Christendom the tide of civilisation, which had so long ebbed, began to flow with a steady
and accelerated course, and a fairer prospect was opened to
the hopes and efforts of the rising generations.   Great was
the success, and rapid the progress, during the two hundred
years of the crusades; and some philosophers have applauded
the propitious influence of these holy wars, which appear to
me to have checked, rather than forwarded, the maturity of
Europe [89] The lives and labours of millions, which were
buried in the East, would have been more profitably employed
in the improvement of their native country the accumulated
stock of industry and wealth would have overflowed in navigation and trade; and the Latins would have been enriched
and enlightened by a pure and friendly correspondence with
the climates of the East.   In one respect I can indeed perceive the accidental operation of the crusades, not so much in
producing a benefit, as in removing an evil.   The larger portion of the inhabitants of Europe was chained to the soil,
without freedom, or property, or knowledge, and the two
orders of ecclesiastics and nobles, whose numbers were
comparatively small, alone deserved the name of citizens and
men.   This oppressive system was supported by the arts of
the clergy and the swords of the barons The authority
of the priests operated in the darker ages as a salutary antidote: they prevented the total extinction of letters, mitigated
the fierceness of the times, sheltered the poor and defenceless,
and preserved or revived the peace and order of civil society.
But the independence, rapine, and discord of the feudal
lords were unmixed with any semblance of good, and every
hope of industry and improvement was crushed by the iron
weight of the martial aristocracy.   Among the causes that

[89] On this interesting subject, the progress of society in Europe, a strong
ray of philosophic light has broke from Scotland in our own times, and it is
with private as well as public regard that I repeat the names of Hume,
Robertson, and Adam Smith

undermined the Gothic edifice, a conspicuous place must be allowed to the crusades. The estates of the barons were dissipated, and their race was often extinguished, in these costly and perilous expeditions. Their poverty extorted from their pride those charters of freedom which unlocked the fetters of the slave, secured the farm of the peasant and the shop of the artificer, and gradually restored a substance and a soul to the most numerous and useful part of the community. The conflagration which destroyed the tall and barren trees of the forest gave air and scope to the vegetation of the smaller and nutritive plants of the soil.

Digression on the Family of Courtenay

THE purple of three emperors who have reigned at Constantinople will authorise or excuse a digression on the origin and singular fortunes of the house of COURTENAY,[90] in the three principal branches I. Of Edessa, II. Of France; and III. Of England; of which the last only has survived the revolutions of eight hundred years.

I. Before the introduction of trade, which scatters riches, and of knowledge, which dispels prejudice, the prerogative of birth is most strongly felt and most humbly acknowledged. In every age the laws and manners of the Germans have discriminated the ranks of society· the dukes and counts, who shared the empire of Charlemagne, converted their office to an inheritance; and to his children each feudal lord bequeathed his honour and his sword. The proudest families are content to lose, in the darkness of the middle ages, the

---

[90] I have applied, but not confined, myself to *A Genealogical History of the Noble and Illustrious Family of Courtenay, by Ezra Cleaveland, Tutor to Sir William Courtenay, and Rector of Honiton*, Exon 1735, in folio The first part is extracted from William of Tyre, the second from Bouchet's French history, and the third from various memorials, public, provincial, and private, of the Courtenays of Devonshire The rector of Honiton has more gratitude than industry, and more industry than criticism.

tree of their pedigree, which, however deep and lofty, must ultimately rise from a plebeian root; and their historians must descend ten centuries below the Christian era, before they can ascertain any lineal succession by the evidence of surnames, of arms, and of authentic records. With the first rays of light [91] we discern the nobility and opulence of Atho, a French knight. his nobility, in the rank and title of a nameless father, his opulence, in the foundation of the castle of Courtenay, in the district of Gatinois, about fifty-six miles to the south of Paris. From the reign of Robert, the son of Hugh Capet, the barons of Courtenay are conspicuous among the immediate vassals of the crown; and Joscelin, the grandson of Atho and a noble dame, is enrolled among the heroes of the first crusade. A domestic alliance (their mothers were sisters) attached him to the standard of Baldwin of Bruges, the second count of Edessa. a princely fief, which he was worthy to receive, and able to maintain, announces the number of his martial followers, and, after the departure of his cousin, Joscelin himself was invested with the county of Edessa on both sides of the Euphrates. By economy in peace his territories were replenished with Latin and Syrian subjects. his magazines with corn, wine, and oil; his castles with gold and silver, with arms and horses. In a holy warfare of thirty years he was alternately a conqueror and a captive; but he died like a soldier, in an horse-litter at the head of his troops; and his last glance beheld the flight of the Turkish invaders who had presumed on his age and infirmities. His son and successor, of the same name, was less deficient in valour than in vigilance; but he sometimes forgot that dominion is acquired and maintained by the same arts. He challenged the hostility of the Turks, without securing the friendship of the prince of Antioch; and, amidst the

[91] The primitive record of the family is a passage of the Continuator of Aimoin, a monk of Fleury, who wrote in the xiith century. See his Chronicle, in the Historians of France (tom. xi. p. 176)

peaceful luxury of Turbessel, in Syria,[92] Joscelin neglected the defence of the Christian frontier beyond the Euphrates. In his absence, Zenghi, the first of the Atabeks, besieged and stormed his capital, Edessa, which was feebly defended by a timorous and disloyal crowd of Orientals; the Franks were oppressed in a bold attempt for its recovery, and Courtenay ended his days in the prison of Aleppo. He still left a fair and ample patrimony But the victorious Turks oppressed on all sides the weakness of a widow and orphan, and, for the equivalent of an annual pension, they resigned to the Greek emperor the charge of defending, and the shame of losing, the last relics of the Latin conquest. The countess-dowager of Edessa retired to Jerusalem with her two children. the daughter, Agnes, became the wife and mother of a king, the son, Joscelin the Third, accepted the office of seneschal, the first of the kingdom, and held his new estates in Palestine by the service of fifty knights. His name appears with honour in all the transactions of peace and war; but he finally vanishes in the fall of Jerusalem; and the name of Courtenay, in this branch of Edessa, was lost by the marriage of his two daughters with a French and a German baron.[93]

II While Joscelin reigned beyond the Euphrates, his elder brother, Milo, the son of Joscelin, the son of Atho, continued, near the Seine, to possess the castle of their fathers, which was at length inherited by Rainaud, or Reginald, the youngest of his three sons. Examples of genius or virtue must be rare in the annals of the oldest families; and, in a remote age, their pride will embrace a deed of rapine and

---

[92] Turbessel, or as it is now styled Telbesher, is fixed by d'Anville four and twenty miles from the great passage over the Euphrates at Zeugma [Tell Bāsher, now Saleri Kaleh, "a large mound with ruins near the village of Tulbashar," two days' journey north of Aleppo (Sir C Wilson, note to Bahā ad-Dīn, p 58)]

[93] His possessions are distinguished in the Assises of Jerusalem (c 326) among the feudal tenures of the kingdom, which must therefore have been collected between the years 1153 and 1187 His pedigree may be found in the Lignages d'Outremer, c. 16.

violence; such, however, as could not be perpetrated without some superiority of courage, or at least of power. A descendant of Reginald of Courtenay may blush for the public robber who stripped and imprisoned several merchants, after they had satisfied the king's duties at Sens and Orleans. He will glory in the offence, since the bold offender could not be compelled to obedience and restitution, till the regent and the count of Champagne prepared to march against him at the head of an army.[94] Reginald bestowed his estates on his eldest daughter, and his daughter on the seventh son of King Louis the Fat; and their marriage was crowned with a numerous offspring. We might expect that a private should have merged in a royal name; and that the descendants of Peter of France and Elizabeth of Courtenay would have enjoyed the title and honours of princes of the blood. But this legitimate claim was long neglected and finally denied; and the causes of their disgrace will represent the story of this second branch   I   Of all the families now extant, the most ancient, doubtless, and the most illustrious is the house of France, which has occupied the same throne above eight hundred years, and descends, in a clear and lineal series of males, from the middle of the ninth century.[95] In the age of the crusades it was already revered both in the East and West.

[94] The rapine and satisfaction of Reginald de Courtenay are preposterously arranged in the epistles of the abbot and regent Suger (cxiv cxvi), the best memorials of the age (Duchesne, Scriptores Hist Franc. tom iv. p. 530)

[95] In the beginning of the xith century, after naming the father and grandfather of Hugh Capet, the monk Glaber is obliged to add, cujus genus valde in-ante reperitur obscurum   Yet we are assured that the great-grandfather of Hugh Capet was Robert the Strong, count of Anjou (A D 863–873), a noble Frank of Neustria, Neustricus   generosæ stirpis, who was slain in the defence of his country against the Normans, dum patriæ fines tuebatur Beyond Robert, all is conjecture or fable   It is a probable conjecture that the third race descended from the second by Childebrand, the brother of Charles Martel   It is an absurd fable that the second was allied to the first by the marriage of Ansbert, a Roman senator and the ancestor of St Arnoul, with Blithilde, a daughter of Clotaire I   The Saxon origin of the house of France is an ancient but incredible opinion   See a judicious memoir of

But from Hugh Capet to the marriage of Peter no more than
five reigns or generations had elapsed, and so precarious
was their title that the eldest sons, as a necessary precaution,
were previously crowned during the lifetime of their fathers
The peers of France have long maintained their precedency
before the younger branches of the royal line, nor had the
princes of the blood, in the twelfth century, acquired that
hereditary lustre which is now diffused over the most remote
candidates for the succession. 2. The barons of Courtenay
must have stood high in their own estimation, and in that of
the world, since they could impose on the son of a king the
obligation of adopting for himself and all his descendants
the name and arms of their daughter and his wife. In the
marriage of an heiress with her inferior or her equal, such
exchange was often required and allowed; but, as they continued to diverge from the regal stem, the sons of Louis the
Fat were insensibly confounded with their maternal ancestors,
and the new Courtenays might deserve to forfeit the honours
of their birth, which a motive of interest had tempted them to
renounce. 3 The shame was far more permanent than the
reward, and a momentary blaze was followed by a long darkness The eldest son of these nuptials, Peter of Courtenay,
had married, as I have already mentioned, the sister of the
counts of Flanders, the two first emperors of Constantinople;
he rashly accepted the invitation of the barons of Romania,
his two sons, Robert and Baldwin, successively held and lost
the remains of the Latin empire in the East, and the grand-
daughter of Baldwin the Second again mingled her blood with
the blood of France and of Valois To support the expenses
of a troubled and transitory reign, their patrimonial estates
were mortgaged or sold, and the last emperors of Constantinople depended on the annual charity of Rome and Naples
  While the elder brothers dissipated their wealth in romantic

M de Foncemagne (Mémoires de l'Académie des Inscriptions, tom xx
p. 548-579) He had promised to declare his own opinion in a second
memoir, which has never appeared

adventures, and the castle of Courtenay was profaned by a plebeian owner, the younger branches of that adopted name were propagated and multiplied. But their splendour was clouded by poverty and time · after the decease of Robert, great butler of France, they descended from princes to barons; the next generations were confounded with the simple gentry; the descendants of Hugh Capet could no longer be visible in the rural lords of Tanlay and of Champignelles. The more adventurous embraced, without dishonour, the profession of a soldier; the least active and opulent might sink, like their cousins of the branch of Dreux, into the condition of peasants. Their royal descent, in a dark period of four hundred years, became each day more obsolete and ambiguous; and their pedigree, instead of being enrolled in the annals of the king-dom, must be painfully searched by the minute diligence of heralds and genealogists. It was not till the end of the six-teenth century, on the accession of a family almost as remote as their own, that the princely spirit of the Courtenays again revived, and the question of the nobility provoked them to assert the royalty of their blood. They appealed to the jus-tice and compassion of Henry the Fourth; obtained a favour-able opinion from twenty lawyers of Italy and Germany, and modestly compared themselves to the descendants of King David, whose prerogatives were not impaired by the lapse of ages, or the trade of a carpenter.[96] But every ear was deaf, and every circumstance was adverse, to their law-ful claims. The Bourbon kings were justified by the neglect

[96] Of the various petitions, apologies, &c , published by the *princes* of Courtenay, I have seen the three following all in octavo   1 De Stirpe et Origine Domus de Courtenay   addita sunt Responsa celeberrimorum Europæ Jurisconsultorum, Paris, 1607   2 Représentation du Procédé tenu a l'instance faicte devant le Roi, par Messieurs de Courtenay, pour la conversation de l'Honneur et Dignité de leur Maison, Branch de la Royalle Maison de France, a Paris, 1613   3 Représentation du subject qui a porté Messieurs de Salles et de Fraville, de la Maison de Courtenays, à se retirer hors du Royaume, 1614   It was an homicide, for which the Courte-nays expected to be pardoned, or tried, as princes of the blood.

of the Valois, the princes of the blood, more recent and lofty, disdained the alliance of this humble kindred; the parliament, without denying their proofs, eluded a dangerous precedent by an arbitrary distinction and established St. Louis as the first father of the royal line.[97] A repetition of complaints and protests was repeatedly disregarded. and the hopeless pursuit was terminated in the present century by the death of the last male of the family.[98] Their painful and anxious situation was alleviated by the pride of conscious virtue; they sternly rejected the temptations of fortune and favour; and a dying Courtenay would have sacrificed his son, if the youth could have renounced, for any temporal interest, the right and title of a legitimate prince of the blood of France.[99]

III. According to the old register of Ford Abbey, the Courtenays of Devonshire are descended from Prince *Florus*, the second son of Peter, and the grandson of Louis the Fat.[100] This fable of the grateful or venal monks was too respectfully

[97] The sense of the parliaments is thus expressed by Thuanus Principis nomen nusquam in Galliâ tributum, nisi iis qui per matres e regibus nostris originem repetunt qui nunc tantum a Ludovico Nono beatæ memoriæ numerantur nam *Cortinaei* et Drocenses, a Ludovico crasso genus ducentes, hodie inter eos minime recensentur — a distinction of expediency rather than justice The sanctity of Louis IX could not invest him with any special prerogative, and all the descendants of Hugh Capet must be included in his original compact with the French nation

[98] The last male of the Courtenays was Charles Roger, who died in the year 1730, without leaving any sons The last female was Helen de Courtenay, who married Louis de Beaufremont Her title of Princesse du Sang Royal de France was suppressed (February 7, 1737) by an *arrêt* of the parliament of Paris

[99] The singular anecdote to which I allude, is related in the Recueil des Pièces intéressantes et peu connues (Maestricht, 1786, in four vols 12mo), and the unknown editor [M de la Place, of Calais] quotes his author, who had received it from Helen de Courtenay, Marquise de Beaufremont

[100] Dugdale, Monasticon Anglicanum, vol 1 p 786 Yet this fable must have been invented before the reign of Edward III The profuse devotion of the three first generations to Ford Abbey was followed by oppression on one side and ingratitude on the other, and in the sixth generation the monks ceased to register the births, actions, and deaths of their patrons

entertained by our antiquaries, Camden [101] and Dugdale; [102] but it is so clearly repugnant to truth and time, that the rational pride of the family now refuses to accept this imaginary founder. Their most faithful historians believe that, after giving his daughter to the king's son, Reginald of Courtenay abandoned his possessions in France, and obtained from the English monarch a second wife and a new inheritance. It is certain, at least, that Henry the Second distinguished in his camps and councils a Reginald, of the name, arms, and, as it may be fairly presumed, of the genuine race of the Courtenays of France. The right of wardship enabled a feudal lord to reward his vassal with the marriage and estate of a noble heiress; and Reginald of Courtenay acquired a fair establishment in Devonshire, where his posterity has been seated above six hundred years. [103] From a Norman baron, Baldwin de Brioniis, who had been invested by the Conqueror, Hawise, the wife of Reginald, derived the honour of Okehampton, which was held by the service of ninety-three knights; and a female might claim the manly offices of hereditary viscount or sheriff, and of captain of the royal castle of Exeter. Their son Robert married the sister of the earl of Devon; at the end of a century, on the failure of the family of Rivers, [104] his great-grandson, Hugh the Second, succeeded to a title which was still considered as a territorial dignity; and twelve earls of Devonshire, of the name of

[101] In his Britannia, in the list of the earls of Devonshire. His expression, e regio sanguine ortos credunt, betrays, however, some doubt or suspicion.

[102] In his Baronage, p. i. p. 634, he refers to his own Monasticon. Should he not have corrected the register of Ford Abbey, and annihilated the phantom Florus, by the unquestionable evidence of the French historians?

[103] Besides the third and most valuable book of Cleaveland's History, I have consulted Dugdale, the father of our genealogical science (Baronage, p. i. p. 634–643).

[104] This great family, de Ripuariis, de Redvers, de Rivers, ended, in Edward the First's time, in Isabella de Fortibus, a famous and potent dowager, who long survived her brother and husband (Dugdale, Baronage, p. i. p. 254–257).

Courtenay, have flourished in a period of two hundred and twenty years They were ranked among the chief of the barons of the realm; nor was it till after a strenuous dispute that they yielded to the fief of Arundel the first place in the parliament of England; their alliances were contracted with the noblest families, the Veres, Despensers, St. Johns, Talbots, Bohuns, and even the Plantagenets themselves; and in a contest with John of Lancaster, a Courtenay, bishop of London, and afterwards archbishop of Canterbury, might be accused of profane confidence in the strength and number of his kindred In peace, the earls of Devon resided in their numerous castles and manors of the west; their ample revenue was appropriated to devotion and hospitality; and the epitaph of Edward, surnamed, from his misfortunes, the *blind*, from his virtues, the *good*, earl, inculcates with much ingenuity a moral sentence, which may, however, be abused by thoughtless generosity After a grateful commemoration of the fifty-five years of union and happiness, which he enjoyed with Mabel his wife, the good earl thus speaks from the tomb: —

> What we gave, we have;
> What we spent, we had;
> What we left, we lost.[105]

But their *losses*, in this sense, were far superior to their gifts and expenses; and their heirs, not less than the poor, were the objects of their paternal care The sums which they paid for livery and seisin attest the greatness of their possessions; and several estates have remained in their family since the thirteenth and fourteenth centuries. In war, the Courtenays of England fulfilled the duties, and deserved the honours, of chivalry They were often entrusted to levy and command the militia of Devonshire and Cornwall; they often attended their supreme lord to the borders of Scotland; and in foreign

---

[105] Cleaveland, p 142 By some it is assigned to a Rivers, earl of Devon, but the English denotes the xvth rather than the xiiith century.

service, for a stipulated price, they sometimes maintained fourscore men at arms and as many archers. By sea and land they fought under the standard of the Edwards and Henries; their names are conspicuous in battles, in tournaments, and in the original list of the order of the Garter; three brothers shared the Spanish victory of the Black Prince; and in the lapse of six generations the English Courtenays had learned to despise the nation and country from which they derived their origin. In the quarrel of the two Roses, the earls of Devon adhered to the house of Lancaster, and three brothers successively died either in the field or on the scaffold. Their honours and estates were restored by Henry the Seventh; a daughter of Edward the Fourth was not disgraced by the nuptials of a Courtenay; their son, who was created marquis of Exeter, enjoyed the favour of his cousin, Henry the Eighth, and in the camp of Cloth of Gold he broke a lance against the French monarch   But the favour of Henry was the prelude of disgrace; his disgrace was the signal of death, and of the victims of the jealous tyrant, the marquis of Exeter is one of the most noble and guiltless   His son Edward lived a prisoner in the Tower, and died an exile at Padua; and the secret love of Queen Mary, whom he slighted, perhaps for the princess Elizabeth, has shed a romantic colour on the story of this beautiful youth   The relics of his patrimony were conveyed into strange families by the marriages of his four aunts; and his personal honours, as if they had been legally extinct, were revived by the patents of succeeding princes.   But there still survived a lineal descendant of Hugh, the first earl of Devon, a younger branch of the Courtenays, who have been seated at Powderham Castle above four hundred years, from the reign of Edward the Third to the present hour.   Their estates have been increased by the grant and improvement of lands in Ireland, and they have been recently restored to the honours of the peerage.   Yet the Courtenays still retain the plaintive motto, which asserts the innocence, and deplores the fall, of their ancient house [106] While they sigh for past greatness, they are doubtless sensible of present blessings, in the long series of the Courtenay annals, the most splendid era is likewise the most unfortunate; nor can an opulent peer of Britain be inclined to envy the emperors of Constantinople, who wandered over Europe to solicit alms for the support of their dignity and the defence of their capital.

[106] *Ubi lapsus! Quid feci?* a motto which was probably adopted by the Powderham branch, after the loss of the earldom of Devonshire, &c. The primitive arms of the Courtenays were, *or, three torteaux, gules*, which seem to denote their affinity with Godfrey of Bouillon and the ancient counts of Boulogne

[Some further information on the family of the Courtenays will be found in a short note in the Gentleman's Magazine for July, 1839, p 39 Cp Smith's note in his ed of Gibbon, vol vii p 354.]

CHAPTER LXII

The Greek Emperors of Nice and Constantinople — Eleva-
tion and Reign of Michael Palæologus — His false Union
with the Pope and the Latin Church — Hostile Designs
of Charles of Anjou — Revolt of Sicily — War of the
Catalans in Asia and Greece — Revolutions and Present
State of Athens

THE loss of Constantinople restored a momentary vigour
to the Greeks. From their palaces the princes and nobles
were driven into the field; and the fragments of the falling
monarchy were grasped by the hands of the most vigorous
or the most skilful candidates. In the long and barren pages
of the Byzantine annals,[1] it would not be an easy task to
equal the two characters of Theodore Lascaris and John
Ducas Vataces,[2] who replanted and upheld the Roman
standard at Nice in Bithynia. The difference of their virtues

[1] For the reigns of the Nicene emperors, more especially of John Vataces
and his son, their minister, George Acropolita, is the only genuine contemporary, but George Pachymer returned to Constantinople with the Greeks,
at the age of nineteen (Hanckius, de Script Byzant. c 33, 34, p 564–578,
Fabric Bibliot Græc tom vi p 448–460). Yet the history of Nicephorus
Gregoras, though of the xivth century, is a valuable narrative from the taking
of Constantinople by the Latins   [We have subsidiary contemporary sources,
such as the autobiography of Nicephorus Blemmydes (recently edited by
A Heisenberg, 1896), who was an important person at the courts of Vatatzes
and Theodore II   See vol ix Appendix 6   The Empire of Nicæa and
Despotate of Epirus have been treated in the histories of Finlay and Hopf,
but more fully in a recently published special work in modern Greek by
Antonios Mêharakês 'Ιστορία τοῦ βασιλείου τῆς Νικαίας καὶ τοῦ δεσποτάτου τῆς
'Ηπείρου, 1898]

[2] Nicephorus Gregoras (l ii c i) distinguishes between the ὀξεῖα ὁρμή
of Lascaris, and the εὐστάθεια of Vataces   The two portraits are in a very
good style.

was happily suited to the diversity of their situation. In his first efforts the fugitive Lascaris commanded only three cities and two thousand soldiers; his reign was the season of generous and active despair; in every military operation he staked his life and crown; and his enemies, of the Hellespont and the Mæander, were surprised by his celerity and subdued by his boldness. A victorious reign of eighteen years expanded the principality of Nice to the magnitude of an empire. The throne of his successor and son-in-law, Vataces, was founded on a more solid basis, a larger scope, and more plentiful resources; and it was the temper as well as the interest of Vataces to calculate the risk, to expect the moment, and to ensure the success of his ambitious designs. In the decline of the Latins I have briefly exposed the progress of the Greeks. the prudent and gradual advances of a conqueror, who, in a reign of thirty-three years, rescued the provinces from national and foreign usurpers, till he pressed on all sides the Imperial city, a leafless and sapless trunk, which must fall at the first stroke of the axe. But his interior and peaceful administration is still more deserving of notice and praise.[3] The calamities of the times had wasted the numbers and the substance of the Greeks, the motives and the means of agriculture were extirpated; and the most fertile lands were left without cultivation or inhabitants. A portion of this vacant property was occupied and improved by the command, and for the benefit, of the emperor; a powerful hand and a vigilant eye supplied and surpassed, by a skilful management, the minute diligence of a private farmer; the royal domain became the garden and granary of Asia; and without impoverishing the people the sovereign acquired a fund of innocent and productive wealth. According to the nature of the soil, his lands were sown with corn or planted with vines;

---

[3] Pachymer, l. i. c. 23, 24; Nic. Greg. l. ii. c. 6. The reader of the Byzantines must observe how rarely we are indulged with such precious details.

the pastures were filled with horses and oxen, with sheep and hogs; and, when Vataces presented to the empress a crown of diamonds and pearls, he informed her with a smile that this precious ornament arose from the sale of the eggs of his innumerable poultry. The produce of his domain was applied to the maintenance of his palace and hospitals, the calls of dignity and benevolence; the lesson was still more useful than the revenue; the plough was restored to its ancient security and honour; and the nobles were taught to seek a sure and independent revenue from their estates, instead of adorning their splendid beggary by the oppression of the people, or (what is almost the same) by the favours of the court. The superfluous stock of corn and cattle was eagerly purchased by the Turks, with whom Vataces preserved a strict and sincere alliance; but he discouraged the importation of foreign manufactures, the costly silks of the East and the curious labours of the Italian looms   "The demands of nature and necessity," was he accustomed to say, "are indispensable; but the influence of passion may rise and sink at the breath of a monarch"; and both his precept and example recommended simplicity of manners and the use of domestic industry. The education of youth and the revival of learning were the most serious objects of his care; and, without deciding the precedency, he pronounced with truth that a prince and a philosopher [4] are the two most eminent characters of human society. His first wife was Irene, the daughter of Theodore Lascaris, a woman more illustrious by her personal merit, the milder virtues of her sex, than by the blood of the Angeli and Comneni, that flowed in her veins and transmitted the inheritance of the empire. After her death, he was contracted to Anne, or Constance, a natural daughter of the emperor Frederic the Second; [5] but, as the bride had

[4] Μόνοι γὰρ ἀπάντων ἀνθρώπων ὀνομαστότατοι βασιλεὺς καὶ φιλόσοφος (Georg. Acropol c. 32) The emperor, in a familiar conversation, examined and encouraged the studies of his future logothete

[5] [Her mother was Bianca Lancia of Piedmont Frederick seems to have

not attained the years of puberty, Vataces placed in his solitary bed an Italian damsel of her train;[6] and his amorous weakness bestowed on the concubine the honours, though not the title, of lawful empress.   His frailty was censured as a flagitious and damnable sin by the monks; and their rude invectives exercised and displayed the patience of the royal lover   A philosophic age may excuse a single vice, which was redeemed by a crowd of virtues, and, in the review of his faults, and the more intemperate passions of Lascaris, the judgment of their contemporaries was softened by gratitude to the second founders of the empire[7]   The slaves of the Latins, without law or peace, applauded the happiness of their brethren who had resumed their national freedom; and Vataces employed the laudable policy of convincing the Greeks of every dominion that it was their interest to be enrolled in the number of his subjects.

A strong shade of degeneracy is visible between John Vataces and his son Theodore; between the founder who sustained the weight, and the heir who enjoyed the splendour, of the Imperial crown.[8]   Yet the character of Theodore was

married her ultimately (towards the close of his life) and legitimised her children (Matthew Paris, ed Lond, vol 7, p 216).   The lady's true name was Constance (as western writers called her), only Greek writers name her Anna, so that she was probably baptised under this name into the Greek church]

[6] [The Greek writers call her the Μαρκεζίνα — Marchioness.   Her liaison with the Emperor caused an incident which produced a quarrel between him and Nicephorus Blemmydes   She entered the Monastery of St Gregory in grand costume   Blemmydes, when he observed her presence, ordered the communion service to be discontinued   Vatatzes refused to punish a just man, as the Marchioness demanded, but showed his resentment by breaking off all relations with him.   Besides Nicephorus Gregoras, i p 45, 46, we have a description of the incident from the pen of Blemmydes himself in his autobiography, c 41 (ed Heisenberg)]

[7] Compare Acropolita (c 18, 52) and the two first books of Nicephorus Gregoras

[8] A Persian saying, that Cyrus was the *father*, and Darius the *master*, of his subjects, was applied to Vataces and his son   But Pachymer (l 1 c 23) has mistaken the mild Darius for the cruel Cambyses, despot or tyrant of his

not devoid of energy; he had been educated in the school of
his father, in the exercise of war and hunting: Constantinople
was yet spared; but in the three years of a short reign he
thrice led his armies into the heart of Bulgaria.[9]   His virtues
were sullied by a choleric and suspicious temper: the first
of these may be ascribed to the ignorance of control; and the
second might naturally arise from a dark and imperfect view
of the corruption of mankind.   On a march in Bulgaria he
consulted on a question of policy his principal ministers;
and the Greek logothete, George Acropolita, presumed to
offend him by the declaration of a free and honest opinion.
The emperor half unsheathed his scymetar; but his more
deliberate rage reserved Acropolita for a baser punishment.
One of the first officers of the empire was ordered to dis-
mount, stripped of his robes, and extended on the ground in
the presence of the prince and army.   In this posture he was
chastised with so many and such heavy blows from the clubs
of two guards or executioners that, when Theodore commanded them to cease, the great logothete was scarcely able
to rise and crawl away to his tent.   After a seclusion of some
days, he was recalled by a peremptory mandate to his seat in
council, and so dead were the Greeks to the sense of honour
and shame that it is from the narrative of the sufferer himself
that we acquire the knowledge of his disgrace.[10]   The cruelty

people   By the institution of taxes, Darius had incurred the less odious, but
more contemptible, name of Κάπηλος, *merchant* or *broker* (Herodotus, iii 89).

[9] Theodore led two expeditions in person against the Bulgarians, in 1256
and 1257   At the end of the second expedition he had a meeting with Theodora Petraleipha, the wife of Michael II , Despot of Epirus, at Thessalonica,
where a marriage was both arranged and celebrated between his daughter
Maria and her son Nicephorus   The third expedition, to which Gibbon
refers, was that of 1258 against Michael II , which however was conducted
not by Theodore but by Michael Palæologus, the future emperor]

[10] Acropolita (c 63) seems to admire his own firmness in sustaining a
beating, and not returning to council till he was called   He relates the exploits of Theodore, and his own services, from c 53 to c 74 of his History.
See the third book of Nicephorus Gregoras   [Among some unpublished
works of this remarkable monarch Theodore Lascaris is an encomium on

of the emperor was exasperated by the pangs of sickness, the approach of a premature end, and the suspicion of poison and magic.[11] The lives and fortunes, the eyes and limbs, of his kinsmen and nobles were sacrificed to each sally of passion, and, before he died, the son of Vataces might deserve from the people, or at least from the Court, the appellation of tyrant A matron of the family of the Palæologi [12] had provoked his anger by refusing to bestow her beauteous daughter on the vile plebeian who was recommended by his caprice. Without regard to her birth or age, her body, as high as the neck, was enclosed in a sack with several cats, who were pricked with pins to irritate their fury against their unfortunate fellow-captive. In his last hours the emperor testified a wish to forgive and be forgiven, a just anxiety for the fate of John, his son and successor, who, at the age of eight years, was condemned to the dangers of a long minority. His last choice entrusted the office of guardian to the sanctity of the patriarch Arsenius, and to the courage of George Muzalon, the great domestic, who was equally distinguished by the royal favour and the public hatred. Since their connection with the Latins, the names and privileges of hereditary rank had insinuated themselves into the Greek monarchy; and the noble families [13] were provoked by the elevation of a worth-

George Acropolites. There is also a rhetorical estimate of his contemporary Frederick II , a work which ought to have been published long ago   George Acropolites made a collection of his letters, some of these are extant but not yet printed   Professor Krumbacher designates Theodore II "as statesman, writer, and man, one of the most interesting figures of Byzantium, a sort of oriental parallel to his great contemporary Frederick II , a degenerate, no doubt, intellectually highly gifted, bodily weak, without moral force, with a nervous system fatally preponderant" (op cit p 478)   On his theological productions cp J Draseke, Byz Zeitschrift, iii p 198 sqq] [Since this note was written, an edition of the Correspondence of Theodore Lascaris was published by N Festa]

[11] [He seems to have suffered from a cerebral disease, and to have been subject to fits of epilepsy   Cp Méharakis, op cit p 479]

[12] [A sister of Michael Palæologus]

[13] Pachymer (l 1 c 21) names and discriminates fifteen or twenty Greek

less favourite, to whose influence they imputed the errors and
calamities of the late reign.   In the first council after the
emperor's death, Muzalon, from a lofty throne, pronounced
a laboured apology of his conduct and intentions : his modesty
was subdued by an unanimous assurance of esteem and
fidelity; and his most inveterate enemies were the loudest to
salute him as the guardian and saviour of the Romans.   Eight
days were sufficient to prepare the execution of the conspiracy.
On the ninth,[14] the obsequies of the deceased monarch were
solemnised in the cathedral of Magnesia,[15] an Asiatic city,
where he expired, on the banks of the Hermus and at the foot
of Mount Sipylus.   The holy rites were interrupted by a
sedition of the guards: Muzalon, his brothers, and his adherents were massacred at the foot of the altar; and the absent
patriarch was associated with a new colleague, with Michael
Palæologus, the most illustrious, in birth and merit, of the
Greek nobles.[16]

Of those who are proud of their ancestors, the far greater
part must be content with local or domestic renown : and few
there are who dare trust the memorials of their family to the
public annals of their country.   As early as the middle of
the eleventh century, the noble race of the Palæologi[17]

families καὶ ὅσοι ἄλλοι, οἷς ἡ μεγαλογενὴς σείρα καὶ χρυσῆ συγκεκρότητο. Does
he mean, by this decoration, a figurative or a real golden chain?   Perhaps
both.

[14] [So Pachymeres, Gregoras, and Phrantzes; but Acropolita says the
third, p. 163, ed. Bonn.]

[15] The old geographers, with Cellarius and d'Anville, and our travellers,
particularly Pocock and Chandler, will teach us to distinguish the two
Magnesias of Asia Minor, of the Mæander and of Sipylus.   The latter, our
present object, is still flourishing for a Turkish city, and lies eight hours, or
leagues, to the north-east of Smyrna (Tournefort, Voyage du Levant, tom. iii.
lettre xxiii. p. 365-370.   Chandler's Travels into Asia Minor, p. 267).

[16] See Acropolita (c. 75, 76, &c.), who lived too near the times; Pachymer
(l. i. c. 13-25); Gregoras (l. iii. c. 3-5).

[17] The pedigree of Palæologus is explained by Ducange (Famil. Byzant.
p. 230, &c.); the events of his private life are related by Pachymer (l. i. c.
7-12), and Gregoras (l. ii. 8, l. iii. 2, 4, l. iv. 1), with visible favour to the
father of the reigning dynasty.

stands high and conspicuous in the Byzantine history it was the valiant George Palæologus who placed the father of the Comneni on the throne; and his kinsmen or descendants continue, in each generation, to lead the armies and councils of the state. The purple was not dishonoured by their alliance; and, had the law of succession, and female succession, been strictly observed, the wife of Theodore Lascaris must have yielded to her elder sister, the mother of Michael Palæologus, who afterwards raised his family to the throne. In his person, the splendour of birth was dignified by the merit of the soldier and statesman: in his early youth he was promoted to the office of *Constable* or commander of the French mercenaries; the private expense of a day never exceeded three pieces of gold; but his ambition was rapacious and profuse; and his gifts were doubled by the graces of his conversation and manners. The love of the soldiers and people excited the jealousy of the court; and Michael thrice escaped from the dangers in which he was involved by his own imprudence or that of his friends. I. Under the reign of Justice and Vataces, a dispute arose [18] between two officers, one of whom accused the other of maintaining the hereditary right of the Palæologi. The cause was decided, according to the new jurisprudence of the Latins, by single combat: the defendant was overthrown; but he persisted in declaring that himself alone was guilty; and that he had uttered these rash or treasonable speeches without the approbation or knowledge of his patron. Yet a cloud of suspicion hung over the innocence of the constable; he was still pursued by the whispers of malevolence, and a subtile courtier, the archbishop of Philadelphia, urged him to accept the judgment of God in the fiery proof of the ordeal [19] Three days before the trial, the

---

[18] Acropolita (c 50) relates the circumstances of this curious adventure, which seems to have escaped the more recent writers

[19] Pachymer (l i c 12), who speaks with proper contempt of this barbarous trial, affirms that he had seen in his youth many persons who had

patient's arm was enclosed in a bag and secured by the royal signet; and it was incumbent on him to bear a red-hot ball of iron three times from the altar to the rails of the sanctuary, without artifice and without injury Palæologus eluded the dangerous experiment with sense and pleasantry. "I am a soldier," said he, "and will boldly enter the lists with my accusers, but a layman, a sinner like myself, is not endowed with the gift of miracles. *Your* piety, most holy prelate, may deserve the interposition of Heaven, and from your hands I will receive the fiery globe, the pledge of my innocence " The archbishop started; the emperor smiled; and the absolution or pardon of Michael was approved by new rewards and new services. II. In the succeeding reign, as he held the government of Nice, he was secretly informed that the mind of the absent prince was poisoned with jealousy; and that death or blindness would be his final reward. Instead of awaiting the return and sentence of Theodore, the constable, with some followers, escaped from the city and the empire; and, though he was plundered by the Turkmans of the desert, he found an hospitable refuge in the court of the sultan. In the ambiguous state of an exile, Michael reconciled the duties of gratitude and loyalty; drawing his sword against the Tartars; admonishing the garrisons of the Roman limit; and promoting, by his influence, the restoration of peace, in which his pardon and recall were honourably included. III. While he guarded the West against the despot of Epirus, Michael was again suspected and condemned in the palace; and such was his loyalty or weakness that he submitted to be led in chains above six hundred miles from Durazzo to Nice. The civility of the messenger alleviated his disgrace; the emperor's sickness dispelled his danger, and the last breath of Theodore, which recommended his infant son,

---

sustained, without injury, the fiery ordeal As a Greek, he is credulous, but the ingenuity of the Greeks might furnish some remedies of art or fraud against their own superstition or that of their tyrant.

at once acknowledged the innocence and the power of
Palæologus.

But his innocence had been too unworthily treated, and his
power was too strongly felt, to curb an aspiring subject in
the fair field that was offered to his ambition [20] In the council after the death of Theodore, he was the first to pronounce,
and the first to violate, the oath of allegiance to Muzalon,
and so dexterous was his conduct that he reaped the benefit,
without incurring the guilt, or at least the reproach, of the
subsequent massacre. In the choice of a regent, he balanced
the interests and passions of the candidates; turned their
envy and hatred from himself against each other, and forced
every competitor to own that, after his own claims, those of
Palæologus were best entitled to the preference Under the
title of Great Duke, he accepted or assumed, during a long
minority, the active powers of government; the patriarch was
a venerable name, and the factious nobles were seduced, or
oppressed, by the ascendant of his genius. The fruits of the
economy of Vataces were deposited in a strong castle on the
banks of the Hermus,[21] in the custody of the faithful Varangians; the constable retained his command or influence over
the foreign troops; he employed the guards to possess the
treasure, and the treasure to corrupt the guards; and, whatsoever might be the abuse of the public money, his character
was above the suspicion of private avarice. By himself, or
by his emissaries, he strove to persuade every rank of subjects
that their own prosperity would rise in just proportion to the
establishment of his authority. The weight of taxes was suspended, the perpetual theme of popular complaint, and he
prohibited the trials by the ordeal and judicial combat. These

[20] Without comparing Pachymer to Thucydides or Tacitus, I will praise
his narrative (l 1 c 13-32, l iii c 1-9), which pursues the ascent of Palæologus with eloquence, perspicuity, and tolerable freedom Acropolita is
more cautious, and Gregoras more concise

[21] [In Astytzion on the Scamander. The treasures here were deposited
by Theodore II]

barbaric institutions were already abolished or undermined in France [22] and England; [23] and the appeal to the sword offended the sense of a civilised, [24] and the temper of an unwarlike, people. For the future maintenance of their wives and children the veterans were grateful, the priest and the philosopher applauded his ardent zeal for the advancement of religion and learning; and his vague promise of rewarding merit was applied by every candidate to his own hopes. Conscious of the influence of the clergy, Michael successfully laboured to secure the suffrage of that powerful order.   Their expensive journey from Nice to Magnesia afforded a decent and ample pretence; the leading prelates were tempted by the liberality of his nocturnal visits; and the incorruptible patriarch was flattered by the homage of his new colleague, who led his mule by the bridle into the town, and removed to a respectful distance the importunity of the crowd. Without renouncing his title by royal descent, Palæologus encouraged a free discussion into the advantages of elective monarchy; and his adherents asked, with the insolence of triumph, What patient would trust his health, or what merchant would abandon his vessel, to the *hereditary* skill of a physician or a

[22] The judicial combat was abolished by St. Louis in his own territories; and his example and authority were at length prevalent in France (Esprit des Loix, l xxviii. c 29).

[23] In civil cases, Henry II gave an option to the defendant; Glanville prefers the proof by evidence, and that by judicial combat is reprobated in the Fleta   Yet the trial by battle has never been abrogated in the English law, and it was ordered by the judges as late as the beginning of the last century.

[24] Yet an ingenious friend has urged to me, in mitigation of this practice, 1 *That*, in nations emerging from barbarism, it moderates the licence of private war and arbitrary revenge   2 *That* it is less absurd than the trials by the ordeal, or boiling water, or the cross, which it has contributed to abolish   3 *That* it served at least as a test of personal courage · a quality so seldom united with a base disposition that the danger of the trial might be some check to a malicious prosecutor, and an useful barrier against injustice supported by power.   The gallant and unfortunate earl of Surrey might probably have escaped his unmerited fate, had not his demand of the combat against his accuser been over-ruled

pilot? The youth of the emperor and the impending dangers of a minority required the support of a mature and experienced guardian; of an associate raised above the envy of his equals, and invested with the name and prerogatives of royalty. For the interest of the prince and people, without any views for himself or his family, the Great Duke consented to guard and instruct the son of Theodore; but he sighed for the happy moment when he might restore to his firmer hands the administration of his patrimony, and enjoy the blessings of a private station. He was first invested with the title and prerogatives of *despot*, which bestowed the purple ornaments, and the second place in the Roman monarchy. It was afterwards agreed that John and Michael should be proclaimed as joint emperors, and raised on the buckler, but that the pre-eminence should be reserved for the birth-right of the former. A mutual league of amity was pledged between the royal partners, and, in case of a rupture, the subjects were bound, by their oath of allegiance, to declare themselves against the aggressor an ambiguous name, the seed of discord and civil war Palæologus was content; but on the day of his coronation, and in the cathedral of Nice, his zealous adherents most vehemently urged the just priority of his age and merit. The unseasonable dispute was eluded by postponing to a more convenient opportunity the coronation of John Lascaris; and he walked with a slight diadem in the train of his guardian, who alone received the Imperial crown from the hands of the patriarch. It was not without extreme reluctance that Arsenius abandoned the cause of his pupil; but the Varangians brandished their battle-axes; a sign of assent was extorted from the trembling youth, and some voices were heard, that the life of a child should no longer impede the settlement of the nation. A full harvest of honours and employments was distributed among his friends by the grateful Palæologus. In his own family he created a despot and two sebastocrators; Alexius Strategopulus was decorated with the title of Cæsar; and that veteran commander soon repaid the obligation, by restoring Constantinople to the Greek emperor.

It was in the second year of his reign, while he resided in the palace and gardens of Nymphæum,[25] near Smyrna, that the first messenger arrived at the dead of night, and the stupendous intelligence was impaited to Michael, after he had been gently waked by the tender precaution of his sister Eulogia. The man was unknown or obscure; he produced no letters from the victorious Cæsar, nor could it easily be credited, after the defeat of Vataces and the recent failure of Palæologus himself, that the capital had been surprised by a detachment of eight hundred soldiers. As an hostage, the doubtful author was confined, with the assurance of death or an ample recompense, and the court was left some hours in the anxiety of hope and fear, till the messengers of Alexius arrived with the authentic intelligence, and displayed the trophies of the conquest, the sword and sceptre,[26] the buskins and bonnet,[27] of the usurper Baldwin, which he had dropt in

[25] The site of Nymphæum is not clearly defined in ancient or modern geography [Turkish Nif, it lay on the road from Smyrna to Sardis   Cp. Ramsay, Asia Minor, p. 108]   But from the last hours of Vataces (Acropolita, c 52) it is evident the palace and gardens of his favourite residence were in the neighbourhood of Smyrna   Nymphæum might be loosely placed in Lydia (Gregoras, l vi 6)   [Pachymeres says that Michael was at Nymphaeum when he received the glad tidings, but Gregoras says Nicaea, and Acropolites says Meteorion   As Acropolites was with Michael at the time, we must follow him (so Mêliarakês, p 509).   Meteorion "must have been in the Hermos valley, and may possibly be the purely Byzantine fortress Gurduk Kalesi, a few miles north of Thyateira, near the site of Attaleia" (Ramsay, *op cit* p. 131)]

[26] This sceptre, the emblem of justice and power, was a long staff, such as was used by the heroes in Homer   By the latter Greeks it was named *Dicanice*, and the Imperial sceptre was distinguished as usual by the red or purple colour

[27] Acropolita affirms (c 87) that this bonnet was after the French fashion; but from the ruby at the point or summit Ducange (Hist de C. P l v c 28, 29) believes that it was the high-crowned hat of the Greeks.   Could Acropolita mistake the dress of his own court?

his precipitate flight. A general assembly of the bishops, senators, and nobles was immediately convened, and never perhaps was an event received with more heartfelt and universal joy. In a studied oration, the new sovereign of Constantinople congratulated his own and the public fortune. "There was a time," said he, "a far-distant time, when the Roman empire extended to the Adriatic, the Tigris, and the confines of Ethiopia. After the loss of the provinces, our capital itself, in these last and calamitous days, has been wrested from our hands by the Barbarians of the West. From the lowest ebb, the tide of prosperity has again returned in our favour; but our prosperity was that of fugitives and exiles; and, when we were asked, Which was the country of the Romans? we indicated with a blush the climate of the globe and the quarter of the heavens. The Divine Providence has now restored to our arms the city of Constantine, the sacred seat of religion and empire; and it will depend on our valour and conduct to render this important acquisition the pledge and omen of future victories." So eager was the impatience of the prince and people that Michael made his triumphal entry into Constantinople only twenty days after the expulsion of the Latins. The golden gate was thrown open at his approach, the devout conqueror dismounted from his horse; and a miraculous image of Mary, the Conductress, was borne before him, that the divine Virgin in person might appear to conduct him to the temple of her Son, the cathedral of St. Sophia. But, after the first transport of devotion and pride, he sighed at the dreary prospect of solitude and ruin. The palace was defiled with smoke and dirt, and the gross intemperance of the Franks; whole streets had been consumed by fire, or were decayed by the injuries of time; the sacred and profane edifices were stripped of their ornaments; and, as if they were conscious of their approaching exile, the industry of the Latins had been confined to the work of pillage and destruction Trade had expired under the pressure of anarchy and distress; and the number of inhabitants had decreased with the opulence of the city It was the first care of the Greek monarch to reinstate the nobles in the palaces of their fathers; and the houses or the ground which they occupied were restored to the families that could exhibit a legal right of inheritance. But the far greater part was extinct or lost, the vacant property had devolved to the lord, he repeopled Constantinople by a liberal invitation to the provinces; and the brave *volunteers* were seated in the capital which had been recovered by their arms. The French barons and the principal families had retired with their emperor; but the patient and humble crowd of Latins was attached to the country, and indifferent to the change of masters Instead of banishing the factories of the Pisans, Venetians, and Genoese, the prudent conqueror accepted their oaths of allegiance, encouraged their industry, confirmed their privileges, and allowed them to live under the jurisdiction of their proper magistrates. Of these nations, the Pisans and Venetians preserved their respective quarters in the city; but the services and powers of the Genoese deserved at the same time the gratitude [28] and the jealousy of the Greeks. Their independent colony was first planted at the sea-port town of Heraclea in Thrace. They were speedily recalled, and settled in the exclusive possession of the suburb of Galata, an advantageous post, in which they revived the commerce, and insulted the majesty, of the Byzantine empire.[29]

The recovery of Constantinople was celebrated as the era of a new empire the conqueror, alone, and by the right of the sword, renewed his coronation in the church of St. Sophia, and the name and honours of John Lascaris, his pupil and lawful sovereign, were insensibly abolished But his claims still lived in the minds of the people; and the royal youth must speedily attain the years of manhood and ambition.

[28] [The Genoese had sent ships, in accordance with the treaty of Nymphaeum, but these had not arrived in time to be of actual service]

[29] See Pachymer (l 2, c 28–33), Acropolita (c 88), Nicephorus Gregoras (l. iv. 7), and for the treatment of the subject Latins, Ducange (l v c 30, 31).

By fear or conscience, Palæologus was restrained from dipping his hands in innocent and royal blood, but the anxiety of an usurper and a parent urged him to secure his throne by one of those imperfect crimes so familiar to the modern Greeks. The loss of sight incapacitated the young prince for the active business of the world instead of the brutal violence of tearing out his eyes, the visual nerve was destroyed by the intense glare of a red-hot bason,[30] and John Lascaris was removed to a distant castle, where he spent many years in privacy and oblivion Such cool and deliberate guilt may seem incompatible with remorse, but, if Michael could trust the mercy of Heaven, he was not inaccessible to the reproaches and vengeance of mankind, which he had provoked by cruelty and treason. His cruelty imposed on a servile court the duties of applause or silence; but the clergy had a right to speak in the name of their invisible master, and their holy legions were led by a prelate, whose character was above the temptations of hope or fear. After a short abdication of his dignity, Arsenius [31] had consented to ascend the ecclesiastical throne of Constantinople, and to preside in the restoration of the church. His pious simplicity was long deceived by the arts of Palæologus; and his patience and submission might soothe the usurper, and protect the safety of the young prince. On the news of his inhuman treatment, the patriarch unsheathed the spiritual sword, and superstition, on this occasion, was enlisted in the cause of humanity and justice.

[30] This milder invention for extinguishing the sight was tried by the philosopher Democritus on himself, when he sought to withdraw his mind from the visible world a foolish story! The word *abacinare*, in Latin and Italian, has furnished Ducange (Gloss Latin) with an opportunity to review the various modes of blinding, the more violent were, scooping, burning with an iron or hot vinegar, and binding the head with a strong cord till the eyes burst from their sockets Ingenious tyrants!

[31] See the first retreat and restoration of Arsenius, in Pachymer (l ii c 15, l iii c 1, 2), and Nicephorus Gregoras (l iii c 1, l iv c 1) Posterity justly accused the ἀφέλεια and ῥᾳθυμία of Arsenius, the virtues of an hermit, the vices of a minister (l xii. c. 2).

In a synod of bishops, who were stimulated by the example
of his zeal, the patriarch pronounced a sentence of excommunication; though his prudence still repeated the name of
Michael in the public prayers.   The Eastern prelates had not
adopted the dangerous maxims of ancient Rome; nor did
they presume to enforce their censures, by deposing princes,
or absolving nations from their oaths of allegiance.   But the
Christian who had been separated from God and the church
became an object of horror; and, in a turbulent and fanatic
capital that horror might arm the hand of an assassin or
inflame a sedition of the people.   Palæologus felt his danger,
confessed his guilt, and deprecated his judge   the act was
irretrievable; the prize was obtained; and the most rigorous
penance, which he solicited, would have raised the sinner to
the reputation of a saint.   The unrelenting patriarch refused
to announce any means of atonement or any hopes of mercy;
and condescended only to pronounce that, for so great a crime,
great indeed must be the satisfaction.   "Do you require,"
said Michael, "that I should abdicate the empire?"   And
at these words he offered, or seemed to offer, the sword of
state.   Arsenius eagerly grasped this pledge of sovereignty;
but, when he perceived that the emperor was unwilling to
purchase absolution at so dear a rate, he indignantly escaped
to his cell, and left the royal sinner kneeling and weeping
before the door.[32]

The danger and scandal of this excommunication subsisted
above three years, till the popular clamour was assuaged by
time and repentance; till the brethren of Arsenius condemned
his inflexible spirit, so repugnant to the unbounded forgiveness of the gospel.   The emperor had artfully insinuated that,
if he were still rejected at home, he might seek, in the Roman
pontiff, a more indulgent judge; but it was far more easy and

[32] The crime and excommunication of Michael are fairly told by Pachymer
(l. iii. c. 10, 14, 19, &c.), and Gregoras (l. iv. c. 4).   His confession and
penance restored their freedom

effectual to find or to place that judge at the head of the Byzantine church. Arsenius was involved in a vague rumour of conspiracy and disaffection, some irregular steps in his ordination and government were liable to censure; a synod deposed him from the episcopal office, and he was transported under a guard of soldiers to a small island of the Propontis. Before his exile, he sullenly requested that a strict account might be taken of the treasures of the church; boasted that his whole riches, three pieces of gold, had been earned by transcribing the Psalms, continued to assert the freedom of his mind; and denied, with his last breath, the pardon which was implored by the royal sinner [33] After some delay, Gregory, bishop of Hadrianople, was translated to the Byzantine throne; but his authority was found insufficient to support the absolution of the emperor; and Joseph, a reverend monk, was substituted to that important function This edifying scene was represented in the presence of the senate and people; at the end of six years, the humble penitent was restored to the communion of the faithful; and humanity will rejoice that a milder treatment of the captive Lascaris was stipulated as a proof of his remorse. But the spirit of Arsenius still survived in a powerful faction of the monks and clergy, who persevered above forty-eight years in an obstinate schism. Their scruples were treated with tenderness and respect by Michael and his son; and the reconciliation of the Arsenites was the serious labour of the church and state In the confidence of fanaticism, they had proposed to try their cause by a miracle; and, when the two papers that contained their own and the adverse cause were cast into a fiery brazier, they expected that the Catholic verity would be respected by the flames. Alas! the two papers were indiscriminately consumed, and this unforeseen accident

[33] Pachymer relates the exile of Arsenius (l v c 1-16), he was one of the commissaries who visited him in the desert island The last testament of the unforgiving patriarch is still extant (Dupin, Bibliothèque Ecclésiastique, tom x p 95).

produced the union of a day, and renewed the quarrel of an age.[34] The final treaty displayed the victory of the Arsenites; the clergy abstained during forty days from all ecclesiastical functions; a slight penance was imposed on the laity; the body of Arsenius was deposited in the sanctuary; and in the name of the departed saint the prince and people were released from the sins of their fathers.[35]

The establishment of his family was the motive, or at least the pretence, of the crime of Palæologus; and he was impatient to confirm the succession, by sharing with his eldest son the honours of the purple Andronicus, afterwards surnamed the Elder, was proclaimed and crowned emperor of the Romans, in the fifteenth year of his age, and, from the first era of a prolix and inglorious reign, he held that august title nine years as the colleague, and fifty as the successor, of his father.   Michael himself, had he died in a private station, would have been thought more worthy of the empire; and the assaults of his temporal and spiritual enemies left him few moments to labour for his own fame or the happiness of his subjects.   He wrested from the Franks several of the noblest islands of the Archipelago, Lesbos, Chios, and Rhodes;[38] his brother Constantine was sent to command in Malvasia and Sparta; and the eastern side of the Morea, from Argos and Napoli to Cape Tænarus, was repossessed by the Greeks.[37]   This effusion of Christian blood was loudly

[34] Pachymer (l vii c 22) relates this miraculous trial like a philosopher, and treats with similar contempt a plot of the Arsenites, to hide a revelation in the coffin of some old saint (l vii c 13)   He compensates this incredulity by an image that weeps, another that bleeds (l vii c 30), and the miraculous cures of a deaf and a mute patient (l xi c 32)

[35] The story of the Arsenites is spread through the thirteen books of Pachymer   Their union and triumph are reserved for Nicephorus Gregoras (l vii c 9), who neither loves nor esteems these sectaries

[36] [These islands were subject to Michael, but not conquered by him; see Appendix 3]

[37] [Michael released William Villehardouin, prince of Achaia, who had been taken prisoner at the battle of Pelagonia (see above, p 34)   For his liberty William undertook to become a vassal of the Empire, and to hand

condemned by the patriarch; and the insolent priest presumed to interpose his fears and scruples between the arms of princes. But, in the prosecution of these Western conquests, the countries beyond the Hellespont were left naked to the Turks; and their depredations verified the prophecy of a dying senator, that the recovery of Constantinople would be the ruin of Asia. The victories of Michael were achieved by his lieutenants, his sword rusted in the palace; and, in the transactions of the emperor with the popes and the king of Naples, his political arts were stained with cruelty and fraud.[38]

I. The Vatican was the most natural refuge of a Latin emperor, who had been driven from his throne; and Pope Urban the Fourth appeared to pity the misfortunes, and vindicate the cause, of the fugitive Baldwin. A crusade, with plenary indulgence, was preached by his command against the schismatic Greeks; he excommunicated their allies and adherents; solicited Louis the Ninth in favour of his kinsman, and demanded a tenth of the ecclesiastic revenues of France and England for the service of the holy war.[39] The subtile Greek, who watched the rising tempest of the West, attempted to suspend or soothe the hostility of the pope, by suppliant embassies and respectful letters; but he insinuated that the establishment of peace must prepare the reconciliation and obedience of the Eastern church. The Roman court could not be deceived by so gross an artifice; and Michael was admonished that the repentance of the son should precede the forgiveness of the father; and that *faith*

over to Michael the fortresses of Misithra, Maina, and Monemvasia See (besides Pachymeres, Gibbon's source) the Chronicle of Morea (in Buchon, Chroniques Etrangères Cp. vol. iv Appendix 6)]

[38] Of the xiii books of Pachymer, the first six (as the ivth and vth of Nicephorus Gregoras) contain the reign of Michael, at the time of whose death he was forty years of age Instead of breaking, like his editor the Père Poussin, his history into two parts, I follow Ducange and Cousin, who number the xiii books in one series

[39] Ducange, Hist de C. P l v. c. 33, &c from the Epistles of Urban IV.

(an ambiguous word) was the only basis of friendship and alliance   After a long and affected delay, the approach of danger and the importunity of Gregory the Tenth compelled him to enter on a more serious negotiation; he alleged the example of the great Vataces, and the Greek clergy, who understood the intentions of their prince, were not alarmed by the first steps of reconciliation and respect   But, when he pressed the conclusion of the treaty, they strenuously declared that the Latins, though not in name, were heretics in fact, and that they despised those strangers as the vilest and most despicable portion of the human race.[40]   It was the task of the emperor to persuade, to corrupt, to intimidate, the most popular ecclesiastics, to gain the vote of each individual, and alternately to urge the arguments of Christian charity and the public welfare.   The texts of the fathers and the arms of the Franks were balanced in the theological and political scale; and, without approving the addition to the Nicene creed, the most moderate were taught to confess that the two hostile propositions of proceeding from the Father BY the Son, and of proceeding from the Father AND the Son, might be reduced to a safe and catholic sense [41]   The supremacy of the pope was a doctrine more easy to conceive, but more painful to acknowledge; yet Michael represented to his monks and prelates that they might submit to name the Roman bishop as the first of the patriarchs, and that their distance and discretion would guard the liberties of the Eastern church from the mischievous consequences of the right of appeal.   He protested that he would sacrifice his

---

[40] From their mercantile intercourse with the Venetians and Genoese, they branded the Latins as κάπηλοι and βάναυσοι (Pachymer, l v c 10)   "Some are heretics in name, others, like the Latins, in fact," said the learned Veccus (l v c 12), who soon afterwards became a convert (c. 15, 16), and a patriarch (c 24)

[41] In this class we may place Pachymer himself, whose copious and candid narrative occupies the vth and vith books of his history   Yet the Greek is silent on the council of Lyons, and seems to believe that the popes always resided in Rome and Italy

life and empire rather than yield the smallest point of orthodox faith or national independence, and this declaration
was sealed and ratified by a golden bull. The patriarch
Joseph withdrew to a monastery, to resign or resume his
throne, according to the event of the treaty, the letters of
union and obedience were subscribed by the emperor, his son
Andronicus, and thirty-five archbishops and metropolitans,
with their respective synods; and the episcopal list was
multiplied by many dioceses which were annihilated under the
yoke of the infidels. An embassy was composed of some
trusty ministers and prelates, they embarked for Italy,
with rich ornaments and rare perfumes for the altar of St.
Peter; and their secret orders authorised and recommended
a boundless compliance. They were received in the general
council of Lyons, by Pope Gregory the Tenth, at the head of
five hundred bishops.[42] He embraced with tears his long-
lost and repentant children, accepted the oath of the ambassadors, who abjured the schism in the name of the two
emperors; adorned the prelates with the ring and mitre;
chaunted in Greek and Latin the Nicene creed, with the
addition of *filioque;* and rejoiced in the union of the East
and West, which had been reserved for his reign To consummate this pious work, the Byzantine deputies were
speedily followed by the pope's nuncios, and their instruction
discloses the policy of the Vatican, which could not be satisfied
with the vain title of supremacy. After viewing the temper
of the prince and people, they were enjoined to absolve the
schismatic clergy who should subscribe and swear their
abjuration and obedience; to establish in all the churches
the use of the perfect creed; to prepare the entrance of a cardinal legate, with the full powers and dignity of his office,
and to instruct the emperor in the advantages which he

---

[42] See the Acts of the Council of Lyons in the year 1274 Fleury, Hist
Ecclésiastique, tom xviii p 181-199 Dupin, Bibliot Eccles tom v p 135
[George Acropolites was the chief ambassador of Michael]

might derive from the temporal protection of the Roman pontiff.[43]

But they found a country without a friend, a nation in which the names of Rome and Union were pronounced with abhorrence. The patriarch Joseph was indeed removed; his place was filled by Veccus,[44] an ecclesiastic of learning and moderation; and the emperor was still urged by the same motives, to persevere in the same professions But, in his private language, Palæologus affected to deplore the pride, and to blame the innovations, of the Latins; and, while he debased his character by this double hypocrisy, he justified and punished the opposition of his subjects. By the joint suffrage of the new and the ancient Rome, a sentence of excommunication was pronounced against the obstinate schismatics; the censures of the church were executed by the sword of Michael; on the failure of persuasion, he tried the arguments of prison and exile, of whipping and mutilation: those touchstones, says an historian, of cowards and the brave. Two Greeks still reigned in Ætolia, Epirus, and Thessaly, with the appellation of despots; they had yielded to the sovereign of Constantinople, but they rejected the chains of the Roman pontiff, and supported their refusal by successful arms. Under their protection, the fugitive monks and bishops assembled in hostile synods, and retorted the name of heretic with the galling addition of apostate; the prince of Trebizond was tempted to assume the forfeit title of emperor; and even the Latins of Negropont, Thebes, Athens, and the Morea forgot the merits of the convert, to join, with open or

[43] This curious instruction, which has been drawn with more or less honesty by Wading and Leo Allatius from the archives of the Vatican, is given in an abstract or version by Fleury (tom xviii p 252-258)

[44] [Johannes Veccus (Patriarch 1275) was the chief theologian who supported the Union His work, On the Union and Peace of the Churches of Old and New Rome, and others on the same subject, were published in the Graecia Orthodoxa of Leo Allatius (vol i, 1652) and will be found in Migne, P G vol 141 His most formidable controversial opponent, Gregory of Cyprus (for whose works see Migne vol 142) became Patriarch in 1283]

clandestine aid, the enemies of Palæologus. His favourite generals, of his own blood and family, successively deserted or betrayed the sacrilegious trust. His sister Eulogia, a niece, and two female cousins conspired against him; another niece, Mary queen of Bulgaria, negotiated his ruin with the sultan of Egypt; and in the public eye their treason was consecrated as the most sublime virtue.[45] To the pope's nuncios, who urged the consummation of the work, Palæologus exposed a naked recital of all that he had done and suffered for their sake. They were assured that the guilty sectaries, of both sexes and every rank, had been deprived of their honours, their fortunes, and their liberty a spreading list of confiscation and punishment, which involved many persons, the dearest to the emperor, or the best deserving of his favour They were conducted to the prison, to behold four princes of the royal blood chained in the four corners, and shaking their fetters in an agony of grief and rage. Two of these captives were afterwards released, the one by submission, the other by death, but the obstinacy of their two companions was chastised by the loss of their eyes; and the Greeks, the least adverse to the union, deplore that cruel and inauspicious tragedy[46] Persecutors must expect the hatred of those whom they oppress; but they commonly find some consolation in the testimony of their conscience, the applause of their party, and, perhaps, the success of their undertaking But the hypocrisy of Michael, which was prompted only by political motives, must have forced him to hate himself, to despise his followers, and to esteem and envy the rebel champions, by whom he was

[45] This frank and authentic confession of Michael's distress is exhibited in barbarous Latin by Ogerius, who signs himself Protonotarius Interpretum, and transcribed by Wading from the MSS of the Vatican (A D 1278, No 3) His Annals of the Franciscan order, the Fratres Minores, in xvii volumes in folio (Rome, 1741), I have now accidentally seen among the waste paper of a bookseller

[46] See the vith book of Pachymer, particularly the chapters 1, 11, 16, 18, 24-27 He is the more credible, as he speaks of this persecution with less anger than sorrow.

detested and despised.[47]   While his violence was abhorred at Constantinople, at Rome his slowness was arraigned and his sincerity suspected; till at length Pope Martin the Fourth excluded the Greek emperor from the pale of a church into which he was striving to reduce a schismatic people.   No sooner had the tyrant expired than the union was dissolved and abjured by unanimous consent; the churches were purified, the penitents were reconciled; and his son Andronicus, after weeping the sins and errors of his youth, most piously denied his father the burial of a prince and a Christian.[48]

II.   In the distress of the Latins, the walls and towers of Constantinople had fallen to decay; they were restored and fortified by the policy of Michael who deposited a plenteous store of corn and salt provisions, to sustain the siege which he might hourly expect from the resentment of the Western powers.   Of these, the sovereign of the Two Sicilies was the most formidable neighbour; but, as long as they were possessed by Mainfroy, the bastard of Frederic the Second, his monarchy was the bulwark rather than the annoyance of the Eastern empire   The usurper, though a brave and active prince, was sufficiently employed in the defence of his throne; his proscription by successive popes had separated Mainfroy from the common cause of the Latins; and the forces that might have besieged Constantinople were detained in a

[47] [Finlay shows no mercy to Michael   "He was a type of the empire he re-established and transmitted to his descendants   He was selfish, hypocritical, able and accomplished, an inborn liar, vain, meddling, ambitious, cruel and rapacious   He has gained renown in history as the restorer of the Eastern Empire; he ought to be execrated as the corrupter of the Greek race, for his reign affords a signal example of the extent to which a nation may be degraded by the misconduct of its sovereign when he is entrusted with despotic power" (vol 3, p 372)]

[48] Pachymer, l vii c 1-11, 17   The speech of Andronicus the Elder (lib xii c 2) is a curious record, which proves that, if the Greeks were the slaves of the emperor, the emperor was not less the slave of superstition and the clergy

crusade against the domestic enemy of Rome The prize of
her avenger, the crown of the Two Sicilies, was won and
worn by the brother of St. Louis, by Charles, count of Anjou
and Provence, who led the chivalry of France on this holy
expedition.[49] The disaffection of his Christian subjects
compelled Mainfroy to enlist a colony of Saracens, whom his
father had planted in Apulia; and this odious succour will
explain the defiance of the Catholic hero, who rejected all
terms of accommodation " Bear this message," said Charles,
"to the sultan of Nocera, that God and the sword are umpire
between us; and that he shall either send me to paradise, or I
will send him to the pit of hell." The armies met, and, though
I am ignorant of Mainfroy's doom in the other world, in this
he lost his friends, his kingdom, and his life, in the bloody
battle of Benevento Naples and Sicily were immediately
peopled with a warlike race of French nobles; and their
aspiring leader embraced the future conquest of Africa,
Greece, and Palestine. The most specious reasons might
point his first arms against the Byzantine empire, and
Palæologus, diffident of his own strength, repeatedly appealed
from the ambition of Charles to the humanity of St. Louis,
who still preserved a just ascendant over the mind of his
ferocious brother. For a while the attention of that brother
was confined at home by the invasion of Conradin, the last
heir of the Imperial house of Swabia; but the hapless boy
sunk in the unequal conflict; and his execution on a public
scaffold taught the rivals of Charles to tremble for their

---

[49] The best accounts, the nearest the time, the most full and entertaining,
of the conquest of Naples by Charles of Anjou, may be found in the Florentine Chronicles of Ricordano Malespina [leg Malespini] (c 175-193) and
Giovanni Villani (l vii c 1-10, 25-30), which are published by Muratori in
the viiith and viiith volumes of the Historians of Italy In his Annals (tom
xi p 56-72), he has abridged these great events, which are likewise described
in the Istoria Civile of Giannone (tom ii l xix , tom iii l xx) [The
chronicle attributed to Malespini has been proved not to be original but to
depend on Villani See Scheffer-Boichorst, in Sybel's Historische Zeitschrift,
24, p. 274 sqq (1870).]

heads as well as their dominions. A second respite was obtained by the last crusade of St Louis to the African coast; and the double motive of interest and duty urged the king of Naples to assist, with his powers and his presence, the holy enterprise The death of St Louis released him from the importunity of a virtuous censor, the king of Tunis confessed himself the tributary and vassal of the crown of Sicily; and the boldest of the French knights were free to enlist under his banner against the Greek empire A treaty and a marriage united his interest with the house of Courtenay; his daughter, Beatrice, was promised to Philip, son and heir of the emperor Baldwin; a pension of six hundred ounces of gold was allowed for his maintenance; and his generous father distributed among his allies the kingdoms and provinces of the East, reserving only Constantinople, and one day's journey round the city, for the Imperial domain.[50] In this perilous moment, Palæologus was the most eager to subscribe the creed, and implore the protection, of the Roman pontiff, who assumed, with propriety and weight, the character of an angel of peace, the common father of the Christians By his voice the sword of Charles was chained in the scabbard; and the Greek ambassadors beheld him, in the pope's antichamber, biting his ivory sceptre in a transport of fury, and deeply resenting the refusal to enfranchise and consecrate his arms. He appears to have respected the disinterested mediation of Gregory the Tenth; but Charles was insensibly disgusted by the pride and partiality of Nicholas the Third, and his attachment to his kindred, the Ursini family, alienated the most strenuous champion from the service of the church. The hostile league against the Greeks, of Philip the Latin emperor, the king of the Two Sicilies, and the republic of Venice, was ripened into execu-

[50] Ducange, Hist de C P l. v. c. 49-56, l vi c 1-13 See Pachymer, l iv. c. 29, l v. c. 7-10, 25, l. vi c 30, 32, 33, and Nicephorus Gregoras, l. iv c l v i 6.

tion; and the election of Martin the Fourth, a French pope, gave a sanction to the cause. Of the allies, Philip supplied his name, Martin, a bull of excommunication, the Venetians, a squadron of forty galleys; and the formidable powers of Charles consisted of forty counts, ten thousand men at arms, a numerous body of infantry, and a fleet of more than three hundred ships and transports. A distant day was appointed for assembling this mighty force in the harbour of Brindisi; and a previous attempt was risked with a detachment of three hundred knights, who invaded Albania and besieged the fortress of Belgrade. Their defeat might amuse with a triumph the vanity of Constantinople; but the more sagacious Michael, despairing of his arms, depended on the effects of a conspiracy; on the secret workings of a rat, who gnawed the bow-string [51] of the Sicilian tyrant.

Among the proscribed adherents of the house of Swabia, John of Procida forfeited a small island of that name in the bay of Naples His birth was noble, but his education was learned; and, in the poverty of exile, he was relieved by the practice of physic, which he had studied in the school of Salerno. Fortune had left him nothing to lose except life; and to despise life is the first qualification of a rebel. Procida was endowed with the art of negotiation, to enforce his reasons and disguise his motives; and, in his various trans-actions with nations and men, he could persuade each party that he laboured solely for *their* interest. The new king-doms of Charles were afflicted by every species of fiscal and military oppression, [52] and the lives and fortunes of his Italian subjects were sacrificed to the greatness of their

[51] The reader of Herodotus will recollect how miraculously the Assyrian host of Sennacherib was disarmed and destroyed (l ii c 141)

[52] According to Sabas Malaspina (Hist Sicula, l iii c 16, in Muratori, tom viii p 832), a zealous Guelph, the subjects of Charles, who had reviled Mainfroy as a wolf, began to regret him as a lamb, and he justifies their discontent by the oppressions of the French government (l vi c 2, 7) See the Sicilian manifesto in Nicholas Specialis (l i c 11, in Muratori, tom v p 930)

master and the licentiousness of his followers. The hatred
of Naples was repressed by his presence; but the looser
government of his vicegerents excited the contempt, as well
as the aversion, of the Sicilians; the island was roused to a
sense of freedom by the eloquence of Procida, and he displayed to every baron his private interest in the common
cause. In the confidence of foreign aid, he successively
visited the courts of the Greek emperor and of Peter, king of
Arragon,[53] who possessed the maritime countries of Valentia
and Catalonia. To the ambitious Peter a crown was presented, which he might justly claim by his marriage with the
sister of Mainfroy, and by the dying voice of Conradin, who
from the scaffold had cast a ring to his heir and avenger.
Palæologus was easily persuaded to divert his enemy from a
foreign war by a rebellion at home, and a Greek subsidy
of twenty-five thousand ounces of gold was most profitably
applied to arm a Catalan fleet, which sailed under an holy
banner to the specious attack of the Saracens of Africa.
In the disguise of a monk or beggar, the indefatigable missionary of revolt flew from Constantinople to Rome, and
from Sicily to Saragossa; the treaty was sealed with the
signet of Pope Nicholas himself, the enemy of Charles; and
his deed of gift transferred the fiefs of St. Peter from the house
of Anjou to that of Arragon. So widely diffused and so
freely circulated, the secret was preserved above two years
with impenetrable discretion; and each of the conspirators
imbibed the maxim of Peter, who declared that he would
cut off his left hand, if it were conscious of the intentions of
his right. The mine was prepared with deep and dangerous
artifice; but it may be questioned whether the instant explosion of Palermo were the effect of accident or design.

On the vigil of Easter, a procession of the disarmed citizens

---

[53] See the character and counsels of Peter of Arragon, in Mariana (Hist
Hispan. l. xiv c 6, tom ii p 133) The reader forgives the Jesuit's defects,
in favour always of his style, and often of his sense.

visited a church without the walls; and a noble damsel was
rudely insulted by a French soldier [54] The ravisher was instantly punished with death; and, if the people was at first
scattered by a military force, their numbers and fury prevailed: the conspirators seized the opportunity; the flame
spread over the island, and eight thousand French were
exterminated in a promiscuous massacre, which has obtained
the name of the SICILIAN VESPERS.[55] From every city the
banners of freedom and the church were displayed; the
revolt was inspired by the presence or the soul of Procida;
and Peter of Arragon, who sailed from the African coast to
Palermo, was saluted as the king and saviour of the isle.
By the rebellion of a people on whom he had so long trampled
with impunity, Charles was astonished and confounded; and
in the first agony of grief and devotion he was heard to
exclaim, "O God! if thou hast decreed to humble me, grant
me at least a gentle and gradual descent from the pinnacle of
greatness" His fleet and army, which already filled the
sea-ports of Italy, were hastily recalled from the service of the
Grecian war; and the situation of Messina exposed that
town to the first storm of his revenge. Feeble in themselves,
and yet hopeless of foreign succour, the citizens would have
repented and submitted, on the assurance of full pardon and
their ancient privileges. But the pride of the monarch was
already rekindled; and the most fervent entreaties of the
legate could extort no more than a promise, that he would
forgive the remainder, after a chosen list of eight hundred
rebels had been yielded to his discretion. The despair of

---

[54] After enumerating the sufferings of his country, Nicholas Specialis adds,
in the true spirit of Italian jealousy, Quæ omnia et graviora quidem, ut arbitror,
patienti animo Siculi tolerassent, nisi (quod primum cunctis dominantibus
cavendum est) alienas fœminas invasissent (l i c 2, p 924)

[55] The French were long taught to remember this bloody lesson "If I
am provoked," said Henry the Fourth, "I will breakfast at Milan, and dine
at Naples" "Your Majesty," replied the Spanish ambassador, "may perhaps arrive in Sicily for vespers"

the Messinese renewed their courage, Peter of Arragon approached to their relief,[56] and his rival was driven back by the failure of provision, and the terrors of the equinox, to the Calabrian shore   At the same moment, the Catalan admiral, the famous Roger de Loria, swept the channel with an invincible squadron   the French fleet, more numerous in transports than in galleys, was either burnt or destroyed; and the same blow assured the independence of Sicily and the safety of the Greek empire.   A few days before his death, the emperor Michael rejoiced in the fall of an enemy whom he hated and esteemed; and perhaps he might be content with the popular judgment that, had they not been matched with each other, Constantinople and Italy must speedily have obeyed the same master[57]   From this disastrous moment, the life of Charles was a series of misfortunes; his capital was insulted, his son was made prisoner, and he sunk into the grave without recovering the isle of Sicily, which, after a war of twenty years, was finally severed from the throne of Naples, and transferred, as an independent kingdom, to a younger branch of the house of Arragon[58]

I shall not, I trust, be accused of superstition; but I must remark that, even in this world, the natural order of events

[56] This revolt, with the subsequent victory, are related by two national writers, Bartholemy a Neocastro (in Muratori, tom xiii [and in Del Re, Cronisti e scrittori, vol 2]) and Nicholas Specialis (in Muratori, tom x), the one a contemporary, the other of the next century   The patriot Specialis disclaims the name of rebellion and all previous correspondence with Peter of Arragon (nullo communicato consilio), who *happened* to be with a fleet and army on the African coast (l 1 c 4, 9)   [For the Sicilian vespers and the sequel, see also the contemporary chronicle of Bernard d'Esclot (an obscure figure), which is published by Buchon in his Chroniques Etrangères (1860), c 81 *sqq* , and also an anonymous contemporary relation of the conspiracy of John Prochyta, in the Sicilian idiom, of which Buchon (*ib.* p 736 *sqq*) has given a French translation]

[57] Nicephorus Gregoras (l v c 6) admires the wisdom of Providence in this equal balance of states and princes   For the honour of Palæologus, I had rather this balance had been observed by an Italian writer

[58] See the Chronicle of Villani, the xith volume of the Annali d'Italia of Muratori, and the xxth and xxist books of the Istoria Civile of Giannone

will sometimes afford the strong appearances of moral retribution. The first Palæologus had saved his empire by involv-
ing the kingdoms of the West in rebellion and blood; and from
these seeds of discord uprose a generation of iron men, who
assaulted and endangered the empire of his son   In modern
times our debts and taxes are the secret poison, which still
corrodes the bosom of peace, but in the weak and disorderly
government of the middle ages it was agitated by the present
evil of the disbanded armies.   Too idle to work, too proud to
beg, the mercenaries were accustomed to a life of rapine:
they could rob with more dignity and effect under a banner
and a chief, and the sovereign, to whom their service was
useless and their presence importunate, endeavoured to
discharge the torrent on some neighbouring countries.   After
the peace of Sicily, many thousands of Genoese, *Catalans*,[59]
&c., who had fought, by sea and land, under the standard
of Anjou or Arragon were blended into one nation by the
resemblance of their manners and interest.   They heard that
the Greek provinces of Asia were invaded by the Turks: they
resolved to share the harvest of pay and plunder; and
Frederic, king of Sicily, most liberally contributed the means
of their departure.   In a warfare of twenty years, a ship, or a
camp, was become their country; arms were their sole profession and property; valour was the only virtue which they
knew; their women had imbibed the fearless temper of their
lovers and husbands; it was reported that, with a stroke of
their broad sword, the Catalans could cleave a horseman and
an horse; and the report itself was a powerful weapon.
Roger de Flor was the most popular of their chiefs; and his
personal merit overshadowed the dignity of his prouder
rivals of Arragon.   The offspring of a marriage between a

[59] In this motley multitude, the Catalans and Spaniards, the bravest of
the soldiery, were styled by themselves and the Greeks *Amogavares* [Al-
mugavari=scouts]   Moncada derives their origin from the Goths, and
Pachymer (l vi c 22) from the Arabs, and, in spite of national and religious
pride, I am afraid the latter is in the right

German gentleman [60] of the court of Frederic the Second and a damsel of Brindisi, Roger was successively a templar, an apostate, a pirate, and at length the richest and most powerful admiral of the Mediterranean.   He sailed from Messina to Constantinople, with eighteen galleys, four great ships, and eight thousand adventurers; and his previous treaty was faithfully accomplished by Andronicus the Elder, who accepted with joy and terror this formidable succour.[61] A palace was allotted for his reception, and a niece of the emperor was given in marriage to the valiant stranger, who was immediately created Great Duke or Admiral of Romania   After a decent repose, he transported his troops over the Propontis, and boldly led them against the Turks; in two bloody battles thirty thousand of the Moslems were slain; he raised the siege of Philadelphia, and deserved the name of the deliverer of Asia.   But, after a short season of prosperity, the cloud of slavery and ruin again burst on that unhappy province.   The inhabitants escaped (says a Greek historian) from the smoke into the flames; and the hostility of the Turks was less pernicious than the friendship of the Catalans.   The lives and fortunes which they had rescued, they considered as their own; the willing or reluctant maid was saved from the race of circumcision for the embraces of a Christian soldier, the exaction of fines and supplies was enforced by licentious rapine and arbitrary executions; and, on the resistance of Magnesia, the Great Duke besieged a city of the Roman empire.[62]   These disorders he excused by the wrongs and passions

[60] [A falconer (Ramon Muntaner, c 194)   His name was Richard Blum It was translated by an Italian equivalent   See Buchon's note]

[61] [Before he went himself, Roger sent envoys to make the terms.   The Emperor's niece, whom he married, was daughter of the Bulgarian Tsar, John Asên IV (whom Muntaner calls the emperador Lantzaura, c 199) As to the numbers of the expedition Muntaner says (c 201) that there were about 36 sail, 1500 horsemen, 4000 almogavars, 1000 foot-soldiers; as well as the oarsmen and sailors]

[62] Some idea may be formed of the population of these cities, from the 36,000 inhabitants of Tralles, which, in the preceding reign, was rebuilt by the emperor, and ruined by the Turks (Pachymer, l vi c 20, 21).

of a victorious army, nor would his own authority or person
have been safe, had he dared to punish his faithful followers,
who were defrauded of the just and covenanted price of their
services. The threats and complaints of Andronicus disclosed
the nakedness of the empire His golden bull had invited no
more than five hundred horse and a thousand foot-soldiers;
yet the crowd of volunteers, who migrated to the East, had
been enlisted and fed by his spontaneous bounty. While
his bravest allies were content with three byzants, or pieces of
gold, for their monthly pay, an ounce or even two ounces of
gold were assigned to the Catalans, whose annual pension
would thus amount to near an hundred pounds sterling; one
of their chiefs had modestly rated at three hundred thousand
crowns the value of his *future* merits; and above a million had
been issued from the treasury for the maintenance of these
costly mercenaries. A cruel tax had been imposed on the
corn of the husbandman one third was retrenched from the
salaries of the public officers, and the standard of the coin
was so shamefully debased that of the four-and-twenty parts
only five were of pure gold.[63] At the summons of the emperor,
Roger evacuated a province which no longer supplied the
materials of rapine, but he refused to disperse his troops;
and, while his style was respectful, his conduct was independent and hostile. He protested that, if the emperor should
march against him, he would advance forty paces to kiss the
ground before him; but, in rising from this prostrate attitude,

---

[63] I have collected these pecuniary circumstances from Pachymer (l. vi
c 21, l. vii. c 4, 5, 8, 14, 19), who describes the progressive degradation of
the gold coin Even in the prosperous times of John Ducas Vataces, the
byzants were composed in equal proportions of the pure and the baser metal
The poverty of Michael Palæologus compelled him to strike a new coin, with
nine parts, or carats, of gold, and fifteen of copper alloy After his death
the standard rose to ten carats, till in the public distress it was reduced to
the moiety The prince was relieved for a moment, while credit and commerce were for ever blasted In France, the gold coin is of twenty-two
carats (one twelfth alloy), and the standard of England and Holland is still
higher

Roger had a life and sword at the service of his friends. The Great Duke of Romania condescended to accept the title and ornaments of Cæsar; but he rejected the new proposal of the government of Asia, with a subsidy of corn and money, on condition that he should reduce his troops to the harmless number of three thousand men. Assassination is the last resource of cowards. The Cæsar was tempted to visit the royal residence of Hadrianople in the apartment, and before the eyes, of the empress, he was stabbed by the Alani [63 a] guards; [64] and, though the deed was imputed to their private revenge, his countrymen, who dwelt at Constantinople in the security of peace, were involved in the same proscription by the prince or people. The loss of their leader intimidated the crowd of adventurers, who hoisted the sails of flight, and were soon scattered round the coasts of the Mediterranean. But a veteran band of fifteen hundred Catalans or French stood firm in the strong fortress of Gallipoli on the Hellespont, displayed the banners of Arragon, and offered to revenge and justify their chief by an equal combat of ten or an hundred warriors. Instead of accepting this bold defiance, the emperor Michael, the son and colleague of Andronicus, resolved to oppress them with the weight of multitudes · every nerve was strained to form an army of thirteen thousand horse and thirty thousand foot; and the Propontis was covered with the ships of the Greeks and Genoese. In two battles by sea and land, these mighty forces were encountered and overthrown by the despair and discipline of the Catalans; the young emperor fled to the palace; and an insufficient guard of light horse was left for the protection of the open country. Victory renewed the hopes and numbers of the adventurers:

[63 a] [Is this a misprint for Alanic or Alan?]

[64] [Roger had crossed to Europe to help the Emperor Andronicus against the Bulgarians Before returning he wished to take leave of the young Emperor "Kyr Michael" who was at Hadrianople, though it was known that Michael bore him a grudge Roger's wife and others tried to dissuade him, in vain (Muntaner, c. 213, 215)]

every nation was blended under the name and standard of
the *great company;* and three thousand Turkish proselytes
deserted from the Imperial service to join this military association.   In the possession of Gallipoli,[65] the Catalans intercepted the trade of Constantinople and the Black Sea, while
they spread their devastations on either side of the Hellespont over the confines of Europe and Asia   To prevent their
approach, the greatest part of the Byzantine territory was
laid waste by the Greeks themselves · the peasants and their
cattle retired into the city; and myriads of sheep and oxen,
for which neither place nor food could be procured, were
unprofitably slaughtered on the same day.   Four times the
emperor Andronicus sued for peace, and four times he was
inflexibly repulsed, till the want of provisions, and the
discord of the chiefs, compelled the Catalans to evacuate the
banks of the Hellespont and the neighbourhood of the capital.
After their separation from the Turks, the remains of the
great company pursued their march through Macedonia and
Thessaly, to seek a new establishment in the heart of Greece.[66]

After some ages of oblivion, Greece was awakened to new
misfortunes by the arms of the Latins.   In the two hundred
and fifty years between the first and the last conquest of Constantinople, that venerable land was disputed by a multitude
of petty tyrants; without the comforts of freedom and genius,

[65] [Ramon Muntaner, the historian of the expedition, was for a long time
captain of Gallipoli, and he describes (c 225) the good time he had]

[66] The Catalan war is most copiously related by Pachymer, in the xith,
xiith, and xiiith books, till he breaks off in the year 1308   Nicephorus
Gregoras (l vii 3-6) is more concise and complete   Ducange, who adopts
these adventurers as French, has hunted their footsteps with his usual diligence (Hist. de C. P l vi c 22-46)   He quotes an Arragonese history,
which I have read with pleasure, and which the Spaniards extol as a model
of style and composition (Expedicion de los Catalines y Arragoneses contra
Turcos y Griegos, Barcelona, 1623, in quarto, Madrid, 1777, in octavo)
Don Francisco de Moncada, Conde de Osona, may imitate Cæsar or Sallust,
he may transcribe the Greek or Italian contemporaries, but he never quotes
his authorities, and I cannot discern any national records of the exploits of
his countrymen   [See vol ix Appendix 6]

her ancient cities were again plunged in foreign and intestine war, and, if servitude be preferable to anarchy, they might repose with joy under the Turkish yoke.   I shall not pursue the obscure and various dynasties that rose and fell on the continent or in the isles, [67] but our silence on the fate of ATHENS [68] would argue a strange ingratitude to the first and purest school of liberal science and amusement.   In the partition of the empire, the principality of Athens and Thebes was assigned to Otho de la Roche, a noble warrior of Burgundy, [69] with the title of Great Duke, [70] which the Latins understood in their own sense, and the Greeks more foolishly derived from the age of Constantine. [71]   Otho followed the standard of the marquis of Montferrat, the ample state, which he acquired by a miracle of conduct or fortune, [72] was

[67] [For a summary of the island dynasties see Appendix 3]

[68] See the laborious history of Ducange, whose accurate table of the French dynasties recapitulates the thirty-five passages in which he mentions the dukes of Athens   [Gregorovius, Geschichte der Stadt Athen im Mittelalter]

[69] He is twice mentioned by Villehardouin with honour (No 151, 235); and under the first passage Ducange observes all that can be known of his person and family.

[70] From these Latin princes of the xivth century, Boccace, Chaucer, and Shakespeare have borrowed their Theseus *Duke* of Athens   [And Dante, Inferno, 12, 17]   An ignorant age transfers its own language and manners to the most distant times   [Otto de la Roche had not the ducal title.   He called himself *sire* (not *grand sire*) or dominus Athenarum   The title is μέγας κύρ in the Chronicle of Morea   The ducal title was first assumed by Guy I in 1260 with permission of Louis IX of France.   Megara went along with Athens as a *pertinence* (cum pertinentia Megaron, in the Act of Partition)]

[71] The same Constantine gave to Sicily a king, to Russia the *magnus dapifer* of the empire, to Thebes the *primicerius* and these absurd fables are properly lashed by Ducange (ad Nicephor Greg l vii c 5)   By the Latins, the lord of Thebes was styled, by corruption, the Megas Kurios, or Grand Sire !   [See last note   He took his title from Athens, not from Thebes]

[72] *Quodam miraculo,* says Alberic   He was probably received by Michael Choniates, the archbishop who had defended Athens against the tyrant Leo Sgurus [A D 1204] (Nicetas in Baldwino [p 805, ed Bonn])   Michael was the brother of the historian Nicetas, and his encomium of Athens is still extant in MS in the Bodleian Library (Fabric Bibliot Grec tom vi p 405)

peaceably inherited by his son and two grandsons,[73] till the family, though not the nation, was changed, by the marriage of an heiress, into the elder branch of the house of Brienne. The son of that marriage, Walter de Brienne, succeeded to the duchy of Athens; and, with the aid of some Catalan mercenaries, whom he invested with fiefs, reduced above thirty castles of the vassal or neighbouring lords. But, when he was informed of the approach and ambition of the great company, he collected a force of seven hundred knights, six thousand four hundred horse, and eight thousand foot, and boldly met them on the banks of the river Cephisus in Bœotia.[74] The Catalans amounted to no more than three thousand five hundred horse and four thousand foot; but the deficiency of numbers was compensated by stratagem and order   They formed round their camp an artificial inundation · the duke and his knights advanced without fear or precaution on the verdant meadow; their horses plunged into the bog, and he was cut in pieces, with the greatest part of the French cavalry. His family and nation were expelled, and his son, Walter de Brienne, the titular duke of Athens, the tyrant of Florence, and the constable of France, lost his life in the field of Poitiers. Attica and Bœotia were the rewards of the victorious Catalans; they married the widows and daughters of the slain; and during fourteen years the great company was the terror of the Grecian states.   Their factions drove them to acknowledge the sovereignty of the house of Arragon,[75] and, during the remainder of the fourteenth century, Athens, as a govern-

[See above, p 7, note 15   It is supposed that Archbishop Akominatos made conditions of surrender with Boniface   The Western soldiers sacrilegiously pillaged the Parthenon church   Akominatos left Athens after its occupation by De la Roche]

[73] [This should be   nephew, two grand-nephews, and a great-grand-nephew, Guy II A D 1287-1308   Guy II 's aunt Isabella had married Hugh de Brienne, Walter de Brienne was their son]

[74] [See Ramon Muntaner, chap 240]

[75] [They also held Neopatras in Thessaly, their title was Duke of Athens and Neopatras, and the kings of Spain retained the title.]

ment or an appanage, was successively bestowed by the kings
of Sicily   After the French and Catalans, the third dynasty
was that of the Accaioli, a family, plebeian at Florence, potent
at Naples, and sovereign in Greece.   Athens, which they
embellished with new buildings, became the capital of a state
that extended over Thebes, Argos, Corinth, Delphi, and a
part of Thessaly; and their reign was finally determined by
Mahomet the Second, who strangled the last duke, and educated his sons in the discipline and religion of the seraglio.[76]

Athens,[77] though no more than the shadow of her former
self, still contains about eight or ten thousand inhabitants·
of these, three fourths are Greeks in religion and language;
and the Turks, who compose the remainder, have relaxed,
in their intercourse with the citizens, somewhat of the pride
and gravity of their national character.   The olive-tree, the
gift of Minerva, flourishes in Attica; nor has the honey of
Mount Hymettus lost any part of its exquisite flavour;[78] but
the languid trade is monopolised by strangers, and the
agriculture of a barren land is abandoned to the vagrant
Walachians.   The Athenians are still distinguished by the
subtlety and acuteness of their understandings; but these
qualities, unless ennobled by freedom and enlightened by
study, will degenerate into a low and selfish cunning; and it
is a proverbial saying of the country, "From the Jews of

[76] [For the Accaioli see Appendix 2]

[77] The modern account of Athens, and the Athenians, is extracted from
Spon (Voyage en Grèce, tom II p 79-199) and Wheler (Travels into Greece,
p 337-414), Stuart (Antiquities of Athens, *passim*), and Chandler (Travels
into Greece, p 23-172)   The first of these travellers visited Greece in the
year 1676, the last 1765, and ninety years had not produced much difference
in the tranquil scene   [At the end of the 12th century Michael Akominatos
deplores the decline of Athens (for his dirge see above, p 7, note 14).   He
says that he has become a Barbarian by living so long in Athens (ed Lampros vol 2, p 44)]

[78] The ancients, or at least the Athenians, believed that all the bees in the
world had been propagated from Mount Hymettus   They taught that health
might be preserved, and life prolonged, by the external use of oil and the
internal use of honey (Geoponica l 15 c 7 p 1089 1090 edit Niclas).

THE ACROPOLIS.

Thessalonica, the Turks of Negropont, and the Greeks of Athens, good Lord, deliver us!" This artful people has eluded the tyranny of the Turkish bashaws by an expedient which alleviates their servitude and aggravates their shame. About the middle of the last century, the Athenians chose for their protector the Kislar Aga, or chief black eunuch of the seraglio. This Æthiopian slave, who possesses the sultan's ear, condescends to accept the tribute of thirty thousand crowns; his lieutenant, the Waywode, whom he annually confirms, may reserve for his own about five or six thousand more; and such is the policy of the citizens that they seldom fail to remove and punish an oppressive governor. Their private differences are decided by the archbishop, one of the richest prelates of the Greek church, since he possesses a revenue of one thousand pounds sterling; and by a tribunal of the eight *geronti* or elders, chosen in the eight quarters of the city. The noble families cannot trace their pedigree above three hundred years, but their principal members are distinguished by a grave demeanour, a fur cap, and the lofty appellation of *archon*. By some, who delight in the contrast, the modern language of Athens is represented as the most corrupt and barbarous of the seventy dialects of the vulgar Greek;[79] this picture is too darkly coloured; but it would not be easy, in the country of Plato and Demosthenes, to find a reader, or a copy, of their works. The Athenians walk with supine indifference among the glorious ruins of antiquity; and such is the debasement of their character that they are incapable of admiring the genius of their predecessors.[80]

[79] Ducange, Glossar Græc Præfat p 8, who quotes for his author Theodosius Zygomalas, a modern grammarian [of the 16th cent] Yet Spon (tom ii p 194), and Wheler (p 355), no incompetent judges, entertain a more favourable opinion of the Attic dialect

[80] Yet we must not accuse them of corrupting the name of Athens, which they still call Athini From the εἰς τὴν ᾿Αθήνην we have formed our own barbarism of *Setines*. [*Setines* comes from (στὰ)s ᾿Αθήνας]

CHAPTER LXIII

*Civil Wars, and Ruin of the Greek Empire — Reigns of An-
dronicus, the Elder and Younger, and John Palæologus
— Regency, Revolt, Reign, and Abdication of John
Cantacuzene — Establishment of a Genoese Colony at
Pera or Galata — Their Wars with the Empire and City
of Constantinople*

THE long reign of Andronicus [1] the Elder is chiefly memorable by the disputes of the Greek church, the invasion of the
Catalans, and the rise of the Ottoman power. He is celebrated as the most learned and virtuous prince of the age;
but such virtue and such learning contributed neither to the
perfection of the individual nor to the happiness of society.
A slave of the most abject superstition, he was surrounded
on all sides by visible and invisible enemies; nor were the
flames of hell less dreadful to his fancy than those of a Catalan
or Turkish war. Under the reign of the Palæologi, the choice
of the patriarch was the most important business of the state;
the heads of the Greek church were ambitious and fanatic
monks; and their vices or virtues, their learning or ignorance,
were equally mischievous or contemptible. By his intemperate discipline, the patriarch Athanasius [2] excited the hatred

---

[1] Andronicus himself will justify our freedom in the invective (Nicephorus
Gregoras, l 1 c 1) which he pronounced against historic falsehood   It is
true that his censure is more pointedly urged against calumny than against
adulation

[2] For the anathema in the pigeon's nest, see Pachymer (l ix c 24), who
relates the general history of Athanasius (l viii c 13–16, 20–24, l x c 27–
29, 31–36, l xi c 1–3, 5, 6, l xiii c 8, 10, 23, 35), and is followed by
Nicephorus Gregoras (l vi c 5, 7, l vii c 1, 9), who includes the second
retreat of this second Chrysostom

of the clergy and people he was heard to declare that the
sinner should swallow the last dregs of the cup of penance;
and the foolish tale was propagated of his punishing a
sacrilegious ass that had tasted the lettuce of a convent-
garden Driven from the throne by the universal clamour,
Athanasius composed, before his retreat, two papers of a very
opposite cast His public testament was in the tone of charity
and resignation, the private codicil breathed the direst
anathemas against the authors of his disgrace, whom he
excluded for ever from the communion of the Holy Trinity,
the angels, and the saints. This last paper he enclosed in
an earthen pot, which was placed, by his order, on the top
of one of the pillars in the dome of St. Sophia, in the distant
hope of discovery and revenge At the end of four years,
some youths, climbing by a ladder in search of pigeons' nests,
detected the fatal secret; and, as Andronicus felt himself
touched and bound by the excommunication, he trembled
on the brink of the abyss which had been so treacherously
dug under his feet A synod of bishops was instantly
convened to debate this important question, the rashness
of these clandestine anathemas was generally condemned;
but, as the knot could be untied only by the same hand, as
that hand was now deprived of the crosier, it appeared that
this posthumous decree was irrevocable by any earthly power.
Some faint testimonies of repentance and pardon were extorted from the author of the mischief, but the conscience
of the emperor was still wounded, and he desired, with no
less ardour than Athanasius himself, the restoration of a
patriarch by whom alone he could be healed. At the dead
of night a monk rudely knocked at the door of the royal bed-
chamber, announcing a revelation of plague and famine, of
inundations and earthquakes Andronicus started from his
bed, and spent the night in prayer, till he felt, or thought that
he felt, a slight motion of the earth The emperor, on foot,
led the bishops and monks to the cell of Athanasius; and,
after a proper resistance, the saint, from whom this message

had been sent, consented to absolve the prince and govern the church of Constantinople. Untamed by disgrace and hardened by solitude, the shepherd was again odious to the flock; and his enemies contrived a singular and, as it proved, a successful mode of revenge. In the night they stole away the foot-stool or foot-cloth of his throne, which they secretly replaced with the decoration of a satirical picture. The emperor was painted with a bridle in his mouth, and Athanasius leading the tractable beast to the feet of Christ. The authors of the libel were detected and punished; but, as their lives had been spared, the Christian priest in sullen indignation retired to his cell; and the eyes of Andronicus, which had been opened for a moment, were again closed by his successor.

If this transaction be one of the most curious and important of a reign of fifty years, I cannot at least accuse the brevity of my materials, since I reduce into some few pages the enormous folios of Pachymer,[3] Cantacuzene,[4] and Nicephorus Gregoras,[5] who have composed the prolix and languid story of the times. The name and situation of the emperor John Cantacuzene might inspire the most lively curiosity His memorials of forty years extend from the revolt of the younger Andronicus to his own abdication of the empire; and it is observed that, like Moses and Cæsar, he was the principal actor in the scenes which he describes But in this eloquent work we should vainly seek the sincerity of an hero or a penitent.

[3] Pachymer, in seven books, 377 folio pages, describes the first twenty-six years of Andronicus the Elder, and marks the date of his composition by the current news or lie of the day (A D. 1308). Either death or disgust prevented him from resuming the pen

[4] After an interval of twelve years from the conclusion of Pachymer, Cantacuzenus takes up the pen, and his first book (c 1–59, p 9–150) relates the civil war and the eight last years of the elder Andronicus The ingenious comparison of Moses and Cæsar is fancied by his French translator, the President Cousin

[5] Nicephorus Gregoras more briefly includes the entire life and reign of Andronicus the Elder (l vi c i, l x c i, p 96–291) This is the part of which Cantacuzene complains as a false and malicious representation of his conduct.

Retired in a cloister from the vices and passions of the world,
he presents not a confession, but an apology, of the life of an
ambitious statesman. Instead of unfolding the true counsels
and characters of men, he displays the smooth and specious
surface of events, highly varnished with his own praises and
those of his friends. Their motives are always pure, their
ends always legitimate; they conspire and rebel without any
views of interest; and the violence which they inflict or suffer
is celebrated as the spontaneous effect of reason and virtue.

After the example of the first of the Palæologi, the elder
Andronicus associated his son Michael to the honours of the
purple; and, from the age of eighteen to his premature death,
that prince was acknowledged, above twenty-five years, as
the second emperor of the Greeks.[8] At the head of an army,
he excited neither the fears of the enemy nor the jealousy of
the court; his modesty and patience were never tempted to
compute the years of his father; nor was that father compelled to repent of his liberality either by the virtues or vices
of his son. The son of Michael was named Andronicus from
his grandfather, to whose early favour he was introduced by
that nominal resemblance The blossoms of wit and beauty
increased the fondness of the elder Andronicus, and, with
the common vanity of the age, he expected to realise in the
second, the hope which had been disappointed in the first,
generation. The boy was educated in the palace as an heir
and a favourite, and, in the oaths and acclamations of the
people, the *august triad* was formed by the names of the father,
the son, and the grandson. But the younger Andronicus was
speedily corrupted by his infant greatness, while he beheld,
with puerile impatience, the double obstacle that hung, and

---

[8] He was crowned May 21, 1295, and died October 12, 1320 (Ducange,
Fam Byz p 239) His brother, Theodore, by a second marriage, inherited
the marquisate of Montferrat, apostatised to the religion and manners of the
Latins (ὅτι καὶ γνώμῃ καὶ πίστει καὶ σχήματι, καὶ γενείων κουρᾷ καὶ πᾶσιν ἔθεσιν
Λατῖνος ἦν ἀκραιφνής, Nic. Greg 1 ix c. 1), and founded a dynasty of Italian
princes, which was extinguished A D 1533 (Ducange, Fam Byz. p. 249-253).

might long hang, over his rising ambition. It was not to
acquire fame, or to diffuse happiness, that he so eagerly
aspired; wealth and impunity were in his eyes the most
precious attributes of a monarch, and his first indiscreet
demand was the sovereignty of some rich and fertile island,
where he might lead a life of independence and pleasure.
The emperor was offended by the loud and frequent intemperance which disturbed his capital; the sums which his
parsimony denied were supplied by the Genoese usurers of
Pera, and the oppressive debt, which consolidated the interest
of a faction, could be discharged only by a revolution. A
beautiful female, a matron in rank, a prostitute in manners,
had instructed the younger Andronicus in the rudiments of
love; but he had reason to suspect the nocturnal visits of a
rival, and a stranger passing through the street was pierced
by the arrows of his guards, who were placed in ambush at
her door. That stranger was his brother, Prince Manuel,
who languished and died of his wound; and the emperor
Michael, their common father, whose health was in a declining state, expired on the eighth day, lamenting the loss of
both his children.[7] However guiltless in his intention, the
younger Andronicus might impute a brother's and a father's
death to the consequence of his own vices; and deep was the
sigh of thinking and feeling men, when they perceived, instead of sorrow and repentance, his ill-dissembled joy on the
removal of two odious competitors. By these melancholy
events, and the increase of his disorders, the mind of the
elder emperor was gradually alienated; and, after many
fruitless reproofs, he transferred on another grandson [8] his

---

[7] We are indebted to Nicephorus Gregoras (l viii c. 1) for the knowledge
of this tragic adventure; while Cantacuzene more discreetly conceals the
vices of Andronicus the Younger, of which he was the witness and perhaps
the associate (l 1 c 1, &c)

[8] His destined heir was Michael Catharus, the bastard of Constantine his
second son In this project of excluding his grandson Andronicus, Nicephorus Gregoras (l viii c. 3 [p 295-6, ed Bonn]) agrees with Cantacuzene
(l 1 c. 1, 2).

hopes and affection. The change was announced by the
new oath of allegiance to the reigning sovereign and the *person* whom he should appoint for his successor, and the acknowledged heir, after a repetition of insults and complaints,
was exposed to the indignity of a public trial Before the
sentence, which would probably have condemned him to a
dungeon or a cell, the emperor was informed that the palace
courts were filled with the armed followers of his grandson;
the judgment was softened to a treaty of reconciliation, and
the triumphant escape of the prince encouraged the ardour
of the younger faction

Yet the capital, the clergy, and the senate adhered to the
person, or at least to the government, of the old emperor, and
it was only in the provinces, by flight, and revolt, and foreign
succour, that the malecontents could hope to vindicate their
cause and subvert his throne. The soul of the enterprise was
the great domestic, John Cantacuzene; the sally from Constantinople is the first date of his actions and memorials,
and, if his own pen be most descriptive of his patriotism,
an unfriendly historian has not refused to celebrate the zeal
and ability which he displayed in the service of the young
emperor. That prince escaped from the capital under the
pretence of hunting; erected his standard at Hadrianople;
and, in a few days, assembled fifty thousand horse and foot,
whom neither honour nor duty could have armed against the
Barbarians. Such a force might have saved or commanded
the empire; but their counsels were discordant, their motions
were slow and doubtful, and their progress was checked by
intrigue and negotiation. The quarrel of the two Andronici
was protracted, and suspended, and renewed, during a ruinous
period of seven years. In the first treaty the relics of the Greek
empire were divided Constantinople, Thessalonica, and the
islands were left to the elder, while the younger acquired the
sovereignty of the greatest part of Thrace, from Philippi to
the Byzantine limit By the second treaty he stipulated the
payment of his troops his immediate coronation and an

adequate share of the power and revenue of the state. The
third civil war was terminated by the surprise of Constantinople, the final retreat of the old emperor, and the sole reign
of his victorious grandson   The reasons of this delay may
be found in the characters of the men and of the times. When
the heir of the monarchy first pleaded his wrongs and his apprehensions, he was heard with pity and applause, and his
adherents repeated on all sides the inconsistent promise that
he would increase the pay of the soldiers and alleviate the
burdens of the people. The grievances of forty years were
mingled in his revolt; and the rising generation was fatigued
by the endless prospect of a reign whose favourites and maxims
were of other times. The youth of Andronicus had been
without spirit, his age was without reverence, his taxes produced an annual revenue of five hundred thousand pounds;
yet the richest of the sovereigns of Christendom was incapable
of maintaining three thousand horse and twenty galleys, to
resist the destructive progress of the Turks.[9] "How different," said the younger Andronicus, "is my situation from that
of the son of Philip! Alexander might complain that his
father would leave him nothing to conquer; alas! my grand-
sire will leave me nothing to lose" But the Greeks were
soon admonished that the public disorders could not be
healed by a civil war; and their young favourite was not
destined to be the saviour of a falling empire. On the first
repulse, his party was broken by his own levity, their intestine discord, and the intrigues of the ancient court, which
tempted each malecontent to desert or betray the cause of
rebellion. Andronicus the Younger was touched with remorse, or fatigued with business, or deceived by negotiation; pleasure rather than power was his aim, and the

---

[9] See Nicephorus Gregoras, l. viii c 6   The younger Andronicus complained that in four years and four months a sum of 350,000 byzants of gold
was due to him for the expenses of his household (Cantacuzen l 1 c 48).
Yet he would have remitted the debt, if he might have been allowed to
squeeze the farmers of the revenue.

licence of maintaining a thousand hounds, a thousand hawks, and a thousand huntsmen was sufficient to sully his fame and disarm his ambition

Let us now survey the catastrophe of this busy plot and the final situation of the principal actors [10] The age of Andronicus was consumed in civil discord, and, amidst the events of war and treaty, his power and reputation continually decayed, till the fatal night in which the gates of the city and palace were opened without resistance to his grandson His principal commander scorned the repeated warnings of danger; and retiring to rest in the vain security of ignorance, abandoned the feeble monarch, with some priests and pages, to the terrors of a sleepless night These terrors were quickly realised by the hostile shouts which proclaimed the titles and victory of Andronicus the Younger; and the aged emperor, falling prostrate before an image of the Virgin, despatched a suppliant message to resign the sceptre and to obtain his life at the hands of the conqueror. The answer of his grandson was decent and pious, at the prayer of his friends, the younger Andronicus assumed the sole administration, but the elder still enjoyed the name and pre-eminence of the first emperor, the use of the great palace, and a pension of twenty-four thousand pieces of gold, one half of which was assigned on the royal treasure, and the other on the fishery of Constantinople. But his impotence was soon exposed to contempt and oblivion; the vast silence of the palace was disturbed only by the cattle and poultry of the neighbourhood, which roved with impunity through the solitary courts; and a reduced allowance of ten thousand pieces of gold [11] was all that he

---

[10] I follow the chronology of Nicephorus Gregoras, who is remarkably exact. It is proved that Cantacuzene has mistaken the dates of his own actions, or rather that his text has been corrupted by ignorant transcribers

[11] I have endeavoured to reconcile the 24,000 [*leg* 12,000] pieces of Cantacuzene (l ii c 1 [vol 1 p 311, ed Bonn]) with the 10,000 of Nicephorus Gregoras (l ix c 2), the one of whom wished to soften, the other to magnify, the hardships of the old emperor

could ask and more than he could hope   His calamities were
embittered by the gradual extinction of sight   his confinement was rendered each day more rigorous; and during the
absence and sickness of his grandson, his inhuman keepers,
by the threats of instant death, compelled him to exchange
the purple for the monastic habit and profession.   The monk
Antony had renounced the pomp of the world: yet he had
occasion for a coarse fur in the winter-season; and, as wine
was forbidden by his confessor, and water by his physician,
the sherbet of Egypt was his common drink.   It was not
without difficulty that the late emperor could procure three
or four pieces to satisfy these simple wants; and, if he
bestowed the gold to relieve the more painful distress of a
friend, the sacrifice is of some weight in the scale of humanity
and religion   Four years after his abdication, Andronicus,
or Antony, expired in a cell, in the seventy-fourth year of his
age, and the last strain of adulation could only promise a
more splendid crown of glory in heaven than he had enjoyed
upon earth [12]

Nor was the reign of the younger, more glorious or fortunate
than that of the elder, Andronicus.[13]   He gathered the fruits
of ambition. but the taste was transient and bitter; in the
supreme station he lost the remains of his early popularity;
and the defects of his character became still more conspicuous
to the world.   The public reproach urged him to march in
person against the Turks; nor did his courage fail in the hour
of trial; but a defeat and wound were the only trophies of his
expedition in Asia, which confirmed the establishment of the
Ottoman monarchy.   The abuses of the civil government

[12] See Nicephorus Gregoras (l ix 6–8, 10, 14, l x c 1)   The historian
had tasted of the prosperity, and shared the retreat, of his benefactor, and
that friendship, which "waits or to the scaffold or the cell," should not
lightly be accused as "a hireling, a prostitute to praise "

[13] The sole reign of Andronicus the Younger is described by Cantacuzene
(l ii c 1–40, p. 191–339) and Nicephorus Gregoras (l ix c 7–l xi c 11,
p 262–361)

attained their full maturity and perfection, his neglect of forms, and the confusion of national dresses, are deplored by the Greeks as the fatal symptoms of the decay of the empire. Andronicus was old before his time, the intemperance of youth had accelerated the infirmities of age, and, after being rescued from a dangerous malady by nature, or physic, or the Virgin, he was snatched away before he had accomplished his forty-fifth year. He was twice married, and, as the progress of the Latins in arms and arts had softened the prejudices of the Byzantine court, his two wives were chosen in the princely houses of Germany and Italy. The first, Agnes at home, Irene in Greece, was daughter of the duke of Brunswick Her father [14] was a petty lord [15] in the poor and savage regions of the north of Germany, [16] yet he derived some revenue from his silver mines; [17] and his family is

[14] Agnes, or Irene, was the daughter of Duke Henry the Wonderful, the chief of the house of Brunswick, and the fourth in descent from the famous Henry the Lion, duke of Saxony and Bavaria, and conqueror of the Salvi on the Baltic coast Her brother Henry was surnamed the *Greek*, from his two journeys into the East, but these journeys were subsequent to his sister's marriage, and I am ignorant *how* Agnes was discovered in the heart of Germany, and recommended to the Byzantine court (Rimius, Memoirs of the House of Brunswick, p 126–137)

[15] Henry the Wonderful was the founder of the branch of Grubenhagen, extinct in the year 1596 (Rimius, p 287) He resided in the castle of Wolfenbuttel, and possessed no more than a sixth part of the allodial estates of Brunswick and Luneburg, which the Guelph family had saved from the confiscation of their great fiefs The frequent partitions among brothers had almost ruined the princely houses of Germany, till that just but pernicious law was slowly superseded by the right of primogeniture The principality of Grubenhagen, one of the last remains of the Hercynian forest, is a woody, mountainous, and barren tract (Busching's Geography, vol vi p 270–286, English translation)

[16] The royal author of the Memoirs of Brandenburg will teach us how justly, in a much later period, the north of Germany deserved the epithets of poor and barbarous (Essai sur les Mœurs, &c) In the year 1306, in the woods of Luneburg, some wild people, of the Vened race, were allowed to bury alive their infirm and useless parents (Rimius, p 136)

[17] The assertion of Tacitus that Germany was destitute of the precious metals must be taken, even in his own time, with some limitation (Germania, c 5, Annal vi 20) According to Spener (Hist Germaniæ Pragmatica, tom

celebrated by the Greeks as the most ancient and noble of the Teutonic name.[18] After the death of this childless princess, Andronicus sought in marriage Jane, the sister of the count of Savoy,[19] and his suit was preferred to that of the French king.[20] The count respected in his sister the superior majesty of a Roman empress; her retinue was composed of knights and ladies, she was regenerated and crowned in St Sophia, under the more orthodox appellation of Anne; and, at the nuptial feast, the Greeks and Italians vied with each other in the martial exercises of tilts and tournaments.

The empress Anne of Savoy survived her husband. Their son, John Palæologus, was left an orphan and an emperor, in the ninth year of his age; and his weakness was protected by the first and most deserving of the Greeks. The long and cordial friendship of his father for John Cantacuzene is alike honourable to the prince and the subject. It had been formed amidst the pleasures of their youth; their families were almost equally noble;[21] and the recent lustre of the purple was amply compensated by the energy of a private

i p 351), *Argentifodinæ* in Hercyniis montibus, imperante Othone magno (A D 968), primum apertæ, largam etiam opes augendi dederunt copiam, but Rimius (p. 258, 259) defers till the year 1016 discovery of the silver mines of Grubenhagen, or the Upper Hartz, which were productive in the beginning of the xivth century, and which still yield a considerable revenue to the house of Brunswick.

[18] Cantacuzene has given a most honourable testimony, ἦν δ' ἐκ Γερμανῶν αὔτη θυγατὴρ δουκὸς ντὶ μπρουζουικ (the modern Greeks employ the ντ for the δ, and the μπ for the β, and the whole will read, in the Italian idiom, di Brunzuic), τοῦ παρ' αὐτοῖς ἐπιφανεστάτου, καὶ λαμπρότητι πάντας τοὺς ὁμοφύλους ὑπερβάλλοντος τοῦ γένους   The praise is just in itself, and pleasing to an English ear

[19] Anne, or Jane, was one of the four daughters of Amédée the Great, by a second marriage, and half-sister of his successor, Edward count of Savoy (Anderson's Tables, p 650). See Cantacuzene (l i c 40-42)

[20] That king, if the fact be true, must have been Charles the Fair, who, in five years (1321–1326), was married to three wives (Anderson, p 628) Anne of Savoy arrived at Constantinople in February, 1326

[21] The noble race of the Cantacuzeni (illustrious from the xith century in the Byzantine annals) was drawn from the Paladins of France, the heroes of those romances which, in the xiiith century, were translated and read by

education. We have seen that the young emperor was saved by Cantacuzene from the power of his grandfather, and, after six years of civil war, the same favourite brought him back in triumph to the palace of Constantinople. Under the reign of Andronicus the Younger, the great domestic ruled the emperor and the empire; and it was by his valour and conduct that the isle of Lesbos and the principality of Ætolia were restored to their ancient allegiance. His enemies confess that, among the public robbers, Cantacuzene alone was moderate and abstemious; and the free and voluntary account which he produces of his own wealth [22] may sustain the presumption that it was devolved by inheritance, and not accumulated by rapine. He does not indeed specify the value of his money, plate, and jewels; yet, after a voluntary gift of two hundred vases of silver, after much had been secreted by his friends and plundered by his foes, his forfeit treasures were sufficient for the equipment of a fleet of seventy galleys. He does not measure the size and number of his estates, but his granaries were heaped with an incredible store of wheat and barley; and the labour of a thousand yoke of oxen might cultivate, according to the practice of antiquity, about sixty-two thousand five hundred acres of arable land.[23] His pastures were stocked with two thousand five hundred brood mares, two hundred camels, three hundred mules, five hundred asses, five thousand horned cattle, fifty thousand hogs, and seventy thousand sheep [24] a precious record of

the Greeks (Ducange, Fam Byzant p 258)   [Monograph on Cantacuzene · V Parisot, Cantacuzène, Homme d'état et historien, 1845]

[22] See Cantacuzene (l iii c. 24, 30, 36)

[23] Saserna, in Gaul, and Columella, in Italy or Spain, allow two yoke of oxen, two drivers, and six labourers, for two hundred jugera (125 English acres) of arable land, and three more men must be added if there be much underwood (Columella de Re Rusticâ, l ii c 13, p 441, edit Gesner)

[24] In this enumeration (l iii c 30), the French translation of the President Cousin is blotted with three palpable and essential errors   1 He omits the 1000 yoke of working oxen   2 He interprets the πεντακόσιαι πρὸς δισχιλίαις, by the number of fifteen hundred   [The mistake has not been corrected in

rural opulence, in the last period of the empire, and in a land, most probably in Thrace, so repeatedly wasted by foreign and domestic hostility   The favour of Cantacuzene was above his fortune.   In the moments of familiarity, in the hour of sickness, the emperor was desirous to level the distance between them, and pressed his friend to accept the diadem and purple.   The virtue of the great domestic, which is attested by his own pen, resisted the dangerous proposal; but the last testament of Andronicus the Younger named him the guardian of his son and the regent of the empire.

Had the regent found a suitable return of obedience and gratitude, perhaps he would have acted with pure and zealous fidelity in the service of his pupil.[25]   A guard of five hundred soliders watched over his person and the palace; the funeral of the late emperor was decently performed; the capital was silent and submissive; and five hundred letters, which Cantacuzene despatched in the first month, informed the provinces of their loss and their duty.   The prospect of a tranquil minority was blasted by the Great Duke or Admiral Apocaucus; and, to exaggerate *his* perfidy, the Imperial historian is pleased to magnify his own imprudence in raising him to that office against the advice of his more sagacious sovereign.   Bold and subtle, rapacious and profuse, the avarice and ambition of Apocaucus were by turns subservient to each other; and his talents were applied to the ruin of his country.   His arrogance was heightened by the command of a naval force and an impregnable castle, and, under the mask of oaths and flattery, he secretly conspired against his benefactor.   The female court of the empress was bribed and directed; he encouraged Anne of Savoy to assert,

the Bonn edition, vol ii p 185]   3 He confounds myriads with chiliads, and gives Cantacuzene no more than 5000 hogs   Put not your trust in translations!

[25] See the regency and reign of John Cantacuzenus, and the whole progress of the civil war, in his own history (l iii c 1–100, p 348–700), and in that of Nicephorus Gregoras (l xii c 1–l xv c 9, p 353–492)

by the law of nature, the tutelage of her son, the love of power was disguised by the anxiety of maternal tenderness; and the founder of the Palæologi had instructed his posterity to dread the example of a perfidious guardian. The patriarch John of Apri was a proud and feeble old man, encompassed by a numerous and hungry kindred. He produced an obsolete epistle of Andronicus, which bequeathed the prince and people to his pious care. the fate of his predecessor Arsenius prompted him to prevent, rather than punish, the crimes of an usurper; and Apocaucus smiled at the success of his own flattery, when he beheld the Byzantine priest assuming the state and temporal claims of the Roman pontiff.[26] Between three persons so different in their situation and character, a private league was concluded · a shadow of authority was restored to the senate, and the people was tempted by the name of freedom. By this powerful confederacy, the great domestic was assaulted at first with clandestine, at length with open, arms. His prerogatives were disputed; his opinions slighted, his friends persecuted, and his safety was threatened both in the camp and city. In his absence on the public service, he was accused of treason; proscribed as an enemy of the church and state, and delivered, with all his adherents, to the sword of justice, the vengeance of the people, and the power of the devil his fortunes were confiscated; his aged mother was cast into prison, all his past services were buried in oblivion, and he was driven by injustice to perpetrate the crime of which he was accused.[27] From the review of his preceding conduct, Cantacuzene appears to have been guiltless of any treasonable designs; and

[26] He assumed the royal privilege of red shoes or buskins; placed on his head a mitre of silk and gold, subscribed his epistles with hyacinth or green ink, and claimed for the new, whatever Constantine had given to the ancient, Rome (Cantacuzen l iii c 36, Nic Gregoras, l xiv c 3)

[27] Nic. Gregoras (l vii c 5) confesses the innocence and virtues of Cantacuzenus, the guilt and flagitious vices of Apocaucus; nor does he dissemble the motive of his personal and religious enmity to the former, νῦν δὲ διὰ κακίαν ἄλλων αἴτιος ὁ πρᾴοτατος τῆς τῶν ὅλων ἔδοξεν εἶναι φθορᾶς.

the only suspicion of his innocence must arise from the vehemence of his protestations, and the sublime purity which he ascribes to his own virtue. While the empress and the patriarch still affected the appearance of harmony, he repeatedly solicited the permission of retiring to a private, and even a monastic, life. After he had been declared a public enemy, it was his fervent wish to throw himself at the feet of the young emperor, and to receive without a murmur the stroke of the executioner: it was not without reluctance that he listened to the voice of reason, which inculcated the sacred duty of saving his family and friends, and proved that he could only save them by drawing the sword and assuming the Imperial title.

In the strong city of Demotica, his peculiar domain, the emperor John Cantacuzenus was invested with the purple buskins; his right leg was clothed by his noble kinsmen, the left by the Latin chiefs, on whom he conferred the order of knighthood   But even in this act of revolt he was still studious of loyalty; and the titles of John Palæologus and Anne of Savoy were proclaimed before his own name and that of his wife Irene.   Such vain ceremony is a thin disguise of rebellion, nor are there perhaps any *personal* wrongs that can authorise a subject to take arms against his sovereign ; but the want of preparation and success may confirm the assurance of the usurper that this decisive step was the effect of necessity rather than of choice.   Constantinople adhered to the young emperor; the king of Bulgaria was invited to the relief of Hadrianople; the principal cities of Thrace and Macedonia, after some hesitation, renounced their obedience to the great domestic, and the leaders of the troops and provinces were induced, by their private interest, to prefer the loose dominion of a woman and a priest.[28]   The army of Cantacuzene, in sixteen divisions, was stationed on the

---

[28] [The people seem to have clung to the legitimate heir, the officials to have supported Cantacuzene]

banks of the Melas, to tempt or intimidate the capital, it
was dispersed by treachery or fear, and the officers, more
especially the mercenary Latins, accepted the bribes, and
embraced the service, of the Byzantine court. After this
loss, the rebel emperor (he fluctuated between the two characters) took the road of Thessalonica with a chosen remnant,
but he failed in his enterprise on that important place; and he
was closely pursued by the Great Duke, his enemy Apocaucus,
at the head of a superior power by sea and land. Driven
from the coast, in his march, or rather flight, into the mountains of Servia, Cantacuzene assembled his troops to scrutinise
those who were worthy and willing to accompany his broken
fortunes A base majority bowed and retired, and his trusty
band was diminished to two thousand, and at last to five
hundred, volunteers. The *cral*,[29] or despot of the Servians,
received him with generous hospitality; but the ally was
insensibly degraded to a suppliant, an hostage, a captive;
and, in this miserable dependence, he waited at the door of
the Barbarian, who could dispose of the life and liberty of a
Roman emperor. The most tempting offers could not persuade the cral to violate his trust; but he soon inclined to the
stronger side; and his friend was dismissed without injury
to a new vicissitude of hopes and perils. Near six years the
flame of discord burnt with various success and unabated

[29] The princes of Servia (Ducange, Famil Dalmaticæ, &c c 2-4, 9) were
styled Despots in Greek, and Cral in their native idiom (Ducange, Gloss
Græc p 751) That title, the equivalent of king, appears to be of Sclavonic
origin, from whence it has been borrowed by the Hungarians, the modern
Greeks, and even by the Turks (Leunclavius, Pandect Turc p 422), who
reserve the name of Padishah for the Emperor. To obtain the latter instead
of the former is the ambition of the French at Constantinople (Avertissement
à l'Histoire de Timur Bec, p 39) [The Servian and Bulgarian *Kral*,
"king," from which the Hungarian *Király*, "king," is borrowed, seems to
be derived from *Karl* the Great, just as the German and Slavonic word for
Emperor is from the name of Caesar We find Κράλ in a Greek diploma
of King (and saint) Stephen of Hungary ἐγὼ Στέφανος Χριστιανὸς ὁ καὶ κράλ
πάσης Οὐγγρίας It is cited in Hunfalvy's Magyarország Ethnographiája,
p. 322]

rage. the cities were distracted by the faction of the nobles and the plebeians — the Cantacuzeni and Palæologi; and the Bulgarians, the Servians, and the Turks were invoked on both sides as the instruments of private ambition and the common ruin. The regent deplored the calamities of which he was the author and victim. and his own experience might dictate a just and lively remark on the different nature of foreign and civil war. "The former," said he, "is the external warmth of summer, always tolerable, and often beneficial; the latter is the deadly heat of a fever, which consumes without a remedy the vitals of the constitution." [30]

The introduction of barbarians and savages into the contests of civilised nations is a measure pregnant with shame and mischief; which the interest of the moment may compel, but which is reprobated by the best principles of humanity and reason. It is the practice of both sides to accuse their enemies of the guilt of the first alliances; and those who fail in their negotiations are loudest in their censure of the example which they envy and would gladly imitate. The Turks of Asia were less barbarous, perhaps, than the shepherds of Bulgaria and Servia; [31] but their religion rendered them the

---

[30] Nic Gregoras, l xii c 14 It is surprising that Cantacuzene has not inserted this just and lively image in his own writings

[31] [The author does not seem to realise, he certainly has not brought out, the dominant position of Servia at this time under its king Stephen Dushan, a name which deserves a place in the history of the Fall of the Roman Empire Servia was the strongest power in the peninsula under Stephen (1331–1355), and its boundaries extended from the Danube to the gulf of Arta "He was a man of great ambition and was celebrated for his gigantic stature and personal courage His subjects boasted of his liberality and success in war, his enemies reproached him with faithlessness and cruelty He had driven his father Stephen VII [Urosh III] from the throne, and the old man had been murdered in prison by the rebellious nobles of Servia, who feared lest a reconciliation should take place with his son Stephen Dushan passed seven years of his youth at Constantinople, where he became acquainted with all the defects of the Byzantine government and with all the vices of Greek society The circumstances in which the rival Emperors were placed during the year 1345 were extremely favourable to his ambitious projects, and he seized the opportunity to extend his conquests in every direction To the

implacable foes of Rome and Christianity. To acquire the friendship of their emirs, the two factions vied with each other in baseness and profusion; the dexterity of Cantacuzene obtained the preference; but the succour and victory were dearly purchased by the marriage of his daughter with an infidel, the captivity of many thousand Christians, and the passage of the Ottomans into Europe, the last and fatal stroke in the fall of the Roman empire. The inclining scale was decided in his favour by the death of Apocaucus, the just, though singular, retribution of his crimes. A crowd of nobles or plebeians, whom he feared or hated, had been seized by his orders in the capital and the provinces, and the old palace of Constantine was assigned for the place of their confinement. Some alterations in raising the walls and narrowing the cells had been ingeniously contrived to prevent their escape and aggravate their misery, and the work was incessantly pressed by the daily visits of the tyrant. His guards watched at the gate, and, as he stood in the inner court to overlook the architects, without fear or suspicion, he was assaulted and laid breathless on the ground, by two resolute prisoners of the Palæologian race,[32] who were armed

cast he rendered himself master of the whole valley of the Strymon, took the large and flourishing city of Serres and garrisoned all the fortresses as far as the wall that defended the pass of Christopolis. He extended his dominions along the shores of the Adriatic, and to the south he carried his arms to the gulf of Ambracia. He subdued the Vallachians of Thessaly, and placed strong garrisons in Achrida, Kastoria and Joannina. Flushed with victory he at last formed the ambitious scheme of depriving the Greeks of their political and ecclesiastical supremacy in the Eastern Empire and transferring them to the Servians" (Finlay, iv p 441–2). In 1346 he was crowned at Skopia as "Tsar of the Serbs and Greeks," and gave his son the title of Kral, and he raised his archbishop to the rank of Patriarch. The prosperity of his reign is better shown by the growth of trade in the Servian towns than by the increase of Servian territory. Moreover Stephen did for Servia what Yaroslav did for Russia, he drew up a code of laws, which might be quoted to modify Gibbon's contemptuous references to the Servians as barbarians. This Zakonik has been repeatedly edited by Shafarik, Miklosich, Novakovich, and Zigel]

[32] The two avengers were both Palæologi, who might resent, with royal

with sticks and animated by despair. On the rumour of revenge and liberty, the captive multitude broke their fetters, fortified their prison, and exposed from the battlements the tyrant's head, presuming on the favour of the people and the clemency of the empress. Anne of Savoy might rejoice in the fall of an haughty and ambitious minister, but, while she delayed to resolve or to act, the populace, more especially the mariners, were excited by the widow of the Great Duke to a sedition, an assault, and a massacre. The prisoners (of whom the far greater part were guiltless or inglorious of the deed) escaped to a neighbouring church, they were slaughtered at the foot of the altar, and in his death the monster was not less bloody and venomous than in his life   Yet his talents alone upheld the cause of the young emperor; and his surviving associates, suspicious of each other, abandoned the conduct of the war, and rejected the fairest terms of accommodation. In the beginning of the dispute, the empress felt and complained that she was deceived by the enemies of Cantacuzene; the patriarch was employed to preach against the forgiveness of injuries; and her promise of immortal hatred was sealed by an oath under the penalty of excommunication [33] But Anne soon learned to hate without a teacher: she beheld the misfortunes of the empire with the indifference of a stranger: her jealousy was exasperated by the competition of a rival empress; and, on the first symptoms of a more yielding temper, she threatened the patriarch to convene a synod and degrade him from his office. Their incapacity and discord would have afforded the most decisive advantage; but the civil war was protracted by the weakness

indignation, the shame of their chains. The tragedy of Apocaucus may deserve a peculiar reference to Cantacuzene (l iii c 86 [*leg* 87–8]) and Nic Gregoras (l xiv c 10)

[33] Cantacuzene accuses the patriarch, and spares the empress, the mother of his sovereign (l iii 33, 34), against whom Nic Gregoras expresses a particular animosity (l xiv 10, 11, xv. 5). It is true that they do not speak exactly of the same time.

of both parties, and the moderation of Cantacuzene has not
escaped the reproach of timidity and indolence   He successively recovered the provinces and cities, [34] and the realm of
his pupil was measured by the walls of Constantinople; but
the metropolis alone counterbalanced the rest of the empire;
nor could he attempt that important conquest, till he had
secured in his favour the public voice and a private correspondence.   An Italian, of the name of Facciolati, [35] had

[34] ["The Greek Empire consisted of several detached provinces when
Cantacuzenos seated himself on the throne, and the inhabitants of these
different parts could only communicate freely by sea. The direct intercourse
by land, even between Constantinople and Thessalonica, by the Egnatian
Way, was interrupted, for the Servian Emperor possessed Amphipolis, and
all the country about the mouth of the Strymon from Philippi to the lake
Bolbe   The nucleus of the imperial power consisted of the city of Constantinople and the greater part of Thrace   On the Asiatic side of the Bosphorus, the Greek possessions were confined to the suburb of Skutari, a few
forts and a narrow strip of coast extending from Chalcedon to the Black
Sea   In Thrace the frontier extended from Sozopolis along the mountains
to the south-west, passing about a day's journey to the north of Adrianople,
and descending to the Aegean Sea at the pass and fortress of Christopolis
It included the districts of Morrah and the Thracian Chalkidike [of which
Gratianopolis was the chief town]   The second portion of the Empire in
importance consisted of the rich and populous city of Thessalonica, with the
western part of the Macedonian Chalkidike and its three peninsulas of Cas-
sandra, Longos and Agionoros ["Αγιον "Ορος]   By land it was entirely
enclosed in the Servian empire   The third detached portion of the empire
consisted of a part of Vallachian Thessaly and of Albanian Epirus, which
formed a small imperial province interposed between the Servian empire and
the Catalan duchy of Athens and Neopatras   The fourth consisted of the
Greek province in the Peloponnesus, which obtained the name of the Despotat
of Misithra, and embraced about one third of the peninsula   Cantacuzenos
conferred the government on his second son, Manuel, who preserved his
place by force of arms after his father was driven from the throne   The remaining fragments of the empire consisted of a few islands in the Aegean
Sea which had escaped the domination of the Venetians, the Genoese, and
the Knights of St John, and of the cities of Philadelphia and Phocaea, which
still recognised the suzerainty of Constantinople, though surrounded by the
territories of the emirs of Aidin and Saroukhan   Such were the relics of the
Byzantine empire " Finlay, iv p 447-8]

[35] The traitor and treason are revealed by Nic Gregoras (l xv c 8), but
the name is more discreetly suppressed by his great accomplice (Cantacuzen
l iii c 99)

succeeded to the office of Great Duke: the ships, the guards, and the golden gate were subject to his command, but his humble ambition was bribed to become the instrument of treachery; and the revolution was accomplished without danger or bloodshed. Destitute of the powers of resistance or the hope of relief, the inflexible Anne would have still defended the palace, and have smiled to behold the capital in flames, rather than in the possession of a rival. She yielded to the prayers of her friends and enemies; and the treaty was dictated by the conqueror, who professed a loyal and zealous attachment to the son of his benefactor The marriage of his daughter with John Palæologus was at length consummated. the hereditary right of the pupil was acknowledged; but the sole administration during ten years was vested in the guardian. Two emperors and three empresses were seated on the Byzantine throne; and a general amnesty quieted the apprehensions, and confirmed the property, of the most guilty subjects. The festival of the coronation and nuptials was celebrated with the appearance of concord and magnificence, and both were equally fallacious. During the late troubles, the treasures of the state, and even the palace, had been alienated or embezzled: the royal banquet was served in pewter or earthenware; and such was the proud poverty of the times that the absence of gold and jewels was supplied by the paltry artifices of glass and gilt leather.[36]

I hasten to conclude the personal history of John Cantacuzene.[37] He triumphed and reigned; but his reign and triumph were clouded by the discontent of his own and the adverse faction. His followers might style the general am-

[36] Nic Greg l xv II There were, however, some pearls, but very thinly sprinkled The rest of the stones had only παντοδαπὴν χροιὰν πρὸς τὸ διαυγές

[37] From his return to Constantinople, Cantacuzene continues his history, and that of the empire, one year beyond the abdication of his son Matthew, A D 1357 (l IV c 1–50, p 705–911) Nicephorus Gregoras ends with the synod of Constantinople, in the year 1351 (l xxii c 3, p 660, the rest, to the conclusion of the xxivth book, p 717, is all controversy), and his fourteen last books are still MSS in the king of France's library. See vol IX App 6]

nesty an act of pardon for his enemies and of oblivion for his friends·[38] in his cause their estates had been forfeited or plundered; and, as they wandered naked and hungry through the streets, they cursed the selfish generosity of a leader who, on the throne of the empire, might relinquish without merit his private inheritance. The adherents of the empress blushed to hold their lives and fortunes by the precarious favour of an usurper; and the thirst of revenge was concealed by a tender concern for the succession, and even the safety, of her son. They were justly alarmed by a petition of the friends of Cantacuzene, that they might be released from their oath of allegiance to the Palæologi and entrusted with the defence of some cautionary towns: a measure supported with argument and eloquence; and which was rejected (says the Imperial historian) "by *my* sublime and almost incredible virtue" His repose was disturbed by the sound of plots and seditions; and he trembled lest the lawful prince should be stolen away by some foreign or domestic enemy, who would inscribe his name and his wrongs in the banners of rebellion. As the son of Andronicus advanced in the years of manhood, he began to feel and to act for himself; and his rising ambition was rather stimulated than checked by the imitation of his father's vices If we may trust his own professions, Cantacuzene laboured with honest industry to correct these sordid and sensual appetites, and to raise the mind of the young prince to a level with his fortune In the Servian expedition [39] the two emperors showed themselves in cordial harmony to the troops and provinces; and

---

[38] The emperor (Cantacuzen l iv c 1) represents his own virtues, and Nic Gregoras (l xv c 11) the complaints of his friends, who suffered by its effects I have lent them the words of our poor cavaliers after the Restoration

[39] [One important consequence of the Servian conquests, and the wars connected therewith, may be noticed here, — the Albanian invasion of Greece The highlanders of northern Epirus, descendants of the ancient Illyrians, and speaking in idiom which represents the old Illyrian language, descended into Thessaly, laid it waste, and were a terror to the Catalan adventurers themselves. They settled in the Thessalian mountains and

the younger colleague was initiated by the elder in the mysteries of war and government. After the conclusion of the peace, Palæologus was left at Thessalonica, a royal residence and a frontier station, to secure by his absence the peace of Constantinople, and to withdraw his youth from the temptations of a luxurious capital. But the distance weakened the powers of control, and the son of Andronicus was surrounded with artful or unthinking companions, who taught him to hate his guardian, to deplore his exile, and to vindicate his rights. A private treaty with the cral or despot of Servia was soon followed by an open revolt; and Cantacuzene, on the throne of the elder Andronicus, defended the cause of age and prerogative, which in his youth he had so vigorously attacked. At his request, the empress-mother undertook the voyage of Thessalonica, and the office of mediation · she returned without success; and unless Anne of Savoy was instructed by adversity, we may doubt the sincerity, or at least the fervour, of her zeal. While the regent grasped the sceptre with a firm and vigorous hand, she had been instructed to declare that the ten years of his legal administration would soon elapse; and that, after a full trial of the vanity of the world, the emperor Cantacuzene sighed for the repose of a cloister, and was ambitious only of an heavenly crown. Had these sentiments been genuine, his voluntary abdication would have restored the peace of the empire, and his conscience would have been relieved by an act of justice. Palæologus alone was responsible for his future government, and, whatever might be his vices, they were surely less formidable than the calamities of a civil war, in which the Barbarians and infidels were again invited to assist the Greeks in their mutual destruction. By the arms of the Turks, who now struck a

spread over Greece, where they formed a new element in the population. The Albanian settlers speak their own language, amid the surrounding Greeks, to the present day, therein differing remarkably from the Slavonic settlers, who adopted the Greek tongue For the Albanians, see Hahn, Albanesische Studien]

deep and everlasting root in Europe, Cantacuzene prevailed
in the third conquest in which he had been involved; and the
young emperor, driven from the sea and land, was compelled
to take shelter among the Latins of the isle of Tenedos. His
insolence and obstinacy provoked the victor to a step which
must render the quarrel irreconcileable, and the association
of his son Matthew, whom he invested with the purple, established the succession in the family of the Cantacuzeni
But Constantinople was still attached to the blood of her ancient princes; and this last injury accelerated the restoration
of the rightful heir A noble Genoese espoused the cause of
Palæologus, obtained a promise of his sister, and achieved
the revolution with two galleys and two thousand five hundred
auxiliaries. Under the pretence of distress they were admitted
into the lesser port; a gate was opened, and the Latin shout
of "Long life and victory to the emperor John Palæologus!"
was answered by a general rising in his favour. A numerous
and loyal party yet adhered to the standard of Cantacuzene;
but he asserts in his history (does he hope for belief?) that his
tender conscience rejected the assurance of conquest: that,
in free obedience to the voice of religion and philosophy, he
descended from the throne and embraced with pleasure the
monastic habit and profession.[40] So soon as he ceased to be
a prince, his successor was not unwilling that he should be a
saint; the remainder of his life was devoted to piety and learning; in the cells of Constantinople and Mount Athos, the
monk Joasaph was respected as the temporal and spiritual
father of the emperor; and, if he issued from his retreat, it
was as the minister of peace, to subdue the obstinacy, and
solicit the pardon, of his rebellious son [41]

[40] The awkward apology of Cantacuzene (l iv c 39-42), who relates, with
visible confusion, his own downfall, may be supplied by the less accurate but
more honest narratives of Matthew Villani (l iv c 46, in the Script Rerum
Ital tom xiv p 268) and Ducas (c 10, 11)

[41] Cantacuzene, in the year 1375, was honoured with a letter from the pope
(Fleury, Hist Ecclés tom xx p 250) His death is placed, by a respectable

Yet in the cloister, the mind of Cantacuzene was still exercised by theological war.   He sharpened a controversial pen
against the Jews and Mahometans,[42] and in every state he
defended with equal zeal the divine light of Mount Thabor,
a memorable question which consummates the religious follies
of the Greeks   The fakirs of India[43] and the monks of the
Oriental church were alike persuaded that in total abstraction
of the faculties of the mind and body the purer spirit may ascend to the enjoyment and vision of the Deity   The opinion
and practice of the monasteries of Mount Athos[44] will be best
represented in the words of an abbot who flourished in the
eleventh century   "When thou art alone in thy cell," says the
ascetic teacher, "shut thy door, and seat thyself in a corner;
raise thy mind above all things vain and transitory, recline
thy beard and chin on thy breast; turn thy eyes and thy
thoughts towards the middle of thy belly, the region of the
navel, and search the place of the heart, the seat of the soul.
At first, all will be dark and comfortless, but, if you persevere
day and night, you will feel an ineffable joy; and no sooner
has the soul discovered the place of the heart than it is involved
in a mystic and ethereal light."   This light, the production of
a distempered fancy, the creature of an empty stomach and
an empty brain, was adored by the Quietists as the pure and

authority, on the 20th of November, 1411 (Ducange, Fam Byzant p 260)
But, if he were of the age of his companion Andronicus the Younger, he must
have lived 116 years a rare instance of longevity, which in so illustrious a
person would have attracted universal notice   [Date of death· A D 1383]

[42] His four discourses, or books, were printed at Basil, 1543 (Fabric
Biblot Græc tom vi p 473) [reprinted in Migne, Patr Gr vol 154, p 372
sqq]   He composed them to satisfy a proselyte who was assaulted with
letters from his friends of Ispahan   Cantacuzene had read the Koran, but
I understand from Maracci that he adopts the vulgar prejudices and fables
against Mahomet and his religion

[43] See the Voyages de Bernier, tom i p 127

[44] Mosheim, Institut Hist Eccles p 522, 523   Fleury, Hist Ecclés tom
xx p 22, 24, 107–114, &c   The former unfolds the causes with the judgment of a philosopher, the latter transcribes and translates with the prejudices
of a Catholic priest.

perfect essence of God himself; and, as long as the folly was confined to Mount Athos, the simple solitaries were not inquisitive how the divine essence could be a *material* substance, or how an *immaterial* substance could be perceived by the eyes of the body. But in the reign of the younger Andronicus these monasteries were visited by Barlaam,[45] a Calabrian monk, who was equally skilled in philosophy and theology, who possessed the languages of the Greeks and Latins, and whose versatile genius could maintain their opposite creeds, according to the interest of the moment. The indiscretion of an ascetic revealed to the curious traveller the secrets of mental prayer; and Barlaam embraced the opportunity of ridiculing the Quietists, who placed the soul in the navel, of accusing the monks of Mount Athos of heresy and blasphemy. His attack compelled the more learned to renounce or dissemble the simple devotion of their brethren; and Gregory Palamas introduced a scholastic distinction between the essence and operation of God [46] His inaccessible essence dwells in the midst of an uncreated and eternal light, and this beatific vision of the saints had been manifested to the disciples on Mount Thabor, in the transfiguration of Christ. Yet this distinction could not escape the reproach of polytheism, the eternity of the light of Thabor was fiercely denied; and Barlaam still charged the Palamites with holding two eternal substances, a visible and an invisible God. From the rage

[45] Basnage (in Canisii Antiq. Lectiones, tom iv p 363-368) has investigated the character and story of Barlaam The duplicity of his opinions had inspired some doubts of the identity of his person See likewise Fabricius (Bibliot. Græc tom x p 427-432) [G Mandolon, Fra Barlaamo Calabrese, maestro del Petrarca, 1888]

[46] [The chief upholders of Barlaam were Gregory Akindynos (for whose works see Migne, P G vol 151) and Nicephorus Gregoras, whose Φλωρέντιος ἢ περὶ σοφίας (in Jahns Archiv, 10, p 485 *sqq*, 1844) is founded on a dispute with Barlaam. The chief opponent was Gregory Palamas, who had lived at Athos, and came forward as defender of the Hesychasts, to whose doctrine he gave a dogmatic basis (cp Ehrhard, ap Krumbacher, p 103) Some of his works are printed in Migne, P G vols 150, 151; a large number are happily buried in MSS.]

of the monks of Mount Athos, who threatened his life, the Calabrian retired to Constantinople, where his smooth and specious manners introduced him to the favour of the great domestic and the emperor. The court and the city were involved in this theological dispute, which flamed amidst the civil war, but the doctrine of Barlaam was disgraced by his flight and apostacy; the Palamites triumphed; and their adversary, the patriarch John of Apri, was deposed by the consent of the adverse factions of the state. In the character of emperor and theologian, Cantacuzene presided in the synod of the Greek church, which established, as an article of faith, the uncreated light of Mount Thabor, and, after so many insults, the reason of mankind was slightly wounded by the addition of a single absurdity. Many rolls of paper or parchment have been blotted; and the impenitent sectaries, who refused to subscribe the orthodox creed, were deprived of the honours of Christian burial, but in the next age the question was forgotten; nor can I learn that the axe or the faggot were employed for the extirpation of the Barlaamite heresy.[47]

For the conclusion of this chapter I have reserved the Genoese war, which shook the throne of Cantacuzene and betrayed the debility of the Greek empire. The Genoese, who, after the recovery of Constantinople, were seated in the suburb of Pera or Galata, received that honourable fief from the bounty of the emperor. They were indulged in the use of their laws and magistrates; but they submitted to the duties of vassals and subjects   the forcible word of *liegemen* [48] was borrowed

[47] See Cantacuzene (l. ii c. 39, 40, l iv c 3, 23–25) and Nic. Gregoras (l xi c 10, l xv 3, 7, &c), whose last books, from the 19th to the 24th, are almost confined to a subject so interesting to the authors   Boivin (in Vit Nic. Gregoræ), from the unpublished books, and Fabricius (Bibliot Græc tom x p 462–473), or rather Montfaucon, from the MSS of the Coislin Library, have added some facts and documents   [Sauli, Colonia dei Genovesi in Galata]

[48] Pachymer (l v. c 10) very properly explains λίζιους (*ligios*) by ιδίους The use of these words in the Greek and Latin of the feudal times may be amply understood from the Glossaries of Ducange (Græc. p 811, 812, Latin. tom   , p   ·   ,)

from the Latin jurisprudence; and their *podestà*, or chief, before he entered on his office, saluted the emperor with loyal acclamations and vows of fidelity Genoa sealed a firm alliance with the Greeks; and, in case of a defensive war, a supply of fifty empty galleys, and a succour of fifty galleys completely armed and manned, was promised by the republic to the empire. In the revival of a naval force it was the aim of Michael Palæologus to deliver himself from a foreign aid; and his vigorous government contained the Genoese of Galata within those limits which the insolence of wealth and freedom provoked them to exceed A sailor threatened that they should soon be masters of Constantinople, and slew the Greek who resented this national affront; and an armed vessel, after refusing to salute the palace, was guilty of some acts of piracy in the Black Sea. Their countrymen threatened to support their cause, but the long and open village of Galata was instantly surrounded by the Imperial troops, till, in the moment of the assault, the prostrate Genoese implored the clemency of their sovereign. The defenceless situation which secured their obedience exposed them to the attack of their Venetian rivals, who, in the reign of the elder Andronicus, presumed to violate the majesty of the throne. On the approach of their fleets, the Genoese, with their families and effects, retired into the city; their empty habitations were reduced to ashes; and the feeble prince, who had viewed the destruction of his suburb, expressed his resentment, not by arms, but by ambassadors. This misfortune, however, was advantageous to the Genoese, who obtained, and imperceptibly abused, the dangerous licence of surrounding Galata with a strong wall, of introducing into the ditch the waters of the sea; of erecting lofty turrets, and of mounting a train of military engines on the rampart The narrow bounds in which they had been circumscribed were insufficient for the growing colony, each day they acquired some addition of landed property; and the adjacent hills were covered with their villas and castles, which they joined and protected by

new fortifications [49]   The navigation and trade of the Euxine
was the patrimony of the Greek emperors, who commanded
the narrow entrance, the gates, as it were, of that inland sea.
In the reign of Michael Palæologus, their prerogative was
acknowledged by the sultan of Egypt, who solicited and obtained the liberty of sending an annual ship for the purchase
of slaves in Circassia and the Lesser Tartary : a liberty pregnant with mischief to the Christian cause, since these youths
were transformed by education and discipline into the formidable Mamalukes [50]   From the colony of Pera the Genoese
engaged with superior advantage in the lucrative trade of the
Black Sea ; and their industry supplied the Greeks with fish
and corn, two articles of food almost equally important to a
superstitious people.   The spontaneous bounty of nature
appears to have bestowed the harvests of the Ukraine, the
produce of a rude and savage husbandry; and the endless
exportation of salt fish and caviar is annually renewed by the
enormous sturgeons that are caught at the mouth of the Don,
or Tanais, in their last station of the rich mud and shallow
water of the Mæotis.[51]   The waters of the Oxus, the Caspian,
the Volga, and the Don opened a rare and laborious passage
for the gems and spices of India ; and, after three months'

[49] The establishment and progress of the Genoese at Pera, or Galata, is
described by Ducange (C P. Christiana, l. 1 p 68, 69), from the Byzantine
historians, Pachymer (l. 11 c 35, l v 10, 30, l ix 15, l xii 6, 9), Nicephorus
Gregoras (l v c 4, l vi c 11, l ix c 5, l xi c 1, l xv. c. 1, 6), and Cantacuzene (l 1. c 12, l. ii c 29, &c)   [The golden Bulls of Michael VIII (A D
1261) and Andronicus the Elder (A D 1304) granting privileges to the Genoese
will found in Zacharia, Jus Graeco-Romanum, iii p 574 *sqq*, p 623 *sqq*]

[50] Both Pachymer (l 111 c 3-5) and Nic Gregoras (l iv c 7) understand
and deplore the effects of this dangerous indulgence   Bibars, sultan of
Egypt, himself a Tartar, but a devout Musulman, obtained from the children
of Zingis the permission to build a stately mosque in the capital of Crimea
(De Guignes, Hist des Huns, tom 111 p 343)

[51] Chardin (Voyages en Perse, tom 1 p 48) was assured at Caffa that
these fishes were sometimes twenty-four or twenty-six feet long, weighed eight
or nine hundred pounds, and yielded three or four quintals of caviar   The
corn of the Bosphorus had supplied the Athenians in [and long before] the
time of Demosthenes

march, the caravans of Carizme met the Italian vessels in the harbours of Crimea.[52] These various branches of trade were monopolised by the diligence and the power of the Genoese. Their rivals of Venice and Pisa were forcibly expelled; the natives were awed by the castles and cities, which arose on the foundations of their humble factories; and their principal establishment of Caffa[53] was besieged without effect by the Tartar powers. Destitute of a navy, the Greeks were oppressed by these haughty merchants, who fed or famished Constantinople, according to their interest. They proceeded to usurp the customs, the fishery, and even the toll of the Bosphorus, and, while they derived from these objects a revenue of two hundred thousand pieces of gold, a remnant of thirty thousand was reluctantly allowed to the emperor[54] The colony of Pera or Galata acted, in peace and war, as an independent state, and, as it will happen in distant settlements, the Genoese podestà too often forgot that he was the servant of his own masters.

These usurpations were encouraged by the weakness of the elder Andronicus, and by the civil wars that afflicted his age and the minority of his grandson. The talents of Cantacuzene were employed to the ruin, rather than the restoration, of the empire; and after his domestic victory he was condemned to an ignominious trial, whether the Greeks or the Genoese should reign in Constantinople. The merchants of Pera were offended by his refusal of some contiguous lands, some commanding heights, which they proposed to cover with new fortifications, and in the absence of the emperor, who was detained at Demotica by sickness, they ventured to brave

[52] De Guignes, Hist des Huns, tom III. p 343, 344. Viaggi di Ramusio, tom I fol 400. But this land or water carriage could only be practicable when Tartary was united under a wise and powerful monarch

[53] Nic Gregoras (l XIII c 12) is judicious and well-informed on the trade and colonies of the Black Sea Chardin describes the present ruins of Caffa, where, in forty days, he saw above 400 sail employed in the corn and fish trade (Voyages en Perse, tom i p 46-48).

[54] See Nic. Gregoras, l. XVII. c. 1.

the debility of a female reign. A Byzantine vessel, which had presumed to fish at the mouth of the harbour, was sunk by these audacious strangers; the fishermen were murdered. Instead of suing for pardon, the Genoese demanded satisfaction; required, in an haughty strain, that the Greeks should renounce the exercise of navigation; and encountered, with regular arms, the first sallies of the popular indignation. They instantly occupied the debateable land, and by the labour of a whole people, of either sex and of every age, the wall was raised, and the ditch was sunk, with incredible speed. At the same time they attacked and burnt two Byzantine galleys; while the three others, the remainder of the Imperial navy, escaped from their hand; the habitations without the gates, or along the shore, were pillaged and destroyed; and the care of the regent, of the empress Irene, was confined to the preservation of the city. The return of Cantacuzene dispelled the public consternation the emperor inclined to peaceful counsels; but he yielded to the obstinacy of his enemies, who rejected all reasonable terms, and to the ardour of his subjects, who threatened, in the style of scripture, to break them in pieces like a potter's vessel. Yet they reluctantly paid the taxes that he imposed for the construction of ships and the expenses of the war; and, as the two nations were masters, the one of the land, the other of the sea, Constantinople and Pera were pressed by the evils of a mutual siege. The merchants of the colony, who had belived that a few days would terminate the war, already murmured at their losses, the succours from their mother-country were delayed by the factions of Genoa; and the most cautious embraced the opportunity of a Rhodian vessel to remove their families and effects from the scene of hostility. In the spring, the Byzantine fleet, seven galleys and a train of smaller vessels, issued from the mouth of the harbour and steered in a single line along the shore of Pera; unskilfully presenting their sides to the beaks of the adverse squadron. The crews were composed of peasants and mechanics nor was their ignorance compensated by the native courage of Barbarians. The wind was strong, the waves were rough; and no sooner did the Greeks perceive a distant and inactive enemy, than they leaped headlong into the sea, from a doubtful to an inevitable peril. The troops that marched to the attack of the lines of Pera were struck at the same moment with a similar panic; and the Genoese were astonished, and almost ashamed, at their double victory. Their triumphant vessels, crowned with flowers, and dragging after them the captive galleys, repeatedly passed and repassed before the palace. The only virtue of the emperor was patience, and the hope of revenge his sole consolation. Yet the distress of both parties interposed a temporary agreement; and the shame of the empire was disguised by a thin veil of dignity and power. Summoning the chiefs of the colony, Cantacuzene affected to despise the trivial object of the debate; and, after a mild reproof, most liberally granted the lands, which had been previously resigned to the seeming custody of his officers.[55]

But the emperor was soon solicited to violate the treaty, and to join his arms with the Venetians, the perpetual enemies of Genoa and her colonies. While he compared the reasons of peace and war, his moderation was provoked by a wanton insult of the inhabitants of Pera, who discharged from their rampart a large stone that fell in the midst of Constantinople. On his just complaint, they coldly blamed the imprudence of their engineer; but the next day the insult was repeated, and they exulted in a second proof that the royal city was not beyond the reach of their artillery. Cantacuzene instantly signed his treaty with the Venetians, but the weight of the Roman empire was scarcely felt in the balance of these opulent and powerful republics.[56] From the straits of Gibraltar to the

[55] The events of this war are related by Cantacuzene (l iv c 11) with obscurity and confusion, and by Nic. Gregoras (l. xvii c 1-7) in a clear and honest narrative The priest was less responsible than the prince for the defeat of the fleet.

[56] The second war is darkly told by Cantacuzene (l iv. c. 18, p 24, 25,

mouth of the Tanais, their fleets encountered each other with various success, and a memorable battle was fought in the narrow sea, under the walls of Constantinople. It would not be an easy task to reconcile the accounts of the Greeks, the Venetians, and the Genoese;[57] and, while I depend on the narrative of an impartial historian,[58] I shall borrow from each nation the facts that redound to their own disgrace and the honour of their foes. The Venetians, with their allies, the Catalans, had the advantage of number; and their fleet, with the poor addition of eight Byzantine galleys, amounted to seventy-five sail; the Genoese did not exceed sixty-four; but in those times their ships of war were distinguished by the superiority of their size and strength. The names and families of their naval commanders, Pisani and Doria, are illustrious in the annals of their country; but the personal merit of the former was eclipsed by the fame and abilities of his rival. They engaged in tempestuous weather, and the tumultuary conflict was continued from the dawn to the extinction of light. The enemies of the Genoese applaud their prowess; the friends of the Venetians are dissatisfied with their behaviour, but all parties agree in praising the skill and boldness of the Catalans, who, with many wounds, sustained the brunt of the action On the separation of the fleets, the event might appear doubtful, but the thirteen Genoese galleys, that had been sunk or taken, were compensated by a double loss of the allies: of fourteen Venetians, ten Catalans, and two Greeks; and even the grief of the conquerors ex-

28–32), who wishes to disguise what he dares not deny I regret this part of Nic Gregoras, which is still in MS at Paris [It has since been edited, see vol. ix Appendix 6]

[57] Muratori (Annali d'Italia, tom vii p 144) refers to the most ancient Chronicles of Venice (Caresinus [Raffaino Carasini, ob 1390], the continuator of Andrew Dandolus, tom vii p 421, 422) and Genoa (George Stella [ob 1420], Annales Genuenses, tom xvii p 1091, 1092), both which I have diligently consulted in his great Collection of the Historians of Italy.

[58] See the Chronicle of Matteo Villani of Florence, l ii c 59, 60, p. 145–147, c. 74, 75, p 156, 157, in Muratori's Collection, tom xiv

pressed the assurance and habit of more decisive victories. Pisani confessed his defeat by retiring into a fortified harbour, from whence, under the pretext of the orders of the senate, he steered with a broken and flying squadron for the isle of Candia, and abandoned to his rivals the sovereignty of the sea. In a public epistle,[59] addressed to the doge and senate, Petrarch employs his eloquence to reconcile the maritime powers, the two luminaries of Italy. The orator celebrates the valour and victory of the Genoese, the first of men in the exercise of naval war; he drops a tear on the misfortunes of their Venetian brethren; but he exhorts them to pursue with fire and sword the base and perfidious Greeks, to purge the metropolis of the East from the heresy with which it was infected. Deserted by their friends, the Greeks were incapable of resistance; and, three months after the battle, the emperor Cantacuzene solicited and subscribed a treaty, which for ever banished the Venetians and Catalans, and granted to the Genoese a monopoly of trade and almost a right of dominion.[60] The Roman empire (I smile in transcribing the name) might soon have sunk into a province of Genoa, if the ambition of the republic had not been checked by the ruin of her freedom and naval power. A long contest of one hundred and thirty years was determined by the triumph of Venice, and the factions of the Genoese compelled them to seek for domestic peace under the protection of a foreign lord, the duke of Milan, or the French king. Yet the spirit of commerce survived that of conquest, and the colony of Pera still awed the capital, and navigated the Euxine, till it was involved by the Turks in the final servitude of Constantinople itself.

[59] The Abbé de Sade (Mémoires sur la Vie de Petrarque, tom iii p 257-263) translates this letter, which he had copied from a MS in the king of France's library. Though a servant of the Duke of Milan, Petrarch pours forth his astonishment and grief at the defeat and despair of the Genoese in the following year (p 323-332)

[60] [Text (the Latin copy) in Sauli, Colonia dei Genovesi in Galata, ii 216, and in Zacharia, Jus Graeco-Romanum, iii 706]

CHAPTER LXIV

Conquests of Zingis Khan and the Moguls from China to
Poland — Escape of Constantinople and the Greeks —
Origin of the Ottoman Turks in Bithynia — Reigns
and Victories of Othman, Orchan, Amurath the First,
and Bajazet the First — Foundation and Progress of
the Turkish Monarchy in Asia and Europe — Danger
of Constantinople and the Greek Empire

FROM the petty quarrels of a city and her suburbs, from the
cowardice and discord of the falling Greeks, I shall now ascend to the victorious Turks, whose domestic slavery was ennobled by martial discipline, religious enthusiasm, and the
energy of the national character.   The rise and progress of
the Ottomans, the present sovereigns of Constantinople, are
connected with the most important scenes of modern history;
but they are founded on a previous knowledge of the great
eruption of the Moguls and Tartars, whose rapid conquests
may be compared with the primitive convulsions of nature,
which have agitated and altered the surface of the globe.
I have long since asserted my claim to introduce the nations,
the immediate or remote authors of the fall of the Roman
empire; nor can I refuse myself to those events which, from
their uncommon magnitude, will interest a philosophic mind
in the history of blood.[1]

From the spacious highlands between China, Siberia, and
the Caspian Sea, the tide of emigration and war has repeatedly
been poured   These ancient seats of the Huns and Turks

---

[1] The reader is invited to review the chapters of the fourth, fifth, sixth, and
seventh volumes, the manners of pastoral nations, the conquests of Atila and
the Huns, which were composed at a time when I entertained the wish,
rather than the hope, of concluding my history.

were occupied in the twelfth century by many pastoral tribes of the same descent and similar manners, which were united and led to conquest by the formidable Zingis In his ascent to greatness, that Barbarian (whose private appellation was Temugin) had trampled on the necks of his equals. His birth was noble; but it was in the pride of victory that the prince or people deduced his seventh ancestor from the immaculate conception of a virgin.[2] His father had reigned over thirteen hordes, which composed about thirty or forty thousand families, above two-thirds refused to pay tithes or obedience to his infant son; and, at the age of thirteen, Temugin fought a battle against his rebellious subjects. The future conqueror of Asia was reduced to fly and to obey; but he rose superior to his fortune, and, in his fortieth year, he had established his fame and dominion over the circumjacent tribes In a state of society in which policy is rude and valour is universal, the ascendant of one man must be founded on his power and resolution to punish his enemies and recompense his friends. His first military league was ratified by the simple rites of sacrificing an horse and tasting of a running stream Temugin pledged himself to divide with his followers the sweets and the bitters of life; and, when he had shared among them his horses and apparel, he was rich in their gratitude and his own hopes. After his first victory, he placed seventy caldrons on the fire, and seventy of the most guilty rebels were cast headlong into the boiling water. The sphere of his attraction was continually enlarged by the ruin of the proud and the submission of the prudent;

[2] [The miraculous origin of the race of Chingiz Khan appears in Turkish and Chinese as well as in Mongol legend The family to which he belonged was called the Borjigen, it seems to have been of Turkish origin on the female side, but Mongol on the male (Cahun, Intr à l'histoire de l'Asie, p 203) It possessed lands and high prestige among the Mongol tribes to the north of China between the rivers Selinga and Orchon It is important to realise that the Mongols were not very numerous. In the Mongol empire, as it is called, which Chingiz Khan created, the Mongolian element was small What he did was to create a great Turkish empire under Mongol domination]

VOL. X — 11

and the boldest chieftains might tremble, when they beheld, enchased in silver, the skull of the khan of the Keraites,[3] who under the name of Prester John had corresponded with the Roman pontiff and the princes of Europe. The ambition of Tegumin condescended to employ the arts of superstition; and it was from a naked prophet, who could ascend to heaven on a white horse, that he accepted the title of Zingis,[4] the *Most Great;* and a divine right to the conquest and dominion of the earth.   In a general *couroultai*, or diet, he was seated on a felt, which was long afterwards revered as a relic, and solemnly proclaimed Great Khan or emperor of the Moguls[5] and Tartars.[6]   Of these kindred though rival

[3] The Khans of the Keraites [Karaits] were most probably incapable of reading the pompous epistles composed in their name by the Nestorian missionaries, who endowed them with the fabulous wonders of an Indian kingdom   Perhaps these Tartars (the Presbyter or Priest John) had submitted to the rites of baptism and ordination (Assemann Bibliot Orient tom iii p ii p 487-503)   [Sir H. Howorth has shown very clearly (Hist of the Mongols, i p 696 *sqq*) that the Karaits were Turks, not Mongols.   Their territory was near the Upper Orchon, between the rivers Selinga and Kernlen   They were Christians   Their chief Tughril received the title of Wang ("king") from the (Manchu) Emperor of Northern China for his services in 1193 against the Naiman Turks of the regions of the Altai and Upper Irtish.   Chingiz also took part in this war, and his services were recognised by the title of Dai Ming, "high Brightness"   For an account of Prester John — the name by which the Karait khans were known in the west — and the legends attached to him, see Howorth, i cap x p 534 *sqq*]

[4] Since the history and tragedy of Voltaire, *Gengis*, at least in French, seems to be the more fashionable spelling, but Abulghazi Khan must have known the true name of his ancestor   His etymology appears just, *Zin*, in the Mogul tongue, signifies *great*, and *gis* is the superlative termination (Hist Généalogique des Tartars, part iii p 194, 195).   From the same idea of magnitude the appellation of *Zingis* is bestowed on the ocean   [Chingiz (= very great, or autocrat) represents the true spelling   He also bore the title Sutu Bodgo, "son of Heaven "]

[5] The name of Moguls has prevailed among the Orientals, and still adheres to the titular sovereign, the Great Mogul of Hindostan   [Mongol, Mogul, and (Arabic) Mughal are all attempts to represent a name which among the true Mongols is pronounced something between Moghol (or Mool) and Mongol, but never with the *u* sound   See Tarīkh-i-Rashīdi, tr Elias and Ross, p 73 note]

[6] The Tartars (more properly Tatars) were descended from Tatar Khan,

names, the former had given birth to the Imperial race; and the latter has been extended, by accident or error, over the spacious wilderness of the North

The code of laws which Zingis dictated to his subjects was adapted to the preservation of domestic peace and the exercise of foreign hostility. The punishment of death was inflicted on the crimes of adultery, murder, perjury, and the capital thefts of an horse or ox, and the fiercest of men were mild and just in their intercourse with each other. The future election of the great khan was vested in the princes of his family and the heads of the tribes; and the regulations of the chase were essential to the pleasures and plenty of a Tartar camp The victorious nation was held sacred from all servile labours, which were abandoned to slaves and strangers; and every labour was servile except the profession of arms The service and discipline of the troops, who were armed with bows, scymetars, and iron maces, and divided by hundreds, thousands, and ten thousands, were the institutions of a veteran commander. Each officer and soldier was made responsible, under pain of death, for the safety and honour of his companions; and the spirit of conquest breathed in the law that peace should never be granted unless to a vanquished and suppliant enemy.[7] But it is the religion of Zingis that best deserves our wonder and applause. The Catholic inquisitors of Europe, who defended nonsense by cruelty, might have been confounded by the example of a

the brother of Mogul Khan (see Abulghazi, part i and ii), and once formed a horde of 70,000 families on the borders of Kitay (p 103-112) In the great invasion of Europe (A D. 1238), they seem to have led the vanguard, and the similitude of the name of *Tartarei* recommended that of Tartars to the Latins (Matth Paris, p 398, &c) [The Tatars seem to have been a mixture of Manchus and Turks On one of the old Turkish inscriptions of A D 733 (see above vol vii p 399) Tatars are mentioned]

[7] [The code drawn up by Chingiz was called Yāsāk or Law (On it, see Sir H. Howorth's paper in the *Indian Antiquary*, July, 1882) The cruelties of Chingiz were always the simple execution of the laws he was never capricious]

Barbarian, who anticipated the lessons of philosophy[8] and established by his laws a system of pure theism and perfect toleration.   His first and only article of faith was the existence of one God, the author of all good, who fills, by his presence, the heavens and earth, which he has created by his power. The Tartars and Moguls were addicted to the idols of their peculiar tribes; and many of them had been converted by the foreign missionaries to the religions of Moses, of Mahomet, and of Christ.   These various systems in freedom and concord were taught and practised within the precincts of the same camp; and the Bonze, the Imam, the Rabbi, the Nestorian, and the Latin priest enjoyed the same honourable exemption from service and tribute.   In the mosch of Bochara, the insolent victor might trample the Koran under his horse's feet, but the calm legislator respected the prophets and pontiffs of the most hostile sects.   The reason of Zingis was not informed by books; the khan could neither read nor write; and, except the tribe of the Igours, the greatest part of the Moguls and Tartars were as illiterate as their sovereign.[9]   The memory of their exploits was preserved by tradition; sixty-eight years after the death of Zingis, these traditions were collected and transcribed;[10] the brevity of their domestic annals

[8] A singular conformity may be found between the religious laws of Zingis Khan and of Mr Locke (Constitutions of Carolina, in his works, vol iv p 535, 4to edition, 1777).

[9] [When Chingiz conquered the Naiman Turks of the Altai regions, c 1203-4, the vizir of the Naiman king passed into his service and became his chancellor. This minister was an Uigur and had Uigur successors   Through these Uigurs, the Uigur alphabet (derived from the Syriac) was adopted by the Mongols, and the old Turkish script (of the Orchon inscriptions, see above vol vii p 399) became obsolete]   On the Uigurs see Vámbéry's Uigurische Sprachmonumente und das Kudatku Bilik, 1870.

[10] In the year 1294, by the command of [Mahmūd Ghāzān] Cazan, khan of Persia, the fourth [fifth] in descent from Zingis   From these traditions, his vizir, Fadlallah [Rashīd ad-Dīn], composed a Mogul history in the Persian language, which has been used by Petit de la Croix (Hist de Genghizcan, p 537-539) [see D'Ohsson, Hist des Mongols, 1 627 sqq   For Rashīd's Jāmi al-Tawārikh see Appendix 1]   The Histoire Généalogique des Tatars (à Leyde, 1726, in 12mo, 2 tomes) was translated by the Swedish prisoners

may be supplied by the Chinese,[11] Persians,[12] Armenians,[13]

in Siberia, from the Mogul MS of Abulgasi Bahadur Khan, a descendant of
Zingis, who reigned over the Usbeks of Charasm, or Carizme (A D 1644–
1663). He is of most value and credit for the names, pedigrees, and manners
of his nation Of his nine parts, the 1st descends from Adam to Mogul
Khan; the 2nd, from Mogul to Zingis, the 3rd is the life of Zingis, the
ivth, vth, vith, and viith, the general history of his four sons and their posterity,
the viiith and ixth, the particular history of the descendants of Sheibani
Khan, who reigned in Maurenahar and Charasm [The work of Abulghazi
has been edited and translated by Des Maisons (St Petersburg, 1870) For
Jūzjānī and Juvainī see Appendix 1]

[11] Histoire de Gentchiscan, et de toute la Dinastie des Mongous ses Suc-
cesseurs, Conquérans de la Chine, tirée de l'Histoire de la Chine, par le
R P Gaubil, de la Société de Jésus, Missionaire à Pekin, à Paris, 1739,
in 4to This translation is stamped with the Chinese character of domestic
accuracy and foreign ignorance [It has been superseded by the Russian
work of the Père Hyacinth, on the first four Khans of the house of Chingiz,
1829 A contemporary Chinese work by Men-Hun has been translated by
Vasiliev in the ivth vol of the Transactions of the Russian Arch Soc,
Oriental Sect]

[12] See the Histoire du Grand Genghizcan, premier Empereur des Mogols
et Tartares, par M Petit de la Croix, à Paris, 1710, in 12mo [it has been
translated into English] a work of ten years' labour, chiefly drawn from
the Persian writers, among whom Nisavi, the secretary of Sultan Gelaleddin,
has the merit and prejudices of a contemporary. A slight air of romance is
the fault of the originals, or the compiler See likewise the articles of
Genghizcan, Mohammed, Gelaleddin, &c, in the Bibliothèque Orientale of
d'Herbelot [Several histories of the Mongols have appeared in this century. D'Ohsson, Histoire des Mongols, 1852, Wolff, Geschichte der Mongolen oder Tataren, 1872, Quatremère, Histoire des Mongoles de la Perse,
1836, Howorth, History of the Mongols, Part 1, 1876, Part 2 (in 2 vols),
1880 (on the "Tartars" of Russia and Central Asia), Part 3, 1888 (on
Mongols of Persia), Cahun, Introduction à l'Histoire de l'Asie, 1896 For
later Mongols of Central Asia, see the Tarikh-i-Rashidi of Mirzā Muhammad
Haidar Dughlāt, transl by E D Ross, ed by N Elias, 1895, for which,
and for Schmidt, Geschichte der Ost-Mongolen, cp Appendix 1 For Chingiz
Khan Erdmann, Temudschin der Unerschutterliche, 1862, R K Douglas,
Life of Jinghiz Khān, 1877, Howorth, op cit Pt 1 Gibbon does not
mention Pallas, Sammlungen historischer Nachrichten uber die Mon-
golischen Volkerschaften, which appeared at St Petersburg in 1776, 2 vols]

[13] Haithonus, or Aithonus, an Armenian prince, and afterwards a monk
of Premontré (Fabric Bibliot. Lat. medii Ævi, tom 1 p 34), dictated, in
the French language, his book De Tartaris, his old fellow-soldiers It was
immediately translated into Latin, and is inserted in the Novus Orbis of
Simon Grynæus (Basil, 1555, in folio) [See above, vol iv p 398 For
Haithon I see Appendix 1]

Syrians,[14] Arabians,[15] Greeks,[16] Russians,[17] Poles,[18] Hungarians,[19] and Latins;[20] and each nation will deserve credit

[14] Zingis Khan, and his first successors, occupy the conclusion of the ixth Dynasty of Abulpharagius (vers Pocock, Oxon 1663, in 4to), and his xth Dynasty is that of the Moguls of Persia Assemannus (Bibliot. Orient tom ii) has extracted some facts from his Syriac writings, and the lives of the Jacobite maphrians or primates of the East

[15] Among the Arabians, in language and religion, we may distinguish Abulfeda, sultan of Hamah in Syria, who fought in person, under the Mamaluke standard, against the Moguls

[16] Nicephorus Gregoras (l ii c 5, 6) has felt the necessity of connecting the Scythian and Byzantine histories He describes, with truth and elegance, the settlement and manners of the Moguls of Persia, but he is ignorant of their origin, and corrupts the names of Zingis and his sons

[17] M Levesque (Histoire de Russie, tom ii) has described the conquest of Russia by the Tartars, from the patriarch Nicon and the old chronicles [See Soloviev, Istoriia Rossii, vol iii cap ii p 820 sqq]

[18] For Poland, I am content with the Sarmatia Asiatica et Europaea of Matthew à Michou, or de Michovia, a canon and physician of Cracow (A D 1506), inserted in the Novus Orbis of Grynæus Fabric Bibliot Latin mediæ et infimæ Ætatis, tom v p 56 [The most important Polish source is the Historia Polonica of Johannes Dlugossius (who lived in the 15th century and died 1480) His works have been edited in 14 vols by Alexander Przezdziecki (1867-87) and the Hist Pol. occupies vols x -xiv Roepell's Geschichte Polens, vol i (1840) Only one contemporary Polish chronicle has survived the Annals of the Cracow Chapter, Mon Germ xix 582 sqq]

[19] I should quote Thuroczius, the oldest general historian (pars ii c 74, p 150), in the first volume of the Scriptores Rerum Hungaricarum, did not the same volume contain the original narrative of a contemporary, an eyewitness, and a sufferer (M Rogerii, Hungari, Varadiensis Capituli Canonici, Carmen miserabile, seu Historia super Destructione Regni Hungariæ, Temporibus Belæ IV Regis per Tartaros factà, p 292-321) [it will be found in Endlicher, Rer Hung Monum Arpadiana, p 255 sqq], the best picture that I have ever seen of all the circumstances of a Barbaric invasion [Gibbon omits to mention another contemporary account (of great importance) of the invasion of Hungary, by Thomas Archdeacon of Spalato, in his Historia Salonitana, published in Schwandtrer's Scriptores Hung , vol iii]

[20] Matthew Paris has represented, from authentic documents, the danger and distress of Europe (consult the word Tartari in his copious Index). [It has been conjectured that among the documents used by Matthew were anti-Semitic fly-leaves, accusing the Jews of inviting and helping the Mongols. Strakosch-Grassmann, Der Einfall der Mongolen, p 116] From motives of zeal and curiosity, the court of the great Khan, in the xiiith century, was visited by two friars, John de Plano Carpini and William Rubruquis, and

in the relation of their own disasters and their own defeats.[21]

The arms of Zingis and his lieutenants successively reduced the hordes of the desert, who pitched their tents between the wall of China and the Volga; and the Mogul emperor became the monarch of the pastoral world, the lord of many millions of shepherds and soldiers, who felt their united strength, and were impatient to rush on the mild and wealthy climates of the South. His ancestors had been the tributaries of the Chinese emperors, and Temugin himself had been disgraced by a title of honour and servitude.[22] The court of Pekin was astonished by an embassy from its former vassal, who in the tone of the king of nations exacted the tribute and obedience which he had paid, and who affected to treat the *Son of Heaven* as the most contemptible of mankind An haughty answer disguised their secret apprehensions; and their fears were soon justified by the march of innumerable squadrons, who pierced on all sides the feeble rampart of the great wall. Ninety cities were stormed, or starved, by

by Marco Polo, a Venetian gentleman The Latin relations of the two former are inserted in the first volume of Hackluyt: the Italian original, or version, of the third (Fabric Bibliot Latin medii Ævi, tom ii p 198, tom. v p 25) may be found in the second tome of Ramusio [Colonel H Yule's English translation, The Book of Ser Marco Polo the Venetian, in 2 vols , 1875, with plans and illustrations, and most valuable elucidations and bibliography, is indispensable to the study of the traveller A new edition of Rubruquis is wanted The account of a journey among the Mongols by another traveller, Ascellinus, is printed in Fejér, Codex diplomaticus Hungariae, iv 1, 428 *sqq*]

[21] In his great History of the Huns, M de Guignes has most amply treated of Zingis Khan and his successors See tom iii l xv –xix , and in the collateral articles of the Seljukians of Roum, tom ii l vi , the Carizmians l xiv , and the Mamalukes, tom iv l xvi , consult likewise the tables of the 1st volume. He is ever learned and accurate , yet I am only indebted to him for a general view, and some passages of Abulfeda, which are still latent in the Arabic text

[22] [The people who ruled over Northern China at this time were the Niu-Chi or Man-Chu (They called themselves Aisin, "golden," which the Chinese translated by Kin, and hence they are generally called the Kin dynasty) They had conquered Northern China in 1120 from the Karā-Khitay Turks, who had held it since 1004 Chingiz, who was always punctili-

the Moguls, ten only escaped; and Zingis, from a knowledge of the filial piety of the Chinese, covered his vanguard with their captive parents, an unworthy and, by degrees, a fruitless abuse of the virtues of his enemies. His invasion was supported by the revolt of an hundred thousand Khitans, who guarded the frontier; yet he listened to a treaty; and a princess of China, three thousand horses, five hundred youths, and as many virgins, and a tribute of gold and silk, were the price of his retreat. In his second expedition, he compelled the Chinese emperor to retire beyond the yellow river to a more southern residence. The siege of Pekin [23] was long and laborious: the inhabitants were reduced by famine to decimate and devour their fellow-citizens; when their ammunition was spent, they discharged ingots of gold and silver from their engines; but the Moguls introduced a mine to the centre of the capital; and the conflagration of the palace burnt above thirty days. China was desolated by Tartar war and domestic faction; and the five northern provinces were added to the empire of Zingis.

ous in matters of form, chose his moment when the Emperor Chang-Tsong, to whom he had taken a feudal oath, was dead (1208), then he openly refused allegiance to the successor. He had prepared the way for the overthrow of the Niu-Chi by the conquest of the land of the Hia (north of Tibet, and west of the great bend of the Hoang Ho. the country of the Tanguts), which was then a republic of brigands, who (with their capital at Ning-Hia on the Hoang Ho), commanding the routes to the west, were a pest both to the southern and the northern Chinese empires   Cahun, Intr. à l'histoire de l'Asie, p 248   Chingiz in conquering the Hia thus appeared as a public benefactor, but really seized a key position both in regard to China and in regard to the routes to the west through Dzungaria and through Cashgaria   On the Kin empire see the Histoire de l'empire de Kin ou empire d'or, Aisin Gurun-i Suduri Bithe, transl by C de Harlez, 1887]

[23] More properly *Yen-king*, an ancient city, whose ruins still appear some furlongs to the south-east of the modern *Pekin*, which was built by Cublai Khan (Gaubel, p 146). Pe-king and Nan-king are vague titles, the courts of the north and of the south   The identity and change of names perplex the most skilful readers of the Chinese geography (p 177) [When the Karā-Khitay Turks (under their chiefs the Ye-Lu family) conquered Northern China in 1004, they took Yen as their capital, it is now called Pe-king, "capital of the north"   "Khitan" is the Chinese form of Khitay]

In the West, he touched the dominions of Mohammed, sultan of Carizme, who reigned from the Persian gulf to the borders of India and Turkestan, and who, in the proud imitation of Alexander the Great, forgot the servitude and ingratitude of his fathers to the house of Seljuk.[24] It was the wish of Zingis to establish a friendly and commercial intercourse with the most powerful of the Moslem princes; nor could he be tempted by the secret solicitations of the caliph of Bagdad, who sacrificed to his personal wrongs the safety of the church and state. A rash and inhuman deed provoked and justified the Tartar arms in the invasion of the southern Asia. A caravan of three ambassadors and one hundred and fifty merchants was arrested and murdered at Otrar,[25] by the command of Mohammed, nor was it till after a demand and denial of justice, till he had prayed and fasted three nights on a mountain, that the Mogul emperor appealed to the judgment of God and his sword. Our European battles, says a philosophic writer,[26] are petty skirmishes, if compared to the numbers that have fought and fallen in the fields of Asia. Seven hundred thousand Moguls and Tartars are said to have marched under the standard of Zingis and his four sons. In the vast plains that extend to the north of

[24] [In the last quarter of the 11th cent, Anushtigīn a Turkish slave was appointed governor of Carizme (Khwārizm) by the Sultan Malik Shāh His son took the title of Carizme Shāh, and his grandson Atsīz made himself independent of the Seljuk sultans in the second quarter of the 12th cent Alā ad-Dīn Mohammad (A D 1199-1220) made this principality of Carizme (which Atsīz and Tukush (1172-1199) had already extended as far as Jand in the north and Ispahan in the west), into a great realm, subduing Persia and Transoxiana, overthrowing the Ghōrid dynasty of Afghanistan, and invaded Eastern Turkestan (the kingdom of the Karā-Khitay)]

[25] [On the middle Jaxartes. It was the capital of the Gūr-Khans of the Turkish kingdom of Karā-Khitay Gibbon omits to mention the conquest of this kingdom (the south-western provinces of the modern empire of China) by Chingiz, before he came face to face with the Carizmian empire]

[26] M de Voltaire, Essai sur l'Histoire Générale, tom iii c 60, p 8 His account of Zingis and the Moguls contains, as usual, much general sense and truth, with some particular errors.

the Sihon or Jaxartes, they were encountered by four hundred thousand soldiers of the sultan; and in the first battle, which was suspended by the night, one hundred and sixty thousand Carizmians were slain. Mohammed was astonished by the multitude and valour of his enemies.[27] he withdrew from the scene of danger, and distributed his troops in the frontier towns, trusting that the Barbarians, invincible in the field, would be repulsed by the length and difficulty of so many regular sieges. But the prudence of Zingis had formed a body of Chinese engineers, skilled in the mechanic arts, informed, perhaps, of the secret of gunpowder, and capable, under his discipline, of attacking a foreign country with more vigour and success than they had defended their own. The Persian historians will relate the sieges and reduction of Otrar, Cogende, Bochara, Samarcand, Carizme, Herat, Merou, Nisabour, Balch, and Candahar; and the conquest of the rich and populous countries of Transoxiana, Carizme, and Chorasan The destructive hostilities of Attila and the Huns have long since been elucidated by the example of Zingis and the Moguls; and in this more proper place I shall be content to observe that, from the Caspian to the Indus, they ruined a tract of many hundred miles, which

[27] [The strategical ability displayed in the campaigns of Chingiz and his successors has been well brought out by Cahun It is wholly an error to regard the Mongol conquests as achieved merely by numbers and intrepid physical bravery The campaigns were carefully planned out — not by Chingiz himself, he only considered, and approved or rejected, the plans submitted to him by his military advisers He knew how to choose able generals (Samuka and Subutai were two of the most illustrious), but he did not interfere with them in their work The invasion of the Carizmian empire was carried out thus a Mongol army which had just conquered the land of Cashgar advanced over the great southern pass into Fergana and descended upon Khojend The main army advanced by the great northern gate, through Dzungaria and the Ili regions, to Otrār on the Jaxartes Half the army spread up the river to take or mask the Carizmian fortresses and join hands at Khojend with the corps from Cashgar The other half, under Chingiz himself, marched straight across the Red Sand Desert upon Bochara Cahun, op cit. p 285 Success was rendered easy by the strategical mistakes of Mohammad]

was adorned with the habitations and labours of mankind, and that five centuries have not been sufficient to repair the ravages of four years. The Mogul emperor encouraged or indulged the fury of his troops, the hope of future possession was lost in the ardour of rapine and slaughter, and the cause of the war exasperated their native fierceness by the pretence of justice and revenge. The downfall and death of the sultan Mohammed, who expired unpitied and alone in a desert island of the Caspian Sea, is a poor atonement for the calamities of which he was the author Could the Carizmian empire have been saved by a single hero, it would have been saved by his son Gelaleddin, whose active valour repeatedly checked the Moguls in the career of victory. Retreating, as he fought, to the banks of the Indus, he was oppressed by their innumerable host, till, in the last moment of despair, Gelaleddin spurred his horse into the waves, swam one of the broadest and most rapid rivers of Asia, and extorted the admiration and applause of Zingis himself. It was in this camp that the Mogul emperor yielded with reluctance to the murmurs of his weary and wealthy troops, who sighed for the enjoyment of their native land. Incumbered with the spoils of Asia, he slowly measured back his footsteps, betrayed some pity for the misery of the vanquished, and declared his intention of rebuilding the cities which had been swept away by the tempest of his arms. After he had repassed the Oxus and Jaxartes, he was joined by two generals, whom he had detached with thirty thousand horse, to subdue the western provinces of Persia. They had trampled on the nations which opposed their passage, penetrated through the gates of Derbend, traversed the Volga and the desert, and accomplished the circuit of the Caspian Sea, by an expedition which had never been attempted and has never been repeated. The return of Zingis was signalised by the overthrow of the rebellious or independent kingdoms of Tartary, and he died in the fulness of years and glory, with his last breath exhorting and instructing his sons to achieve the conquest of the Chinese empire.

The harem of Zingis was composed of five hundred wives and concubines; and of his numerous progeny, four sons, illustrious by their birth and merit, exercised under their father the principal offices of peace and war.   Toushi [28] was his great huntsman, Zagatai [29] his judge, Octai his minister, and Tuli his general, and their names and actions are often conspicuous in the history of his conquests.   Firmly united for their own and the public interest, the three brothers and their families were content with dependent sceptres; and Octai, by general consent, was proclaimed Great Khan, or emperor of the Moguls and Tartars.   He was succeeded by his son Gayuk, after whose death the empire devolved to his cousins, Mangou and Cublai, the sons of Tuli, and the grandsons of Zingis.[30]   In the sixty-eight years of his four first successors, the Moguls subdued almost all Asia and a large portion of Europe.   Without confining myself to the order of time, without expatiating on the detail of events, I shall present a general picture of the progress of their arms. I. In the East; II. In the South; III. In the West; and, IV. In the North.

I.   Before the invasion of Zingis, China was divided into

[28] [Jūjī received the realm of Karā-Khitay, and his son Bātū obtained possession of the Khanate of Kipchak, see below, p. 145]

[29] Zagatai [Chagatāy] gave his name to his dominions of Maurenahar [Mā-warā-l-nahr], or Transoxiana [along with part of Kashgar, Balkh, and Ghazna], and the Moguls of Hindostan, who emigrated from that country, are styled Zagatais by the Persians   This certain etymology, and the similar example of Uzbek, Nogai, &c may warn us not absolutely to reject the derivations of a national, from a personal, name. [The succession of the Chagatāy Khans of Transoxiana is very uncertain.   On this branch see Mr Oliver's monograph, "The Chaghatai Mughals," in Journ R As Soc, vol xv.   Cp the list in Lane-Poole's Mohammadan Dynasties, p 242]

[30] [Mangū (1251-1257) appointed his brother Khubilāy governor of the southern provinces   On Mangū's death, Khubilāy defeated the attempts of the line of Jūjī to recover the chief Khanate, and reigned till 1294   He transferred the royal residence from Karakorum to Peking]

two empires or dynasties of the North and South,[31] and the difference of origin and interest was smoothed by a general conformity of laws, language, and national manners. The Northern empire, which had been dismembered by Zingis, was finally subdued seven years after his death. After the loss of Pekin, the emperor had fixed his residence at Kaifong, a city many leagues in circumference, and which contained, according to the Chinese annals, fourteen hundred thousand families of inhabitants and fugitives. He escaped from thence with only seven horsemen, and made his last stand in a third capital, till at length the hopeless monarch, protesting his innocence and accusing his fortune, ascended a funeral pile, and gave orders that, as soon as he had stabbed himself, the fire should be kindled by his attendants. The dynasty of the *Song*, the native and ancient sovereigns of the whole empire, survived above forty-five years the fall of the Northern usurpers; and the perfect conquest was reserved for the arms of Cublai. During this interval, the Moguls were often diverted by foreign wars; and, if the Chinese seldom dared to meet their victors in the field, their passive courage presented an endless succession of cities to storm and of millions to slaughter. In the attack and defence of places, the engines of antiquity and the Greek fire were alternately employed; the use of gunpowder, in cannon and bombs, appears as a familiar practice;[32] and the sieges were conducted by the Mahometans and Franks, who had been liberally invited

[31] In Marco Polo and the Oriental geographers, the names of Cathay and Mangi distinguish the Northern and Southern empires, which, from A D 1234 to 1279, were those of the Great Khan and of the Chinese The search of Cathay, after China had been found, excited and misled our navigators of the sixteenth century, in their attempts to discover the north-east passage [Cp Cathay and the Way Thither a collection of all minor notices of China previous to the sixteenth century, translated and edited by Col H Yule, 2 vols 1866]

[32] I depend on the knowledge and fidelity of the Père Gaubil, who translates the Chinese text of the annals of the Moguls or Yuen (p 71, 93, 153), but I am ignorant at what time these annals were composed and published The

into the service of Cublai. After passing the great river, the troops and artillery were conveyed along a series of canals, till they invested the royal residence of Hamcheu, or Quinsay, in the country of silk, the most delicious climate of China. The emperor, a defenceless youth, surrendered his person and sceptre; and, before he was sent in exile into Tartary, he struck nine times the ground with his forehead, to adore in prayer or thanksgiving the mercy of the Great Khan. Yet the war (it was now styled a rebellion) was still maintained in the southern provinces from Hamcheu to Canton, and the obstinate remnant of independence and hostility was transported from the land to the sea. But, when the fleet of the *Song* was surrounded and oppressed by a superior armament, their last champion leaped into the waves with his infant emperor in his arms. "It is more glorious," he cried, "to die a prince than to live a slave." An hundred thousand Chinese imitated his example, and the whole empire, from Tonkin to the great wall, submitted to the dominion of Cublai. His boundless ambition aspired to the conquest of Japan; his fleet was twice shipwrecked; and the lives of an hundred thousand Moguls and Chinese were sacrificed in the fruitless expedition. But the circumjacent kingdoms, Corea, Tonkin, Cochinchina, Pegu, Bengal, and Thibet, were reduced in different degrees of tribute and obedience by the effort or terror of his arms. He explored the Indian Ocean with a fleet of a thousand ships, they sailed in sixty-eight days, most probably to the isle of Borneo, under the equinoctial line; and, though they returned not without spoil or

two uncles of Marco Polo, who served as engineers at the siege of Siengyangfou (l n c 61, in Ramusio, tom ii , see Gaubil, p 155, 157) must have felt and related the effects of this destructive powder, and their silence is a weighty and almost decisive objection. I entertain a suspicion that the recent discovery was carried from Europe to China by the caravans of the xvth century, and falsely adopted as an old national discovery before the arrival of the Portuguese and Jesuits in the xviith Yet the Père Gaubil affirms that the use of gunpowder has been known to the Chinese above 1600 years [For Chinese Annals see Appendix 1]

glory, the emperor was dissatisfied that the savage king had escaped from their hands.

II. The conquest of Hindostan by the Moguls was reserved in a later period for the house of Timour, but that of Iran, or Persia, was achieved by Holagou [33] Khan, the grandson of Zingis, the brother and lieutenant of the two successive emperors, Mangou and Cublai I shall not enumerate the crowd of sultans, emirs, and atabeks, whom he trampled into dust; but the extirpation of the *Assassins*, or Ismaelians [34] of Persia, may be considered as a service to mankind. Among the hills to the south of the Caspian, these odious sectaries had reigned with impunity above an hundred and sixty years; and their prince, or imam, established his lieutenant to lead and govern the colony of Mount Libanus, so famous and formidable in the history of the crusades.[35] With the fanaticism of the Koran, the Ismaelians had blended the Indian transmigration and the visions of their own prophets; and it was their first duty to devote their souls and bodies in blind obedience to the vicar of God. The daggers of his missionaries were felt both in the East and West; the Christians and the Moslems enumerate, and perhaps multiply, the illustrious victims that were sacrificed to the zeal, avarice, or resentment of *the old man* (as he was corruptly styled) *of the mountain*. But these daggers, his only arms, were broken

[33] [Hūlāgū His reign in Persia began in A D 1256. His dynasty was called the Il Khāns, that is "Khāns of the Ils" or tribes (i e provincial). Hammer has made them the subject of a book. Geschichte der Ilchane, 1842.]

[34] All that can be known of the Assassins of Persia and Syria, is poured from the copious, and even profuse, erudition of M Falconet, in two *Mémoires* read before the Academy of Inscriptions (tom xvii p 127-170) [One of the princes Jelal ad-Dīn Hasan had sent his submission to Chingiz it was his son Rukn ad-Dīn who fought with Hūlāgū. On the Assassins see Hammer's History of the Assassins, transl by O C Wood, 1835]

[35] The Ismaelians of Syria, 40,000 assassins, had acquired or founded ten castles in the hills above Tortosa About the year 1280, they were extirpated by the Mamalukes [See Guyard, Un grand-Maître des Assassins, in the Journal asiatique, 1877]

by the sword of Holagou, and not a vestige is left of the enemies of mankind, except the word *assassin*, which, in the most odious sense, has been adopted in the languages of Europe. The extinction of the Abbassides cannot be indifferent to the spectators of their greatness and decline. Since the fall of their Seljukian tyrants, the caliphs had recovered their lawful dominion of Bagdad and the Arabian Irak; but the city was distracted by theological factions, and the commander of the faithful was lost in a harem of seven hundred concubines. The invasion of the Moguls he encountered with feeble arms and haughty embassies. "On the divine decree," said the caliph Mostasem, "is founded the throne of the sons of Abbas. and their foes shall surely be destroyed in this world and in the next. Who is this Holagou that dares to arise against them? If he be desirous of peace, let him instantly depart from the sacred territory, and perhaps he may obtain from our clemency the pardon of his fault." This presumption was cherished by a perfidious vizir, who assured his master that, even if the Barbarians had entered the city, the women and children, from the terraces, would be sufficient to overwhelm them with stones. But, when Holagou touched the phantom, it instantly vanished into smoke. After a siege of two months, Bagdad was stormed and sacked by the Moguls, and their savage commander pronounced the death of the caliph Mostasem, the last of the temporal successors of Mahomet, whose noble kinsmen, of the race of Abbas, had reigned in Asia above five hundred years. Whatever might be the designs of the conqueror, the holy cities of Mecca and Medina [36] were protected by the Arabian desert, but the Moguls spread beyond the Tigris and Euphrates, pillaged Aleppo and Damascus, and threatened to join the Franks in the deliverance of Jerusalem. Egypt was lost,

[36] As a proof of the ignorance of the Chinese in foreign transactions, I must observe that some of their historians extend the conquests of Zingis himself to Medina, the country of Mahomet (Gaubil, p 42).

had she been defended only by her feeble offspring, but the
Mamalukes had breathed in their infancy the keenness of
a Scythian air. equal in valour, superior in discipline, they
met the Moguls in many a well-fought field; and drove back
the stream of hostility to the eastward of the Euphrates.
But it overflowed with resistless violence the kingdoms
of Armenia and Anatolia, of which the former was possessed
by the Christians, and the latter by the Turks. The sultans
of Iconium opposed some resistance to the Mogul arms, till
Azzadin sought a refuge among the Greeks of Constantinople,
and his feeble successors, the last of the Seljukian dynasty,
were finally extirpated by the khans of Persia.

III. No sooner had Octai subverted the Northern empire
of China, than he resolved to visit with his arms the most
remote countries of the West.[37] Fifteen hundred thousand
Moguls and Tartars were inscribed on the military roll;
of these the Great Khan selected a third [38] which he entrusted
to the command of his nephew Batou, the son of Tuli;[39]
who reigned over his father's conquests to the north of the
Caspian Sea. After a festival of forty days, Batou set forwards on this great expedition, and such was the speed and
ardour of his innumerable squadrons that in less than six
years they had measured a line of ninety degrees of longitude,
a fourth part of the circumference of the globe. The great
rivers of Asia and Europe, the Volga and Kama, the Don and
Borysthenes, the Vistula and Danube, they either swam with
their horses, or passed on the ice, or traversed in leathern

[37] [On the history of the Mongols in the West and the Golden Horde, see
Hammer's Geschichte der goldenen Horde, 1840, and Howorth's History of
the Mongols, part ii   In May 1334 the Moorish traveller Ibn Batūta visited
the camp of Uzbeg Khan of the Golden Horde (Voyages, ed and transl
Defrémery and Sanguinetti, vol ii 1877)]

[38] [The numbers given in the western sources are mere metaphors for
immensity Cp Cahun, *op cit* p 343-344, Strakosch-Grassmann, Der
Einfall der Mongolen in Mitteleuropa, p 182-184 The total number of
the Mongols may have been about 100,000]

[39] [Bātū was son of Jūjī (not of Tulūy).]

boats, which followed the camp and transported their waggons and artillery. By the first victories of Batou,[40] the remains of national freedom were eradicated in the immense
plains of Turkestan and Kipzak.[41] In his rapid progress,
he overran the kingdoms, as they are now styled, of Astracan
and Cazan, and the troops which he detached towards
Mount Caucasus, explored the most secret recesses of Georgia
and Circassia. The civil discord of the great dukes or princes
of Russia betrayed their country to the Tartars. They spread
from Livonia to the Black Sea, and both Moscow and Kiow,
the modern and the ancient capitals, were reduced to ashes:
a temporary ruin, less fatal than the deep and perhaps indelible mark which a servitude of two hundred years has
imprinted on the character of the Russians.[42] The Tartars
ravaged with equal fury the countries which they hoped to
possess and those which they were hastening to leave. From
the permanent conquest of Russia, they made a deadly,
though transient, inroad into the heart of Poland and as far
as the borders of Germany. The cities of Lublin and Cracow were obliterated; they approached the shores of the
Baltic; and in the battle of Lignitz, they defeated the dukes

[40] [Bâtû was only nominally the leader. The true commander was Subutai,
who deserves to be remembered among the great generals of the world for
the brilliant campaign of 1241. See Appendix 4.]

[41] The *Dashte Kipzak* [Dasht-i-Kipchāk] or plain of Kipzak, extends on
either side of the Volga, in a boundless space towards the Jaik and Borysthenes,
and is supposed to contain the primitive name and nation of the Cossacks.

[42] [Riazan was taken 21st December, 1237, then Moscow, then Vladimir,
the Grand Duke's capital, 7th January, 1238, then the Grand Duke's army
was routed, 4th March. Subutai did not go farther north-westward than
Torjok; he turned to subdue the Caucasian regions, the valley of the Don
and the land of the Kipchaks. This occupied him till the end of 1239.
Then he advanced on Kiev, and ruined it, with an exceptional and deliberate
malice, which requires some explanation. Kiev was at this time a most
prosperous and important centre of commerce with the East. From this
time forward Venice had a monopoly of trade with the extreme East. Now
the Venetian merchants of the Crimea were on very good terms with the
Mongols. It has been plausibly suggested by M. Cahun that in the destruction of Kiev the Mongols acted under Venetian influence (*op. cit.* p. 350).]

of Silesia, the Polish palatines, and the great master of the
Teutonic order,[43] and filled nine sacks with the right ears of
the slain   From Lignitz, the extreme point of their western
march, they turned aside to the invasion of Hungary,[44]
and the presence or spirit of Batou inspired the host of five
hundred thousand men · the Carpathian hills could not be
long impervious to their divided columns, and their approach
had been fondly disbelieved till it was irresistibly felt   The
king, Bela the Fourth, assembled the military force of his
counts and bishops; but he had alienated the nation by
adopting a vagrant horde of forty thousand families of Comans,
and these savage guests were provoked to revolt by the suspicion of treachery and the murder of their prince. The
whole country north of the Danube was lost in a day, and
depopulated in a summer; and the ruins of cities and churches
were overspread with the bones of the natives, who expiated
the sins of their Turkish ancestors. An ecclesiastic, who
fled from the sack of Waradin, describes the calamities which
he had seen or suffered , and the sanguinary rage of sieges
and battles is far less atrocious than the treatment of the
fugitives, who had been allured from the woods under a
promise of peace and pardon, and who were coolly slaughtered
as soon as they had performed the labours of the harvest and
vintage.   In the winter, the Tartars passed the Danube
on the ice, and advanced to Gran or Strigonium, a German
colony, and the metropolis of the kingdom   Thirty engines
were planted against the walls; the ditches were filled with
sacks of earth and dead bodies; and, after a promiscuous
massacre, three hundred noble matrons were slain in the presence of the khan   Of all the cities and fortresses of Hungary,
three alone survived the Tartar invasion, and the unfortunate Bela hid his head among the islands of the Adriatic.

[43] [And a band of Knights Templar of France]
[44] [This is not correct   The battle of Liegnitz was gained by the right
wing of the Mongol army   The advance into Hungary, under Bātū and
Subutai, was simultaneous. See Appendix 4.]

The Latin world was darkened by this cloud of savage hostility; a Russian fugitive carried the alarm to Sweden, and the remote nations of the Baltic and the ocean trembled at the approach of the Tartars,[45] whom their fear and ignorance were inclined to separate from the human species. Since the invasion of the Arabs in the eighth century, Europe had never been exposed to a similar calamity, and, if the disciples of Mahomet would have oppressed her religion and liberty, it might be apprehended that the shepherds of Scythia would extinguish her cities, her arts, and all the institutions of civil society. The Roman pontiff attempted to appease and convert these invincible Pagans by a mission of Franciscan and Dominican friars; but he was astonished by the reply of the khan, that the sons of God and of Zingis were invested with a divine power to subdue or extirpate the nations, and that the pope would be involved in the universal destruction, unless he visited in person, and as a suppliant, the royal horde. The emperor Frederic the Second embraced a more generous mode of defence, and his letters to the kings of France and England and the princes of Germany represented the common danger, and urged them to arm their vassals in this just and rational crusade.[46] The Tartars themselves were awed by the fame and valour of the Franks; the town

[45] In the year 1238, the inhabitants of Gothia (*Sweden*) and Frise were prevented, by their fear of the Tartars, from sending, as usual, their ships to the herring fishery on the coast of England, and, as there was no exportation, forty or fifty of these fish were sold for a shilling (Matthew Paris, p 396) It is whimsical enough that the orders of a Mogul Khan, who reigned on the borders of China, should have lowered the price of herrings in the English market

[46] I shall copy his characteristic or flattering epithets of the different countries of Europe Furens ac fervens ad arma Germania, strenuæ militiæ genetrix et alumna Francia, bellicosa et audax Hispania, virtuosa viris et classe munita fertilis Anglia, impetuosis bellatoribus referta Alemannia, navalis Dacia, indomita Italia, pacis ignara Burgundia, inquieta Apulia, cum maris Græci, Adriatici, et Tyrrheni insulis pyraticis et invictis, Cretâ, Cypro, Siciliâ, cum Oceano conterminis, insulis, et regionibus, cruenta Hybernia, cum agili Walliâ, palustris Scotia, glacialis Norwegia, suam electam militiam sub vexillo Crucis destinabunt, &c. (Matthew Paris, p 498)

of Neustadt in Austria was bravely defended against them by fifty knights and twenty crossbows; and they raised the siege on the appearance of a German army. After wasting the adjacent kingdoms of Servia, Bosnia, and Bulgaria, Batou slowly retreated from the Danube to the Volga to enjoy the rewards of victory in the city and palace of Serai, which started at his command from the midst of the desert.[47]

IV. Even the poor and frozen regions of the North attracted the arms of the Moguls. Sheibani Khan, the brother of the great Batou, led an horde of fifteen thousand families into the wilds of Siberia; and his descendants reigned at Tobolskoy above three centuries, till the Russian conquest. The spirit of enterprise which pursued the course of the Oby and Yenisei must have led to the discovery of the Icy Sea. After brushing away the monstrous fables, of men with dogs' heads and cloven feet, we shall find that, fifteen years after the death of Zingis, the Moguls were informed of the name and manners of the Samoyedes in the neighbourhood of the polar circle, who dwelt in subterraneous huts, and derived their furs and their food from the sole occupation of hunting.[48]

While China, Syria, and Poland were invaded at the same time by the Moguls and Tartars, the authors of the mighty

[47] [The news of the death of the Grand Khan Ogotai recalled Bātū and Subutai to the East. The Mongols left Siebenbürgen in summer, 1242, Bulgaria in the following winter Europe did not deceive itself It was fully conscious that the Mongols could have extended their conquests if they had chosen. As Roger puts it, they disdained to conquer Germany — Tartari aspernabantur Theutomain expugnare (Miserabile Carmen, in M G H 29, p 564). On the position of the capital of the Golden Horde, Serai, the chief works are Grigor'ev, O miestopolozhenii stolitsy zolotoi Ordy Saraia, 1845, and Brun, O rezidentsii chanov zolotoi Ordy do vremen Dzhanibeka (in the publications of the 3rd Archeological Congress at Kiev), 1878 Brun attempts to show that there were two (old) Serais, — the elder, nearer the Caspian Sea, not far from the village of Selitrian, the later at Tsarev]

[48] See Carpin's relation in Hakluyt, vol 1 p 30 The pedigree of the khans of Siberia is given by Abulghazi (part viii p 485-495). Have the Russians found no Tartar chronicles at Tobolskoi?

mischief were content with the knowledge and declaration
that their word was the sword of death.   Like the first caliphs,
the first successors of Zingis seldom appeared in person at
the head of their victorious armies   On the banks of the
Onon and Selinga, the royal or *golden horde* exhibited the
contrast of simplicity and greatness, of the roasted sheep
and mare's milk which composed their banquets, and of a
distribution in one day of five hundred waggons of gold and
silver.   The ambassadors and princes of Europe and Asia
were compelled to undertake this distant and laborious pilgrimage, and the life and reign of the great dukes of Russia,
the kings of Gregoria and Armenia, the sultans of Iconium,
and the emirs of Persia were decided by the frown or smile
of the Great Khan.   The sons and grandsons of Zingis had
been accustomed to the pastoral life; but the village of
Caracorum [49] was gradually ennobled by their election and
residence.   A change of manners is implied in the removal
of Octai and Mangou from a tent to an house; and their
example was imitated by the princes of their family and the
great officers of the empire.   Instead of the boundless forest,
the enclosure of a park afforded the more indolent pleasures
of the chase; their new habitations were decorated with paint-
ing and sculpture, their superfluous treasures were cast in
fountains, and basons, and statues of massy silver, and the
artists of China and Paris vied with each other in the service
of the Great Khan.[50]   Caracorum contained two streets, the

---

[49] The Map of d'Anville and the Chinese Itineraries (de Guignes, tom i
p 57) seem to mark the position of Holin, or Caracorum, about six hundred
miles to the north-west of Pekin   The distance between Selinginsky and
Pekin is near 2000 Russian versts, between 1300 and 1400 English miles
(Bell's Travels, vol ii p 67)   [For the situation of Caracorum, at a place
still called Kara-Kharam, on the north bank of the Orchon, see Geographical
Magazine for July 1874, p 137, Yule's Marco Polo, vol i p 228-229]

[50] Rubruquis found at Caracorum his countryman *Guillaume Boucher*,
orfèvre de Paris, who had executed, for the khan, a silver tree, supported
by four lions, and ejecting four different liquors   Abulghazi (part iv p 336)
mentions the painters of Kitay or China.

one of Chinese mechanics, the other of Mahometan traders;
and the places of religious worship, one Nestorian church,
two moschs, and twelve temples of various idols, may represent, in some degree, the number and division of inhabitants
Yet a French missionary declares that the town of St. Denys,
near Paris, was more considerable than the Tartar capital,
and that the whole palace of Mangou was scarcely equal to
a tenth part of that Benedictine abbey. The conquests of
Russia and Syria might amuse the vanity of the Great Khans,
but they were seated on the borders of China; the acquisition
of that empire was the nearest and most interesting object,
and they might learn from their pastoral economy that it is
for the advantage of the shepherd to protect and propagate
his flock. I have already celebrated the wisdom and virtue
of a mandarin who prevented the desolation of five populous
and cultivated provinces. In a spotless administration of
thirty years, this friend of his country and of mankind continually laboured to mitigate or suspend the havoc of war;
to save the monuments, and to rekindle the flame, of science;
to restrain the military commander by the restoration of civil
magistrates; and to instil the love of peace and justice into
the minds of the Moguls He struggled with the barbarism
of the first conquerors; but his salutary lessons produced
a rich harvest in the second generation. The northern and
by degrees the southern empire acquiesced in the government of Cublai, the lieutenant and afterwards the successor
of Mangou, and the nation was loyal to a prince who had
been educated in the manners of China. He restored the
forms of her venerable constitution; and the victors submitted
to the laws, the fashions, and even the prejudices of the vanquished people. This peaceful triumph, which has been
more than once repeated, may be ascribed, in a great measure,
to the numbers and servitude of the Chinese. The Mogul
army was dissolved in a vast and populous country, and their
emperors adopted with pleasure a political system which
gives to the prince the solid substance of despotism and leaves

to the subject the empty names of philosophy, freedom, and filial obedience. Under the reign of Cublai, letters and commerce, peace and justice, were restored, the great canal of five hundred miles was opened from Nankin to the capital; he fixed his residence at Pekin,[51] and displayed in his court the magnificence of the greatest monarch of Asia. Yet this learned prince declined from the pure and simple religion of his great ancestor; he sacrificed to the idol Fo; and his blind attachment to the lamas of Thibet and the bonzes of China [52] provoked the censure of the disciples of Confucius. His successors polluted the palace with a crowd of eunuchs, physicians, and astrologers, while thirteen millions of their subjects were consumed in the provinces by famine. One hundred and forty years after the death of Zingis, his degenerate race, the dynasty of the Yuen, was expelled by a revolt of the native Chinese; [53] and the Mogul emperors were lost in the oblivion of the desert. Before this revolution, they had forfeited their supremacy over the dependent branches of their house, the khans of Kipzak and Russia, the khans of Zagatai or Transoxiana, and the khans of Iran or Persia. By their distance and power, these royal lieutenants had soon been released from the duties of obedience; and, after the death of Cublai, they scorned to accept a sceptre or a title from his unworthy successors. According to their respective situation, they maintained the simplicity of the pastoral life or assumed the luxury of the cities of Asia; but the princes and their hordes were alike disposed for the reception of a foreign worship. After some hesitation between the Gospel and the Koran, they

[51] [Which was called Khān Bāligh, City of the Khān]

[52] The attachment of the khans, and the hatred of the mandarins, to the bonzes and lamas (Duhalde, Hist de la Chine, tom i p 502, 503) seems to represent them as the priests of the same god, of the Indian *Fo*, whose worship prevails among the sects of Hindostan, Siam, Thibet, China, and Japan But this mysterious subject is still lost in a cloud, which the researches of our Asiatic Society may gradually dispel

[53] [Under Chu Yuen Chang, who became emperor and founded the Ming dynasty.]

conformed to the religion of Mahomet; and, while they adopted for their brethren the Arabs and Persians, they renounced all intercourse with the ancient Moguls, the idolaters of China.

In this shipwreck of nations, some surprise may be excited by the escape of the Roman empire, whose relics, at the time of the Mogul invasion, were dismembered by the Greeks and Latins. Less potent than Alexander, they were pressed, like the Macedonian, both in Europe and Asia, by the shepherds of Scythia, and, had the Tartars undertaken the siege, Constantinople must have yielded to the fate of Pekin, Samarcand, and Bagdad. The glorious and voluntary retreat of Batou from the Danube was insulted by the vain triumph of the Franks and Greeks,[54] and in a second expedition death surprised him in full march to attack the capital of the Cæsars. His brother Borga carried the Tartar arms into Bulgaria and Thrace; but he was diverted from the Byzantine war by a visit to Novogorod, in the fifty-seventh degree of latitude, where he numbered the inhabitants and regulated the tributes of Russia. The Mogul khan formed an alliance with the Mamalukes against his brethren of Persia; three hundred thousand horse penetrated through the gates of Derbend; and the Greeks might rejoice in the first example of domestic war. After the recovery of Constantinople, Michael Palæologus,[55] at a distance from his court and army, was surprised and surrounded in a Thracian castle by twenty thousand Tartars. But the object of their march was a private interest; they came to the deliverance of Azzadin,[56] the Turkish sultan; and were content with his person and

[54] Some repulse of the Moguls in Hungary (Matthew Paris, p 545, 546) might propagate and colour the report of the union and victory of the kings of the Franks on the confines of Bulgaria Abulpharagius (Dynast p 310), after forty years, beyond the Tigris, might be easily deceived

[55] See Pachymer, l iii c 25, and l iv c 26, 27, and the false alarm at Nice, l iii c 27 [28] Nicephorus Gregoras, l iv. c 6

[56] [Izz ad-Din II. reigned A D 1245-1257]

the treasure of the emperor. Their general Noga, whose name is perpetuated in the hordes of Astracan, raised a formidable rebellion against Mengo Timour, the third of the khans of Kipzak; obtained in marriage Maria, the natural daughter of Palæologus; and guarded the dominions of his friend and father. The subsequent invasions of a Scythian cast were those of outlaws and fugitives; and some thousands of Alani and Comans, who had been driven from their native seats, were reclaimed from a vagrant life and enlisted in the service of the empire. Such was the influence in Europe of the invasion of the Moguls. The first terror of their arms secured rather than disturbed the peace of the Roman Asia. The sultan of Iconium solicited a personal interview with John Vataces, and his artful policy encouraged the Turks to defend their barrier against the common enemy.[57] That barrier indeed was soon overthrown; and the servitude and ruin of the Seljukians exposed the nakedness of the Greeks. The formidable Holagou threatened to march to Constantinople at the head of four hundred thousand men; and the groundless panic of the citizens of Nice will present an image of the terror which he had inspired. The accident of a procession, and the sound of a doleful litany, "From the fury of the Tartars, good Lord, deliver us," had scattered the hasty report of an assault and massacre. In the blind credulity of fear, the streets of Nice were crowded with thousands of both sexes, who knew not from what or to whom they fled; and some hours elapsed before the firmness of the military officers could relieve the city from this imaginary foe. But the ambition of Holagou and his successors was fortunately diverted by the conquest of Bagdad and a long vicissitude of Syrian wars; their hostility to the Moslems inclined them to unite with the Greeks and Franks,[58] and their

[57] G Acropolita, p 36, 37 [c 41] Nic Gregoras, l ii c 6, l iv c. 5
[58] Abulpharagius, who wrote in the year 1284, declares that the Moguls, since the fabulous defeat of Batou had not attacked either the Franks or

generosity or contempt had offered the kingdom of Anatolia as the reward of an Armenian vassal The fragments of the Seljukian monarchy were disputed by the emirs who had occupied the cities or the mountains, but they all confessed the supremacy of the khans of Persia; and he often interposed his authority, and sometimes his arms, to check their depredations, and to preserve the peace and balance of his Turkish frontier. The death of Cazan,[59] one of the greatest and most accomplished princes of the house of Zingis, removed this salutary control; and the decline of the Moguls gave a free scope to the rise and progress of the OTTOMAN EMPIRE.[60]

After the retreat of Zingis, the sultan Gelaleddin of Carisme had returned from India to the possession and defence of his Persian kingdoms. In the space of eleven years, that hero fought in person fourteen battles, and such was his activity that he led his cavalry, in seventeen days, from Teflis to Kerman, a march of a thousand miles.[61] Yet he was oppressed by the jealousy of the Moslem princes and the innumerable armies of the Moguls; and after his last defeat Gelaleddin perished ignobly in the mountains of Curdistan. His death dissolved a veteran and adventurous army, which included under the name of Carizmians, or Corasmins, many Turkman hordes that had attached themselves to the sultan's fortune. The bolder and more powerful chiefs invaded

Greeks; and of this he is a competent witness Hayton, likewise, the Armeniac prince, celebrates their friendship for himself and his nation

[59] Pachymer gives a splendid character of Cazan Khan, the rival of Cyrus and Alexander (l xii c 1) In the conclusion of his history (l xiii c 36), he *hopes* much from the arrival of 30,000 Tochars, or Tartars, who were ordered by the successor of Cazan [Ghāzān Mahmūd, A D 1295-1304, his successor was Uljāitu, A. D. 1304-1316] to restrain the Turks of Bithynia, A D 1308

[60] The origin of the Ottoman dynasty is illustrated by the critical learning of MM de Guignes (Hist des Huns, tom iv. p 329-337), and d'Anville (Empire Turc, p 14-22), two inhabitants of Paris, from whom the Orientals may learn the history and geography of their own country.

[61] [Jalāl ad-Din Mangbarti, A D 1220-1231]

Syria and violated the holy sepulchre of Jerusalem; the more
humble engaged in the service of Aladin, sultan of Iconium;
and among these were the obscure fathers of the Ottoman
line.[62] They had formerly pitched their tents near the southern banks of the Oxus, in the plains of Mahan and Nesa;
and it is somewhat remarkable that the same spot should
have produced the first authors of the Parthian and Turkish
empires. At the head or in the rear of a Carizmian army,
Soliman Shah was drowned in the passage of the Euphrates;
his son, Orthogrul, became the soldier and subject of Aladin,
and established at Surgut,[63] on the banks of the Sangar, a
camp of four hundred families, or tents, whom he governed
fifty-two years both in peace and war. He was the father
of Thaman, or Athman, whose Turkish name has been melted
into the appellation of the caliph Othman;[64] and, if we describe that pastoral chief as a shepherd and a robber, we must
separate from those characters all idea of ignominy and baseness. Othman possessed, and perhaps surpassed, the ordinary virtues of a soldier; and the circumstances of time and
place were propitious to his independence and success.
The Seljukian dynasty was no more; and the distance and
decline of the Mogul khans soon enfranchised him from the
control of a superior. He was situate on the verge of the
Greek empire, the Koran sanctified his *gazi*, or holy war,
against the infidels; and their political errors unlocked the
passes of Mount Olympus, and invited him to descend into
the plains of Bithynia. Till the reign of Palæologus, these
passes had been vigilantly guarded by the militia of the country, who were repaid by their own safety and an exemption

[62] [They were a clan of the tribe of Oghuz]

[63] [Sugut (Turkish name ="willow"), south of Malagina on the way to
Dorylæum, is mentioned by Anna Comnena (Σαγουδάους, xv 2)   Othmān was
born in A D 1258   Gibbon has shown his critical faculty in neglecting the
confused and false accounts of the Greek historians, Phrantzes and Chalcondyles, of the deeds of Ertughrul]

[64] [This is the correct form of the name — Othmān.   The name of the
people is Othmānli   Ottoman is a corruption.]

from taxes   The emperor abolished their privilege and assumed their office, but the tribute was rigorously collected,
the custody of the passes was neglected, and the hardy moun-
taineers degenerated into a trembling crowd of peasants
without spirit or discipline.   It was on the twenty-seventh
of July, in the year twelve hundred and ninety-nine of the
Christian era, that Othman first invaded the territory of
Nicomedia;[65] and the singular accuracy of the date seems
to disclose some foresight of the rapid and destructive growth
of the monster.   The annals of the twenty-seven years of
his reign would exhibit a repetition of the same inroads;
and his hereditary troops were multiplied in each campaign
by the accession of captives and volunteers.   Instead of
retreating to the hills, he maintained the most useful and de-
fensible posts, fortified the towns and castles which he had
first pillaged; and renounced the pastoral life for the baths
and palaces of his infant capitals.   But it was not till Othman was oppressed by age and infirmities that he received
the welcome news of the conquest of Prusa, which had been
surrendered by famine or treachery to the arms of his son
Orchan.   The glory of Othman is chiefly founded on that
of his descendants; but the Turks have transcribed or composed a royal testament of his last counsels of justice and
moderation.[66]

[65] See Pachymer, l x c. 25, 26, l xiii. c. 33, 34, 36; and concerning the
guard of the mountains, l i c 3-6, Nicephorus Gregoras, l vii c 1, and
the first book of Laonicus Chalcondyles, the Athenian

[66] I am ignorant whether the Turks have any writers older than Mahomet
II, nor can I reach beyond a meagre chronicle (Annales Turcici ad annum
1550), translated by John Gaudier, and published by Leunclavius (ad calcem
Laonic Chalcond p 311-350), with copious pandects, or commentaries.
The History of the Growth and Decay (A D 1300-1683) of the Othman empire was translated into English from the Latin MS of Demetrius Cantemir,
Prince of Moldavia (London, 1734, in folio)   The author is guilty of strange
blunders in Oriental History, but he was conversant with the language, the
annals, and institutions of the Turks   Cantemir partly draws his materials
from the Synopsis of Saadi Effendi of Larissa, dedicated in the year 1696
to Sultan Mustapha, and a valuable abridgment of the original historians

From the conquest of Prusa we may date the true era of
the Ottoman empire　The lives and possessions of the Christian subjects were redeemed by a tribute or ransom of thirty
thousand crowns of gold, and the city, by the labours of
Orchan, assumed the aspect of a Mahometan capital, Prusa
was decorated with a mosch, a college, and an hospital
of royal foundation; the Seljukian coin was changed for the
name and impression of the new dynasty; and the most
skilful professors of human and divine knowledge attracted
the Persian and Arabian students from the ancient schools
of Oriental learning　The office of vizir was instituted for
Aladin, the brother of Orchan; and a different habit distinguished the citizens from the peasants, the Moslems from
the infidels. All the troops of Othman had consisted of
loose squadrons of Turkman cavalry, who served without pay
and fought without discipline; but a regular body of infantry
was first established and trained by the prudence of his son.[67]

In one of the Ramblers, Dr Johnson praises Knolles (a General History of
the Turks to the present year, London, 1603), as the first of historians, unhappy only in the choice of his subject　Yet I much doubt whether a partial
and verbose compilation from Latin writers, thirteen hundred folio pages
of speeches and battles, can either instruct or amuse an enlightened age,
which requires from the historian some tincture of philosophy and criticism
[See Appendix 1]
[67] [Alā ad-Dīn was a political thinker.　Having resigned all claim to a
share in Othman's inheritance he spent some years in retirement and thought,
and then gave to his brother the result of his meditations.　Orchan made
him vizir and followed his suggestions　The chief reforms introduced by
Alā ad-Dīn were three.　(1) The regulation of Turkish dress is mentioned in
the text.　(2) The introduction of an independent Ottoman coinage　Hitherto
the Seljuk money circulated　The historian Sad ad-Dīn (transl Bratutti, i.
p 40) states that the first Ottoman coins, gold and silver, with Orchan's
name, were issued in 1328　There are no dates on Orchan's coins.　(3) The
institution of the Janissaries (Yani Chari, "new soldiery"), probably in A D
1330 (cp Sad ad-Dīn, ib p 42)　This used to be wrongly ascribed to
Murad I (so Marsigli, Stato militare, i 67, and Gibbon)　Compare Hammer,
Gesch des osmanischen Reiches, i 97 sqq　Alā ad-Dīn clearly grasped the
fact that an establishment of well-trained infantry was indispensable.　A
regular body of cavalry was also established at the same time　The regular
troops received pay, whereas the great general levy of cavalry performed
military service for their fiefs.]

A great number of volunteers was enrolled with a small stipend, but with the permission of living at home, unless they were summoned to the field; their rude manners and seditious temper disposed Orchan to educate his young captives as his soldiers and those of the prophet; but the Turkish peasants were still allowed to mount on horseback and follow his standard, with the appellation and the hopes of *freebooters*. By these arts he formed an army of twenty-five thousand Moslems; a train of battering engines was framed for the use of sieges, and the first successful experiment was made on the cities of Nice and Nicomedia. Orchan granted a safe-conduct to all who were desirous of departing with their families and effects, but the widows of the slain were given in marriage to the conquerors; and the sacrilegious plunder, the books, the vases, and the images were sold or ransomed at Constantinople. The emperor, Andronicus the Younger, was vanquished and wounded by the son of Othman, [68] he subdued the whole province or kingdom of Bithynia, as far as the shores of the Bosphorus and Hellespont; and the Christians confessed the justice and clemency of a reign which claimed the voluntary attachment of the Turks of Asia. Yet Orchan was content with the modest title of emir; and in the list of his compeers, the princes of Roum or Anatolia, [69] his military forces were surpassed by the emirs of Ghermian and Caramania, each of whom could bring into

[68] Cantacuzene, though he relates the battle and heroic flight of the younger Andronicus (l ii c 6–8), dissembles, by his silence, the loss of Prusa, Nice, and Nicomedia, which are fairly confessed by Nicephorus Gregoras (l viii. 15, ix 9, 13, vi 6) It appears that Nice was taken by Orchan in 1330, and Nicomedia in 1339, which are somewhat different from the Turkish dates [Capture of Nicomedia, A D 1326, battle of Philocrene, A D 1330; capture of Nicæa, A D 1330, reduction of Karāsī (the ancient Mysia, including Pergamus) after A D 1340 See Zinkeisen, Gesch des osmanischen Reiches in Europa, i 102–117]

[69] The partition of the Turkish emirs is extracted from two contemporaries, the Greek Nicephorus Gregoras (l. vii 1), and the Arabian Marakeschi (de Guignes, tom ii P ii p 76, 77) See likewise the first book of Laonicus Chalcondyles

the field an army of forty thousand men. Their dominions
were situate in the heart of the Seljukian kingdom; but the
holy warriors, though of inferior note, who formed new
principalities on the Greek empire, are more conspicuous
in the light of history. The maritime country from the
Propontis to the Mæander and the isle of Rhodes, so long
threatened and so often pillaged, was finally lost about the
thirtieth year of Andronicus the Elder.[70] Two Turkish
chieftains, Sarukhan and Aidin, left their names to their
conquests and their conquests to their posterity. The captivity or ruin of the *seven* churches of Asia was consummated;
and the Barbarous lords of Ionia and Lydia still trample on
the monuments of classic and Christian antiquity. In the
loss of Ephesus, the Christians deplored the fall of the first
angel, the extinction of the first candlestick of the Revelations; [71] the desolation is complete; and the temple of Diana

[70] Pachymer, l. xiii c 13   [The western coast of Asia Minor south of
Karāsī (Mysia) was not incorporated in the Ottoman realm till the reign of
Bayezid I   The most powerful rival of the Ottomans in Asia, at this time,
was the state of Caramania (which reached from the Sangarius to the Pam-
phylian sea, and included Galatia, Eastern Phrygia, Lycaonia, Pisidia and
Pamphylia)   Murad took Angora (Ancyra) in A D 1360, and in 1386 he
inflicted a demoralising defeat on the Caramanian Sultan in the battle of
Iconium   In 1391 the prince of Sarūkhān (the regions of the Hermus, including Sardis and Magnesia) and the prince of Aidin (south of Sarūkhān,
reaching to south of the Mæander) submitted, and likewise the lord of
Mentesia (Caria, including Miletus)   At the same time Bayezid subdued
Kermiyān (Western Phrygia) and Tekka (Lycia), and the western part of
Caramania   In 1393 the principality of Kastamuniyā (in Paphlagonia,
including Sinope) was conquered; and with the exception of the eastern
parts of Caramania all the little Seljuk states of Anatolia were in the hands
of the Ottomans   Cp the table in S Lane-Poole's Mohammadan Dynasties,
p 134   See below, p 34]
[71] See the Travels of Wheler and Spon, of Pocock and Chandler, and
more particuarly Smith's Survey of the Seven Churches of Asia, p 205–276
The more pious antiquaries labour to reconcile the promises and threats of
the author of the Revelations with the *present* state of the seven cities   Perhaps it would be more prudent to confine his predictions to the characters
and events of his own times. [For Ephesus and the temple of Diana see
Wood's Discoveries at Ephesus, 1877]

or the church of Mary will equally elude the search of the curious traveller The circus and three stately theatres of Laodicea are now peopled with wolves and foxes; Sardes is reduced to a miserable village; the God of Mahomet, without a rival or a son, is invoked in the moschs of Thyatira and Pergamus, and the populousness of Smyrna is supported by the foreign trade of the Franks and Armenians. Philadelphia alone has been saved by prophecy, or courage. At a distance from the sea, forgotten by the emperors, encompassed on all sides by the Turks, her valiant citizens defended their religion and freedom above four-score years, and at length capitulated with the proudest of the Ottomans. Among the Greek colonies and churches of Asia, Philadelphia is still erect, a column in a scene of ruins: a pleasing example that the paths of honour and safety may sometimes be the same.[72] The servitude of Rhodes was delayed above two centuries by the establishment of the knights of St. John of Jerusalem [73] Under the discipline of the order that island emerged into fame and opulence; the noble and warlike monks were renowned by land and sea; and the bulwark of Christendom provoked and repelled the arms of the Turks and Saracens.

The Greeks, by their intestine divisions, were the authors of their final ruin.[74] During the civil wars of the elder and

[72] [The date of the Ottoman capture of Philadelphia is uncertain (cp Finlay, History of Greece, iii p 469, note) Probably A D 1391]

[73] Consult the fourth book of the Histoire de l'Ordre de Malthe, par l'Abbé de Vertot That pleasing writer betrays his ignorance in supposing that Othman, a freebooter of the Bithynian hills, could besiege Rhodes by sea and land

[74] [For the success of the Ottomans, "the last example of the conquest of a numerous Christian population by a small number of Musulman invaders, and of the colonisation of civilised countries by a race ruder than the native population," Finlay assigns three particular causes (History of Greece, iii p 475). "1 The superiority of the Ottoman tribe over all contemporary nations in religious convictions and in moral and military conduct 2 The number of different races that composed the population of the country between the Adriatic and the Black Sea, the Danube, and the Aegean. 3 The

younger Andronicus, the son of Othman achieved, almost without resistance, the conquest of Bithynia, and the same disorders encouraged the Turkish emirs of Lydia and Ionia to build a fleet, and to pillage the adjacent islands and the sea-coast of Europe. In the defence of his life and honour, Cantacuzene was tempted to prevent or imitate his adversaries by calling to his aid the public enemies of his religion and country   Amir, the son of Aidin, concealed under a Turkish garb the humanity and politeness of a Greek; he was united with the great domestic by mutual esteem and reciprocal services; and their friendship is compared, in the vain rhetoric of the times, to the perfect union of Orestes and Pylades.[75] On the report of the danger of his friend, who was persecuted by an ungrateful court, the prince of Ionia assembled at Smyrna a fleet of three hundred vessels, with an army of twenty-nine thousand men; sailed in the depth of winter, and cast anchor at the mouth of the Hebrus   From thence, with a chosen band of two thousand Turks, he marched along the banks of the river, and rescued the empress, who was besieged in Demotica by the wild Bulgarians.   At that disastrous moment the life or death of his beloved Cantacuzene was concealed by his flight into Servia; but the grateful Irene, impatient to behold her deliverer, invited him to enter the city, and accompanied her message with a present of rich apparel and an hundred horses.   By a peculiar strain of delicacy the gentle Barbarian refused, in the absence of an unfortunate friend, to visit his wife or to taste the luxuries of the palace, sustained in his tent the rigour of the winter; and rejected the hospitable gift, that he might share the hard-

depopulation of the Greek empire, the degraded state of its judicial and civil administration, and the demoralisation of the Hellenic race "]

[75] Nicephorus Gregoras has expatiated with pleasure on this amiable character (l xii 7, xiii 4, 10, xiv. 1, 9 xvi 6)   Cantacuzene speaks with honour and esteem of his ally (l iii c 56, 57, 63, 64, 66–68, 86, 89, 95, 96) , but he seems ignorant of his own sentimental passion for the Turk, and indirectly denies the possibility of such unnatural friendship (l. iv. c. 40).

ships of two thousand companions, all as deserving as himself of that honour and distinction. Necessity and revenge
might justify his predatory excursions by sea and land;
he left nine thousand five hundred men for the guard of his
fleet; and persevered in the fruitless search of Cantacuzene,
till his embarkation was hastened by a fictitious letter, the
severity of the season, the clamours of his independent troops,
and the weight of his spoil and captives. In the prosecution
of the civil war, the prince of Ionia twice returned to Europe;
joined his arms with those of the emperor, besieged Thessalonica, and threatened Constantinople Calumny might
affix some reproach on his imperfect aid, his hasty departure,
and a bribe of ten thousand crowns, which he accepted from
the Byzantine court, but his friend was satisfied; and the
conduct of Amir is excused by the more sacred duty of defending against the Latins his hereditary dominions. The
maritime power of the Turks had united the pope, the king
of Cyprus, the republic of Venice, and the order of St. John,
in a laudable crusade; their galleys invaded the coast of Ionia;
and Amir was slain with an arrow, in the attempt to wrest
from the Rhodian knights the citadel of Smyrna [76] Before
his death, he generously recommended another ally of his
own nation, not more sincere or zealous than himself, but
more able to afford a prompt and powerful succour, by his
situation along the Propontis and in the front of Constantinople. By the prospect of a more advantageous treaty, the
Turkish prince of Bithynia was detached from his engagements with Anne of Savoy; and the pride of Orchan dictated
the most solemn protestations that, if he could obtain the
daughter of Cantacuzene, he would invariably fulfil the duties
of a subject and a son Parental tenderness was silenced
by the voice of ambition; the Greek clergy connived at the

[76] After the conquest of Smyrna by the Latins, the defence of this fortress
was imposed by Pope Gregory XI on the Knights of Rhodes (see Vertot,
l v.)

marriage of a Christian princess with a sectary of Mahomet, and the father of Theodora describes, with shameful satisfaction, the dishonour of the purple.[77] A body of Turkish cavalry attended the ambassadors, who disembarked from thirty vessels before his camp of Selybria   A stately pavilion was erected, in which the empress Irene passed the night with her daughters.   In the morning, Theodora ascended a throne, which was surrounded with curtains of silk and gold; the troops were under arms; but the emperor alone was on horseback.   At a signal the curtains were suddenly withdrawn, to disclose the bride, or the victim, encircled by kneeling eunuchs and hymenæal torches· the sound of flutes and trumpets proclaimed the joyful event; and her pretended happiness was the theme of the nuptial song, which was chaunted by such poets as the age could produce.   Without the rites of the church, Theodora was delivered to her Barbarous lord; but it had been stipulated that she should preserve her religion in the harem of Boursa; and her father celebrates her charity and devotion in this ambiguous situation.   After his peaceful establishment on the throne of Constantinople, the Greek emperor visited his Turkish ally, who, with four sons, by various wives, expected him at Scutari, on the Asiatic shore.   The two princes partook, with seeming cordiality, of the pleasures of the banquet and the chase, and Theodora was permitted to repass the Bosphorus, and to enjoy some days in the society of her mother.   But the friendship of Orchan was subservient to his religion and interest; and in the Genoese war he joined without a blush the enemies of Cantacuzene.

In the treaty with the empress Anne, the Ottoman prince

[77] See Cantacuzenus, l iii c 95   Nicephorus Gregoras, who, for the light of Mount Thabor, brands the emperor with the names of tyrant and Herod, excuses, rather than blames, this Turkish marriage, and alleges the passion and power of Orchan, ἐγγύτατος, καὶ τῇ δυνάμει τοὺς κατ' αὐτὸν ἤδη Περσικοὺς (Turkish) ὑπεραίρων Σατράπας (l xv 5)   He afterwards celebrates his kingdom and armies. See his reign in Cantemir, p 24-30

had inserted a singular condition, that it should be lawful for him to sell his prisoners at Constantinople or transport them into Asia A naked crowd of Christians of both sexes and every age, of priests and monks, of matrons and virgins, was exposed in the public market, the whip was frequently used to quicken the charity of redemption; and the indigent Greeks deplored the fate of their brethren, who were led away to the worst evils of temporal and spiritual bondage.[78] Cantacuzene was reduced to subscribe the same terms; and their execution must have been still more pernicious to the empire; a body of ten thousand Turks had been detached to the assistance of the empress Anne, but the entire forces of Orchan were exerted in the service of his father. Yet these calamities were of a transient nature; as soon as the storm had passed away, the fugitives might return to their habitations; and at the conclusion of the civil and foreign wars Europe was completely evacuated by the Moslems of Asia. It was in his last quarrel with his pupil that Cantacuzene inflicted the deep and deadly wound, which could never be healed by his successors, and which is poorly expiated by his theological dialogues against the prophet Mahomet. Ignorant of their own history, the modern Turks confound their first and their final passage of the Hellespont,[79] and describe the son of Orchan as a nocturnal robber, who, with eighty companions, explores by stratagem an hostile and unknown shore. Soli-

[78] The most lively and concise picture of this captivity may be found in the history of Ducas (c 8), who fairly transcribes what Cantacuzene confesses with a guilty blush!

[79] In this passage, and the first conquests in Europe, Cantemir (p 27, &c) gives a miserable idea of his Turkish guides, nor am I much better satisfied with Chalcondyles (l 1 p 12, &c [p 25 ed Bonn]) They forget to consult the most authentic record, the ivth book of Cantacuzene I likewise regret the last books, which are still manuscript, of Nicephorus Gregoras [They have been since published See above, vol iv p 384-5. The Ottomans captured the little fortress of Tzympe, near Gallipoli, in 1356, and Gallipoli itself in 1358 For Tzympe, cp Cantacuzenus, iv. 33, vol iii p. 242 ed Bonn]

man, at the head of ten thousand horse, was transported in the vessels, and entertained as the friend, of the Greek emperor.   In the civil wars of Roumania, he performed some service and perpetrated more mischief, but the Chersonesus was insensibly filled with a Turkish colony; and the Byzantine court solicited in vain the restitution of the fortresses of Thrace.   After some artful delays between the Ottoman prince and his son, their ransom was valued at sixty thousand crowns, and the first payment had been made, when an earthquake shook the walls and cities of the provinces; the dismantled places were occupied by the Turks, and Gallipoli, the key of the Hellespont, was rebuilt and repeopled by the policy of Soliman.   The abdication of Cantacuzene dissolved the feeble bands of domestic alliance, and his last advice admonished his countrymen to decline a rash contest, and to compare their own weakness with the numbers and valour, the discipline and enthusiasm, of the Moslems.   His prudent counsels were despised by the headstrong vanity of youth, and soon justified by the victories of the Ottomans. But, as he practised in the field the exercise of the *jerid*, Soliman was killed by a fall from his horse; and the aged Orchan wept and expired on the tomb of his valiant son.

But the Greeks had not time to rejoice in the death of their enemies; and the Turkish scymetar was wielded with the same spirit by Amurath the First, the son of Orchan and the brother of Soliman.   By the pale and fainting light of the Byzantine annals,[80] we can discern that he subdued without resistance the whole province of Roumania or Thrace, from the Hellespont to Mount Hæmus and the verge of the capital; and that Hadrianople was chosen for the royal seat of his government and religion in Europe.[81]   Constantinople,

[80] After the conclusion of Cantacuzene and Gregoras, there follows a dark interval of an hundred years   George Phranza, Michael Ducas, and Laonicus Chalcondyles, all three wrote after the taking of Constantinople.

[81] [Hadrianople was taken in 1361, Philippopolis in 1362   In the next year (1363) a federate army of the Servians (under Urosh V), Bosnians, and

whose decline is almost coeval with her foundation, had often, in the lapse of a thousand years, been assaulted by the Barbarians of the East and West, but never till this fatal hour had the Greeks been surrounded, both in Asia and Europe, by the arms of the same hostile monarchy. Yet the prudence or generosity of Amurath postponed for a while this easy conquest; and his pride was satisfied with the frequent and humble attendance of the emperor John Palæologus and his four sons, who followed at his summons the court and camp of the Ottoman prince He marched against the Sclavonian nations between the Danube and the Adriatic, the Bulgarians, Servians, Bosnians, and Albanians; and these warlike tribes, who had so often insulted the majesty of the empire, were repeatedly broken by his destructive inroads. Their countries did not abound either in gold or silver; nor were their rustic hamlets and townships enriched by commerce or decorated by the arts of luxury. But the natives of the soil have been distinguished in every age by their hardiness of mind and body; and they were converted by a prudent institution into the firmest and most faithful supporters of the Ottoman greatness [82] The vizir of Amurath reminded his sovereign that, according to the Mahometan law, he was entitled to a fifth part of the spoil and captives; and that the duty might easily be levied, if vigilant officers were stationed at Gallipoli, to watch the passage, and to select for his use the stoutest and most beautiful of the Christian youth. The advice was followed; the edict was proclaimed; many thousands of the European captives were educated in religion

Walachians marched to deliver Hadrianople, but were defeated by a far inferior force on the banks of the Maritza (Cp Sad ad-Din, tr Bratutti, 1 p. 91 *sqq*) In 1365 Murad established his residence at Hadrianople In 1373-4 he pressed into Macedonia In 1375 the Bulgarian prince Sisman became his vassal In 1385 Sophia was captured It should be noted that in 1365 Murad made a treaty with the important commercial city of Ragusa]

[82] See Cantemir, p 37-41, with his own large and curious annotations [The institution of the Janissaries is here wrongly ascribed to Murad, it belongs to the reign of Orchan See above, p 158, note 67]

and arms; and the new militia was consecrated and named by a celebrated dervish.   Standing in the front of their ranks, he stretched the sleeve of his gown over the head of the foremost soldier, and his blessing was delivered in these words. "Let them be called Janizaries (*Yengi cheri*, or new soldiers), may their countenance be ever bright! their hand victorious! their sword keen! may their spear always hang over the heads of their enemies, and, wheresoever they go, may they return with a *white face!*" [83]   Such was the origin of these haughty troops, the terror of the nations, and sometimes of the sultans themselves.   Their valour has declined, their discipline is relaxed, and their tumultuary array is incapable of contending with the order and weapons of modern tactics; [84] but at the time of their institution, they possessed a decisive superiority in war; since a regular body of infantry, in constant exercise and pay, was not maintained by any of the princes of Christendom   The Janizaries fought with the zeal of proselytes against their *idolatrous* countrymen; and in the battle of Cossova the league and independence of the Sclavonian tribes was finally crushed. [85]   As the conqueror walked over

[83] *White* and *black* face are common and proverbial expressions of praise and reproach in the Turkish language   Hic *niger* est, hunc tu Romane caveto, was likewise a Latin sentence

[84] [They were abolished (massacred) by the sultan Mahmūd II in 1826]

[85] [Lazarus, the Kral of Servia, won important successes over Ottoman invaders of Bosnia in 1387   This emboldened the other Slavs of the Balkan peninsula   Shishman of Bulgaria revolted, and this led to the direct incorporation of Bulgaria in the Ottoman empire   The Servian Kral, who was the leader of the Slavs in their struggle to maintain their independence, took the field at the head of a federate army in spring 1389   He was supported by the King of Bosnia, the princes of Croatia, Albania, and Chlum (afterwards Herzegovina) and Walachia, and there were some Bulgarians (who had escaped the wreck of their country) and Hungarian auxiliaries in his army   The battle was fought, 15th June, on the Kosovo-polje or Amselfeld (blackbird field) on the banks of the Lab, west of Pristina   The name of the Servian who stabbed Murad was Milosh Obilić (or Kobilović)   See the Turkish historian Nesri's account of the campaign (Hungarian translation by Thúry in Torok torténetirók, i p 32 *sqq*)   For the general history of the Slavonic struggles against the Turks see Rački's articles in the Rad (South Slavonic Journal), vols ii iii and iv , on the battle of Kosovo, iii p 91]

the field, he observed that the greatest part of the slain consisted of beardless youths, and listened to the flattering reply of his vizir, that age and wisdom would have taught them not to oppose his irresistible arms. But the sword of his Janizaries could not defend him from the dagger of despair; a Servian soldier started from the crowd of dead bodies, and Amurath was pierced in the belly with a mortal wound   The grandson of Othman was mild in his temper, modest in his apparel, and a lover of learning and virtue; but the Moslems were scandalised at his absence from public worship, and he was corrected by the firmness of the mufti, who dared to reject his testimony in a civil cause   a mixture of servitude and freedom not unfrequent in Oriental history.[86]

The character of Bajazet, the son and successor of Amurath, is strongly expressed in his surname of *Ilderim*, or the lightning; and he might glory in an epithet which was drawn from the fiery energy of his soul and the rapidity of his destructive march.   In the fourteenth year of his reign,[87] he incessantly moved at the head of his armies, from Boursa to Hadrianople, from the Danube to the Euphrates, and, though he strenuously laboured for the propagation of the law, he invaded, with impartial ambition, the Christian and Mahometan princes of Europe and Asia.   From Angora to Amasia and Erzeroum, the northern regions of Anatolia were reduced to his obedience; he stripped of their hereditary possessions his brother emirs, of Ghermian and Caramania, of Aidin and

---

[86] See the life and death of Morad, or Amurath I , in Cantemir (p 33-45), the 1st book of Chalcondyles, and the Annales Turcici of Leunclavius   According to another story, the sultan was stabbed by a Croat in his tent: and this accident was alleged to Busbequius (Epist 1 p 98), as an excuse for the unworthy precaution of pinioning, as it were, between two attendants, an ambassador's arms when he is introduced to the royal presence

[87] The reign of Bajazet I or Ilderim Bayazid, is contained in Cantemir (p 46), the 11d book of Chalcondyles, and the Annales Turcici   The surname of Ilderim, or lightning, is an example that the conquerors and poets of every age have *felt* the truth of a system which derives the sublime from the principle of terror

Sarukhan; and after the conquest of Iconium the ancient kingdom of the Seljukians again revived in the Ottoman dynasty   Nor were the conquests of Bajazet less rapid or important in Europe.   No sooner had he imposed a regular form of servitude on the Servians and Bulgarians, than he passed the Danube to seek new enemies and new subjects in the heart of Moldavia.[88]   Whatever yet adhered to the Greek empire in Thrace, Macedonia, and Thessaly acknowledged a Turkish master.   An obsequious bishop led him through the gates of Thermopylæ into Greece; and we may observe, as a singular fact, that the widow of a Spanish chief, who possessed the ancient seat of the oracle of Delphi, deserved his favour by the sacrifice of a beauteous daughter. The Turkish communication between Europe and Asia had been dangerous and doubtful, till he stationed at Gallipoli a fleet of galleys, to command the Hellespont and intercept the Latin succours of Constantinople.   While the monarch indulged his passions in a boundless range of injustice and cruelty, he imposed on his soldiers the most rigid laws of modesty and abstinence, and the harvest was peaceably reaped and sold within the precincts of his camp.[89]   Provoked by the loose and corrupt administration of justice, he collected, in a house, the judges and lawyers of his dominions, who expected that in a few moments the fire would be kindled to reduce them to ashes.   His ministers trembled in silence; but an Æthiopian buffoon presumed to insinuate the true cause of the evil; and future venality was left without excuse by annexing an adequate salary to the office of Cadhi.[90]   The

---

[88] Cantemir, who celebrates the victories of the great Stephen over the Turks (p 47), had composed the ancient and modern state of his principality of Moldavia, which has been long promised, and is still unpublished.

[89] [The reign of Bayezid [Bāyezīd] was marked by a general corruption of morals and manners, propagated by the example of the court — especially of Bayezid himself and his grand vizir, Ali Pasha. See Zinkeisen. Gesch des osm Reiches, 1 p 384-6]

[90] Leunclav Annal Turcici, p. 318, 319   The venality of the cadhis has long been an object of scandal and satire; and, if we distrust the observations

humble title of Emir was no longer suitable to the Ottoman greatness, and Bajazet condescended to accept a patent of Sultan from the caliphs who served in Egypt under the yoke of the Mamalukes [91] a last and frivolous homage that was yielded by force to opinion, by the Turkish conquerors to the house of Abbas and the successors of the Arabian prophet. The ambition of the sultan was inflamed by the obligation of deserving this august title; and he turned his arms against the kingdom of Hungary, the perpetual theatre of the Turkish victories and defeats Sigismond, the Hungarian king, was the son and brother of the emperors of the West, his cause was that of Europe and the church; and, on the report of his danger, the bravest knights of France and Germany were eager to march under his standard and that of the cross. In the battle of Nicopolis, Bajazet defeated a confederate army of an hundred thousand Christians, who had proudly boasted that, if the sky should fall, they could uphold it on their lances. The far greater part were slain or driven into the Danube; and Sigismond, escaping to Constantinople by the river and the Black Sea, returned after a long circuit to his exhausted kingdom.[92] In the pride of victory, Bajazet threatened that he would besiege Buda, that he would subdue

of our travellers, we may consult the feeling of the Turks themselves (d'Herbelot, Bibliot Orientale, p 216, 217, 229, 230).

[91] The fact, which is attested by the Arabic history of Ben Schounah [Ibn-Shihna], a contemporary Syrian (de Guignes, Hist des Huns, tom iv p 336), destroys the testimony of Saad Effendi and Cantemir (p 14, 15), of the election of Othman to the dignity of Sultan

[92] See the Decades Rerum Hungaricarum (Dec. in l. ii p 379) of Bonfinius, an Italian, who, in the xvith century, was invited into Hungary to compose an eloquent history of that kingdom Yet, if it be extant and accessible, I should give the preference to some homely chronicle of the time and country [There is an account of the battle by John Schiltberger of Munich (who was made prisoner), in his story of his Bondage and Travels, 1394-1427, which has been translated into English by J B Telfer, 1879 (Hakluyt Society) Mirtschea the Great, prince of Walachia, who had been made prisoner at Kosovo, was also engaged at Nicopolis, as the ally of Sigismund, but seeing that the battle was hopeless, he drew off his forces in good time. He was followed by a Turkish force to Walachia, and defeated

the adjacent counties of Germany and Italy; and that he would feed his horse with a bushel of oats on the altar of St. Peter at Rome. His progress was checked, not by the miraculous interposition of the apostle, not by a crusade of the Christian powers, but by a long and painful fit of the gout The disorders of the moral, are sometimes corrected by those of the physical, world; and an acrimonious humour falling on a single fibre of one man may prevent or suspend the misery of nations.

Such is the general idea of the Hungarian war; but the disastrous adventure of the French has procured us some memorials which illustrate the victory and character of Bajazet.[93] The duke of Burgundy, sovereign of Flanders, and uncle of Charles the Sixth, yielded to the ardour of his son, John count of Nevers, and the fearless youth was accompanied by four princes, *his* cousins, and those of the French monarch. Their inexperience was guided by the Sire de Coucy, one of the best and oldest captains of Christendom;[94] but the constable, admiral, and marshal of France[95] com-

it near Craiova   On the confusion in the Turkish historians on the Nicopolis campaign, see Thúry, Torok torténetírók, i p 50 note.]

[93] I should not complain of the labour of this work, if my materials were always derived from such books as the Chronicle of honest Froissard (vol. iv c 67, 69, 72, 74, 79-83, 85, 87, 89), who read little, inquired much, and believed all   The original Mémoires of the Maréchal de Boucicault (Partie i c 22-28) add some facts, but they are dry and deficient, if compared with the pleasant garrulity of Froissard   [Very important is the Chronique du religieux de Saint Denys, published in a French translation under the title Histoire de Charles VI, roy de France, in 1663   The original Latin was first published by Bellaguet (in 6 vols) in 1839-52   There is a study on the work by H Delaborde, La vraie Chronique du Religieux de Saint Denis, 1890]

[94] An accurate Memoir on the life of Enguerrand VII Sire de Coucy, has been given by the Baron de Zurlauben (Hist de l'Académie des Inscriptions, tom xxv)   His rank and possessions were equally considerable in France and England, and, in 1375, he led an army of adventurers into Switzerland, to recover a large patrimony which he claimed in right of his grandmother, the daughter of the emperor Albert I of Austria (Sinner, Voyage dans la Suisse Occidentale, tom i p 118-124)

[95] That military office, so respectable at present, was still more con-

manded an army which did not exceed the number of a thousand knights and squires. Those splendid names were the
source of presumption and the bane of discipline. So many
might aspire to command that none were willing to obey,
their national spirit despised both their enemies and their
allies, and in the persuasion that Bajazet *would* fly or *must*
fall, they began to compute how soon they should visit Constantinople, and deliver the holy sepulchre. When their
scouts announced the approach of the Turks,[96] the gay and
thoughtless youths were at table, already heated with wine;
they instantly clasped their armour, mounted their horses,
rode full speed to the vanguard, and resented as an affront
the advice of Sigismond, which would have deprived them of
the right and honour of the foremost attack. The battle
of Nicopolis would not have been lost, if the French would
have obeyed the prudence of the Hungarians; but it might
have been gloriously won, had the Hungarians imitated the
valour of the French. They dispersed the first line, consisting
of the troops of Asia; forced a rampart of stakes, which had
been planted against the cavalry; broke, after a bloody
conflict, the Janizaries themselves, and were at length overwhelmed by the numerous squadrons [97] that issued from the
woods, and charged on all sides this handful of intrepid
warriors. In the speed and secrecy of his march, in the order
and evolutions of the battle, his enemies felt and admired the
military talents of Bajazet. They accuse his cruelty in the
use of victory. After reserving the count of Nevers, and four-
and-twenty lords, whose birth and riches were attested by his
Latin interpreters, the remainder of the French captives, who

spicuous when it was divided between two persons (Daniel, Hist. de la Milice
Françoise, tom ii p 5). One of these, the marshal of the crusade, was the
famous Boucicault, who afterwards defended Constantinople, governed
Genoa, invaded the coast of Asia, and died in the field of Azincour.

[96] [Bajezid was engaged in besieging Constantinople when he received
news that the Franks were besieging Nicopolis]

[97] [About half the Turkish army, which amounted altogether to about
100,000]

had survived the slaughter of the day, were led before his throne; and, as they refused to abjure their faith, were successively beheaded in his presence   The sultan was exasperated by the loss of his bravest Janizaries; and if it be true that, on the eve of the engagement, the French had mas-sacred their Turkish prisoners,[98] they might impute to them-selves the consequences of a just retaliation.   A knight, whose life had been spared, was permitted to return to Paris, that he might relate the deplorable tale and solicit the ran-som of the noble captives.   In the meanwhile the count of Nevers, with the princes and barons of France, were dragged along in the marches of the Turkish camp, exposed as a grateful trophy to the Moslems of Europe and Asia, and strictly confined at Boursa, as often as Bajazet resided in his capital.   The sultan was pressed each day to expiate with their blood the blood of his martyrs; but he had pronounced that they should live, and either for mercy or destruction his word was irrevocable.   He was assured of their value and impor-tance by the return of the messenger, and the gifts and inter-cessions of the kings of France and of Cyprus.   Lusignan presented him with a gold salt-cellar of curious workmanship and of the price of ten thousand ducats; and Charles the Sixth despatched by the way of Hungary a cast of Norwegian hawks, and six horse-loads of scarlet cloth, of fine linen of Rheims, and of Arras tapestry, representing the battles of the great Alexander.   After much delay, the effect of distance rather than of art, Bajazet agreed to accept a ransom of two hundred thousand ducats for the count of Nevers and the surviving princes and barons, the marshal Boucicault, a famous warrior, was of the number of the fortunate; but the admiral of France had been slain in the battle, and the con-stable, with the Sire de Coucy, died in the prison of Boursa.

---

[98] For this odious fact, the Abbé de Vertot quotes the Hist Anonyme de St Denys [see above note 93], l xvi c. 10, 11 (Ordre de Malthe, tom. ii p 310).

This heavy demand, which was doubled by incidental costs, fell chiefly on the duke of Burgundy, or rather on his Flemish subjects, who were bound by the feudal laws to contribute for the knighthood and captivity of the eldest son of their lord. For the faithful discharge of the debt, some merchants of Genoa gave security to the amount of five times the sum: a lesson to those warlike times that commerce and credit are the links of the society of nations. It had been stipulated in the treaty that the French captives should swear never to bear arms against the person of their conqueror, but the onerous restraint was abolished by Bajazet himself. "I despise," said he to the heir of Burgundy, "thy oaths and thy arms Thou art young, and mayest be ambitious of effacing the disgrace of misfortune of thy first chivalry. Assemble thy powers, proclaim thy design, and be assured that Bajazet will rejoice to meet thee a second time in a field of battle." Before their departure, they were indulged in the freedom and hospitality of the court of Boursa. The French princes admired the magnificence of the Ottoman, whose hunting and hawking equipage was composed of seven thousand huntsmen, and seven thousand falconers.[99] In their presence, and at his command, the belly of one of his chamberlains was cut open, on a complaint against him for drinking the goat's milk of a poor woman. The strangers were astonished by this act of justice, but it was the justice of a sultan who disdains to balance the weight of evidence or to measure the degrees of guilt.

After his enfranchisement from an oppressive guardian, John Palæologus remained thirty-six years the helpless and,

[99] Sherefeddin Ali (Hist de Timour Bec, l v c. 13) allows Bajazet a round number of 12,000 officers and servants of the chase. A part of his spoils was afterwards displayed in a hunting-match of Timour 1 Hounds with satin housings, 2 Leopards with collars set with jewels, 3 Grecian greyhounds, and, 4 dogs from Europe, as strong as African lions (idem, l vi c 15) Bajazet was particularly fond of flying his hawks at cranes (Chalcondyles, l. ii. p 35 [p 67 ed Bonn])

as it should seem, the careless spectator of the public ruin.[100]
Love, or rather lust, was his only vigorous passion; and in
the embraces of the wives and virgins of the city the Turkish
slave forgot the dishonour of the emperor of the *Romans*.
Andronicus, his eldest son, had formed, at Hadrianople,
an intimate and guilty friendship with Sauzes, the son
of Amurath; and the two youths conspired against the
authority and lives of their parents. The presence of Amurath in Europe soon discovered and dissipated their rash
counsels; and, after depriving Sauzes of his sight,[101] the
Ottoman threatened his vassal with the treatment of an
accomplice and an enemy, unless he inflicted a similar
punishment on his own son. Palæologus trembled and
obeyed; and a cruel precaution involved in the same sentence
the childhood and innocence of John, the son of the criminal.
But the operation was so mildly, or so unskilfully, performed
that the one retained the sight of an eye and the other was
afflicted only with the infirmity of squinting. Thus excluded from the succession, the two princes were confined
in the tower of Anema; and the piety of Manuel, the second
son of the reigning monarch, was rewarded with the gift of the
Imperial crown   But at the end of two years the turbulence
of the Latins and the levity of the Greeks produced a revolution; and the two emperors were buried in the tower from
whence the two prisoners were exalted to the throne. Another
period of two years afforded Palæologus and Manuel the
means of escape. It was contrived by the magic or subtlety
of a monk, who was alternately named the angel or the devil.
They fled to Scutari; their adherents armed in their cause;
and the two Byzantine factions displayed the ambition and
animosity with which Cæsar and Pompey had disputed the

[100] For the reigns of John Palæologus and his son Manuel, from 1354 to
1402, see Ducas, c 9–15, Phranza, l 1 c 16–21, and the 1st and 2d books of
Chalcondyles, whose proper subject is drowned in a sea of episode

[101] [And beheading him   The prince's name, Saudshi, is given rightly by
Chalcondyles Saûzes, but Ducas and Phrantzes give wrong names.]

empire of the world. The Roman world was now contracted to a corner of Thrace, between the Propontis and the Black Sea, about fifty miles in length and thirty in breadth, a space of ground not more extensive than the lesser principalities of Germany or Italy, if the remains of Constantinople had not still represented the wealth and populousness of a kingdom. To restore the public peace, it was found necessary to divide this fragment of the empire, and, while Palæologus and Manuel were left in possession of the capital, almost all that lay without the walls was ceded to the blind princes, who fixed their residence at Rhodosto and Selybria [102] In the tranquil slumber of royalty, the passions of John Palæologus survived his reason and his strength; he deprived his favourite and heir of a blooming princess of Trebizond; and, while the feeble emperor laboured to consummate his nuptials, Manuel, with an hundred of the noblest Greeks, was sent on a peremptory summons to the Ottoman *porte*. They served with honour in the wars of Bajazet; but a plan of fortifying Constantinople excited his jealousy, he threatened their lives; the new works were instantly demolished; and we shall bestow a praise, perhaps above the merit of Palæologus, if we impute this last humiliation as the cause of his death.

The earliest intelligence of that event was communicated to Manuel, who escaped with speed and secrecy from the palace of Boursa to the Byzantine throne. Bajazet affected a proud indifference at the loss of this valuable pledge, and, while he pursued his conquests in Europe and Asia, he left the emperor to struggle with his blind cousin, John of Selybria, who, in eight years of civil war, asserted his right of primogeniture. At length the ambition of the victorious sultan pointed to the conquest of Constantinople, but he listened to the advice of his vizir, who represented that such an enterprise might unite the powers of Christendom in a second and more formidable

---

[102] [A confirmation of this treaty by the Patriarch Nilus (1380-8) is published in the Sitzungsberichte of the Vienna Academy 1851, p 345]

crusade   His epistle to the emperor was conceived in these
words: "By the divine clemency, our invincible scymetar
has reduced to our obedience almost all Asia, with many and
large countries in Europe, excepting only the city of Constantinople, for beyond the walls thou hast nothing left.
Resign that city, stipulate thy reward, or tremble for thyself
and thy unhappy people at the consequences of a rash refusal." But his ambassadors were instructed to soften their
tone, and to propose a treaty, which was subscribed with submission and gratitude. A truce of ten years was purchased
by an annual tribute of thirty thousand crowns of gold; the
Greeks deplored the public toleration of the law of Mahomet;
and Bajazet enjoyed the glory of establishing a Turkish
cadhi and founding a royal mosch in the metropolis of the
Eastern church.[103]   Yet this truce was soon violated by the
restless sultan. In the cause of the prince of Selybria, the
lawful emperor,[104] an army of Ottomans again threatened
Constantinople; and the distress of Manuel implored the
protection of the king of France. His plaintive embassy
obtained much pity, and some relief; and the conduct of the
succour was entrusted to the marshal Boucicault,[105] whose
religious chivalry was inflamed by the desire of revenging his
captivity on the infidels. He sailed with four ships of war
from Aiguesmortes to the Hellespont; forced the passage,
which was guarded by seventeen Turkish galleys, landed at
Constantinople a supply of six hundred men at arms and
sixteen hundred archers, and reviewed them in the adjacent
plain, without condescending to number or array the multitude of Greeks. By his presence, the blockade was raised

[103] Cantemir, p 50–53   Of the Greeks, Ducas alone (c. 13, 15) acknowledges the Turkish cadhi at Constantinople   Yet even Ducas dissembles the mosch

[104] [The Sultan had forced John to come forward as pretender to the throne,
extorting a secret promise that he would hand over Constantinople to himself]

[105] Mémoires du bon Messire Jean le Maingre, dit *Boucicault*, Maréchal
de France, partie 1. c. 30–35.

both by sea and land; the flying squadrons of Bajazet were driven to a more respectful distance; and several castles in Europe and Asia were stormed by the emperor and the marshal, who fought with equal valour by each other's side But the Ottomans soon returned with an increase of numbers; and the intrepid Boucicault, after a year's struggle, resolved to evacuate a country which could no longer afford either pay or provisions for his soldiers. The marshal offered to conduct Manuel to the French court, where he might solicit in person a supply of men and money; and advised in the meanwhile that, to extinguish all domestic discord, he should leave his blind competitor on the throne. The proposal was embraced, the prince of Selybria was introduced to the capital, and such was the public misery that the lot of the exile seemed more fortunate than that of the sovereign Instead of applauding the success of his vassal, the Turkish sultan claimed the city as his own; and, on the refusal of the emperor John, Constantinople was more closely pressed by the calamities of war and famine. Against such an enemy prayers and resistance were alike unavailing; and the savage would have devoured his prey, if, in the fatal moment, he had not been overthrown by another savage stronger than himself. By the victory of Timour, or Tamerlane, the fall of Constantinople was delayed about fifty years; and this important though accidental service may justly introduce the life and character of the Mogul conqueror.

CHAPTER LXV

*Elevation of Timour, or Tamerlane, to the Throne of Samar-
cand — His Conquests in Persia, Georgia, Tartary,
Russia, India, Syria, and Anatolia — His Turkish
War — Defeat and Captivity of Bajazet — Death of
Timour — Civil War of the Sons of Bajazet — Restora-
tion of the Turkish Monarchy by Mahomet the First —
Siege of Constantinople by Amurath the Second*

THE conquest and monarchy of the world was the first
object of the ambition of TIMOUR. To live in the memory
and esteem of future ages was the second wish of his
magnanimous spirit   All the civil and military transactions
of his reign were diligently recorded in the journals of his
secretaries;[1] the authentic narrative was revised by the
persons best informed of each particular transaction; and
it is believed in the empire and family of Timour that
the monarch himself composed the *commentaries*[2] of his

---

[1] These journals were communicated to Sherefeddin, or Cherefeddin Ali, a
native of Yezd, who composed in the Persian language a history of Timour
Beg [entitled Zafar Nāma = Book of Victory] which has been translated
into French by M Petis de la Croix (Paris, 1722, in 4 vols 12mo), and has
always been my faithful guide   [Translated into English under the title,
The History of Timur Beg (in 2 vols), 1723] His geography and chronology are wonderfully accurate , and he may be trusted for public facts, though
he servilely praises the virtue and fortune of the hero   Timour's attention
to procure intelligence from his own and foreign countries may be seen in the
Institutions, p 215, 217, 349, 351   [There is an older Life of Timur, bearing
the same title as that of Sheref ad-Dīn (Book of Victory). It was written by
Nizām Shāmī, at the command of Timur himself. The work has never
been published, but an edition is promised by Professor E Denison Ross
from a MS. in the British Museum dated 1434   See note in Skrine and Ross,
The Heart of Asia, p 168]

[2] These commentaries are yet unknown in Europe but Mr White gives

life and the *institutions* [3] of his government [4] But these cares were ineffectual for the preservation of his fame, and these precious memorials in the Mogul or Persian language were concealed from the world, or at least from the knowledge of Europe. The nations which he vanquished exercised a base and impotent revenge, and ignorance has long repeated the tale of calumny,[5] which had disfigured the birth and character, the person, and even the name of *Tamerlane*.[6] Yet his real merit would be enhanced, rather than debased, by the elevation of a peasant to the throne of Asia, nor can his lameness be a theme of reproach, unless he had the weakness to blush at a natural, or perhaps an honourable, infirmity.

some hope that they may be imported and translated by his friend Major Davy, who had read in the East this "minute and faithful narrative of an interesting and eventful period" [See Appendix 1]

[3] I am ignorant whether the original institution, in the Turkish or Mogul language, be still extant. The Persic version, with an English translation and most valuable index, was published (Oxford, 1783, in 4to) by the joint labours of Major Davy and Mr White, the Arabic professor This work has been since translated from the Persic into French (Paris, 1787) by M Langlès, a learned Orientalist, who has added the Life of Timour and many curious notes

[4] Shaw Allum, the present Mogul, reads, values, but cannot imitate the institutions of his great ancestor The English translator relies on their internal evidence, but, if any suspicions should arise of fraud and fiction, they will not be dispelled by Major Davy's letter The Orientals have never cultivated the art of criticism, the patronage of a prince, less honourable perhaps, is not less lucrative than that of a bookseller, nor can it be deemed incredible that a Persian, the *real* author, should renounce the credit, to raise the value and price, of the work.

[5] The original of the tale is found in the following work, which is much esteemed for its florid elegance of style *Ahmedis Arabsiadæ* (Ahmed Ebn Arabshaw) *Vitæ et Rerum gestarum Timuri Arabice et Latine Edidit Samuel Henricus Manger Franequeræ*, 1767, 2 tom in 4to This Syrian author is ever a malicious and often an ignorant enemy, the very titles of his chapters are injurious, as how the wicked, as how the impious, as how the viper, &c The copious article of TIMUR in Bibliothèque Orientale, is of a mixed nature, as d'Herbelot indifferently draws his materials (p 877-888) from Khondemir, Ebn Schounah, and the Lebtarikh.

[6] *Demir* or *Timour* [Timūr] signifies, in the Turkish language, iron, and *Beg* is the appellation of a lord or prince By the change of a letter or accent

In the eyes of the Moguls, who held the indefeasible succession of the house of Zingis, he was doubtless a rebel-subject;
yet he sprang from the noble tribe of Berlass: his fifth ancestor, Carashar Nevian, had been the vizir of Zagatai, in his
new realm of Transoxiana; and, in the ascent of some generations, the branch of Timour is confounded, at least by the
females,[7] with the Imperial stem [8] He was born forty miles
to the south of Samarcand, in the village of Sebzar,[9] in the
fruitful territory of Cash, of which his fathers were the hereditary chiefs, as well as of a toman of ten thousand horse.[10]
His birth [11] was cast on one of those periods of anarchy which

it is changed into *Lenc* [Lang], or lame, and a European corruption confounds the two words in the name of Tamerlane   [Timur's lameness was
due to an arrow wound in the foot, received in a battle in Sîstân, when he was
conquering the countries south of the Oxus, before he won Transoxiana]

[7] After relating some false and foolish tales of Timour *Lenc*, Arabshah is
compelled to speak truth, and to own him for a kinsman of Zingis, per
mulieres (as he peevishly adds) laqueos Satanæ (pars i c. 1. p 25)   The
testimony of Abulghazi Khan (p ii c 5, p v c. 4) is clear, unquestionable,
and decisive   [M Cahun also agrees that the claim to connection with the
family of Chingiz was justified]

[8] According to one of the pedigrees, the fourth ancestor of Zingis, and the
ninth of Timour, were brothers, and they agreed that the posterity of the
elder should succeed to the dignity of Khan, and that the descendants of
the younger should fill the office of their minister and general   This tradition was at least convenient to justify the *first* steps of Timour's ambition
(Institutions, p 24, 25, from the MS fragments of Timour's History).

[9] [Not Sebzewâr but Shehr-i-sebz   The province of Kesh had been given
as a fief to Taragai, Timur's father, by Kazghan, the emir or governor of
Transoxiana]

[10] See the preface of Sherefeddin, and Abulfeda's Geography (Chorasmiæ,
&c Descriptio, p 60, 61), in the 3d volume of Hudson's Minor Greek Geographers   [Timur's family, the Barlas, belonged to the clan of the Kurikan
(or Kureken) a Turkish clan mentioned in one of the old Turkish inscriptions of A D 733 (see above, vol vii p 399)   Thus Timur was a Turk not a
Mongol   Cp Cahun, Intr á l'histoire de l'Asie, p 444–445]

[11] See his nativity in Dr Hyde (Syntagma Dissertat tom ii p 466), as it
was cast by the astrologers of his grandson Ulugh Beg   He was born A D.
1336, 9th April, 11° 57′ P M lat 36   I know not whether they can prove
the great conjunction of the planets from whence, like other conquerors and
prophets, Timour derived the surname of Saheb Keran, or master of the
conjunctions (Bibliot Orient p 878)   [Ulugh Beg founded his observatory

announce the fall of the Asiatic dynasties and open a new field
to adventurous ambition   The khans of Zagatai were extinct;
the emirs aspired to independence, and their domestic feuds
could only be suspended by the conquest and tyranny of the
khans of Kashgar, who, with an army of Getes or Calmucks,[12]
invaded the Transoxian kingdom.   From the twelfth year of
his age Timour had entered the field of action, in the twenty-
fifth, he stood forth as the deliverer of his country;[13] and the
eyes and wishes of the people were turned towards an hero
who suffered in their cause.   The chiefs of the law and of the
army had pledged their salvation to support him with their
lives and fortunes, but in the hour of danger they were silent
and afraid, and, after waiting seven days on the hills of Samarcand, he retreated to the desert with only sixty horsemen.
The fugitives were overtaken by a thousand Getes, whom
he repulsed with incredible slaughter, and his enemies were

at Samarcand in 1428   The "Gurganian" astronomical tables were cal-
culated there]

[12] In the institutions of Timour, these subjects of the Khan of Kashgar
are most improperly styled Ouzbegs, or Uzbeks, a name which belongs to
another branch and country of Tartars (Abulghazi, p v c 5; p vii c. 5)
Could I be sure that this word is in the Turkish original, I would boldly
pronounce that the Institutions were framed a century after the death of
Timour, since the establishment of the Uzbeks in Transoxiana   [The people
of the Kirghiz steppes now came to be known as Uzbegs, and the reading in
Timur's Institutes is quite genuine   Gibbon, with others, probably thought
the Jātā were Getæ   It is like the inveterate mistake (into which he also
falls) of confounding the Goths with the Getæ (who were Dacians)   Jātā
is regularly used for Mogolistān in the Zafar Nāma   It is a nickname,
meaning "ne'er-do-well," applied to Central Asian Mongols by their neighbours   Petis de la Croix translated it Geta]

[13] [Timur had not entered the field of action so early   He says in his
Memoirs that from the age of twelve he could receive his visitors with dignity
At eighteen, he was a good knight, skilled in the science of venery, and
amused himself with reading pious books, playing chess, and exercising himself in arms   At twenty-two, we find him taking part (A D 1458) in an
expedition of Kazghan the emir against the Iranians of Khorasan   On
Kazghan's death, Timur (by the advice of the religious orders of Islam)
supported the Chagatāy sultan Taghlak-Timur, who first made him emir of
Transoxiana, and then deposed him in favour of his own son   Then Timur
took to the desert]

forced to exclaim, "Timour is a wonderful man; fortune and the divine favour are with him." But in this bloody action his own followers were reduced to ten, a number which was soon diminished by the desertion of three Carizmians [14] He wandered in the desert with his wife, seven companions, and four horses, and sixty-two days was he plunged in a loathsome dungeon, from whence he escaped by his own courage and the remorse of the oppressor. After swimming the broad and rapid stream of the Jihoon, or Oxus, he led during some months the life of a vagrant and outlaw, on the borders of the adjacent states. But his fame shone brighter in adversity; he learned to distinguish the friends of his person, the associates of his fortune, and to apply the various characters of men for their advantage, and above all for his own. On his return to his native country, Timour was successively joined by the parties of his confederates, who anxiously sought him in the desert, nor can I refuse to describe, in his pathetic simplicity, one of their fortunate encounters. He presented himself as a guide to three chiefs, who were at the head of seventy horse. "When their eyes fell upon me," says Timour, "they were overwhelmed with joy; and they alighted from their horses; and they came and kneeled; and they kissed my stirrup. I also came down from my horse, and took each of them in my arms. And I put my turban on the head of the first chief; and my girdle, rich in jewels and wrought with gold, I bound on the loins of the second; and the third I clothed in my own coat. And they wept, and I wept also; and the hour of prayer was arrived, and we prayed. And we mounted our horses and came to my dwelling; and I collected my people and made a feast." His trusty bands were soon increased by the bravest of the tribes; he led them against a superior foe; and after some vicissitudes of war the Getes were

[14] [Timur himself says he had ten left, Sheref ad-Din says seven. The name of Timur's brave wife, who was with him throughout his adventures, was Oljai]

finally driven from the kingdom of Transoxiana. He had done much for his own glory, but much remained to be done, much art to be exerted, and some blood to be spilt, before he could teach his equals to obey him as their master. The birth and power of emir Houssein compelled him to accept a vicious and unworthy colleague, whose sister was the best beloved of his wives. Their union was short and jealous, but the policy of Timour, in their frequent quarrels, exposed his rival to the reproach of injustice and perfidy, and, after a small defeat, Houssein was slain by some sagacious friends, who presumed, for the last time, to disobey the commands of their lord. At the age of thirty-four,[15] and in a general diet, or *couroultai*, he was invested with *Imperial* command; but he affected to revere the house of Zingis, and, while the emir Timour reigned over Zagatai and the East, a nominal khan served as a private officer in the armies of his servant. A fertile kingdom, five hundred miles in length and in breadth, might have satisfied the ambition of a subject; but Timour aspired to the dominion of the world; and before his death the crown of Zagatai was one of the twenty-seven crowns which he had placed on his head. Without expatiating on the victories of thirty-five campaigns; without describing the lines of march, which he repeatedly traced over the continent of Asia; I shall briefly represent his conquests in I Persia, II. Tartary, and III. India;[16] and from thence proceed to the more interesting narrative of his Ottoman war.

I. For every war, a motive of safety or revenge, of honour or zeal, of right or convenience, may be readily found in the

[15] The 1st book of Sherefeddin is employed on the private life of the hero, and he himself, or his secretary (Institutions, p. 3-77), enlarges with pleasure on the thirteen designs and enterprises which most truly constitute his *personal* merit. It even shines through the dark colouring of Arabshah, p 1 c 1-12.

[16] The conquests of Persia, Tartary, and India are represented in the iid and iiid books of Sherefeddin, and by Arabshah, c. 13-55. Consult the excellent Indexes to the Institutions

jurisprudence of conquerors. No sooner had Timour reunited to the patrimony of Zagatai the dependent countries
of Carizme and Candahar, than he turned his eyes towards
the kingdoms of Iran or Persia. From the Oxus to the Tigris
that extensive country was left without a lawful sovereign since
the death of Abousaid, the last of the descendants of the great
Holacou.[17] Peace and justice had been banished from the
land above forty years, and the Mogul invader might seem
to listen to the cries of an oppressed people. Their petty
tyrants might have opposed him with confederate arms; they
separately stood, and successively fell; and the difference of
their fate was only marked by the promptitude of submission
or the obstinacy of resistance. Ibrahim, prince of Shirwan or
Albania, kissed the footstool of the Imperial throne. His
peace-offerings of silks, horses, and jewels were composed,
according to the Tartar fashion, each article of nine pieces;
but a critical spectator observed that there were only eight
slaves "I myself am the ninth," replied Ibrahim, who was
prepared for the remark; and his flattery was rewarded by the
smile of Timour [18] Shah Mansour, prince of Fars or the
proper Persia, was one of the least powerful, but most dangerous, of his enemies In a battle under the walls of Shiraz,
he broke, with three or four thousand soldiers, the *coul* or
main body of thirty thousand horse, where the emperor fought
in person. No more than fourteen or fifteen guards remained
near the standard of Timour; he stood firm as a rock, and
received on his helmet two weighty strokes of a scymetar; [19]
the Moguls rallied; the head of Mansour was thrown at his feet,

---

[17] [Rather Mūsā A D 1336 Abū Sa'īd reigned 1316–1335 See Lane-
Poole, Mohammadan Dynasties, p 220]

[18] The reverence of the Tartars for the mysterious number of *nine* is
declared by Abulghazi Khan, who, for that reason, divides his Genealogical
History into nine parts

[19] According to Arabshah (p i c 28, p 183), the coward Timour ran
away to his tent, and hid himself from the pursuit of Shah Mansour under
the women's garments. Perhaps Sherefeddin (l ii c 25) has magnified his
courage

and he declared his esteem of the valour of a foe by extirpating
all the males of so intrepid a race. From Shiraz, his troops advanced to the Persian Gulf; and the richness and weakness of
Ormuz [20] were displayed in an annual tribute of six hundred
thousand dinars of gold. Bagdad was no longer the city of
peace, the seat of the caliphs; but the noblest conquest of
Houlacou could not be overlooked by his ambitious successor.
The whole course of the Tigris and Euphrates, from the mouth
to the sources of those rivers, was reduced to his obedience. He
entered Edessa; and the Turkmans of the black sheep were
chastised for the sacrilegious pillage of a caravan of Mecca.
In the mountains of Georgia, the native Christians still braved
the law and the sword of Mahomet, by three expeditions
he obtained the merit of the *gazie*, or holy war, and the Prince
of Teflis became his proselyte and friend

II. A just retaliation might be urged for the invasion of
Turkestan, or the Eastern Tartary. The dignity of Timour
could not endure the impunity of the Getes; he passed the
Sihoon, subdued the kingdom of Cashgar, and marched seven
times into the heart of their country. His most distant camp
was two months' journey, or four hundred and eighty leagues
to the north-east of Samarcand, and his emirs, who traversed the
river Irtish, engraved in the forests of Siberia a rude memorial
of their exploits. The conquest of Kipzak, or the Western Tartary,[21] was founded on the double motive of aiding the dis-

[20] The history of Ormuz is not unlike that of Tyre   The old city, on the
continent, was destroyed by the Tartars, and renewed [in the 14th cent] in
a neighbouring island without fresh water or vegetation   The kings of
Ormuz, rich in the Indian trade and the pearl fishery, possessed large territories both in Persia and Arabia, but they were at first the tributaries of
the sultans of Kerman, and at last were delivered (A D 1505) by the Portuguese
tyrants from the tyranny of their own vizirs (Marco Polo, l i c. 15, 16, fol 7,
8, Abulfeda Geograph tabul xi p 261, 262, an original Chronicle of
Ormuz, in Texeira, or Stevens' History of Persia, p 376-416, and the
Itineraries inserted in the 1st volume of Ramusio, of Ludovico Barthema
(1503), fol 167, of Andrea Corsali (1517), fol 202, 203; and of Odoardo
Barbessa (in 1516), fol 315-318).
[21] Arabshah had travelled into Kipzak, and acquired a singular know-

tressed and chastising the ungrateful. Toctamish, a fugitive prince, was entertained and protected in his court, the ambassadors of Auruss Khan were dismissed with an haughty denial, and followed on the same day by the armies of Zagatai, and their success established Toctamish in the Mogul empire of the North   But, after a reign of ten years, the new khan forgot the merits and the strength of his benefactor, the base usurper, as he deemed him, of the sacred rights of the house of Zingis.   Through the gates of Derbend, he entered Persia at the head of ninety thousand horse; with the innumerable forces of Kipzak, Bulgaria, Circassia, and Russia, he passed the Sihoon, burnt the palaces of Timour, and compelled him, amidst the winter snows, to contend for Samarcand and his life   After a mild expostulation, and a glorious victory, the emperor resolved on revenge; and by the east and the west of the Caspian and the Volga, he twice invaded Kipzak with such mighty [22] powers that thirteen miles were

ledge of the geography, cities, and revolutions of that Northern region (p i c 45–49)   [The position of Tôktämish cannot be understood without a knowledge of the relations of the rulers of the Golden Horde   Orda, the eldest son of Jūjī (eldest son of Chingiz Khan) had succeeded his father in the rule over the tribes north of the Jaxartes   The tribes of the Western Kipchak (the regions of the Volga and Ural, north of the Caspian) had been conquered by Bātū, a younger son of Jūjī (see above, p 144–147)   Tūka-Tīmūr, another son, ruled over Great Bulgaria on the Middle Volga, and a fourth, named Shaybān, was lord of the Kirghiz Kazaks, in Siberia, to the north of Orda's land   The tribes ruled over by all these brothers and their descendants were included under the "Golden Horde," which derived its name from the Sir Orda, the *golden camp* of the Khan   The tribes under the line of Orda were called the White Horde, and the Khans of this line were nominally the head of the family   The tribes subject to Bātū's line were the Blue Horde, and they were far the most important   The line of Bātū came to an end in 1358, and after 20 years of anarchy Tôktämish won the Khanate with Timur's help in 1378   Tôktämish was a descendant of Orda, and had won the lordship of the White Horde in 1376   Under him the Khanate of the Golden Horde reasserted itself in Russia, and Moscow was burned in 1382]

[22] [Timur routed Tôktämish in 1391 at Urtupa, and in 1395 on the Terek By thus destroying the power of the Khanate of the Golden Horde, Timur involuntarily delivered Russia]

measured from his right to his left wing. In a march of five months, they rarely beheld the footsteps of man; and their daily subsistence was often trusted to the fortune of the chase. At length the armies encountered each other; but the treachery of the standard-bearer, who, in the heat of action, reversed the Imperial standard of Kipzak, determined the victory of the Zagatais; and Toctamish (I speak the language of the Institutions) gave the tribe of Toushi to the wind of desolation.[23] He fled to the Christian duke of Lithuania; again returned to the banks of the Volga; and, after fifteen battles with a domestic rival, at last perished in the wilds of Siberia. The pursuit of a flying enemy carried Timour into the tributary provinces of Russia; a duke of the reigning family was made prisoner amidst the ruins of his capital, and Yeletz, by the pride and ignorance of the Orientals, might easily be confounded with the genuine metropolis of the nation   Moscow trembled at the approach of the Tartar, and the resistance would have been feeble, since the hopes of the Russians were placed in a miraculous image of the Virgin, to whose protection they ascribed the casual and voluntary retreat of the conqueror. Ambition and prudence recalled him to the south, the desolate country was exhausted, and the Mogul soldiers were enriched with an immense spoil of precious furs, of linen of Antioch,[24] and of ingots of gold and silver [25]   On the banks of the Don, or Tanais, he received an humble deputation from the consuls

[23] Institutions of Timour, p 123, 125   Mr. White, the editor, bestows some animadversion on the superficial account of Sherefeddin (l m c 12-14), who was ignorant of the designs of Timour, and the true springs of action [M Charmoy contributed to the 3rd vol of the Transactions of the Academy of St Petersburg an important account of these campaigns of Timur]
[24] The furs of Russia are more credible than the ingots. But the linen of Antioch has never been famous; and Antioch was in ruins   I suspect that it was some manufacture of Europe, which the Hanse merchants had imported by the way of Novogorod
[25] M Levesque (Hist de Russie, tom ii p 247. Vie de Timour, p 64-67, before the French version of the Institutes) has corrected the error of Sherefeddin, and marked the true limit of Timour's conquests   His arguments are superfluous, and a simple appeal to the Russian annals is suffi-

and merchants of Egypt,[26] Venice, Genoa, Catalonia, and Biscay, who occupied the commerce and city of Tana, or Azoph, at the mouth of the river. They offered their gifts, admired his magnificence, and trusted his royal word. But the peaceful visit of an emir, who explored the state of the magazines and harbour, was speedily followed by the destructive presence of the Tartars. The city was reduced to ashes; the Moslems were pillaged and dismissed; but all the Christians who had not fled to their ships were condemned either to death or slavery.[27] Revenge prompted him to burn the cities of Serai and Astrachan, the monuments of rising civilisation; and his vanity proclaimed that he had penetrated to the region of perpetual daylight, a strange phenomenon, which authorised his Mahometan doctors to dispense with the obligation of evening prayer.[28]

III. When Timour first proposed to his princes and emirs the invasion of India or Hindostan,[29] he was answered by a murmur of discontent: "The rivers! and the mountains and

cient to prove that Moscow, which six years before had been taken by Toctamish [A.D. 1382], escaped the arms of a more formidable invader.

[26] An Egyptian consul from Grand Cairo is mentioned in Barbaro's voyage to Tana in 1436, after the city had been rebuilt (Ramusio, tom. ii. fol. 92).

[27] The sack of Azoph is described by Sherefeddin (l. iii. c. 55), and much more particularly by the author of an Italian chronicle (Andreas de Redusiis de Quero, in Chron. Tarvisiano, in Muratori Script. Rerum Italicarum, tom. xix. p. 802-805). He had conversed with the Mianis, two Venetian brothers, one of whom had been sent a deputy to the camp of Timour, and the other had lost at Azoph three sons and 12,000 ducats. [After the disintegration of the Golden Horde by Timūr, the house of Tūka-Timūr (see above note 21) begins to come into prominence. Members of this house established the three Khanates of Kazan, the Crimea, and Kazimov.]

[28] Sherefeddin only says (l. iii. c. 13) that the rays of the setting, and those of the rising, sun were scarcely separated by any interval: a problem which may be solved in the latitude of Moscow (the 56th degree) with the aid of the Aurora Borealis and a long summer twilight. But a *day* of forty days (Khondemir apud d'Herbelot, p. 880) would rigorously confine us within the polar circle.

[29] For the Indian war, see the Institutions (p. 129-139), the fourth book of Sherefeddin, and the history of Ferishta (in Dow, vol. ii. p. 1-20), which throws a general light on the affairs of Hindostan.

deserts! and the soldiers clad in armour! and the elephants, destroyers of men!'" But the displeasure of the emperor was more dreadful than all these terrors; and his superior reason was convinced that an enterprise of such tremendous aspect was safe and easy in the execution. He was informed by his spies of the weakness and anarchy of Hindostan, the soubahs of the provinces had erected the standard of rebellion; and the perpetual infancy of Sultan Mahmoud was despised even in the harem of Delhi. The Mogul army moved in three great divisions, and Timour observes with pleasure that the ninety-two squadrons of a thousand horse most fortunately corresponded with the ninety-two names or epithets of the prophet Mahomet. Between the Jihoon and the Indus, they crossed one of the ridges of mountains, which are styled by the Arabian geographers the Stony Girdles of the Earth. The high-land robbers were subdued or extirpated; but great numbers of men and horses perished in the snow; the emperor himself was let down a precipice on a portable scaffold, the ropes were one hundred and fifty cubits in length; and, before he could reach the bottom, this dangerous operation was five times repeated. Timour crossed the Indus at the ordinary passage of Attok; and successively traversed, in the footsteps of Alexander, the *Punjab*, or five rivers,[30] that fall into the master-stream. From Attok to Delhi the high-road measures no more than six hundred miles; but the two conquerors deviated to the south-east; and the motive of Timour was to join his grandson who had achieved by his command the conquest of Moultan. On the eastern bank of the Hyphasis, on the edge of the desert, the Macedonian hero halted and wept; the Mogul entered the desert, reduced the fortress of Batnir, and stood in arms before the gates of Delhi, a great and flourishing city, which had subsisted three centuries under the

[30] The rivers of the Punjab, the five eastern branches of the Indus, have been laid down for the first time with truth and accuracy in Major Rennell's incomparable map of Hindostan In his Critical Memoir he illustrates with judgment and learning the marches of Alexander and Timour.

dominion of the Mahometan kings. The siege, more especially of the castle, might have been a work of time; but he tempted, by the appearance of weakness, the sultan Mahmoud and his vizir to descend into the plain, with ten thousand cuirassiers, forty thousand of his foot-guards, and one hundred and twenty elephants, whose tusks are said to have been armed with sharp and poisoned daggers. Against these monsters, or rather against the imagination of his troops, he condescended to use some extraordinary precautions of fire and a ditch, of iron spikes and a rampart of bucklers; but the event taught the Moguls to smile at their own fears; and, as soon as these unwieldy animals were routed, the inferior species (the men of India) disappeared from the field. Timour made his triumphal entry into the capital of Hindostan; and admired, with a view to imitate, the architecture of the stately mosch; but the order or licence of a general pillage and massacre polluted the festival of his victory. He resolved to purify his soldiers in the blood of the idolaters, or Gentoos, who still surpass, in the proportion of ten to one, the numbers of the Moslems. In this pious design, he advanced one hundred miles to the north-east of Delhi, passed the Ganges, fought several battles by land and water, and penetrated to the famous rock of Coupele, the statue of the cow, that *seems* to discharge the mighty river, whose source is far distant among the mountains of Thibet.[31] His return was along the skirts of the northern hills; nor could this rapid campaign of one year justify the strange foresight of his emirs that their children in a warm climate would degenerate into a race of Hindoos.

[31] The two great rivers, the Ganges and Burrampooter [Brahmapootra], rise in Thibet, from the opposite ridges of the same hills, separate from each other to the distance of 1200 miles, and, after a winding course of 2000 miles, again meet in one point near the gulf of Bengal. Yet, so capricious is fame that the Burrampooter is a late discovery, while his brother Ganges has been the theme of ancient and modern story. Coupele, the scene of Timour's last victory, must be situate near Loldong, 1100 miles from Calcutta; and, in 1774, a British camp! (Rennell's Memoir, p. 7, 59, 90, 91, 99).

It was on the banks of the Ganges that Timour was informed, by his speedy messengers, of the disturbances which had arisen on the confines of Georgia and Anatolia, of the revolt of the Christians, and the ambitious designs of the sultan Bajazet. His vigour of mind and body was not impaired by sixty-three years and innumerable fatigues; and, after enjoying some tranquil months in the palace of Samarcand, he proclaimed a new expedition of seven years into the western countries of Asia.[32] To the soldiers who had served in the Indian war, he granted the choice of remaining at home or following their prince; but the troops of all the provinces and kingdoms of Persia were commanded to assemble at Ispahan and wait the arrival of the Imperial standard. It was first directed against the Christians of Georgia, who were strong only in their rocks, their castles, and the winter-season; but these obstacles were overcome by the zeal and perseverance of Timour; the rebels submitted to the tribute or the Koran; and, if both religions boasted of their martyrs, that name is more justly due to the Christian prisoners, who were offered the choice of abjuration or death. On his descent from the hills, the emperor gave audience to the first ambassadors of Bajazet, and opened the hostile correspondence of complaints and menaces, which fermented two years before the final explosion. Between two jealous and haughty neighbours, the motives of quarrel will seldom be wanting. The Mogul and Ottoman conquests now touched each other in the neighbourhood of Erzeroum and the Euphrates; nor had the doubtful limit been ascertained by time and treaty. Each of these ambitious monarchs might accuse his rival of violating his territory, of threatening his vassals, and protecting his rebels; and, by the name of rebels, each understood the fugitive princes, whose kingdoms he had usurped and whose life or liberty he implacably pursued. The resemblance of character

[32] See the Institutions, p 141, to the end of the 1st book, and Sherefeddin (l. v. c 1-16), to the entrance of Timour into Syria

\ 'I x   ' ,

was still more dangerous than the opposition of interest; and, in their victorious career, Timour was impatient of an equal, and Bajazet was ignorant of a superior. The first epistle [33] of the Mogul emperor must have provoked instead of reconciling the Turkish sultan, whose family and nation he affected to despise. [34] "Dost thou not know that the greatest part of Asia is subject to our arms and our laws? that our invincible forces extend from one sea to the other? that the potentates of the earth form a line before our gate? and that we have compelled Fortune herself to watch over the prosperity of our empire? What is the foundation of thy insolence and folly? Thou hast fought some battles in the woods of Anatolia; contemptible trophies! Thou hast obtained some victories over the Christians of Europe; thy sword was blessed by the apostle of God; and thy obedience to the precept of the Koran, in waging war against the infidels, is the sole consideration that prevents us from destroying thy country, the frontier and bulwark of the Moslem world. Be wise in time; reflect; repent; and avert the thunder of our vengeance, which is yet suspended over thy head. Thou art no more than a pismire; why wilt thou seek to provoke the elephants? Alas! they will trample thee under their feet." In his replies, Bajazet poured forth the indignation of a soul which was deeply stung by such unusual contempt. After retorting the basest reproaches on the thief and rebel of the desert, the Ottoman recapitulates his boasted victories in Iran,

[33] We have three copies of these hostile epistles in the Institutions (p. 147), in Sherefeddin (l. v. c. 14), and in Arabshah (tom. ii. c. 19, p. 183–201), which agree with each other in the spirit and substance, rather than in the style. It is probable that they have been translated, with various latitude, from the Turkish original into the Arabic and Persian tongues. [The genuineness of these letters is doubtful.]

[34] The Mogul emir distinguishes himself and his countrymen by the name of *Turks*, and stigmatises the race and nation of Bajazet with the less honourable epithet of *Turkmans*. Yet I do not understand how the Ottomans could be descended from a Turkman sailor; those inland shepherds were so remote from the sea and all maritime affairs.

Touran, and the Indies; and labours to prove that Timour had never triumphed, unless by his own perfidy and the vices of his foes. "Thy armies are innumerable be they so; but what are the arrows of the flying Tartar against the scymetars and battle-axes of my firm and invincible Janizaries? I will guard the princes who have implored my protection; seek them in my tents. The cities of Arzingan and Erzeroum are mine; and, unless the tribute be duly paid, I will demand the arrears under the walls of Tauris and Sultania." The ungovernable rage of the sultan at length betrayed him to an insult of a more domestic kind. "If I fly from my arms," said he, "may *my* wives be thrice divorced from my bed; but, if thou hast not courage to meet me in the field, mayest thou again receive *thy* wives after they have thrice endured the embraces of a stranger." [35] Any violation, by word or deed, of the secrecy of the harem is an unpardonable offence among the Turkish nations, [36] and the political quarrel of the two monarchs was embittered by private and personal resentment Yet in his first expedition Timour was satisfied with the siege and destruction of Suvas, or Sebaste, a strong city on the borders of Anatolia, and he revenged the indiscretion of the Ottoman on a garrison of four thousand Armenians, who were buried alive for the brave and faithful discharge of their duty [37] As a Musulman, he seemed to respect the pious occupation of Bajazet, who was still engaged in the blockade of Constantinople; and, after this salutary lesson, the Mogul conqueror

[35] According to the Koran (c ii p 27, and Sale's Discourses, p 134), a Musulman who had thrice divorced his wife (who had thrice repeated the words of a divorce) could not take her again, till after she had been married *to*, and repudiated *by*, another husband, an ignominious transaction, which it is needless to aggravate by supposing that the first husband must see her enjoyed by a second before his face (Rycaut's State of the Ottoman Empire, l ii c 21)

[36] The common delicacy of the Orientals, in never speaking of their women, is ascribed in a much higher degree by Arabshah to the Turkish nations, and it is remarkable enough that Chalcondyles (l ii p 55 [p 105, ed Bonn]) had some knowledge of the prejudice and the insult

[37] [And he put to death Bajezid's eldest son Ertogrul]

checked his pursuit, and turned aside to the invasion of Syria and Egypt. In these transactions, the Ottoman prince, by the Orientals, and even by Timour, is styled the *Kaissar of Roum*, the Cæsar of the Romans: a title which, by a small anticipation, might be given to a monarch who possessed the provinces, and threatened the city, of the successors of Constantine.[38]

The military republic of the Mamalukes still reigned in Egypt and Syria; but the dynasty of the Turks was overthrown by that of the Circassians;[39] and their favourite Barkok, from a slave and a prisoner, was raised and restored to the throne. In the midst of rebellion and discord, he braved the menaces, corresponded with the enemies, and detained the ambassadors of the Mogul, who patiently expected his decease, to revenge the crimes of the father on the feeble reign of his son Farage. The Syrian emirs[40] were assembled at Aleppo to repel the invasion; they confided in the fame and discipline of the Mamalukes, in the temper of their swords and lances, of the purest steel of Damascus, in the strength of their walled cities, and in the populousness of sixty thousand villages; and, instead of sustaining a siege, they threw open their gates and arrayed their forces in the

[38] For the style of the Moguls, see the Institutions (p. 131, 147), and for the Persians, the Bibliothèque Orientale (p. 882); but I do not find that the title of Cæsar has been applied by the Arabians, or assumed by the Ottomans themselves. [From Timur to Bayezid the name is an insult; he will not give him a Musulman title.]

[39] See the reigns of Barkok and Pharadge, in M. de Guignes (tom. iv. l. xxii.), who from the Arabic texts of Aboulmahasen, Ebn Schounah, and Aintabi has added some facts to our common stock of materials. [In 1390 the Bahri dynasty made way for the Burji dynasty, founded by Al-Zâhir Sayf al-Dîn Barkûk, who in 1398 was succeeded by Al-Nâsir Nâsir al-Dîn Faraj.]

[40] For these recent and domestic transactions, Arabshah, though a partial, is a credible, witness (tom. i. c. 64-68; tom. ii. c. 1-14). Timour must have been odious to a Syrian; but the notoriety of facts would have obliged him, in some measure, to respect his enemy and himself. His bitters may correct the luscious sweets of Sherefeddin (l. v. c. 17-29).

plain. But these forces were not cemented by virtue and union; and some powerful emirs had been seduced to desert or betray their more loyal companions. Timour's front was covered with a line of Indian elephants, whose turrets were filled with archers and Greek fire, the rapid evolutions of his cavalry completed the dismay and disorder; the Syrian crowds fell back on each other, many thousands were stifled or slaughtered in the entrance of the great street; the Moguls entered with the fugitives, and, after a short defence, the citadel, the impregnable citadel of Aleppo, was surrendered by cowardice or treachery. Among the supplants and captives, Timour distinguished the doctors of the law, whom he invited to the dangerous honour of a personal conference.[41] The Mogul prince was a zealous Musulman; but his Persian schools had taught him to revere the memory of Ali and Hosein; and he had imbibed a deep prejudice against the Syrians, as the enemies of the son of the daughter of the apostle of God. To these doctors he proposed a captious question, which the casuists of Bochara, Samarcand, and Herat were incapable of resolving. "Who are the true martyrs, of those who are slain on my side, or on that of my enemies?" But he was silenced, or satisfied, by the dexterity of one of the cadhis of Aleppo, who replied, in the words of Mahomet himself, that the motive, not the ensign, constitutes the martyr; and that the Moslems of either party, who fight only for the glory of God, may deserve that sacred appellation. The true succession of the caliphs was a controversy of a still more delicate nature, and the frankness of a doctor, too honest for his situation, provoked the emperor to exclaim, "Ye are as false as those of Damascus: Moawiyah was an usurper, Yezid a tyrant, and Ali alone is the lawful successor of the prophet." A prudent explanation restored his tran-

---

[41] These interesting conversations appear to have been copied by Arabshah (tom i c 68, p 625-645) from the cadhi and historian Ebn Schounah, a principal actor. Yet how could he be alive seventy-five years afterwards (d'Herbelot, p. 792)?

quillity; and he passed to a more familiar topic of conversation. "What is your age?" said he to the cadhi. "Fifty years." "It would be the age of my eldest son. You see me here (continued Timour) a poor, lame, decrepit mortal. Yet by my arm has the Almighty been pleased to subdue the kindgoms of Iran, Touran, and the Indies. I am not a man of blood; and God is my witness that in all my wars I have never been the aggressor, and that my enemies have always been the authors of their own calamity." During this peaceful conversation, the streets of Aleppo streamed with blood, and re-echoed with the cries of mothers and children, with the shrieks of violated virgins. The rich plunder that was abandoned to his soldiers might stimulate their avarice; but their cruelty was enforced by the peremptory command of producing an adequate number of heads, which, according to his custom, were curiously piled in columns and pyramids; the Moguls celebrated the feast of victory, while the surviving Moslems passed the night in tears and in chains. I shall not dwell on the march of the destroyer from Aleppo to Damascus, where he was rudely encountered, and almost overthrown, by the armies of Egypt. A retrograde motion was imputed to his distress and despair: one of his nephews deserted to the enemy; and Syria rejoiced in the tale of his defeat, when the sultan was driven, by the revolt of the Mamalukes, to escape with precipitation and shame to his palace of Cairo. Abandoned by their prince, the inhabitants of Damascus still defended their walls; and Timour consented to raise the siege, if they would adorn his retreat with a gift or ransom; each article of nine pieces. But no sooner had he introduced himself into the city, under colour of a truce, than he perfidiously violated the treaty; imposed a contribution of ten millions of gold; and animated his troops to chastise the posterity of those Syrians who had executed or approved the murder of the grandson of Mahomet. A family which had given honourable burial to the head of Hosein, and a colony of artificers whom he sent to labour at Samarcand, were alone reserved in the general massacre; and, after a period of seven centuries, Damascus was reduced to ashes, because a Tartar was moved by religious zeal to avenge the blood of an Arab [42] The losses and fatigues of the campaign obliged Timour to renounce the conquest of Palestine and Egypt, but in his return to the Euphrates he delivered Aleppo to the flames; and justified his pious motive by the pardon and reward of two thousand sectaries of Ali, who were desirous to visit the tomb of his son I have expatiated on the personal anecdotes which mark the character of the Mogul hero, but I shall briefly mention [43] that he erected on the ruins of Bagdad a pyramid of ninety thousand heads; again visited Georgia; encamped on the banks of Araxes; and proclaimed his resolution of marching against the Ottoman emperor. Conscious of the importance of the war, he collected his forces from every province; eight hundred thousand men were enrolled on his military list; [44] but the splendid commands of five and ten thousand horse may be rather expressive of the rank and pension of the chiefs than of the genuine number of effective soldiers. [45] In the pillage

[42] [The destruction attributed to Timur has been greatly exaggerated That he did not burn the mosque of Damascus is proved by its remains (It had been partly burnt in a tumult in 1068) Compare the remarks of Cahun, *op cit* p 495-497]

[43] The marches and occupations of Timour between the Syrian and Ottoman wars are represented by Sherefeddin (I v c 29-43) and Arabshah (tom ii c 15-18)

[44] This number of 800,000 was extracted by Arabshah, or rather by Ebn Schounah, ex rationario Timuri, on the faith of a Carizmian officer (tom. i c 68, p 617), and it is remarkable enough that a Greek historian (Phranza, l 1 c 29) adds no more than 20,000 men Poggius reckons 1,000,000, another Latin contemporary (Chron Tarvisianum, apud Muratori, tom xix p 800) 1,100,000, and the enormous sum of 1,600,000 is attested by a German soldier who was present at the battle of Angora (Leunclav ad Chalcondyl l iii p 82) Timour, in his Institutions, has not deigned to calculate his troops, his subjects, or his revenues

[45] A wide latitude of non-effectives was allowed by the Great Mogul for his own pride and the benefit of his officers Bernier's patron was Penge-Hazari, commander of 5000 horse, of which he maintained no more than 500 (Voyages, tom i p 288, 289).

of Syria, the Moguls had acquired immense riches; but the delivery of their pay and arrears for seven years more firmly attached them to the Imperial standard.

During this diversion of the Mogul arms, Bajazet had two years to collect his forces for a more serious encounter. They consisted of four hundred thousand horse and foot,[46] whose merit and fidelity were of an unequal complexion. We may discriminate the Janizaries, who have been gradually raised to an establishment of forty thousand men; a national cavalry, the Spahis of modern times; twenty thousand cuirassiers of Europe, clad in black and impenetrable armour; the troops of Anatolia, whose princes had taken refuge in the camp of Timour, and a colony of Tartars, whom he had driven from Kipzak, and to whom Bajazet had assigned a settlement in the plains of Hadrianople. The fearless confidence of the sultan urged him to meet his antagonist; and, as if he had chosen that spot for revenge, he displayed his banners near the ruins of the unfortunate Suvas. In the meanwhile, Timour moved from the Araxes through the countries of Armenia and Anatolia: his boldness was secured by the wisest precautions; his speed was guided by order and discipline; and the woods, the mountains, and the rivers were diligently explored by the flying squadrons, who marked his road and preceded his standard. Firm in his plan of fighting in the heart of the Ottoman kingdom, he avoided their camp; dexterously inclined to the left; occupied Cæsarea; traversed the salt desert and the river Halys; and invested Angora: while the sultan, immoveable and ignorant in his post, compared the Tartar swiftness to the crawling of a snail.[47] He returned on the wings of indignation to the

[46] Timour himself fixes at 400,000 men the Ottoman army (Institutions, p. 153), which is reduced to 150,000 by Phranza (l. i. c. 29), and swelled by the German soldier to 1,400,000. It is evident that the Moguls were the more numerous. [The forces of Bayezid are put at 90,000 by Sad ad-Din (tr. Bratutti, 214). Of course the number given by Timur cannot be accepted.]

[47] It may not be useless to mark the distances between Angora and the

relief of Angora; and, as both generals were alike impatient
for action, the plains round that city were the scene of a memorable battle, which has immortalised the glory of Timour
and the shame of Bajazet. For this signal victory, the
Mogul emperor was indebted to himself, to the genius of the
moment, and the discipline of thirty years.   He had improved
the tactics, without violating the manners, of his nation,[48]
whose force still consisted in the missile weapons, and rapid
evolutions, of a numerous cavalry   From a single troop to a
great army, the mode of attack was the same · a foremost line
first advanced to the charge, and was supported in a just
order by the squadrons of the great vanguard. The general's eye watched over the field, and at his command the
front and rear of the right and left wings successively moved
forwards in their several divisions, and in a direct or oblique
line; the enemy was pressed by eighteen or twenty attacks;
and each attack afforded a chance of victory. If they all
proved fruitless or unsuccessful, the occasion was worthy of
the emperor himself, who gave the signal of advancing to the
standard and main body, which he led in person [49] But in
the battle of Angora, the main body itself was supported, on
the flanks and in the rear, by the bravest squadrons of the
reserve, commanded by the sons and grandsons of Timour.
The conqueror of Hindostan ostentatiously shewed a line of
elephants, the trophies, rather than the instruments, of victory :
the use of the Greek fire was familiar to the Moguls and
Ottomans; but, had they borrowed from Europe the recent
invention of gunpowder and cannon, the artificial thunder,

neighbouring cities, by the journeys of the caravans, each of twenty or
twenty-five miles, to Smyrna 20, to Kiotahia 10, to Boursa 10, to Cæsarea
8, to Sinope 10, to Nicomedia 9, to Constantinople 12 or 13 (see Tournefort,
Voyage au Levant, tom ii lettre 21)
    [48] See the Systems of Tactics in the Institutions, which the English editors
have illustrated with elaborate plans (p 373-407).
    [49] The Sultan himself (says Timour) must then put the foot of courage
into the stirrup of patience   A Tartar metaphor, which is lost in the English,
but preserved in the French version of the Institutes (p 156 157)

in the hands of either nation, must have turned the fortune of the day.[50] In that day, Bajazet displayed the qualities of a soldier and a chief, but his genius sunk under a stronger ascendant, and, from various motives, the greatest part of his troops failed him in the decisive moment. His rigour and avarice had provoked a mutiny among the Turks; and even his son Soliman too hastily withdrew from the field. The forces of Anatolia, loyal in their revolt, were drawn away to the banners of their lawful princes. His Tartar allies had been tempted by the letters and emissaries of Timour;[51] who reproached their ignoble servitude under the slaves of their fathers, and offered to their hopes the dominion of their new, or the liberty of their ancient, country. In the right wing of Bajazet, the cuirassiers of Europe charged with faithful hearts and irresistible arms; but these men of iron were soon broken by an artful flight and headlong pursuit; and the Janizaries, alone, without cavalry or missile weapons, were encompassed by the circle of the Mogul hunters. Their valour was at length oppressed by heat, thirst, and the weight of numbers; and the unfortunate sultan, afflicted with the gout in his hands and feet, was transported from the field on the fleetest of his horses. He was pursued and taken by the titular khan of Zagatai; and after his capture, and the defeat of the Ottoman powers, the kingdom of Anatolia submitted to the conqueror, who planted his standard at Kiotahia, and dispersed on all sides the ministers of rapine and destruction. Mirza Mehemmed Sultan, the eldest and best beloved of his grandsons, was despatched to Boursa with thirty thousand

[50] The Greek fire, on Timour's side, is attested by Sherefeddin (l. v. c. 47), but Voltaire's strange suspicion that some cannon, inscribed with strange characters, must have been sent by that monarch to Delhi is refuted by the universal silence of contemporaries

[51] Timour has dissembled this secret and important negotiation with the Tartars, which is indisputably proved by the joint evidence of the Arabian (tom. i. c. 47, p. 391), Turkish (Annal. Leunclav. p. 321), and Persian historians (Khondemir, apud d'Herbelot, p. 882) [And cp. Ducas, p. 35 ed. Bonn.]

horse; and such was his youthful ardour that he arrived with only four thousand at the gates of the capital, after performing in five days a march of two hundred and thirty miles Yet fear is still more rapid in its course, and Soliman, the son of Bajazet, had already passed over to Europe with the royal treasure. The spoil, however, of the palace and city was immense, the inhabitants had escaped, but the buildings, for the most part of wood, were reduced to ashes. From Boursa, the grandson of Timour advanced to Nice, even yet a fair and flourishing city; and the Mogul squadrons were only stopped by the waves of the Propontis. The same success attended the other mirzas and emirs in their excursions; and Smyrna, defended by the zeal and courage of the Rhodian knights, alone deserved the presence of the emperor himself. After an obstinate defence, the place was taken by storm; all that breathed was put to the sword, and the heads of the Christian heroes were launched from the engines, on board of two carracks, or great ships of Europe, that rode at anchor in the harbour. The Moslems of Asia rejoiced in their deliverance from a dangerous and domestic foe, and a parallel was drawn between the two rivals, by observing that Timour, in fourteen days, had reduced a fortress which had sustained seven years the siege, or at least the blockade, of Bajazet.[52]

The *iron cage* in which Bajazet was imprisoned by Tamerlane, so long and so often repeated as a moral lesson, is now rejected as a fable by the modern writers, who smile at the vulgar credulity.[53] They appeal with confidence to the

[52] For the war of Anatolia, or Roum, I add some hints in the Institutions, to the copious narratives of Sherefeddin (l v c 44-65) and Arabshah (tom ii c 20-35) On this part only of Timour's history, it is lawful to quote the Turks (Cantemir, p 53-55, Annal Leunclav p 320-322), and the Greeks (Phranza, l i c 29, Ducas, c 15-17, Chalcondyles, l iii) [Add Sad ad-Din's account of the battle, tr Bratutti, i p 213 *sqq*]

[53] The scepticism of Voltaire (Essai sur l'Histoire Générale, c 88) is ready on this, as on every, occasion to reject a popular tale, and to diminish the magnitude of vice and virtue, and on most occasions his incredulity is

Persian history of Sherefeddin Ali, which has been given to our curiosity in a French version, and from which I shall collect and abridge a more specious narrative of this memorable transaction. No sooner was Timour informed [54] that the captive Ottoman was at the door of his tent, than he graciously stepped forwards to receive him, seated him by his side, and mingled with just reproaches a soothing pity for his rank and misfortune. "Alas!" said the emperor, "the decree of fate is now accomplished by your own fault · it is the web which you have woven, the thorns of the tree which yourself have planted. I wished to spare, and even to assist, the champion of the Moslems; you braved our threats, you despised our friendship; you forced us to enter your kingdom with our invincible armies Behold the event. Had you vanquished, I am not ignorant of the fate which you reserved for myself and my troops. But I disdain to retaliate; your life and honour are secure; and I shall express my gratitude to God by my clemency to man." The royal captive shewed some signs of repentance, accepted the humiliation of a robe of honour, and embraced with tears his son Mousa, who, at his request, was sought and found among the captives of the field. The Ottoman princes were lodged in a splendid pavilion; and the respect of the guards could be surpassed only by their vigilance. On the arrival of the harem from Boursa, Timour restored the queen Despina and

reasonable [The fable of the iron cage is fully discussed by Hammer (Gesch des osmanischen Reiches, 1 252–6), who refers to three points unknown to Gibbon (1) the silence of the eye-witness, John Schiltberger, whom we have already seen captured in the battle of Nicopolis, and who was again captured by the Mongols at Angora, (2) the evidence of the two oldest Ottoman historians, Neshri and Ashikpashazādé, (3) the discussion and denial of the story by the later Ottoman historian Sad ad-Din Hammer points out that the story arose out of a misconception of the words of Ashikpashazādé and Neshri, who state that a litter, furnished with bars like a cage, was provided for Bayezid Such litters were the kind of vehicle regularly used for conveying a prince's harem]

[54] [According to Ducas, Timur was playing chess at the moment of Bayezid's arrival (p. 17)]

her daughter to their father and husband; but he piously required that the Servian princess, who had hitherto been indulged in the profession of Christianity, should embrace without delay the religion of the prophet. In the feast of victory, to which Bajazet was invited, the Mogul emperor placed a crown on his head and a sceptre in his hand, with a solemn assurance of restoring him with an increase of glory to the throne of his ancestors. But the effect of this promise was disappointed by the sultan's untimely death amidst the care of the most skilful physicians, he expired of an apoplexy at Akshehr, the Antioch of Pisidia, about nine months after his defeat. The victor dropped a tear over his grave; his body, with royal pomp, was conveyed to the mausoleum which he had erected at Boursa; and his son Mousa, after receiving a rich present of gold and jewels, of horses and arms, was invested by a patent in red ink with the kingdom of Anatolia.

Such is the portrait of a generous conqueror, which has been extracted from his own memorials, and dedicated to his son and grandson, nineteen years after his decease;[55] and, at a time when the truth was remembered by thousands, a manifest falsehood would have implied a satire on his real conduct Weighty, indeed, is this evidence, adopted by all the Persian histories;[56] yet flattery, more especially in the East, is base and audacious; and the harsh and ignominious treatment of Bajazet is attested by a chain of witnesses, some of whom shall be produced in the order of their time and country. 1. The reader has not forgot the garrison of French, whom the marshal Boucicault left behind him for the

[55] See the history of Sherefeddin (l v c 49, 52, 53, 59, 60) This work was finished at Shiraz, in the year 1424, and dedicated to Sultan Ibrahim, the son of Sharokh, the son of Timour, who reigned in Farsistan in his father's lifetime

[56] After the perusal of Khondemir, Ebn Schounah, &c. the learned d'Herbelot (Bibliot Orientale, p 882) may affirm that this fable is not mentioned in the most authentic histories, but his denial of the visible testimony of Arabshah leaves some room to suspect his accuracy

defence of Constantinople. They were on the spot to receive
the earliest and most faithful intelligence of the overthrow of
their great adversary; and it is more than probable that some
of them accompanied the Greek embassy to the camp of
Tamerlane. From their account, the *hardships* of the prison
and death of Bajazet are affirmed by the marshal's servant
and historian, within the distance of seven years.[57] 2. The
name of Poggius the Italian [58] is deservedly famous among the
revivers of learning in the fifteenth century. His elegant
dialogue on the vicissitudes of fortune [59] was composed in his
fiftieth year, twenty-eight years after the Turkish victory of
Tamerlane,[60] whom he celebrates as not inferior to the illustrious Barbarians of antiquity. Of his exploits and discipline, Poggius was informed by several ocular witnesses;
nor does he forget an example so opposite to his theme as the
Ottoman monarch, whom the Scythian confined like a wild
beast in an iron cage and exhibited a spectacle to Asia. I
might add the authority of two Italian chronicles, perhaps
of an earlier date, which would prove at least that the same
story, whether false or true, was imported into Europe with

[57] Et fut lui-même (*Bajazet*) pris, et mené en prison, en laquelle mourut
de *dure mort!* Mémoires de Boucicault, p 1 c 37   These Memoirs were
composed while the Marshal was still governor of Genoa, from whence he
was expelled in the year 1409 by a popular insurrection (Muratori Annali
d'Italia, tom. xii. p 473, 474)   [On Boucicaut's Memoirs and Life see
Delaville Le Roulx, La France en Orient au 14ᵐᵉ siècle   Expéditions du
Maréchal Boucicaut, 2 vols, 1886]

[58] The reader will find a satisfactory account of the life and writings of
Poggius, in the Poggiana, an entertaining work of M Lenfant [A D 1720],
and in the Bibliotheca Latina mediæ et infimæ Ætatis of Fabricius (tom v.
p 305-308)   Poggius was born in the year 1380, and died in 1459

[59] The dialogue de Varictate Fortunæ (of which a complete and elegant
edition has been published at Paris in 1723, in 4to) was composed a short
time before the death of Pope Martin V (p 5), and consequently about the
end of the year 1430

[60] See a splendid and elegant encomium of Tamerlane, p 36-39, ipse
enim novi (says Poggius) qui fuere in ejus castris   . .   Regem vivum
cepit, caveâque in modum feræ inclusum per omnem Asiam circumtulit
egregium admirandumque spectaculum fortunæ

the first tidings of the revolution [61]   3   At the time when
Poggius flourished at Rome, Ahmed Ebn Arabshah composed
at Damascus the florid and malevolent history of Timour,
for which he had collected materials in his journeys over
Turkey and Tartary.[62]   Without any possible correspondence
between the Latin and the Arabian writer, they agree in the
fact of the iron cage; and their agreement is a striking proof
of their common veracity.   Ahmed Arabshah likewise relates another outrage, which Bajazet endured, of a more
domestic and tender nature.   His indiscreet mention of
women and divorces was deeply resented by the jealous
Tartar.   In the feast of victory, the wine was served by female
cup-bearers; and the sultan beheld his own concubines and
wives confounded among the slaves, and exposed, without a
veil, to the eyes of intemperance.   To escape a similar
indignity, it is said that his successors, except in a single instance, have abstained from legitimate nuptials; and the
Ottoman practice and belief, at least in the sixteenth century,
is attested by the observing Busbequius,[63] ambassador from
the court of Vienna to the great Soliman.   4.   Such is the
separation of language that the testimony of a Greek is not
less independent than that of a Latin or an Arab.   I suppress
the names of Chalcondyles and Ducas, who flourished in a
later period, and who speak in a less positive tone, but
more attention is due to George Phranza,[64] protovestiare of the
last emperors, and who was born a year before the battle of

[61] The Chronicon Tarvisianum (in Muratori, Script Rerum Italicarum,
tom xix p 800), and the Annales Estenses (tom xviii p 974)   The two
authors, Andrea de Redusiis de Quero and James de Delayto, were both
contemporaries, and both chancellors, the one of Trevigi, the other of
Ferrera   The evidence of the former is the most positive

[62] See Arabshah, tom ii c. 28, 34   He travelled in regiones Rumæas,
A H 839 (A D 1435, 27th July), tom ii c 2, p 13

[63] Busbequius in Legatione Turcicâ, epist 1 p 52   Yet his respectable
authority is somewhat shaken by the subsequent marriages of Amurath II
with a Servian, and of Mahomet II with an Asiatic, princess (Cantemir,
p 83, 93)

[64] See the testimony of George Phranza (l 1 c 29), and his life in Hanckius

Angora. Twenty-two years after that event, he was sent ambassador to Amurath the Second; and the historian might converse with some veteran Janizaries, who had been made prisoners with the sultan and had themselves seen him in his iron cage. 5. The last evidence, in every sense, is that of the Turkish annals, which have been consulted or transcribed by Leunclavius, Pocock, and Cantemir.[65] They unanimously deplore the captivity of the iron cage; and some credit may be allowed to national historians, who cannot stigmatise the Tartar without uncovering the shame of their king and country.

From these opposite premises, a fair and moderate conclusion may be deduced. I am satisfied that Sherefeddin Ali has faithfully described the first ostentatious interview, in which the conqueror, whose spirits were harmonised by success, affected the character of generosity. But his mind was insensibly alienated by the unseasonable arrogance of Bajazet, the complaints of his enemies, the Anatolian princes, were just and vehement, and Timour betrayed a design of leading his royal captive in triumph to Samarcand. An attempt to facilitate his escape, by digging a mine under the tent, provoked the Mogul emperor to impose a harsher restraint; and, in his perpetual marches, an iron cage on a waggon might be invented, not as a wanton insult, but as a rigorous precaution. Timour had read in some fabulous history a similar treatment of one of his predecessors, a king of Persia; and Bajazet was condemned to represent the person, and expiate the guilt, of the Roman Cæsar.[66] But the strength of his mind and body

(de Script Byzant p 1 c 40). Chalcondyles and Ducas speak in general terms of Bajazet's *chains*

[65] Annales Leunclav p 321, Pocock, Prolegomen. ad Abulpharag Dynast , Cantemir, p 55 [See above note 53]

[66] A Sapor, king of Persia, had been made prisoner, and enclosed in the figure of a cow's hide, by Maximian, or Galerius Cæsar Such is the fable related by Eutychius (Annal tom i p 421, vers Pocock) The recollection of the true history (Decline and Fall, &c vol ii p 171 *sqq*) will teach us to appreciate the knowledge of the Orientals of the ages which precede the H' u)' '

fainted under the trial, and his premature death might, without injustice, be ascribed to the severity of Timour. He warred not with the dead; a tear and a sepulchre were all that he could bestow on a captive who was delivered from his power; and, if Mousa, the son of Bajazet, was permitted to reign over the ruins of Boursa, the greatest part of the province of Anatolia had been restored by the conqueror to their lawful sovereigns.

From the Irtish and Volga to the Persian Gulf, and from the Ganges to Damascus and the Archipelago, Asia was in the hand of Timour; his armies were invincible, his ambition was boundless, and his zeal might aspire to conquer and convert the Christian kingdoms of the West, which already trembled at his name. He touched the utmost verge of the land; but an insuperable, though narrow, sea rolled between the two continents of Europe and Asia, [67] and the lord of so many *tomans*, or myriads of horse, was not master of a single galley. The two passages of the Bosphorus and Hellespont, of Constantinople and Gallipoli, were possessed, the one by the Christians, the other by the Turks. On this great occasion, they forgot the difference of religion, to act with union and firmness in the common cause. The double straits were guarded with ships and fortifications; and they separately withheld the transports which Timour demanded of either nation, under the pretence of attacking their enemy. At the same time, they soothed his pride with tributary gifts and suppliant embassies, and prudently tempted him to retreat with the honours of victory. Soliman, the son of Bajazet, implored his clemency for his father and himself, accepted, by a red patent, the investiture of the kingdom of Romania, which he already held by the sword; and reiterated

[67] Arabshah (tom ii c 25) describes, like a curious traveller, the straits of Gallipoli and Constantinople. To acquire a just idea of these events, I have compared the narratives and prejudices of the Moguls, Turks, Greeks, and Arabians The Spanish ambassador mentions this hostile union of the Christians and Ottomans (Vie de Timour, p 96).

his ardent wish of casting himself in person at the feet of the king of the world. The Greek emperor [68] (either John or Manuel) submitted to pay the same tribute which he had stipulated with the Turkish sultan, and ratified the treaty by an oath of allegiance, from which he could absolve his conscience as soon as the Mogul arms had retired from Anatolia. But the fears and fancy of nations ascribed to the ambitious Tamerlane a new design of vast and romantic compass: a design of subduing Egypt and Africa, marching from the Nile to the Atlantic Ocean, entering Europe by the Straits of Gibraltar, and, after imposing his yoke on the kingdoms of Christendom, of returning home by the deserts of Russia and Tartary. This remote and perhaps imaginary danger was averted by the submission of the sultan of Egypt; the honours of the prayer and the coin attested at Cairo the supremacy of Timour; and a rare gift of a *giraffe*, or camelopard, and nine ostriches represented at Samarcand the tribute of the African world. Our imagination is not less astonished by the portrait of a Mogul, who, in his camp before Smyrna, meditates and almost accomplishes the invasion of the Chinese empire.[69] Timour was urged to this enterprise by national honour and religious zeal. The torrents which he had shed of Musulman blood could be expiated only by an equal destruction of the infidels; and, as he now stood at the gates of paradise, he might best secure his glorious entrance by demolishing the idols of China, founding moschs in every city, and establishing the profession of faith in one God and his prophet Mahomet. The recent expulsion of the house of Zingis was an insult on the Mogul

[68] Since the name of Cæsar had been transferred to the sultans of Roum, the Greek princes of Constantinople (Sherefeddin, l v c 54) were confounded with the Christian *lords* of Gallipoli, Thessalonica, &c under the title of *Tekkur*, which is derived by corruption from the genitive τοῦ κυρίου (Cantemir, p 51)

[69] See Sherefeddin, l v c. 4, who marks, in a just itinerary, the road to China, which Arabshah (tom ii c. 33) paints in vague and rhetorical colours.

name; and the disorders of the empire afforded the fairest opportunity for revenge. The illustrious Hongvou, founder of the dynasty of *Ming*, died four years before the battle of Angora, and his grandson, a weak and unfortunate youth, was burnt in a palace, after a million of Chinese had perished in the civil war.[70] Before he evacuated Anatolia, Timour despatched beyond the Sihoon a numerous army, or rather colony, of his old and new subjects, to open the road, to subdue the Pagan Calmucks and Mungals, and to found cities and magazines in the desert; and, by the diligence of his lieutenant, he soon received a perfect map and description of the unknown regions from the source of the Irtish to the wall of China. During these preparations, the emperor achieved the final conquest of Georgia; passed the winter on the banks of the Araxes; appeased the troubles of Persia; and slowly returned to his capital, after a campaign of four years and nine months.

On the throne of Samarcand,[71] he displayed, in a short repose, his magnificence and power; listened to the complaints of the people, distributed a just measure of rewards and punishments; employed his riches in the architecture of palaces and temples, and gave audience to the ambassadors of Egypt, Arabia, India, Tartary, Russia, and Spain, the last of whom presented a suit of tapestry which eclipsed the pencil of the Oriental artists. The marriage of six of the emperor's grandsons was esteemed an act of religion as well as of paternal tenderness; and the pomp of the ancient caliphs was revived in their nuptials. They were celebrated in the gardens of Canighul, decorated with innumerable tents and pavilions, which displayed the luxury of a great city and the

[70] Synopsis Hist. Sinicæ, p 74-76 (in the ivth part of the Relations de Thévenot), Duhalde, Hist de la Chine (tom i p 507, 508, folio edition), and for the chronology of the Chinese Emperors, de Guignes, Hist des Huns, tom i p 71, 72

[71] For the return, triumph, and death of Timour, see Sherefeddin (l vi c 1-30) and Arabshah (tom. ii c. 35-47).

spoils of a victorious camp. Whole forests were cut down to
supply fuel for the kitchens; the plain was spread with pyramids of meat and vases of every liquor, to which thousands
of guests were courteously invited. The orders of the state
and the nations of the earth were marshalled at the royal
banquet; nor were the ambassadors of Europe (says the
haughty Persian) excluded from the feast; since even the
casses, the smallest of fish, find their place in the ocean [72]
The public joy was testified by illuminations and masquer-
ades; the trades of Samarcand passed in review; and every
trade was emulous to execute some quaint device, some mar-
vellous pageant, with the materials of their peculiar art.
After the marriage-contracts had been ratified by the cadhis,
the bridegrooms and their brides retired to their nuptial
chambers; nine times, according to the Asiatic fashion,
they were dressed and undressed, and at each change of
apparel pearls and rubies were showered on their heads, and
contemptuously abandoned to their attendants. A general
indulgence was proclaimed; every law was relaxed, every
pleasure was allowed; the people was free, the sovereign was
idle; and the historian of Timour may remark that, after
devoting fifty years to the attainment of empire, the only
happy period of his life were the two months in which he
ceased to exercise his power. But he was soon awakened to
the cares of government and war. The standard was un-
furled for the invasion of China: the emirs made their report
of two hundred thousand, the select and veteran soldiers of

[72] Sherefeddin (l vi c 24) mentions the ambassadors of one of the most
potent sovereigns of Europe. We know that it was Henry III King of
Castile, and the curious relation of his two embassies is still extant, Mariana,
Hist Hispan l xix c 11, tom ii p 329, 330   Advertissement à l'Hist
de Timur Bec, p 28–33   There appears likewise to have been some correspondence between the Mogul emperor, and the court of Charles VII King
of France (Histoire de France, par Velly et Villaret, tom xii p 336)   [The
account of Ruy Gonzalez de Clavijo of his embassy to the court of Timur
in 1403–6 has been translated, with elucidations, by Sir Clements R. Mark-
ham, for the Hakluyt Society, 1859]

Iran and Turan, their baggage and provisions were transported by five hundred great waggons, and an immense train of horses and camels; and the troops might prepare for a long absence, since more than six months were employed in the tranquil journey of a caravan from Samarcand to Pekin Neither age nor the severity of the winter could retard the impatience of Timour; he mounted on horseback, passed the Sihoon on the ice, marched seventy-six parasangs, three hundred miles, from his capital, and pitched his last camp in the neighbourhood of Otrar, where he was expected by the angel of death. Fatigue, and the indiscreet use of iced water, accelerated the progress of his fever; and the conqueror of Asia expired in the seventieth year of his age, thirty-five years after he had ascended the throne of Zagati. His designs were lost, his armies were disbanded; China was saved; and, fourteen years after his decease, the most powerful of his children sent an embassy of friendship and commerce to the court of Pekin.[73]

The fame of Timour has pervaded the East and West; his posterity is still invested with the Imperial *title;* and the admiration of his subjects, who revered him almost as a deity, may be justified in some degree by the praise or confession of his bitterest enemies.[74] Although he was lame of

[73] See the translation of the Persian account of their embassy, a curious and original piece (in the ivth part of the Relations de Thévenot) They presented the emperor of China with an old horse which Timour had formerly rode. It was in the year 1419, that they departed from the court of Herat, to which place they returned in 1422 from Pekin [Timur died in February, 1405, see Elias and Ross, Tarīkh-i-Rashīdī, p 54 note]

[74] From Arabshah, tom ii c. 96 The bright or softer colours are borrowed from Sherefeddin, d'Herbelot, and the Institutions [In one important respect Gibbon's account of Timur and his work is deficient He has not realised, or brought out, the fact that the greatest result of Timur's empire was the victory of Islam in Central Asia Timur acted from the beginning in close co-operation with the Musulman ecclesiastics of Transoxiana, and when he won supreme power, he did away with the Mongol and Turkish legislative system of Chingiz and substituted the law of Islam In regard to the very foundations of the political constitution there is a vast

an hand and foot, his form and stature were not unworthy of his rank, and his vigorous health, so essential to himself and to the world, was corroborated by temperance and exercise. In his familiar discourse he was grave and modest, and, if he was ignorant of the Arabic language, he spoke with fluency and elegance the Persian and Turkish idioms. It was his delight to converse with the learned on topics of history and science; and the amusement of his leisure hours was the game of chess, which he improved or corrupted with new refinements.[75] In his religion, he was a zealous, though not perhaps an orthodox, Musulman;[76] but his sound understanding may tempt us to believe that a superstitious reverence for omens and prophecies, for saints and astrologers, was only affected as an instrument of policy. In the government of a vast empire, he stood alone and absolute, without a rebel to oppose his power, a favourite to seduce his affections, or a minister to mislead his judgment. It was his firmest maxim that, whatever might be the consequence, the word of the prince should never be disputed or recalled; but his foes

difference between the two systems. Chingiz and his successors were subject to the law (the Yāsāk) and bound by its provisions, whereas according to the principles of Islam the head of the state is not bound by the law, but is responsible only to God. Thus the will of the sovereign is set above the law. Timur then broke completely with the Mongol tradition, such as it had been developed under Chinese influence, and drew the Turks of Central Asia out of touch with the far East. As the Mongol power in China was overthrown about the same time by the revolution which set the Ming dynasty on the throne (A.D. 1370), this period marks a general decline of Mongol influence in Asia.]

[75] His new system was multiplied from 32 pieces and 64 squares, to 56 pieces and 110 or 130 squares. But, except in his court, the old game has been thought sufficiently elaborate. The Mogul emperor was rather pleased than hurt with the victory of a subject, a chess-player will feel the value of this encomium!

[76] See Sherefeddin, l. v. c. 15, 25. Arabshah (tom. ii. c. 96, p. 801, 803) reproves the impiety of Timour and the Moguls, who almost preferred to the Koran the Yacsa, or Law of Zingis (cui Deus maledicat) nor will he believe that Sharokh had abolished the use and authority of that Pagan code.

have maliciously observed that the commands of anger and destruction were more strictly executed than those of beneficence and favour His sons and grandsons, of whom Timour left six-and-thirty at his decease, were his first and most submissive subjects, and, whenever they deviated from their duty, they were corrected, according to the laws of Zingis, with the bastonade, and afterwards restored to honour and command. Perhaps his heart was not devoid of the social virtues; perhaps he was not incapable of loving his friends and pardoning his enemies; but the rules of morality are founded on the public interest; and it may be sufficient to applaud the *wisdom* of a monarch, for the liberality by which he is not impoverished, and for the justice by which he is strengthened and enriched To maintain the harmony of authority and obedience, to chastise the proud, to protect the weak, to reward the deserving, to banish vice and idleness from his dominions, to secure the traveller and merchant, to restrain the depredations of the soldier, to cherish the labours of the husbandman, to encourage industry and learning, and, by an equal and modern assessment, to increase the revenue without increasing the taxes, are indeed the duties of a prince; but, in the discharge of these duties, he finds an ample and immediate recompense. Timour might boast that, at his accession to the throne, Asia was the prey of anarchy and rapine, whilst under his prosperous monarchy, a child, fearless and unhurt, might carry a purse of gold from the East to the West. Such was his confidence of merit that from this reformation he derived excuse for his victories and a title to universal dominion. The four following observations will serve to appreciate his claim to the public gratitude, and perhaps we shall conclude that the Mogul emperor was rather the scourge than the benefactor of mankind. 1 If some partial disorders, some local oppressions, were healed by the sword of Timour, the remedy was far more pernicious than the disease. By their rapine, cruelty, and discord, the petty tyrants of Persia might afflict their subjects; but whole nations were crushed under the footsteps of the reformer. The ground which had been occupied by flourishing cities was often marked by his abominable trophies, by columns or pyramids of human heads. Astracan, Carizme, Delhi, Ispahan, Bagdad, Aleppo, Damascus, Boursa, Smyrna, and a thousand others were sacked, or burnt, or utterly destroyed, in his presence, and by his troops; and perhaps his conscience would have been startled if a priest or philosopher had dared to number the millions of victims whom he had sacrificed to the establishment of peace and order.[77] 2. His most destructive wars were rather inroads than conquests. He invaded Turkestan, Kipzak, Russia, Hindostan, Syria, Anatolia, Armenia, and Georgia, without a hope or a desire of preserving those distant provinces. From thence he departed, laden with spoil; but he left behind him neither troops to awe the contumacious, nor magistrates to protect the obedient, natives. When he had broken the fabric of their ancient government, he abandoned them to the evils which his invasion had aggravated or caused; nor were these evils compensated by any present or possible benefits. 3. The kingdoms of Transoxiana and Persia were the proper field which he laboured to cultivate and adorn as the perpetual inheritance of his family. But his peaceful labours were often interrupted, and sometimes blasted, by the absence of the conqueror. While he triumphed on the Volga or the Ganges, his servants, and even his sons, forgot their master and their duty. The public and private injuries were poorly redressed by the tardy rigour of inquiry and punishment; and we must be content to praise the Institutions of Timour, as the spe-

---

[77] Besides the bloody passages of this narrative, I must refer to an anticipation in the sixth volume of the Decline and Fall, which, in a single note (p 16, note 26) accumulates near 300,000 heads of the monuments of his cruelty. Except in Rowe's play on the fifth of November, I did not expect to hear of Timour's amiable moderation (White's preface, p 7) Yet I can excuse a generous enthusiasm in the reader, and still more in the editor, of the Institutions.

cious idea of a perfect monarchy.   4 Whatsoever might be
the blessings of his administration, they evaporated with his
life.   To reign, rather than to govern, was the ambition of his
children and grandchildren,[78] the enemies of each other and
of the people   A fragment of the empire was upheld with
some glory by Sharokh, his youngest son; but after *his* decease, the scene was again involved in darkness and blood,
and before the end of a century Transoxiana and Persia were
trampled by the Uzbeks from the North, and the Turkmans of
the black and white sheep.   The race of Timour would have
been extinct, if an hero, his descendant in the fifth degree,
had not fled before the Uzbek arms to the conquest of Hindostan.   His successors (the Great Moguls [79]) extended their
sway from the mountains of Cashmir to Cape Comorin, and
from Candahar to the Gulf of Bengal.   Since the reign of
Aurungzebe, their empire has been dissolved; their treasures
of Delhi have been rifled by a Persian robber, and the riches
of their kingdoms is now possessed by a company of Christian merchants, of a remote island in the Northern Ocean.

Far different was the fate of the Ottoman monarchy.   The
massy trunk was bent to the ground, but no sooner did the
hurricane pass away than it again rose with fresh vigour and
more lively vegetation.   When Timour, in every sense, had
evacuated Anatolia, he left the cities without a palace, a
treasure, or a king.   The open country was overspread with
hordes of shepherds and robbers of Tartar or Turkman origin;
the recent conquests of Bajazet were restored to the emirs,
one of whom, in base revenge, demolished his sepulchre; and

[78] Consult the last chapters of Sherefeddin and Arabshah, and M de
Guignes (Hist des Huns, tom iv 1 xv), Fraser's History of Nadir Shah
(p 1–62)   The story of Timour's descendants is imperfectly told; and the
second and third parts of Sherefeddin are unknown

[79] Shah Allum [Shāh-Ālam, A D 1759–1806], the present Mogul, is in the
fourteenth [rather fifteenth from Bābar, who was fifth from Timur] degree
from Timour by Miran Shah, his third son   See the iid volume of Dow's
History of Hindustan   [The shadowy survival of the Mogul empire ceased
to exist in 1857]

his five sons were eager, by civil discord, to consume the remnant of their patrimony. I shall enumerate their names in the order of their age and actions [80] 1. It is doubtful, whether I relate the story of the true *Mustapha*, or of an impostor who personated that lost prince.[81] He fought by his father's side in the battle of Angora; but, when the captive sultan was permitted to inquire for his children, Mousa alone could be found; and the Turkish historians, the slaves of the triumphant faction, are persuaded that his brother was confounded among the slain. If Mustapha escaped from that disastrous field, he was concealed twelve years from his friends and enemies, till he emerged in Thessaly and was hailed by a numerous party as the son and successor of Bajazet. His first defeat would have been his last, had not the true, or false, Mustapha been saved by the Greeks and restored, after the decease of his brother Mahomet, to liberty and empire. A degenerate mind seemed to argue his spurious birth; and, if, on the throne of Hadrianople, he was adored as the Ottoman sultan, his flight, his fetters, and an ignominious gibbet delivered the impostor to popular contempt. A similar character and claim was asserted by several rival pretenders; thirty persons are said to have suffered under the name of Mustapha, and these frequent executions may perhaps insinuate that the Turkish court was not perfectly secure of the death of the lawful prince. 2. After his father's captivity, Isa [82] reigned for some time in the neighbourhood of

[80] The civil wars, from the death of Bajazet to that of Mustapha, are related, according to the Turks, by Demetrius Cantemir (p 58-82). Of the Greeks, Chalcondyles (l iv and v), Phranza (l 1 c 30-32), and Ducas (c 18-27), the last is the most copious and best informed

[81] [It is difficult to decide whether he was an impostor, as the Ottoman, or genuine, as the Greek, historians allege Zinkeisen leaves the question open (i 383-384) but with an inclination to the former opinion, Hammer argues for the view that the claimant was the true Mustapha, i 297]

[82] Arabshah, tom ii c 26, whose testimony on this occasion is weighty and valuable The existence of Isa (unknown to the Turks) is likewise confirmed by Sherefeddin (l v c 57)

Angora, Sinope, and the Black Sea; and his ambassadors were dismissed from the presence of Timour with fair promises and honourable gifts But their master was soon deprived of his province and life by a jealous brother, the sovereign of Amasia; and the final event [83] suggested a pious allusion that the law of Moses and Jesus, of *Isa* and *Mousa*, had been abrogated by the greater *Mahomet*. 3 *Soliman* is not numbered in the list of the Turkish emperors; yet he checked the victorious progress of the Moguls, and after their departure united for a while the thrones of Hadrianople and Boursa. In war, he was brave, active, and fortunate, his courage was softened by clemency; but it was likewise inflamed by presumption, and corrupted by intemperance and idleness He relaxed the nerves of discipline in a government where either the subject or the sovereign must continually tremble; his vices alienated the chiefs of the army and the law, and his daily drunkenness, so contemptible in a prince and a man, was doubly odious in a disciple of the prophet In the slumber of intoxication, he was surprised by his brother Mousa; and, as he fled from Hadrianople towards the Byzantine capital, Soliman was overtaken and slain in a bath, after a reign of seven years and ten months 4 The investiture of Mousa degraded him as the slave of the Moguls; his tributary kingdom of Anatolia was confined within a narrow limit, nor could his broken militia and empty treasury contend with the hardy and veteran bands of the sovereign of Romania. Mousa fled in disguise from the palace of Boursa; traversed the Propontis in an open boat; wandered over the Walachian and Servian hills; and, after some vain attempts, ascended the throne of Hadrianople, so recently stained with the blood of Soliman In a reign of three years and a half, his troops were victorious against the Christians of Hungary and the Morea; but Mousa was ruined by his timorous dis-

[83] [Mohammad defeated Isa in battle at Ulubad, A D 1403, and again in 1404 (Sad ad-Din, transl. Bratutti, p 284)]

position and unseasonable clemency. After resigning the
sovereignty of Anatolia, he fell a victim to the perfidy of his
ministers and the superior ascendant of his brother Mahomet.
5. The final victory of Mahomet was the just recompense of
his prudence and moderation. Before his father's captivity,
the royal youth had been entrusted with the government of
Amasia, thirty days' journey from Constantinople and the
Turkish frontier against the Christians of Trebizond and
Georgia. The castle, in Asiatic warfare, was esteemed impregnable; and the city of Amasia,[84] which is equally divided
by the river Iris, rises on either side in the form of an amphi-
theatre, and represents, on a smaller scale, the image of Bagdad. In his rapid career, Timour appears to have overlooked this obscure and contumacious angle of Anatolia;
and Mahomet, without provoking the conqueror, maintained
his silent independence, and chased from the province the
last stragglers of the Tartar host. He relieved himself from
the dangerous neighbourhood of Isa; but in the contests of
their more powerful brethren his firm neutrality was respected;
till, after the triumph of Mousa, he stood forth the heir and
avenger of the unfortunate Soliman. Mahomet obtained
Anatolia by treaty and Romania by arms; and the soldier
who presented him with the head of Mousa was rewarded
as the benefactor of his king and country. The eight years
of his sole and peaceful reign were usefully employed in
banishing the vices of civil discord, and restoring, on a firmer
basis, the fabric of the Ottoman monarchy.[85] His last care
was the choice of two vizirs, Bajazet and Ibrahim,[86] who
might guide the youth of his son Amurath; and such was their

[84] Arabshah, *loc citat* Abulfeda, Geograph tab xvii p 302   Busbequius, epist i p 96, 97, in Itinere C P et Amasiano

[85] [Mohammad's character was marked by justice, mildness, and freedom
from fanaticism]

[86] The virtues of Ibrahim are praised by a contemporary Greek (Ducas,
c 25) His descendants are the sole nobles in Turkey, they content themselves with the administration of his pious foundations, are excused from
public offices, and receive two annual visits from the sultan (Cantemir, p 76).

union and prudence that they concealed, above forty days, the emperor's death, till the arrival of his successor in the palace of Boursa. A new war was kindled in Europe by the prince, or impostor, Mustapha; the first vizir lost his army and his head; but the more fortunate Ibrahim, whose name and family are still revered, extinguished the last pretender to the throne of Bajazet, and closed the scene of domestic hostility.

In these conflicts, the wisest Turks, and indeed the body of the nation, were strongly attached to the unity of the empire; and Romania and Anatolia, so often torn asunder by private ambition, were animated by a strong and invincible tendency of cohesion. Their efforts might have instructed the Christian powers; and, had they occupied, with a confederate fleet, the straits of Gallipoli, the Ottomans, at least in Europe, must have been speedily annihilated. But the schism of the West, and the factions and wars of France and England, diverted the Latins from this generous enterprise; they enjoyed the present respite without a thought of futurity; and were often tempted by a momentary interest to serve the common enemy of their religion. A colony of Genoese,[87] which had been planted at Phocæa [88] on the Ionian coast, was enriched by the lucrative monopoly of alum;[89] and their tranquillity,

---

[87] See Pachymer (l v c 29), Nicephorus Gregoras (l ii. c i), Sherefeddin (l v c 57), and Ducas (c 25) The last of these, a curious and careful observer, is entitled, from his birth and station, to particular credit in all that concerns Ionia and the islands Among the nations that resorted to New Phocæa he mentions the English ('Ιγγλῆνοι); an early evidence of Mediterranean trade

[88] For the spirit of navigation and freedom of ancient Phocæa, or rather of the Phocæans, consult the first book of Herodotus, and the Geographical Index of his last and learned French translator, M Larcher (tom vii p 299)

[89] Phocæa is not enumerated by Pliny (Hist Nat xxxv 52) among the places productive of alum; he reckons Egypt as the first, and for the second the isle of Melos, whose alum mines are described by Tournefort (tom i lettre iv), a traveller and a naturalist After the loss of Phocæa, the Genoese, in 1459, found that useful mineral in the isle of Ischia (Ismael Bouillaud, ad Ducam, c 25).

under the Turkish empire, was secured by the annual payment of tribute.   In the last civil war of the Ottomans, the
Genoese governor, Adorno, a bold and ambitious youth,
embraced the party of Amurath, and undertook, with seven
stout galleys, to transport him from Asia to Europe   The sultan and five hundred guards embarked on board the admiral's ship, which was manned by eight hundred of the
bravest Franks   His life and liberty were in their hands;
nor can we, without reluctance, applaud the fidelity of Adorno,
who, in the midst of the passage, knelt before him, and grate-
fully accepted a discharge of his arrears of tribute.   They
landed in sight of Mustapha and Gallipoli; two thousand
Italians, armed with lances and battle-axes, attended Amurath to the conquest of Hadrianople; and this venal service
was soon repaid by the ruin of the commerce and colony of
Phocæa.

If Timour had generously marched at the request, and to the
relief of, the Greek emperor, he might be entitled to the praise
and gratitude of the Christians.[90]   But a Musulman, who
carried into Georgia the sword of persecution, and respected
the holy warfare of Bajazet, was not disposed to pity or succour the *idolaters* of Europe   The Tartar followed the impulse of ambition; and the deliverance of Constantinople was
the accidental consequence.   When Manuel abdicated the
government, it was his prayer, rather than his hope, that the
ruin of the church and state might be delayed beyond his
unhappy days; and, after his return from a Western pilgrimage, he expected every hour the news of the sad catastrophe
On a sudden, he was astonished and rejoiced by the intelli-

---

[90] The writer who has the most abused this fabulous generosity is our
ingenious Sir William Temple (his Works, vol iii. p 349, 350, 8vo edition),
that lover of exotic virtue   After the conquest of Russia, &c and the passage of the Danube, his Tartar hero relieves, visits, admires, and refuses the
city of Constantine   His flattering pencil deviates in every line from the
truth of history, yet his pleasing fictions are more excusable than the gross
errors of Cantemir.

gence of the retreat, the overthrow, and the captivity of the Ottoman Manuel [91] immediately sailed from Modon in the Morea; ascended the throne of Constantinople; and dismissed his blind competitor to an easy exile in the isle of Lesbos. The ambassadors of the son of Bajazet were soon introduced to his presence; but their pride was fallen, their tone was modest; they were awed by the just apprehension lest the Greeks should open to the Moguls the gates of Europe Soliman saluted the emperor by the name of father; solicited at his hands the government or gift of Romania, and promised to deserve his favour by inviolable friendship, and the restitution of Thessalonica, with the most important places along the Strymon, the Propontis, and the Black Sea The alliance of Soliman exposed the emperor to the enmity and revenge of Mousa. The Turks appeared in arms before the gates of Constantinople; but they were repulsed by sea and land; and, unless the city was guarded by some foreign mercenaries, the Greeks must have wondered at their own triumph. But, instead of prolonging the division of the Ottoman powers, the policy or passion of Manuel was tempted to assist the most formidable of the sons of Bajazet. He concluded a treaty with Mahomet, whose progress was checked by the insuperable barrier of Gallipoli the sultan and his troops were transported over the Bosphorus; he was hospitably entertained in the capital; and his successful sally was the first step to the conquest of Romania The ruin was suspended by the prudence and moderation of the conqueror, he faithfully discharged his own obligations, and those of Soliman; respected the laws of gratitude and peace; and left the emperor guardian of his two younger sons, in the vain hope of saving them from the jealous cruelty of their brother Amurath. But the execution of his last testament would have

---

[91] For the reigns of Manuel and John, of Mahomet I and Amurath II , see the Othman history of Cantemir (p 70-95), and the three Greeks, Chalcondyles, Phranza, and Ducas, who is still superior to his rivals

offended the national honour and religion; and the divan unanimously pronounced that the royal youths should never be abandoned to the custody and education of a Christian dog. On this refusal, the Byzantine councils were divided; but the age and caution of Manuel yielded to the presumption of his son John; and they unsheathed a dangerous weapon of revenge, by dismissing the true or false Mustapha, who had long been detained as a captive and hostage, and for whose maintenance they received an annual pension of three hundred thousand aspers.[92] At the door of his prison, Mustapha subscribed to every proposal, and the keys of Gallipoli, or rather of Europe, were stipulated as the price of his deliverance. But no sooner was he seated on the throne of Romania than he dismissed the Greek ambassadors with a smile of contempt, declaring, in a pious tone, that, at the day of judgment, he would rather answer for the violation of an oath than for the surrender of a Musulman city into the hands of the infidels. The emperor was at once the enemy of the two rivals; from whom he had sustained, and to whom he had offered, an injury; and the victory of Amurath was followed, in the ensuing spring, by the siege of Constantinople.[93]

The religious merit of subduing the city of the Cæsars attracted from Asia a crowd of volunteers, who aspired to the crown of martyrdom. Their military ardour was inflamed

[92] The Turkish asper (from the Greek ἄσπρος [= white]) is, or was, a piece of *white* or silver money, at present much debased, but which was formerly equivalent to the 54th part, at least, of a Venetian ducat, or sequin, and the 300,000 aspers, a princely allowance or royal tribute, may be computed at 2500l sterling (Leunclav Pandect Turc p 406-408) [Cantacuscino (in Sansovino, Historia Universale de Turchi, fol 11 v) counts 54 aspers to a sultanin or ducat, and this was still the value about the beginning of the 16th century, but in the reign of Selim I , before 1520, 60 aspers went to a ducat, and this value was maintained during the reign of Sulayman and Selim II]

[93] For the siege of Constantinople in 1422, see the particular and contemporary narrative of John Cananus, published by Leo Allatius, at the end of his edition of Acropolita (p 188-199)

by the promise of rich spoils and beautiful females; and the sultan's ambition was consecrated by the presence and prediction of Seid Bechar, a descendant of the prophet,[94] who arrived in the camp, on a mule, with a venerable train of five hundred disciples. But he might blush, if a fanatic could blush, at the failure of his assurances The strength of the walls resisted an army of two hundred thousand Turks;[95] their assaults were repelled by the sallies of the Greeks and their foreign mercenaries; the old resources of defence were opposed to the new engines of attack, and the enthusiasm of the dervish, who was snatched to heaven in visionary converse with Mahomet, was answered by the credulity of the Christians, who *beheld* the Virgin Mary, in a violet garment, walking on the rampart and animating their courage.[96] After a siege of two months, Amurath was recalled to Boursa by a domestic revolt, which had been kindled by Greek treachery, and was soon extinguished by the death of a guiltless brother. While he led his Janizaries to new conquests in Europe and Asia, the Byzantine empire was indulged in a servile and precarious respite of thirty years. Manuel sank into the grave, and John Palæologus was permitted to reign, for an annual tribute of three hundred thousand aspers, and the dereliction of almost all that he held beyond the suburbs of Constantinople.

In the establishment and restoration of the Turkish empire, the first merit must doubtless be assigned to the personal

---

[94] Cantemir, p 80 Cananus, who describes Seid Bechar, without naming him, supposes that the friend of Mahomet assumed, in his amours, the privilege of a prophet, and that the fairest of the Greek nuns were promised to the saint and his disciples

[95] [This number, given by Ducas and Phrantzes, is obviously a gross exaggeration, perhaps a slip of the pen Cp Zinkeisen, 1 524 (and 527), who thinks the besiegers did not exceed 40,000 or 50,000 According to Cananus the first corps brought against the city was 10,000, then followed "another army" like a hail storm, p 459 ed Bonn]

[96] For this miraculous apparition, Cananus appeals to the Musulman saint, but who will bear testimony for Seid Bechar?

qualities of the sultans; since, in human life, the most important scenes will depend on the character of a single actor. By some shades of wisdom and virtue they may be discriminated from each other, but, except in a single instance, a period of nine reigns and two hundred and sixty-five years is occupied from the elevation of Othman to the death of Soliman, by a rare series of warlike and active princes, who impressed their subjects with obedience and their enemies with terror. Instead of the slothful luxury of the seraglio, the heirs of royalty were educated in the council and the field; from early youth they were entrusted by their fathers with the command of provinces and armies, and this manly institution, which was often productive of civil war, must have essentially contributed to the discipline and vigour of the monarchy. The Ottomans cannot style themselves, like the Arabian caliphs, the descendants or successors of the apostle of God; and the kindred which they claim with the Tartar khans of the house of Zingis appears to be founded in flattery rather than in truth [97] Their origin is obscure; but their sacred and indefeasible right, which no time can erase and no violence can infringe, was soon and unalterably implanted in the minds of their subjects. A weak or vicious sultan may be deposed and strangled; but his inheritance devolves to an infant or an idiot; nor has the most daring rebel presumed to ascend the throne of his lawful sovereign.[98] While the transient dynasties of Asia have been continually subverted by a crafty vizir in the palace or a victorious general in the

[97] See Rycaut (l i c 13)   The Turkish sultans assume the title of Khan Yet Abulghazi is ignorant of his Ottoman cousins

[98] The third grand vizir of the name of Kiuperli, who was slain at the battle of Salankamen in 1691 (Cantemir, p 382), presumed to say that all the successors of Soliman had been fools or tyrants, and that it was time to abolish the race (Marsigli Stato Militare, &c. p 28)   This political heretic was a good Whig, and justified, against the French ambassador, the revolution of England (Mignot, Hist des Ottomans, tom iii. p 434).   His presumption condemns the singular exception of continuing offices in the same family

camp), the Ottoman succession has been confirmed by the practice of five centuries, and is now incorporated with the vital principle of the Turkish nation.

To the spirit and constitution of that nation a strong and singular influence may, however, be ascribed. The primitive subjects of Othman were the four hundred families of wandering Turkmans, who had followed his ancestors from the Oxus to the Sangar, and the plains of Anatolia are still covered with the white and black tents of their rustic brethren But this original drop was dissolved in the mass of voluntary and vanquished subjects who, under the name of Turks, are united by the common ties of religion, language, and manners. In the cities, from Erzeroum to Belgrade, that national appellation is common to all the Moslems, the first and most honourable inhabitants, but they have abandoned, at least in Romania, the villages and the cultivation of the land to the Christian peasants. In the vigorous age of the Ottoman government, the Turks were themselves excluded from all civil and military honours; and a servile class, an artificial people, was raised by the discipline of education to obey, to conquer, and to command [99] From the time of Orchan and the first Amurath, the sultans were persuaded that a government of the sword must be renewed in each generation with new soldiers; and that such soldiers must be sought, not in effeminate Asia, but among the hardy and warlike natives of Europe. The provinces of Thrace, Macedonia, Albania, Bulgaria, and Servia became the perpetual seminary of the Turkish army; and, when the royal fifth of the captives was diminished by conquest, an inhuman tax, of the fifth child, or of every fifth year, was rigorously levied on the Christian families.[100] At the age of twelve or fourteen

[99] Chalcondyles (l v) and Ducas (c 23) exhibit the rude lineaments of the Ottoman policy, and the transmutation of Christian children into Turkish soldiers

[100] [It is uncertain at what time the rule of levying this tribute every 5th year was introduced; it had become established by the time of Selim I.,

years,[101] the most robust youths were torn from their parents, their names were enrolled in a book; and from that moment they were clothed, taught, and maintained for the public service. According to the promise of their appearance, they were selected for the royal schools of Boursa, Pera, and Hadrianople, entrusted to the care of the bashaws, or dispersed in the houses of the Anatolian peasantry. It was the first care of their masters to instruct them in the Turkish language; their bodies were exercised by every labour that could fortify their strength; they learned to wrestle, to leap, to run, to shoot with the bow, and afterwards with the musket; till they were drafted into the chambers and companies of the Janizaries, and severely trained in the military or monastic discipline of the order. The youths most conspicuous for birth, talents, and beauty were admitted into the inferior class of *Agiamoglans*, or the more liberal rank of *Ichoglans*, of whom the former were attached to the palace, and the latter to the person of the prince. In four successive schools, under the rod of the white eunuchs, the arts of horsemanship and of darting the javelin were their daily exercise, while those of a more studious cast applied themselves to the study of the Koran and the knowledge of the Arabic and Persian tongues. As they advanced in seniority and merit, they were gradually dismissed to military, civil, and even ecclesiastical employments; the longer their stay, the higher was their expectation; till, at a mature period, they were admitted into the number of the forty agas, who stood before the sultan, and were promoted by his choice to the government of provinces and the first honours of the empire.[102] Such a mode of institution was

---

but the tribute was sometimes exacted oftener, and many witnesses say "every three years " Cp Zinkeisen, iii p 216]

[101] [In earlier times, the age seems to have been younger — six or seven]

[102] This sketch of the Turkish education and discipline is chiefly borrowed from Rycaut's State of the Ottoman Empire, the Stato Militare del' Imperio Ottomano of Count Marsigli (in Haya, 1732, in folio), and a Description of

admirably adapted to the form and spirit of a despotic monarchy. The ministers and generals were, in the strictest sense, the slaves of the emperor, to whose bounty they were indebted for their instruction and support. When they left the seraglio, and suffered their beards to grow as the symbol of enfranchisement, they found themselves in an important office, without faction or friendship, without parents and without heirs, dependent on the hand which had raised them from the dust, and which, on the slightest displeasure, could break in pieces these statues of glass, as they are aptly termed by the Turkish proverb [103] In the slow and painful steps of education, their character and talents were unfolded to a discerning eye the *man*, naked and alone, was reduced to the standard of his personal merit; and, if the sovereign had wisdom to choose, he possessed a pure and boundless liberty of choice The Ottoman candidates were trained by the virtues of abstinence to those of action; by the habits of submission, to those of command. A similar spirit was diffused among the troops, and their silence and sobriety, their patience and modesty, have extorted the reluctant praise of their Christian enemies.[104] Nor can the victory appear doubtful, if we compare the discipline and exercise of the Janizaries with the pride of birth, the independence of chivalry, the ignorance of the new levies, the mutinous temper of the veterans, and the vices of intemperance and disorder which so long contaminated the armies of Europe

the Seraglio, approved by Mr Greaves himself, a curious traveller, and inserted in the second volume of his works [One important feature of the Ottoman education was that pains were taken to discover the natural faculties of each individual and to train him for the work to which he was best adapted. On the history of the Janissaries, their organisation and duties, the variations in their effective strength, see A Djevad Bey, Etat militaire Ottoman, vol 1 1882 There is a good brief account of the military establishment in Ranke's little work on the Ottoman Empire (Engl transl by Kelly, 1843)]

[103] From the series of 115 vizirs till the siege of Vienna (Marsigli, p 13), their place may be valued at three years and a half purchase

[104] See the entertaining and judicious letters of Busbequius.

The only hope of salvation for the Greek empire and the adjacent kingdoms would have been some more powerful weapon, some discovery in the art of war, that should give them a decisive superiority over their Turkish foes. Such a weapon was in their hands, such a discovery had been made in the critical moment of their fate. The chymists of China or Europe had found, by casual or elaborate experiments, that a mixture of saltpetre, sulphur, and charcoal produces, with a spark of fire, a tremendous explosion. It was soon observed that, if the expansive force were compressed in a strong tube, a ball of stone or iron might be expelled with irresistible and destructive velocity. The precise era of the invention and application of gunpowder [105] is involved in doubtful traditions and equivocal language; yet we may clearly discern that it was known before the middle of the fourteenth century, and that, before the end of the same, the use of artillery in battles and sieges, by sea and land, was familiar to the states of Germany, Italy, Spain, France, and England.[106] The priority of nations is of small account; none could derive any exclusive benefit from their previous or superior knowledge; and in the common improvement they stood on the same level of relative power and military science. Nor was it possible to circumscribe the secret within the pale of the church; it was disclosed to the

[105] The 1st and 2d volumes of Dr Watson's Chemical Essays contain two valuable discourses on the discovery and composition of gunpowder

[106] On this subject, modern testimonies cannot be trusted   The original passages are collected by Ducange (Gloss Latin tom 1 p 675, *Bombarda*) But in the early doubtful twilight, the name, sound, fire, and effect, that seem to express *our* artillery, may be fairly interpreted of the old engines and the Greek fire. For the English cannon at Crecy, the authority of John Villani (Chron l xii c 65) must be weighed against the silence of Froissard [and the English authorities]   Yet Muratori (Antiquit Italiæ medii Ævi, tom ii Dissert xxvi p 514, 515) has produced a decisive passage from Petrarch (de Remedus utriusque Fortunæ Dialog), who, before the year 1344, execrates this terrestrial thunder, *nuper* rara, *nunc* communis. [La Cabane, De la poudre á canon et de son introduction en France, 1845. Reinaud et Favé Du feu grégois et des origines de la poudre à canon, 1860]

Turks by the treachery of apostates and the selfish policy of rivals; and the sultans had sense to adopt, and wealth to reward, the talents of a Christian engineer. The Genoese who transported Amurath into Europe must be accused as his preceptors, and it was probably by their hands that his cannon was cast and directed at the siege of Constantinople [107] The first attempt was indeed unsuccessful, but in the general warfare of the age the advantage was on *their* side who were most commonly the assailants, for a while the proportion of the attack and defence was suspended, and this thundering artillery was pointed against the walls and turrets which had been erected only to resist the less potent engines of antiquity. By the Venetians, the use of gunpowder was communicated without reproach to the sultans of Egypt and Persia, their allies against the Ottoman power. The secret was soon propagated to the extremities of Asia, and the advantage of the European was confined to his easy victories over the savages of the new world. If we contrast the rapid progress of this mischievous discovery with the slow and laborious advances of reason, science, and the arts of peace, a philosopher, according to his temper, will laugh or weep at the folly of mankind.

[107] The Turkish cannon, which Ducas (c 30) first introduces before Belgrade (A.D. 1436), is mentioned by Chalcondyles (l v p 123 [p 231 ed Bonn]) in 1422, at the siege of Constantinople.

CHAPTER LXVI

Applications of the Eastern Emperors to the Popes — Visits to the West, of John the First, Manuel, and John the Second, Palæologus — Union of the Greek and Latin Churches, promoted by the Council of Basil, and concluded at Ferrara and Florence — State of Literature at Constantinople — Its Revival in Italy by the Greek Fugitives — Curiosity and Emulation of the Latins

In the four last centuries of the Greek emperors, their friendly or hostile aspect towards the pope and the Latins may be observed as the thermometer of their prosperity or distress, as the scale of the rise and fall of the Barbarian dynasties.[1] When the Turks of the house of Seljuk pervaded Asia and threatened Constantinople, we have seen at the council of Placentia the suppliant ambassadors of Alexius imploring the protection of the common father of the Christians. No sooner had the arms of the French pilgrims removed the sultan from Nice to Iconium than the Greek princes resumed, or avowed, their genuine hatred and contempt for the schismatics of the West, which precipitated the first downfall of their empire. The date of the Mogul invasion is marked in the soft and charitable language of John Vataces. After the recovery of Constantinople, the throne

---

[1] [The following works deal with the general history of the schism of the Greek and Latin Churches and the attempts at reunion: Maimbourg, Histoire du Schisme des Grecs, 2 vols., 1677; Pitzipios, L'église orientale, 1855, Pichler, Geschichte der kirchlichen Trennung zwischen Orient und Occident, 2 vols., 1864–5, Demitrakopulos, Ἱστορία τοῦ σχίσματος τῆς Λατινικῆς ἐκκλησίας ἀπὸ τῆς ὀρθοδόξου Ἑλληνικῆς, 1867, Lebedev, History of the Byzantine-Oriental Church from the end of the 11th to the middle of the 15th century (in Russian), 1892.]

of the first Palæologus was encompassed by foreign and domestic enemies; as long as the sword of Charles was suspended over his head, he basely courted the favour of the Roman pontiff, and sacrificed to the present danger his faith, his virtue, and the affection of his subjects. On the decease of Michael, the prince and people asserted the independence of their church and the purity of their creed, the elder Andronicus neither feared nor loved the Latins, in his last distress, pride was the safeguard of superstition, nor could he decently retract in his age the firm and orthodox declarations of his youth. His grandson, the younger Andronicus, was less a slave in his temper and situation; and the conquest of Bithynia by the Turks admonished him to seek a temporal and spiritual alliance with the Western princes. After a separation and silence of fifty years, a secret agent, the monk Barlaam, was despatched to Pope Benedict the Twelfth; and his artful instructions appear to have been drawn by the master-hand of the great domestic.[2] "Most holy father," was he commissioned to say, "the emperor is not less desirous than yourself of an union between the two churches; but in this delicate transaction he is obliged to respect his own dignity and the prejudices of his subjects. The ways of union are twofold, force and persuasion. Of force, the inefficacy has been already tried; since the Latins have subdued the empire, without subduing the minds, of the Greeks. The method of persuasion, though slow, is sure and permanent. A deputation of thirty or forty of our doctors would probably agree with those of the Vatican, in the love of truth and the unity of belief, but on their return, what would be the use, the recompense, of such agreement? the

---

[2] This curious instruction was transcribed (I believe) from the Vatican archives by Odoricus Raynaldus, in his Continuation of the Annals of Baronius (Romæ, 1646-1677, in 10 volumes in folio) I have contented myself with the Abbé Fleury (Hist Ecclésiastique, tom. xx. p 1-8), whose extracts I have always found to be clear, accurate, and impartial [For Barlaam the Calabrian see below, p 276-6]

scorn of their brethren, and the reproaches of a blind and
obstinate nation   Yet that nation is accustomed to reverence
the general councils which have fixed the articles of our
faith ; and, if they reprobate the decrees of Lyons, it is because
the Eastern churches were neither heard nor represented in
that arbitrary meeting   For this salutary end it will be expedient, and even necessary, that a well-chosen legate should
be sent into Greece, to convene the patriarchs of Constantinople, Alexandria, Antioch, and Jerusalem, and, with their
aid, to prepare a free and universal synod. But at this
moment," continued the subtle agent, "the empire is assaulted
and endangered by the Turks, who have occupied four of the
greatest cities of Anatolia. The Christian inhabitants have
expressed a wish of returning to their allegiance and religion ;
but the forces and revenues of the emperor are insufficient
for their deliverance ; and the Roman legate must be accompanied, or preceded, by an army of Franks, to expel the infidels and open a way to the holy sepulchre." If the suspicious Latins should require some pledge, some previous
effect of the sincerity of the Greeks, the answers of Barlaam
were perspicuous and rational. "1. A general synod can
alone consummate the union of the churches · nor can such
a synod be held till the three Oriental patriarchs, and a great
number of bishops, are enfranchised from the Mahometan
yoke. 2. The Greeks are alienated by a long series of oppression and injury. they must be reconciled by some act
of brotherly love, some effectual succour, which may fortify
the authority and arguments of the emperor and the friends
of the union. 3 If some difference of faith or ceremonies
should be found incurable, the Greeks, however, are the
disciples of Christ, and the Turks are the common enemies
of the Christian name. The Armenians, Cyprians, and
Rhodians are equally attacked ; and it will become the piety
of the French princes to draw their swords in the general
defence of religion. 4. Should the subjects of Andronicus
be treated   the   of schismatic   of heretic   of pagans,

a judicious policy may yet instruct the powers of the West to embrace an useful ally, to uphold a sinking empire, to guard the confines of Europe; and rather to join the Greeks against the Turks than to expect the union of the Turkish arms with the troops and treasures of captive Greece." The reasons, the offers, and the demands of Andronicus were eluded with cold and stately indifference. The kings of France and Naples declined the dangers and glory of a crusade   the pope refused to call a new synod to determine old articles of faith; and his regard for the obsolete claims of the Latin emperor and clergy engaged him to use an offensive superscription   "To the *moderator* [3] of the Greeks, and the persons who style themselves the patriarchs of the Eastern churches." For such an embassy, a time and character less propitious could not easily have been found. Benedict the Twelfth [4] was a dull peasant, perplexed with scruples, and immersed in sloth and wine; his pride might enrich with a third crown the papal tiara, but he was alike unfit for the regal and the pastoral office.

After the decease of Andronicus, while the Greeks were distracted by intestine war, they could not presume to agitate a general union of the Christians   But, as soon as Cantacuzene had subdued and pardoned his enemies, he was anxious to justify, or at least to extenuate, the introduction of the Turks into Europe and the nuptials of his daughter with a

---

[3] The ambiguity of this title is happy or ingenious, and *moderator*, as synonymous to *rector*, *gubernator*, is a word of classical, and even Ciceronian, Latinity, which may be found, not in the Glossary of Ducange, but in the Thesaurus of Robert Stephens

[4] The first epistle (sine titulo) of Petrarch exposes the danger of the *bark* and the incapacity of the *pilot*   Hæc inter, vino madidus, ævo gravis ac soporifero rore perfusus, jamjam nutitat, dormitat, jam somno præceps, atque (utinam solus) ruit   Heu quanto felicius patrio terram sulcasset aratro, quam scalmum piscatorium ascendisset   This satire engages his biographer to weigh the virtues and vices of Benedict XII , which have been exaggerated by Guelphs and Ghibelines, by Papists and Protestants (see Mémoires sur la Vie de Pétrarque, tom i p 259, n not 15, p 13-16) He gave occasion to the saying Bibamus papaliter.

Musulman prince.   Two officers of state, with a Latin interpreter, were sent in his name to the Roman court, which was
transplanted to Avignon, on the banks of the Rhone, during
a period of seventy years, they represented the hard necessity
which had urged him to embrace the alliance of the miscreants, and pronounced by his command the specious and
edifying sounds of union and crusade.   Pope Clement the
Sixth,[5] the successor of Benedict, received them with hospitality and honour, acknowledged the innocence of their
sovereign, excused his distress, applauded his magnanimity,
and displayed a clear knowledge of the state and revolutions
of the Greek empire, which he had imbibed from the honest
accounts of a Savoyard lady, an attendant of the empress
Anne.[6]   If Clement was ill endowed with the virtues of a
priest, he possessed, however, the spirit and magnificence of
a prince, whose liberal hand distributed benefices and kingdoms with equal facility   Under his reign, Avignon was the
seat of pomp and pleasure, in his youth he had surpassed
the licentiousness of a baron; and the palace, nay, the bed-
chamber, of the pope was adorned, or polluted, by the visits
of his female favourites.   The wars of France and England
were adverse to the holy enterprise; but his vanity was amused
by the splendid idea; and the Greek ambassadors returned
with two Latin bishops, the ministers of the pontiff.   On
their arrival at Constantinople, the emperor and the nuncios
admired each other's piety and eloquence, and their frequent
conferences were filled with mutual praises and promises,

[5] See the original Lives of Clement VI in Muraton (Script Rerum
Italicarum, tom III p II p 550-589), Matteo Villani (Chron l III c 43,
in Muratori, tom xiv. p 186), who styles him, molto cavalleresco, poco
religioso, Fleury (Hist Ecclés tom. xx p 126), and the Vie de Pétrarque
(tom II p 42-45)   The Abbé de Sade treats him with the most indulgence,
but *he* is a gentleman as well as a priest

[6] Her name (most probably corrupted) was Zampea   She had accompanied and alone remained with her mistress at Constantinople, where her
prudence, erudition, and politeness deserved the praises of the Greeks them-
sel--- (Cant--- --- l - - ;)

by which both parties were amused and neither could be deceived. "I am delighted," said the devout Cantacuzene, "with the project of our holy war, which must redound to my personal glory as well as to the public benefit of Christendom. My dominions will give a free passage to the armies of France: my troops, my galleys, my treasures, shall be consecrated to the common cause, and happy would be my fate, could I deserve and obtain the crown of martyrdom. Words are insufficient to express the ardour with which I sigh for the re-union of the scattered members of Christ. If my death could avail, I would gladly present my sword and my neck; if the spiritual phœnix could arise from my ashes, I would erect the pile and kindle the flame with my own hands." Yet the Greek emperor presumed to observe that the articles of faith which divided the two churches had been introduced by the pride and precipitation of the Latins   he disclaimed the servile and arbitrary steps of the first Palæologus, and firmly declared that he would never submit his conscience, unless to the decrees of a free and universal synod. "The situation of the times," continued he, "will not allow the pope and myself to meet either at Rome or Constantinople, but some maritime city may be chosen on the verge of the two empires, to unite the bishops, and to instruct the faithful, of the East and West." The nuncios seemed content with the proposition, and Cantacuzene affects to deplore the failure of his hopes, which were soon overthrown by the death of Clement and the different temper of his successor. His own life was prolonged, but it was prolonged in a cloister, and, except by his prayers, the humble monk was incapable of directing the counsels of his pupil or the state.[7]

Yet, of all the Byzantine princes, that pupil, John Palæ-

---

[7] See this whole negotiation in Cantacuzene (l iv c 9), who, amidst the praises and virtues which he bestows on himself, reveals the uneasiness of a guilty conscience.

ologus, was the best disposed to embrace, to believe, and to obey the shepherd of the West   His mother, Anne of Savoy, was baptised in the bosom of the Latin church   her marriage with Andronicus imposed a change of name, of apparel, and of worship, but her heart was still faithful to her country and religion; she had formed the infancy of her son, and she governed the emperor, after his mind, or at least his stature, was enlarged to the size of man.   In the first year of his deliverance and restoration, the Turks were still masters of the Hellespont; the son of Cantacuzene was in arms at Hadrianople; and Palæologus could depend neither on himself nor on his people.   By his mother's advice, and in the hope of foreign aid, he abjured the rights both of the church and state; and the act of slavery,[8] subscribed in purple ink and sealed with the *golden* bull, was privately entrusted to an Italian agent.   The first article of the treaty is an oath of fidelity and obedience to Innocent the Sixth and his successors, the supreme pontiffs of the Roman and Catholic church.   The emperor promises to entertain, with due reverence, their legates and nuncios, to assign a palace for their residence, and a temple for their worship; and to deliver his second son Manuel as the hostage of his faith.   For these condescensions, he requires a prompt succour of fifteen galleys, with five hundred men at arms and a thousand archers, to serve against his Christian and Musulman enemies.   Palæologus engages to impose on his clergy and people the same spiritual yoke; but, as the resistance of the Greeks might be justly foreseen, he adopts the two effectual methods of corruption and education   The legate was empowered to distribute the vacant benefices among the ecclesiastics who should subscribe the creed of the Vatican; three schools were instituted to instruct the youth of Constantinople in the language and

---

[8] See this ignominious treaty in Fleury (Hist Ecclés p 151-154), from Raynaldus, who drew it from the Vatican archives.   It was not worth the trouble of a pious forgery.

doctrine of the Latins; and the name of Andronicus, the heir of the empire, was enrolled as the first student. Should he fail in the measures of persuasion or force, Palæologus declares himself unworthy to reign, transfers to the pope all regal and paternal authority; and invests Innocent with full power to regulate the family, the government, and the marriage of his son and successor. But this treaty was neither executed nor published. The Roman galleys were as vain and imaginary as the submission of the Greeks, and it was only by the secrecy, that their sovereign escaped the dishonour, of this fruitless humiliation.

The tempest of the Turkish arms soon burst on his head, and, after the loss of Hadrianople and Romania, he was enclosed in his capital, the vassal of the haughty Amurath, with the miserable hope of being the last devoured by the savage. In this abject state, Palæologus embraced the resolution of embarking for Venice and casting himself at the feet of the pope. He was the first of the Byzantine princes who had ever visited the unknown regions of the West, yet in them alone he could seek consolation or relief, and with less violation of his dignity he might appear in the sacred college than at the Ottoman *Porte*. After a long absence, the Roman pontiffs were returning from Avignon to the banks of the Tiber; Urban the Fifth,[9] of a mild and virtuous character, encouraged or allowed the pilgrimage of the Greek prince, and, within the same year, enjoyed the glory of receiving in the Vatican the two Imperial shadows who represented the majesty of Constantine and Charlemagne. In this suppliant visit, the emperor of Constantinople, whose vanity was lost in his distress, gave more than could be expected of empty sounds and formal submissions. A previous trial was im-

---

[9] See the two first original Lives of Urban V (in Muratori, Script. Rerum Italicarum, tom. iii p. ii p. 623, 635), and the Ecclesiastical Annals of Spondanus (tom. i p. 573, A.D. 1369, No 7) and Raynaldus (Fleury, Hist. Ecclés. tom. xx p. 223, 224). Yet, from some variations, I suspect the papal writers of slightly magnifying the genuflexions of Palæologus.

posed; and, in the presence of four cardinals, he acknowledged, as a true Catholic, the supremacy of the pope and the
double procession of the Holy Ghost. After this purifica-
tion, he was introduced to a public audience in the church
of St. Peter: Urban, in the midst of the cardinals, was seated
on his throne, the Greek monarch, after three genuflexions,
devoutly kissed the feet, the hands, and at length the mouth
of the holy father, who celebrated high mass in his presence,
allowed him to lead the bridle of his mule, and treated him
with a sumptuous banquet in the Vatican. The entertain-
ment of Palæologus was friendly and honourable; yet some
difference was observed between the emperors of the East
and West, [10] nor could the former be entitled to the rare
privilege of chanting the gospel in the rank of a deacon.[11]   In
favour of his proselyte Urban strove to rekindle the zeal of
the French king and the other powers of the West, but he
found them cold in the general cause and active only in their
domestic quarrels.   The last hope of the emperor was in an
English mercenary, John Hawkwood,[12] or Acuto, who, with
a band of adventurers, the White Brotherhood, had ravaged
Italy from the Alps to Calabria; sold his services to the hostile
states, and incurred a just excommunication by shooting his

[10] Paullo minus quam si fuisset Imperator Romanorum. Yet his title of
Imperator Græcorum was no longer disputed (Vit Urban V p 623).

[11] It was confined to the successors of Charlemagne, and to them only on
Christmas Day. On all other festivals, these Imperial deacons were content
to serve the pope, as he said mass, with the book and the *corporal*   Yet the
Abbé de Sade generously thinks that the merits of Charles IV might have
entitled him, though not on the proper day (A D 1368, 1st November), to
the whole privilege   He seems to affix a just value on the privilege and the
man (Vie de Pétrarque, tom iii p 735)

[12] Through some Italian corruptions, the etymology of *Falcone in bosco*
(Matteo [rather, Filippo, the Continuer of Matteo] Villani, l xi c. 79, in
Muratori, tom xiv p 746) suggests the English word *Hawkwood*, the true
name of our adventurous countryman (Thomas Walsingham, Hist Anglican
inter Scriptores Camdeni, p 184). After two and twenty victories and one
defeat, he died, in 1394, General of the Florentines, and was buried with
such honours as the republic has not paid to Dante or Petrarch (Muratori,
Annali d'Italia, tom xii p. 212-371)

arrows against the papal residence. A special licence was
granted to negotiate with the outlaw; but the forces, or the
spirit, of Hawkwood were unequal to the enterprise, and it
was for the advantage perhaps of Palæologus to be disappointed of a succour that must have been costly, that could
not be effectual, and which might have been dangerous.[13]
The disconsolate Greek [14] prepared for his return, but even
his return was impeded by a most ignominious obstacle. On
his arrival at Venice, he had borrowed large sums at exorbi-
tant usury; but his coffers were empty, his creditors were
impatient, and his person was detained as the best security
for the payment. His eldest son Andronicus, the regent of
Constantinople, was repeatedly urged to exhaust every resource, and, even by stripping the churches, to extricate his
father from captivity and disgrace. But the unnatural youth
was insensible of the disgrace, and secretly pleased with the
captivity of the emperor; the state was poor, the clergy was
obstinate; nor could some religious scruple be wanting to
excuse the guilt of his indifference and delay. Such un-
dutiful neglect was severely reproved by the piety of his
brother Manuel, who instantly sold or mortgaged all that he
possessed, embarked for Venice, relieved his father, and
pledged his own freedom to be responsible for the debt.
On his return to Constantinople, the parent and king distinguished his two sons with suitable rewards; but the faith
and manners of the slothful Palæologus had not been improved by his Roman pilgrimage; and his apostacy or con-

[13] This torrent of English (by birth or service) overflowed from France into
Italy after the peace of Bretigny in 1360. Yet the exclamation of Muratori
(Annali, tom xii p 197) is rather true than civil "Ci mancava ancor
questo, che dopo essere calpestrata l'Italia da tanti masnadieri Tedeschi ed
Ungheri, venissero fin dall' Inghilterra nuovi *cani* a finire di divorarla."
[14] Chalcondyles, l. 1 p 25, 26 [p 50 ed Bonn] The Greek supposes his
journey to the king of France, which is sufficiently refuted by the silence
of the national historians Nor am I much more inclined to believe that
Palæologus departed from Italy, valde bene consolatus et contentus (Vit.
Urban V p 623)

version, devoid of any spiritual or temporal effects, was speedily forgotten by the Greeks and Latins.[15]

Thirty years after the return of Palæologus, his son and successor, Manuel, from a similar motive, but on a larger scale, again visited the countries of the West. In a preceding chapter, I have related his treaty with Bajazet, the violation of that treaty, the siege or blockade of Constantinople, and the French succour under the command of the gallant Boucicault.[16] By his ambassadors, Manuel had solicited the Latin powers; but it was thought that the presence of a distressed monarch would draw tears and supplies from the hardest Barbarians;[17] and the marshal who advised the journey, prepared the reception, of the Byzantine prince The land was occupied by the Turks; but the navigation of Venice was safe and open; Italy received him as the first, or at least as the second, of the Christian princes; Manuel was pitied as the champion and confessor of the faith; and the dignity of his behaviour prevented that pity from sinking into contempt. From Venice he proceeded to Padua and Pavia; and even the duke of Milan, a secret ally of Bajazet, gave him safe and honourable conduct to the verge of his dominions.[18] On the confines of France,[19] the royal officers undertook the care of his person, journey, and expenses;

[15] His return in 1370, and the coronation of Manuel, 25th September, 1373 (Ducange, Fam Byzant p 241), leaves some intermediate era for the conspiracy and punishment of Andronicus

[16] Mémoires de Boucicault, p i c 35, 36

[17] His journey into the west of Europe is slightly, and I believe reluctantly, noticed by Chalcondyles (l ii p 44-50 [p 84 sqq ed Bonn]) and Ducas (c 14)

[18] Muratori, Annali d'Italia, tom. xii. p 406   John Galeazzo was the first and most powerful duke of Milan His connection with Bajazet is attested by Froissard, and he contributed to save and deliver the French captives of Nicopolis

[19] For the reception of Manuel at Paris, see Spondanus (Annal Eccles tom. i p 676, 677, A D 1400, No 5), who quotes Juvenal des Ursins [Histoire de Charles vi, 1380-1422 (ed in Buchon's Choix de Chroniques, vol iv)] and the monk of St Denys, and Villaret (Hist de France, tom xii. p 331-334), who quotes nobody, according to the last fashion of the French writers

THE APPIAN WAY.

and two thousand of the richest citizens, in arms and on horseback, came forth to meet him as far as Charenton, in the
neighbourhood of the capital. At the gates of Paris, he was
saluted by the chancellor and the parliament; and Charles
the Sixth, attended by his princes and nobles, welcomed his
brother with a cordial embrace. The successor of Constantine
was clothed in a robe of white silk and mounted on a milk-
white steed — a circumstance, in the French ceremonial, of
singular importance. The white colour is considered as the
symbol of sovereignty; and, in a late visit, the German emperor, after an haughty demand and a peevish refusal, had
been reduced to content himself with a black courser Manuel
was lodged in the Louvre; a succession of feasts and balls,
the pleasures of the banquet and the chase, were ingeniously
varied by the politeness of the French, to display their magnificence and amuse his grief He was indulged in the liberty
of his chapel, and the doctors of the Sorbonne were astonished,
and possibly scandalised, by the language, the rites, and the
vestments of his Greek clergy. But the slightest glance on
the state of the kingdom must teach him to despair of any
effectual assistance. The unfortunate Charles, though he
enjoyed some lucid intervals, continually relapsed into
furious or stupid insanity; the reins of government were
alternately seized by his brother and uncle, the dukes of
Orleans and Burgundy, whose factious competition prepared
the miseries of civil war. The former was a gay youth, dissolved in luxury and love; the latter was the father of John,
count of Nevers, who had so lately been ransomed from
Turkish captivity, and, if the fearless son was ardent to
revenge his defeat, the more prudent Burgundy was content
with the cost and peril of the first experiment. When Manuel
had satiated the curiosity, and perhaps fatigued the patience,
of the French, he resolved on a visit to the adjacent island.
In his progress from Dover, he was entertained at Canterbury with due reverence by the prior and monks of St. Austin;
and, on Blackheath, King Henry the Fourth, with the English

court, saluted the Greek hero (I copy our old historian), who, during many days, was lodged and treated in London as Emperor of the East [20] But the state of England was still more adverse to the design of the holy war. In the same year, the hereditary sovereign had been deposed and murdered; the reigning prince was a successful usurper, whose ambition was punished by jealousy and remorse, nor could Henry of Lancaster withdraw his person or forces from the defence of a throne incessantly shaken by conspiracy and rebellion. He pitied, he praised, he feasted, the emperor of Constantinople; but, if the English monarch assumed the cross, it was only to appease his people, and perhaps his conscience, by the merit or semblance of this pious intention [21] Satisfied, however, with gifts and honours, Manuel returned to Paris; and, after a residence of two years in the West, shaped his course through Germany and Italy, embarked at Venice, and patiently expected, in the Morea, the moment of his ruin or deliverance. Yet he had escaped the ignominious necessity of offering his religion to public or private sale. The Latin church was distracted by the great schism; the kings, the nations, the universities, of Europe were divided in their obedience between the popes of Rome and Avignon; and the emperor, anxious to conciliate the friendship of both parties, abstained from any correspondence with the indigent and unpopular rivals. His journey coincided with the year of the jubilee; but he passed through Italy without desiring or deserving the plenary indulgence which abolished the guilt or penance of the sins

[20] A short note of Manuel in England is extracted by Dr Hody from a MS at Lambeth (de Græcis illustribus, p 14), C P Imperator, diu variisque et horrendis Paganorum insultibus coartatus, ut pro eisdem resistentiam triumphalem perquireret Anglorum Regem visitare decrevit, &c. Rex (says Walsingham, p 364) nobili apparatu   suscepit (ut debuit) tantum Heroa, duxitque Londonias, et per multos dies exhibuit gloriose, pro expensis hospitii sui solvens, et eum respiciens [dignis] tanto fastigio donativis   He repeats the same in his Upodigma Neustriæ (p 556)

[21] Shakespeare begins and ends the play of Henry IV with that prince's vow of a crusade, and his belief that he should die in Jerusalem.

of the faithful. The Roman pope was offended by this neglect, accused him of irreverence to an image of Christ; and exhorted the princes of Italy to reject and abandon the obstinate schismatic.[22]

During the period of the crusades, the Greeks beheld, with astonishment and terror, the perpetual stream of emigration that flowed, and continued to flow, from the unknown climates of the West. The visits of their last emperors removed the veil of separation, and they disclosed to their eyes the powerful nations of Europe, whom they no longer presumed to brand with the name of Barbarians. The observations of Manuel and his more inquisitive followers have been preserved by a Byzantine historian of the times;[23] his scattered ideas I shall collect and abridge; and it may be amusing enough, perhaps instructive, to contemplate the rude pictures of Germany, France, and England, whose ancient and modern state are so familiar to *our* minds. I. GERMANY (says the Greek Chalcondyles) is of ample latitude from Vienna to the Ocean, and it stretches (a strange geography!) from Prague in Bohemia to the river Tartessus and the Pyrenæan Mountains.[24] The soil, except in figs and olives, is sufficiently fruitful; the air is salubrious; the bodies of the natives are

[22] This fact is preserved in the Historia Politica, A.D. 1391-1478, published by Martin Crusius (Turco-Græci, p 1-43) The image of Christ which the Greek emperor refused to worship was probably a work of sculpture.

[23] The Greek and Turkish history of Laonicus Chalcondyles ends with the winter of 1463, and the abrupt conclusion seems to mark that he laid down his pen in the same year We know that he was an Athenian, and that some contemporaries of the same name contributed to the revival of the Greek language in Italy But in his numerous digressions the modest historian has never introduced himself, and his editor Leunclavius, as well as Fabricius (Bibliot Græc. tom vi p 474), seems ignorant of his life and character For his descriptions of Germany, France, and England, see l ii p 36, 37 [p 70 *sqq*], 44-50 [p 85 *sqq*]

[24] I shall not animadvert on the geographical errors of Chalcondyles In this instance, he perhaps followed and mistook Herodotus (l ii c 33), whose text may be explained (Herodote de Larcher, tom ii p 219, 220), or whose ignorance may be excused Had these modern Greeks never read Strabo, or any of their lesser geographers?

robust and healthy; and these cold regions are seldom visited
with the calamities of pestilence or earthquakes.   After the
Scythians or Tartars, the Germans are the most numerous of
nations, they are brave and patient, and, were they united
under a single head, their force would be irresistible.   By the
gift of the pope, they have acquired the privilege of choosing
the Roman emperor;[25] nor is any people more devoutly
attached to the faith and obedience of the Latin patriarch.
The greatest part of the country is divided among the princes
and prelates; but Strasburg, Cologne, Hamburg, and more
than two hundred free cities are governed by sage and equal
laws, according to the will, and for the advantage, of the whole
community.   The use of duels, or single combats on foot,
prevails among them in peace and war; their industry excels
in all the mechanic arts, and the Germans may boast of the
invention of gunpowder and cannon, which is now diffused
over the greatest part of the world.   II. The kingdom of
FRANCE is spread above fifteen or twenty days' journey from
Germany to Spain, and from the Alps to the British Ocean,
containing many flourishing cities, and among these Paris,
the seat of the king, which surpasses the rest in riches and
luxury   Many princes and lords alternately wait in his
palace and acknowledge him as their sovereign; the most
powerful are the dukes of Bretagne and Burgundy, of whom
the latter possesses the wealthy province of Flanders, whose
harbours are frequented by the ships and merchants of our
own and the more remote seas.   The French are an ancient
and opulent people, and their language and manners, though
somewhat different, are not dissimilar from those of the
Italians   Vain of the Imperial dignity of Charlemagne, of
their victories over the Saracens, and of the exploits of their

[25] A citizen of new Rome, while new Rome survived, would have scorned to
dignify the German 'Ρήξ with the titles of Βασιλεύς, or Αὐτοκράτωρ 'Ρωμαίων;
but all pride was extinct in the bosom of Chalcondyles, and he describes the
Byzantine prince and his subject, by the proper, though humble names of
Ἕλληνες, and Βασιλεὺς Ἑλλήνων   [Cp above, vol x p 279]

heroes, Oliver and Rowland,[26] they esteem themselves the
first of the Western nations, but this foolish arrogance has
been recently humbled by the unfortunate events of their
wars against the English, the inhabitants of the British Island
III. Britain, in the ocean and opposite to the shores of
Flanders, may be considered either as one or as three islands;
but the whole is united by a common interest, by the same
manners, and by a similar government   The measure of
its circumference is five thousand stadia   the land is overspread with towns and villages; though destitute of wine,
and not abounding in fruit-trees, it is fertile in wheat and
barley, in honey and wool; and much cloth is manufactured
by the inhabitants   In populousness and power, in riches
and luxury, London,[27] the metropolis of the isle, may claim
a pre-eminence over all the cities of the West.   It is situate
on the Thames, a broad and rapid river, which, at the distance of thirty miles, falls into the Gallic Sea; and the daily
flow and ebb of the tide affords a safe entrance and departure
to the vessels of commerce.   The king is the head of a powerful and turbulent aristocracy   his principal vassals hold their
estates by a free and unalterable tenure; and the laws define
the limits of his authority and their obedience.   The kingdom has been often afflicted by foreign conquest and domestic
sedition; but the natives are bold and hardy, renowned in
arms and victorious in war.   The form of their shields or
targets is derived from the Italians, that of their swords from

[26] Most of the old romances were translated in the xivth century into
French prose, and soon became the favourite amusement of the knights and
ladies in the court of Charles VI   If a Greek believed in the exploits of Rowland and Oliver, he may surely be excused, since the monks of St Denys, the
national historians, have inserted the fables of Archbishop Turpin in their
Chronicles of France

[27] Λονδύνη . . δέ τε πόλις δυνάμει τε προέχουσα τῶν ἐν τῇ νήσῳ ταύτῃ
πασῶν πόλεων, ὄλβῳ τε καὶ τῇ ἄλλῃ εὐδαιμονίᾳ οὐδεμιᾶς τῶν πρὸς ἑσπέραν
λειπομένη [ii p 93 ed Bonn]   Even since the time of Fitzstephen (the xiith
century), London appears to have maintained this pre-eminence of wealth
and magnitude, and her gradual increase has at least kept pace with the
general improvement of Europe.

the Greeks; the use of the long bow is the peculiar and decisive advantage of the English. Their language bears no
affinity to the idioms of the continent; in the habits of
domestic life, they are not easily distinguished from their
neighbours of France; but the most singular circumstance
of their manners is their disregard of conjugal honour and of
female chastity. In their mutual visits, as the first act of
hospitality, the guest is welcomed in the embraces of their
wives and daughters; among friends, they are lent and borrowed without shame; nor are the islanders offended at this
strange commerce and its inevitable consequences.[28] Informed as we are of the customs of old England, and assured
of the virtue of our mothers, we may smile at the credulity,
or resent the injustice, of the Greek, who must have confounded
a modest salute [29] with a criminal embrace. But his credulity
and injustice may teach an important lesson: to distrust the
accounts of foreign and remote nations, and to suspend our
belief of every tale that deviates from the laws of nature and
the character of man.[30]

After his return, and the victory of Timour, Manuel reigned
many years in prosperity and peace. As long as the sons of
Bajazet solicited his friendship and spared his dominions, he
was satisfied with the national religion; and his leisure was

[28] If the double sense of the verb κύω (osculor, and in utero gero) be equivocal, the context and pious horror of Chalcondyles can leave no doubt of his
meaning and mistake (p 49). [There is no ambiguity Chalcondyles uses
the middle form κύεσθαι instead of the active κύειν which is used in classical
Greek, but there is no second sense Neither κύω nor κυῶ is ever used in the
sense of κυνῶ (kiss) It is only in the aorist (ἔκῦσα· ἔκῦσα) that there would
be a danger of confusion — Cp Phrantzes, iii 2]

[29] Erasmus (Epist Fausto Andrelino) has a pretty passage on the English
fashion of kissing strangers on their arrival and departure, from whence,
however, he draws no scandalous inferences

[30] Perhaps we may apply this remark to the community of wives among the
old Britons, as it is supposed by Cæsar and Dion (Dion Cassius, l lxii tom
ii p 1007 [c 6]), with Reimar's judicious annotation The *Arreoy* of
Otaheite, so certain at first, is become less visible and scandalous, in proportion as we have studied the manners of that gentle and amorous people.

employed in composing twenty theological dialogues for its defence [31] The appearance of the Byzantine ambassadors at the council of Constance [32] announces the restoration of the Turkish power, as well as of the Latin church; the conquest of the sultans, Mahomet and Amurath, reconciled the emperor to the Vatican, and the siege of Constantinople almost tempted him to acquiesce in the double procession of the Holy Ghost. When Martin the Fifth ascended, without a rival, the chair of St. Peter, a friendly intercourse of letters and embassies was revived between the East and West Ambition on one side and distress on the other dictated the same decent language of charity and peace The artful Greek expressed a desire of marrying his six sons to Italian princesses, and the Roman, not less artful, despatched the daughter of the marquis of Montferrat, with a company of noble virgins, to soften, by their charms, the obstinacy of the schismatics. Yet, under this mask of zeal, a discerning eye will perceive that all was hollow and insincere in the court and church of Constantinople. According to the vicissitudes of danger and repose, the emperor advanced or retreated; alternately instructed and disavowed his ministers; and escaped from an importunate pressure by urging the duty of inquiry, the obligation of collecting the sense of his patriarchs and bishops, and

[31] [Manuel composed in 26 dialogues a defence of orthodox Christianity against Islam. The whole work was entitled Διάλογος περὶ τῆς τῶν Χριστιανῶν θρησκείας πρός τινα Πέρσην, and grew out of conversations which Manuel had had at Ancyra in 1390 with a Turkish muterizis Only the two first dialogues have been published (Migne, P G 156, p. 126 sqq) Manuel wrote much, and most of his published works will be found in Migne, tom cit His letters have been edited by Legrand, 1893, and this volume contains the interesting essay of Manuel, "What Timur may have said to the conquered Bajazet" There is an excellent monograph on Manuel and his writings by Berger de Xivrey in the Mémoires de l'Institut de France, Ac des Inscr. xix 1 sqq (1853)]

[32] See Lenfant, Hist du Concile de Constance, tom ii p 576, and for the ecclesiastical history of the times, the Annals of Spondanus, the Bibliothèque of Dupin, tom xii , and xxist and xxiid volumes of the History, or rather the Continuation, of Fleury.

the impossibility of convening them at a time when the
Turkish arms were at the gates of his capital. From a
review of the public transactions, it will appear that the Greeks
insisted on three successive measures, a succour, a council,
and a final reunion, while the Latins eluded the second, and
only promised the first as a consequential and voluntary
reward of the third. But we have an opportunity of unfolding
the most secret intentions of Manuel, as he explained them in
a private conversation without artifice or disguise. In his
declining age the emperor had associated John Palæologus, the
second of the name and the eldest of his sons, on whom he
devolved the greatest part of the authority and weight of
government. One day, in the presence only of the historian
Phranza,[33] his favourite chamberlain, he opened to his
colleague and successor the true principle of his negotiations
with the pope.[34] "Our last resource," said Manuel, "against
the Turks is their fear of our union with the Latins, of the
warlike nations of the West, who may arm for our relief, and
for their destruction. As often as you are threatened by the
miscreants, present this danger before their eyes. Propose
a council; consult on the means; but ever delay and avoid
the convocation of an assembly, which cannot tend either to
our spiritual or temporal emolument. The Latins are proud;
the Greeks are obstinate: neither party will recede or retract;

[33] From his early youth, George Phranza, or Phranzes, was employed in the
service of the state and palace, and Hanckius (de Script Byzant p 1 c 40)
has collected his life from his own writings. He was no more than four and
twenty years of age at the death of Manuel, who recommended him, in the
strongest terms, to his successor Imprimis vero hunc Phranzen tibi com-
mendo, qui ministravit mihi fideliter et diligenter (Phranzes, l ii c 1)   Yet
the emperor John was cold, and he preferred the service of the despots of
Peloponnesus

[34] See Phranzes, l ii c 13   While so many manuscripts of the Greek
original are extant in the libraries of Rome, Milan, the Escurial, &c it is a
matter of shame and reproach that we should be reduced to the Latin version,
or abstract, of James Pontanus, ad calcem Theophylact Simocattæ (Ingol-
stadt, 1604), so deficient in accuracy and elegance (Fabric Bibliot Græc.
tom vi p 615-620)   [See Appendix 1]

and the attempt of a perfect union will confirm the schism, alienate the churches, and leave us, without hope or defence, at the mercy of the Barbarians." Impatient of this salutary lesson, the royal youth arose from his seat and departed in silence; and the wise monarch (continues Phranza) casting his eyes on me, thus resumed his discourse· "My son deems himself a great and heroic prince; but alas! our miserable age does not afford scope for heroism or greatness. His daring spirit might have suited the happier times of our ancestors, but the present state requires not an emperor, but a cautious steward of the last relics of our fortunes. Well do I remember the lofty expectations which he built on our alliance with Mustapha; and much do I fear that his rash courage will urge the ruin of our house, and that even religion may precipitate our downfall" Yet the inexperience and authority of Manuel preserved the peace and eluded the council; till, in the seventy-eighth year of his age, and in the habit of a monk, he terminated his career, dividing his precious moveables among his children and the poor, his physicians, and his favourite servants. Of his six sons,[35] Andronicus the Second was invested with the principality of Thessalonica, and died of a leprosy soon after the sale of that city to the Venetians and its final conquest by the Turks. Some fortunate incidents had restored Peloponnesus, or the Morea, to the empire; and in his more prosperous days Manuel had fortified the narrow isthmus of six miles[36] with a stone wall and one hundred and fifty-three towers. The wall was overthrown by the first blast of the Ottomans; the fertile peninsula might have been sufficient for the four younger brothers, Theodore and Constantine, Demetrius

---

[35] See Ducange, Fam Byzant p 243-248

[36] The exact measure of the Hexamilion from sea to sea, was 3800 orgygiæ, or *toises*, of six Greek feet (Phranzes, l i c 38), which would produce a Greek mile, still smaller than that of 660 French *toises*, which is assigned by d'Anville as still in use in Turkey Five miles are commonly reckoned for the breadth of the Isthmus See the Travels of Spon, Wheler, and Chandler.

and Thomas; but they wasted, in domestic contests, the remains of their strength, and the least successful of the rivals were reduced to a life of dependence in the Byzantine palace.

The eldest of the sons of Manuel, John Palæologus the Second, was acknowledged, after his father's death, as the sole emperor of the Greeks. He immediately proceeded to repudiate his wife and to contract a new marriage with the princess of Trebizond; beauty was in his eye the first qualification of an empress; and the clergy had yielded to his firm assurance that, unless he might be indulged in a divorce, he would retire to a cloister and leave the throne to his brother Constantine. The first, and in truth the only, victory of Palæologus was over a Jew,[37] whom, after a long and learned dispute, he converted to the Christian faith, and this momentous conquest is carefully recorded in the history of the times. But he soon resumed the design of uniting the East and West; and, regardless of his father's advice, listened, as it should seem, with sincerity to the proposal of meeting the pope in a general council beyond the Adriatic. This dangerous project was encouraged by Martin the Fifth, and coldly entertained by his successor Eugenius, till, after a tedious negotiation, the emperor received a summons from a Latin assembly of a new character, the independent prelates of Basil, who styled themselves the representatives and judges of the Catholic church

The Roman pontiff had fought and conquered in the cause of ecclesiastical freedom, but the victorious clergy were soon exposed to the tyranny of their deliverer; and his sacred character was invulnerable to those arms which they found so keen and effectual against the civil magistrate. Their great charter, the right of election, was annihilated by appeals, evaded by trusts or commendams, disappointed by rever-

[37] The first objection of the Jews is on the death of Christ: if it were voluntary, Christ was a suicide, which the emperor parries with a mystery. They then dispute on the conception of the Virgin, the sense of the proph-

sionary grants, and superseded by previous and arbitrary reservations.[38] A public auction was instituted in the court of Rome· the cardinals and favourites were enriched with the spoils of nations; and every country might complain that the most important and valuable benefices were accumulated on the heads of aliens and absentees.　During their residence at Avignon, the ambition of the popes subsided in the meaner passions of avarice[39] and luxury. they rigorously imposed on the clergy the tributes of first-fruits and tenths, but they freely tolerated the impunity of vice, disorder, and corruption. These manifold scandals were aggravated by the great schism of the West, which continued above fifty years.　In the furious conflicts of Rome and Avignon, the vices of the rivals were mutually exposed; and their precarious situation degraded their authority, relaxed their discipline, and multiplied their wants and exactions.　To heal the wounds, and restore the monarchy, of the church, the synods of Pisa and Constance[40] were successively convened; but these great

---

[38] In the treatise delle Materie Beneficiarie of Fra Paolo (in the ivth volume of the last and best edition of his works), the papal system is deeply studied and freely described　Should Rome and her religion be annihilated, this golden volume may still survive, a philosophical history and a salutary warning

[39] Pope John XXII (in 1334) left behind him, at Avignon, eighteen millions of gold florins, and the value of seven millions more in plate and jewels　See the Chronicle of John Villani (l. xi c. 20, in Muratori's Collection, tom xiii p 765), whose brother received the account from the Papal treasurers　A treasure of six or eight millions sterling in the xivth century is enormous, and almost incredible.

[40] A learned and liberal Protestant, M Lenfant, has given a fair history of the councils of Pisa, Constance, and Basil, in six volumes in quarto, but the last part is the most hasty and imperfect, except in the account of the troubles of Bohemia　[For the Council of Pisa see Erler, Zur Geschichte des Pisaner Conzils, 1884　The history of the Council of Constance has been rewritten by L Tosti, Storia del concilio di Costanza, 1853 (in 2 vols), a work which has been translated into German by W Arnold (1860)　See also F Stuhr, Die Organisation und Geschäftsordnung des Pisaner und Costanzer Konzils, 1891, and the document (Ein Tagebuch-fragment über das Kostanzer Konzil) edited by Knopfler in the Historisches Jahrbuch der Gorresgesellschaft, vol. xi p 267 sqq, 1890　Gibbon does not mention the big work

assemblies, conscious of their strength, resolved to vindicate the privileges of the Christian aristocracy. From a personal sentence against two pontiffs, whom they rejected, and a third, their acknowledged sovereign, whom they deposed, the fathers of Constance proceeded to examine the nature and limits of the Roman supremacy; nor did they separate till they had established the authority, above the pope, of a general council. It was enacted that, for the government and reformation of the church, such assemblies should be held at regular intervals; and that each synod, before its dissolution, should appoint the time and place of the subsequent meeting By the influence of the court of Rome, the next convocation at Sienna was easily eluded, but the bold and vigorous proceedings of the council of Basil [41] had almost been fatal to the reigning pontiff, Eugenius the Fourth. A just suspicion of his design prompted the fathers to hasten the promulgation of their first decree, that the representatives of the church-militant on earth were invested with a divine and spiritual jurisdiction over all Christians, without excepting the pope, and that a general council could not be dissolved, prorogued, or transferred, unless by their free deliberation and consent. On the notice that Eugenius had fulminated a bull for that purpose, they ventured to summon, to admonish, to threaten, to censure, the contumacious successor of St. Peter. After many delays, to allow time for repentance, they finally declared that, unless he submitted within the term of sixty

of Hardt Magnum oecumenicum Constantiense concilium (6 vols), 1697–1700 (Index, 1742)]

[41] The original acts or minutes of the council of Basil are preserved in the public library, in twelve volumes in folio Basil was a free city, conveniently situate on the Rhine, and guarded by the arms of the neighbouring and confederate Swiss In 1459, the university was founded by Pope Pius II (Æneas Sylvius), who had been secretary to the council But what is a council, or an university, to the presses of Froben and the studies of Erasmus? [The first 3 vols (1853–94) of the Vienna Monumenta conciliorum generalium are devoted to the council of Basil For the union question see Mugnier, L'Expédition du concile de Bâle à Constantinople pour l'union de l'église grecque à l'église latine (1437–8), 1892]

days, he was suspended from the exercise of all temporal and ecclesiastical authority. And to mark their jurisdiction over the prince as well as the priest, they assumed the government of Avignon, annulled the alienation of the sacred patrimony, and protected Rome from the imposition of new taxes. Their boldness was justified, not only by the general opinion of the clergy, but by the support and power of the first monarchs of Christendom the emperor Sigismond declared himself the servant and protector of the synod; Germany and France adhered to their cause; the duke of Milan was the enemy of Eugenius; and he was driven from the Vatican by an insurrection of the Roman people. Rejected at the same time by his temporal and spiritual subjects, submission was his only choice, by a most humiliating bull, the pope repealed his own acts and ratified those of the council; incorporated his legates and cardinals with that venerable body; and *seemed* to resign himself to the decrees of the supreme legislature. Their fame pervaded the countries of the East; and it was in their presence that Sigismond received the ambassadors of the Turkish sultan,[42] who laid at his feet twelve large vases, filled with robes of silk and pieces of gold. The fathers of Basil aspired to the glory of reducing the Greeks, as well as the Bohemians, within the pale of the church, and their deputies invited the emperor and patriarchs of Constantinople to unite with an assembly which possessed the confidence of the Western nations. Palæologus was not averse to the proposal, and his ambassadors were introduced with due honours into the Catholic senate But the choice of the place appeared to be an insuperable obstacle, since he refused to pass the Alps or the sea of Sicily, and positively required that the synod should be adjourned to some convenient city in Italy, or at least on the Danube The other articles of this treaty were more readily stipulated. it was

---

[42] This Turkish embassy, attested only by Crantzius, is related with some doubt by the annalist Spondanus, A D 1433, No 25, tom 1 p. 824

agreed to defray the travelling expenses of the emperor, with a train of seven hundred persons,[43] to remit an immediate sum of eight thousand ducats [44] for the accommodation of the Greek clergy, and in his absence to grant a supply of ten thousand ducats, with three hundred archers, and some galleys for the protection of Constantinople. The city of Avignon advanced the funds for the preliminary expenses; and the embarkation was prepared at Marseilles with some difficulty and delay.

In his distress, the friendship of Palæologus was disputed by the ecclesiastical powers of the West, but the dexterous activity of a monarch prevailed over the slow debates and inflexible temper of a republic. The decrees of Basil continually tended to circumscribe the despotism of the pope and to erect a supreme and perpetual tribunal in the church. Eugenius was impatient of the yoke; and the union of the Greeks might afford a decent pretence for translating a rebellious synod from the Rhine to the Po. The independence of the fathers was lost if they passed the Alps; Savoy or Avignon, to which they acceded with reluctance, were described at Constantinople as situate far beyond the Pillars of Hercules;[45] the emperor and his clergy were apprehensive

[43] Syropulus, p 19 In this list, the Greeks appear to have exceeded the real numbers of the clergy and laity which afterwards attended the emperor and patriarch, but which are not clearly specified by the great ecclesiarch The 75,000 florins which they asked in this negotiation of the pope (p. 9) were more than they could hope or want

[44] I use indifferently the words *ducat* and *florin*, which derive their names, the former from the *dukes* of Milan, the latter from the republic of *Florence*. These gold pieces, the first that were coined in Italy, perhaps in the Latin world, may be compared, in weight and value, to one third of the English guinea

[45] At the end of the Latin version of Phranzes, we read a long Greek epistle or declamation of George of Trebizond, who advises the emperor to prefer Eugenius and Italy He treats with contempt the schismatic assembly of Basil, the Barbarians of Gaul and Germany, who had conspired to transport the chair of St Peter beyond the Alps οἱ ἄθλιοι (says he) σὲ καὶ τὴν μετὰ σοῦ σύνοδον ἔξω τῶν 'Ηρακλείων στηλῶν καὶ πέρα Γαδήρων ἐξάξουσι. Was

of the dangers of a long navigation, they were offended by an haughty declaration that, after suppressing the *new* heresy of the Bohemians, the council would soon eradicate the *old* heresy of the Greeks.[46] On the side of Eugenius, all was smooth and yielding and respectful; and he invited the Byzantine monarch to heal, by his presence, the schism of the Latin, as well as of the Eastern, church. Ferrara, near the coast of the Adriatic, was proposed for their amicable interview, and with some indulgence of forgery and theft a surreptitious decree was procured, which transferred the synod, with its own consent, to that Italian city. Nine galleys were equipped for this service at Venice and in the isle of Candia; their diligence anticipated the slower vessels of Basil. The Roman admiral was commissioned to burn, sink, and destroy;[47] and these priestly squadrons might have encountered each other in the same seas where Athens and Sparta had formerly contended for the pre-eminence of glory. Assaulted by the importunity of the factions, who were ready to fight for the possession of his person, Palæologus hesitated before he left his palace and country on a perilous experiment His father's advice still dwelt on his memory; and reason must suggest that, since the Latins were divided among themselves, they could never unite in a foreign cause. Sigismond dissuaded the unseasonable adventure, his advice was impartial, since he adhered to the council; and it was enforced by the strange belief that the German Cæsar would nominate

Constantinople unprovided with a map? [The writings of the humanist George of Trebizond, on the union question, will be found in Migne, P G vol 161, 829 *sqq*]

[46] Syropulus (p 26-31) attests his own indignation, and that of his countrymen, and the Basil deputies, who excused the rash declaration, could neither deny nor alter an act of the council

[47] Condolmieri, the pope's nephew and admiral, expressly declared, ὅτι ὁρισμὸν ἔχει παρὰ τοῦ Πάπα ἵνα πολεμήσῃ ὅπου ἂν εὕρῃ τὰ κάτεργα τῆς Συνόδου, καὶ εἰ δυνήθῃ καταδύσῃ καὶ ἀφανίσῃ The naval orders of the synod were less peremptory, and, till the hostile squadrons appeared, both parties tried to conceal their quarrel from the Greeks

a Greek his heir and successor in the empire of the West.[48]
Even the Turkish sultan was a counsellor whom it might be
unsafe to trust, but whom it was dangerous to offend. Amurath was unskilled in the disputes, but he was apprehensive
of the union, of the Christians. From his own treasures, he
offered to relieve the wants of the Byzantine court; yet he declared, with seeming magnanimity, that Constantinople should
be secure and inviolate in the absence of her sovereign.[49]
The resolution of Palæologus was decided by the most
splendid gifts and the most specious promises. He wished
to escape, for a while, from a scene of danger and distress;
and, after dismissing, with an ambiguous answer, the messengers of the council, he declared his intention of embarking
in the Roman galleys. The age of the patriarch Joseph was
more susceptible of fear than of hope, he trembled at the
perils of the sea, and expressed his apprehension that his
feeble voice, with thirty, perhaps, of his orthodox brethren,
would be oppressed in a foreign land by the power and numbers of a Latin synod. He yielded to the royal mandate, to
the flattering assurance that he would be heard as the oracle
of nations, and to the secret wish of learning from his brother
of the West to deliver the church from the yoke of kings.[50]
The five *cross-bearers*, or dignitaries of St. Sophia, were bound
to attend his person; and one of these, the great ecclesiarch

[48] Syropulus mentions the hopes of Palæologus (p. 36), and the last advice
of Sigismond (p 57). At Corfu, the Greek emperor was informed of his
friend's death, had he known it sooner, he would have returned home
(p 79)

[49] Phranzes himself, though from different motives, was of the advice of
Amurath (l ii c 13). Utinam ne synodus ista unquam fuisset, si tantas
offensiones et detrimenta paritura erat This Turkish embassy is likewise
mentioned by Syropulus (p 58), and Amurath kept his word He might
threaten (p 125, 219), but he never attacked, the city

[50] The reader will smile at the simplicity with which he imparted these
hopes to his favourites τοιαύτην πληροφορίαν σχήσειν ἤλπιζε καὶ διὰ τοῦ
Ἱάπα ἐθάρρει ἐλευθερῶσαι τὴν ἐκκλησίαν ἀπὸ τῆς ἀποτεθείσης αὐτοῦ δουλείας
παρὰ τοῦ βασιλέω (p 92) Yet it would have been difficult for him to have
practised the lessons of Gregory VII.

or preacher, Sylvester Syropulus,[51] has composed[52] a free
and curious history of the *false* union.[53] Of the clergy that
reluctantly obeyed the summons of the emperor and the patriarch, submission was the first duty, and patience the most
useful virtue. In a chosen list of twenty bishops, we discover the metropolitan titles of Heraclea and Cyzicus, Nice
and Nicomedia, Ephesus and Trebizond, and the personal
merit of Mark and Bessarion, who, in the confidence of their
learning and eloquence, were promoted to the episcopal
rank. Some monks and philosophers were named to display the science and sanctity of the Greek church; and the
service of the choir was performed by a select band of singers
and musicians. The patriarchs of Alexandria, Antioch,
and Jerusalem appeared by their genuine or fictitious deputies, the primate of Russia represented a national church,
and the Greeks might contend with the Latins in the extent
of their spiritual empire. The precious vases of St. Sophia
were exposed to the winds and waves, that the patriarch
might officiate with becoming splendour; whatever gold the

[51] The Christian name of Sylvester is borrowed from the Latin Calendar.
In modern Greek, πουλος, as a diminutive, is added to the end of words,
nor can any reasoning of Creyghton, the editor, excuse his changing into
*Sguro*pulus (Sguros, fuscus) the Syropulus of his own manuscript, whose
name is subscribed with his own hand in the acts of the council of Florence
Why might not the author be of Syrian extraction? [The name Syropulos
occurs repeatedly in the Collection of Letters (dating from the 14th century)
in the Florentine Codex S Marco 356 See Krumbacher, Gesch der
byzantinischen Litteratur, p 485]

[52] From the conclusion of the history, I should fix the date to the year 1444,
four years after the synod, when the great ecclesiarch had abdicated his
office (sectio vii p 330-350) His passions were cooled by time and retirement, and, although Syropulus is often partial, he is never intemperate

[53] *Vera historia unionis non veræ inter Græcos et Latinos* (*Hagæ Comitis*,
1660, in folio) was first published with a loose and florid version, by Robert
Creyghton, chaplain to Charles II in his exile The zeal of the editor
has prefixed a polemic title, for the beginning of the original is wanting
Syropulus may be ranked with the best of the Byzantine writers for the
merit of his narration, and even of his style, but he is excluded from the
orthodox collections of the councils.

emperor could procure was expended in the massy ornaments
of his bed and chariot, [54] and, while they affected to maintain
the prosperity of their ancient fortune, they quarrelled for the
division of fifteen thousand ducats, the first alms of the Roman
pontiff.   After the necessary preparations, John Palæologus,
with a numerous train, accompanied by his brother Demetrius,
and the most respectable persons of the church and state,
. embarked in eight vessels with sails and oars, which steered
through the Turkish straits of Gallipoli to the Archipelago,
the Morea and the Adriatic Gulf.[55]

After a tedious and troublesome navigation of seventy-
seven days, this religious squadron cast anchor before Venice;
and their reception proclaimed the joy and magnificence of
that powerful republic.   In the command of the world, the
modest Augustus had never claimed such honours from his
subjects as were paid to his feeble successor by an independent
state.   Seated on the poop, on a lofty throne, he received the
visit, or, in the Greek style, the *adoration*, of the Doge and
senators.[56]   They sailed in the Bucentaur, which was accompanied by twelve stately galleys, the sea was overspread
with innumerable gondolas of pomp and pleasure, the air
resounded with music and acclamations, the mariners, and
even the vessels, were dressed in silk and gold; and in all the

----

[54] Syropulus (p 63) simply expresses his intention ἵν' οὕτω πομπάων ἐν
'Ιταλοις μέγας βασιλεὺς παρ' ἐκείνων νομίζοιτο, and the Latin of Creyghton
may afford a specimen of his florid paraphrase   Ut pompâ circumductus
noster Imperator Italiæ populis aliquis deauratus Jupiter crederetur, aut
Crœsus ex opulentâ Lydiâ   [In the Greek citation πομπάων is unintelligible,
but so it stands in Creyghton's text   Evidently Syropulus wrote πομπεύων]

[55] Although I cannot stop to quote Syropulus for every fact, I will observe
that the navigation of the Greeks from Constantinople to Venice and Ferrara
is contained in the ivth section (p 67–100), and that the historian has the
uncommon talent of placing each scene before the reader's eye

[56] At the time of the synod, Phranzes was in Peloponnesus; but he received
from the despot Demetrius a faithful account of the honourable reception
of the emperor and patriarch, both at Venice and Ferrara (Dux   .   seden-
tem Imperatorem *adorat*), which are more slightly mentioned by the Latins
(l. ii. c 14–16)

emblems and pageants the Roman eagles were blended with
the lions of St. Mark. The triumphal procession, ascending
the great canal, passed under the bridge of the Rialto, and the
Eastern strangers gazed with admiration on the palaces, the
churches, and the populousness of a city that seems to float
on the bosom of the waves [57] They sighed to behold the
spoils and trophies with which it had been decorated after
the sack of Constantinople. After an hospitable entertain-
ment of fifteen days, Palæologus pursued his journey by land
and water, from Venice to Ferrara; and on this occasion the
pride of the Vatican was tempered by policy to indulge the
ancient dignity of the emperor of the East He made his
entry on a *black* horse; but a milk-white steed, whose trap-
pings were embroidered with golden eagles, was led before
him; and the canopy was borne over his head by the princes
of Este, the sons or kinsmen of Nicholas, marquis of the city,
and a sovereign more powerful than himself [58] Palæologus
did not alight till he reached the bottom of the staircase;
the pope advanced to the door of the apartment; refused
his proffered genuflexion, and, after a paternal embrace,
conducted the emperor to a seat on his left hand Nor
would the patriarch descend from his galley, till a ceremony,
almost equal, had been stipulated between the bishops of
Rome and Constantinople. The latter was saluted by his
brother with a kiss of union and charity; nor would any of
the Greek ecclesiastics submit to kiss the feet of the Western
primate. On the opening of the synod, the place of honour
in the centre was claimed by the temporal and ecclesiastical

[57] The astonishment of a Greek prince and a French ambassador (Mémoires de Philippe de Comines, l vii c. 18) at the sight of Venice abundantly
proves that in the xvth century it was the first and most splendid of the
Christian cities For the spoils of Constantinople at Venice, see Syropulus
(p 87)

[58] Nicholas III of Este reigned forty-eight years (A D 1393-1441), and was
lord of Ferrara, Modena, Reggio, Parma, Rovigo, and Commachio See his
life in Muratori (Antichità Estense, tom. ii. p 159-201).

chiefs; and it was only by alleging that his predecessors had
not assisted in person at Nice or Chalcedon that Eugenius
could evade the ancient precedents of Constantine and
Marcian   After much debate, it was agreed that the right
and left sides of the church should be occupied by the two
nations; that the solitary chair of St. Peter should be raised
the first of the Latin line; and that the throne of the Greek
emperor, at the head of his clergy, should be equal and
opposite to the second place, the vacant seat of the emperor
of the West [59]

But, as soon as festivity and form had given place to a
more serious treaty, the Greeks were dissatisfied with their
journey, with themselves, and with the pope. The artful
pencil of his emissaries had painted him in a prosperous
state; at the head of the princes and prelates of Europe,
obedient, at his voice, to believe and to arm. The thin
appearance of the universal synod of Ferrara betrayed his
weakness, and the Latins opened the first session with only
five archbishops, eighteen bishops, and ten abbots, the
greatest part of whom were the subjects or countrymen of the
Italian pontiff. Except the duke of Burgundy, none of the
potentates of the West condescended to appear in person or
by their ambassadors, nor was it possible to suppress the
judicial acts of Basil against the dignity and person of
Eugenius, which were finally concluded by a new election.
Under these circumstances, a truce or delay was asked and
granted, till Palæologus could expect from the consent of the
Latins some temporal reward for an unpopular union; and,
after the first session, the public proceedings were adjourned

[59] The Latin vulgar was provoked to laughter at the strange dresses of the
Greeks, and especially the length of their garments, their sleeves, and their
beards, nor was the emperor distinguished, except by the purple colour, and
his diadem or tiara with a jewel on the top (Hody de Græcis Illustribus, p 31).
Yet another spectator confesses that the Greek fashion was piu grave e piu
degna than the Italian (Vespasiano, in Vit Eugen IV. in Muratori, tom
xxv p. 261).

above six months. The emperor, with a chosen band of his
favourites and *Janizaries*, fixed his summer residence at a
pleasant spacious monastery, six miles from Ferrara; forgot,
in the pleasures of the chase, the distress of the church and
state; and persisted in destroying the game, without listen-
ing to the just complaints of the marquis or the husbandman.[60]
In the meanwhile, his unfortunate Greeks were exposed to all
the miseries of exile and poverty, for the support of each
stranger, a monthly allowance was assigned of three or four
gold florins; and, although the entire sum did not amount
to seven hundred florins, a long arrear was repeatedly incurred by the indigence or policy of the Roman court.[61]
They sighed for a speedy deliverance, but their escape was
prevented by a triple chain a passport from their superiors
was required at the gates of Ferrara; the government of
Venice had engaged to arrest and send back the fugitives;
and inevitable punishment awaited them at Constantinople.
excommunication, fines, and a sentence which did not respect
the sacerdotal dignity, that they should be stripped naked and
publicly whipped.[62]   It was only by the alternative of hunger
or dispute that the Greeks could be persuaded to open the
first conference; and they yielded with extreme reluctance to

[60] For the emperor's hunting, see Syropulus (p 143, 144, 191)   The pope
had sent him eleven miserable hawks but he bought a strong and swift
horse that came from Russia   The name of *Janizaries* may surprise, but
the name, rather than the institution, had passed from the Ottoman to the
Byzantine court, and is often used in the last age of the empire

[61] The Greeks obtained, with much difficulty, that, instead of provisions,
money should be distributed, four florins *per* month to the persons of honourable rank, and three florins to their servants, with an addition of thirty more
to the emperor, twenty-five to the patriarch, and twenty to the prince or despot
Demetrius   The payment of the first month amounted to 691 florins, a sum
which will not allow us to reckon above 200 Greeks of every condition
(Syropulus, p 104, 105)   On the 20th October 1438, there was an arrear of
four months, in April 1439, of three, and of five and a half in July, at the
time of the union (p. 172, 225, 271)

[62] Syropulus (p 141, 142, 204, 221) deplores the imprisonment of the
Greeks, and the tyranny of the emperor and patriarch.

attend, from Ferrara to Florence, the rear of a flying synod. This new translation was urged by inevitable necessity: the city was visited by the plague; the fidelity of the marquis might be suspected; the mercenary troops of the duke of Milan were at the gates; and, as they occupied Romagna, it was not without difficulty and danger that the pope, the emperor, and the bishops explored their way through the unfrequented paths of the Apennine.[63]

Yet all these obstacles were surmounted by time and policy. The violence of the fathers of Basil rather promoted than injured the cause of Eugenius; the nations of Europe abhorred the schism, and disowned the election, of Felix the Fifth, who was successively a duke of Savoy, an hermit, and a pope; and the great princes were gradually reclaimed by his competitor to a favourable neutrality and a firm attachment. The legates, with some respectable members, deserted to the Roman army, which insensibly rose in numbers and reputation the council of Basil was reduced to thirty-nine bishops and three hundred of the inferior clergy,[64] while the Latins of Florence could produce the subscriptions of the pope himself, eight cardinals, two patriarchs, eight archbishops, fifty-two bishops, and forty-five abbots, or chiefs of religious orders. After the labour of nine months, and the debates of twenty-five sessions, they attained the advantage and glory of the reunion of the Greeks. Four principal questions had been agitated between the two churches· 1. The use of unleavened bread in the communion of Christ's

[63] The wars of Italy are most clearly represented in the xiiith volume of the Annals of Muratori. The schismatic Greek, Syropulus (p 145), appears to have exaggerated the fear and disorder of the pope in his retreat from Ferrara to Florence, which is proved by the acts to have been somewhat more decent and deliberate

[64] Syropulus is pleased to reckon seven hundred prelates in the council of Basil. The error is manifest, and perhaps voluntary That extravagant number could not be supplied by *all* the ecclesiastics, of every degree, who were present at the council, nor by *all* the absent bishops of the West, who, expressly or tacitly, might adhere to its decrees

body; 2 The nature of purgatory, 3. The supremacy of the pope; and 4. The single or double procession of the Holy Ghost The cause of either nation was managed by ten theological champions: the Latins were supported by the inexhaustible eloquence of Cardinal Julian, and Mark of Ephesus and Bessarion of Nice were the bold and able leaders of the Greek forces. We may bestow some praise on the progress of human reason by observing that the first of these questions was *now* treated as an immaterial rite, which might innocently vary with the fashion of the age and country. With regard to the second, both parties were agreed in the belief of an intermediate state of purgation for the venal sins of the faithful; and, whether their souls were purified by elemental fire was a doubtful point, which in a few years might be conveniently settled on the spot by the disputants. The claims of supremacy appeared of a more weighty and substantial kind; yet, by the Orientals, the Roman bishop had ever been respected as the first of the five patriarchs; nor did they scruple to admit that his jurisdiction should be exercised agreeable to the holy canons · a vague allowance which might be defined or eluded by occasional convenience. The procession of the Holy Ghost from the Father alone, or from the Father and the Son, was an article of faith which had sunk much deeper into the minds of men; and in the sessions of Ferrara and Florence the Latin addition of *filioque* was subdivided into two questions, whether it were legal, and whether it were orthodox. Perhaps it may not be necessary to boast on this subject of my own impartial indifference, but I must think that the Greeks were strongly supported by the prohibition of the council of Chalcedon against adding any article whatsoever to the creed of Nice or rather of Constantinople.[65] In earthly affairs, it is not easy to

---

[65] The Greeks, who disliked the union, were unwilling to sally from this strong fortress (p 178, 193, 195, 202, of Syropulus) The shame of the Latins was aggravated by their producing an old MS of the second council of Nice, with *filioque* in the Nicene creed. A palpable forgery! (p 173).

conceive how an assembly of legislators can bind their successors invested with powers equal to their own. But the
dictates of inspiration must be true and unchangeable, nor
should a private bishop, or a provincial synod, have presumed
to innovate against the judgment of the Catholic church. On
the substance of the doctrine, the controversy was equal
and endless· reason is confounded by the procession of a
deity; the gospel, which lay on the altar, was silent; the
various texts of the fathers might be corrupted by fraud or
entangled by sophistry; and the Greeks were ignorant of the
characters and writings of the Latin saints.[66] Of this, at
least, we way be sure, that neither side could be convinced
by the arguments of their opponents. Prejudice may be
enlightened by reason, and a superficial glance may be
rectified by a clear and more perfect view of an object adapted
to our faculties. But the bishops and monks had been taught
from their infancy to repeat a form of mysterious words;
their national and personal honour depended on the repetition
of the same sounds, and their narrow minds were hardened
and inflamed by the acrimony of a public dispute.

While they were lost in a cloud of dust and darkness, the
pope and emperor were desirous of a seeming union, which
could alone accomplish the purposes of their interview; and
the obstinacy of public dispute was softened by the arts of
private and personal negotiation. The patriarch Joseph
had sunk under the weight of age and infirmities; his dying
voice breathed the counsels of charity and concord, and his
vacant benefice might tempt the hopes of the ambitious clergy.
The ready and active obedience of the archbishops of Russia
and Nice, of Isidore and Bessarion, was prompted and recom-
pensed by their speedy promotion to the dignity of cardinals.
Bessarion, in the first debates, had stood forth the most

---

[66] Ὡς ἐγὼ (said an eminent Greek) ὅταν εἰς ναὸν εἰσέλθω Λατίνων οὐ προ-
σκυνῶ τινα τῶν ἐκεῖσε ἀγίων, ἐπεὶ οὐδὲ γνωρίζω τινά (Syropulus, p 109) See
the perplexity of the Greeks (p 217, 218, 252, 253, 273)

strenuous and eloquent champion of the Greek church; and, if the apostate, the bastard, was reprobated by his country,[67] he appears in ecclesiastical story a rare example of a patriot who was recommended to court favour by loud opposition and well timed compliance With the aid of his two spiritual coadjutors, the emperor applied his arguments to the general situation and personal characters of the bishops, and each was successively moved by authority and example Their revenues were in the hands of the Turks, their persons in those of the Latins, an episcopal treasure, three robes and forty ducats, were soon exhausted;[68] the hopes of their return still depended on the ships of Venice and the alms of Rome, and such was their indigence that their arrears, the payment of a debt, would be accepted as a favour and might operate as a bribe.[69] The danger and relief of Constantinople might excuse some prudent and pious dissimulation; and it was insinuated that the obstinate heretics who should resist the consent of the East and West would be abandoned in a hostile land to the revenge or justice of the Roman pontiff.[70]

[67] See the polite altercation of Mark and Bessarion in Syropulus (p 257), who never dissembles the vices of his own party, and fairly praises the virtues of the Latins. [The works of Bessarion are collected in Migne's Greek Patrology, vol clvi, where Bandini's monograph on his life and writings (1777) is reprinted There are two recent monographs Le Cardinal Bessarion, by H Vast (1878), and a Russian monograph by A Sadov (1883). The writings of his opponent Markos Eugenikos, metropolitan of Ephesus, will be found in Migne, P G vols clx and clxi There is a Greek work on these two men by N Kalogeras (Μάρκος ὁ Εὐγενικὸς καὶ Βησσαρίων ὁ Καρδινάλις, 1893) Cp J Draseke, Byzantinische Zeitschrift, iv p 145 sqq]

[68] For the poverty of the Greek bishops, see a remarkable passage of Ducas (c 31) One had possessed, for his whole property, three old gowns, &c By teaching one-and-twenty years in his monastery, Bessarion himself had collected forty gold florins, but of these, the archbishop had expended twenty-eight in his voyage from Peloponnesus, and the remainder at Constantinople (Syropulus, p 127)

[69] Syropulus denies that the Greeks received any money before they had subscribed the act of union (p 283), yet he relates some suspicious circumstances, and their bribery and corruption are positively affirmed by the historian Ducas

[70] The Greeks most piteously express their own fears of exile and per-

In the first private assembly of the Greeks, the formulary of union was approved by twenty-four, and rejected by twelve, members; but the five *cross-bearers* of St. Sophia, who aspired to represent the patriarch, were disqualified by ancient discipline; and their right of voting was transferred to an obsequious train of monks, grammarians, and profane laymen. The will of the monarch produced a false and servile unanimity, and no more than two patriots had courage to speak their own sentiments, and those of their country   Demetrius, the emperor's brother, retired to Venice, that he might not be witness of the union, and Mark of Ephesus, mistaking perhaps his pride for his conscience, disclaimed all communion with the Latin heretics, and avowed himself the champion and confessor of the orthodox creed [71]   In the treaty between the two nations several forms of consent were proposed, such as might satisfy the Latins without dishonouring the Greeks; and they weighed the scruples of words and syllables, till the theological balance trembled with a slight preponderance in favour of the Vatican.   It was agreed (I must entreat the attention of the reader), that the Holy Ghost proceeds from the Father *and* the Son, as from one principle and one substance; that he proceeds *by* the Son, being of the same nature and substance; and that he proceeds from the Father *and* the Son, by one *spiration* and production.   It is less difficult to understand the articles of the preliminary treaty · that the pope should defray all the expenses of the Greeks in their return home, that he should annually maintain two galleys and three hundred soldiers for the defence of Constantinople, that all the ships which transported pilgrims to Jerusalem

petual slavery (Syropul p 196), and they were strongly moved by the emperor's threats (p 260)

[71] I had forgot another popular and orthodox protester: a favourite hound, who usually lay quiet on the foot-cloth of the emperor's throne, but who barked most furiously while the act of union was reading, without being silenced by the soothing or the lashes of the royal attendants (Syropul. p. 265-266)

should be obliged to touch at that port; that, as often as they were required, the pope should furnish ten galleys for a year, or twenty-six months; and that he should powerfully solicit the princes of Europe, if the emperor had occasion for land-forces.

The same year, and almost the same day, were marked by the deposition of Eugenius at Basil, and, at Florence, by his reunion of the Greeks and Latins. In the former synod (which he styled indeed an assembly of demons), the pope was branded with the guilt of simony, perjury, tyranny, heresy, and schism,[72] and declared to be incorrigible in his vices, unworthy of any title, and incapable of holding any ecclesiastical office. In the latter, he was revered as the true and holy vicar of Christ, who, after a separation of six hundred years, had reconciled the Catholics of the East and West, in one fold and under one shepherd. The act of union was subscribed by the pope, the emperor, and the principal members of both churches; even by those who, like Syropulus,[73] had been deprived of the right of voting. Two copies might have sufficed for the East and West, but Eugenius was not satisfied, unless four authentic and similar transcripts were signed and attested as the monuments of his victory.[74] On a memorable day, the sixth of July, the suc-

[72] From the original Lives of the Popes, in Muratori's Collection (tom iii p 2, tom xxv), the manners of Eugenius IV appear to have been decent, and even exemplary His situation, exposed to the world and to his enemies, was a restraint, and is a pledge

[73] Syropulus, rather than subscribe, would have assisted, as the least evil, at the ceremony of the union He was compelled to do both; and the great ecclesiarch poorly excuses his submission to the emperor (p 290-292)

[74] None of these original acts of union can at present be produced Of the ten MSS that are preserved (five at Rome, and the remainder at Florence, Bologna, Venice, Paris, and London), nine have been examined by an accurate critic (M de Brequigny), who condemns them for the variety and imperfections of the Greek signatures Yet several of these may be esteemed as authentic copies, which were subscribed at Florence before (26th August 1439) the final separation of the Pope and emperor (Mémoires de l'Académie des Inscriptions, tom xliii p 287-311) [On these copies see Hefele, Conciliengeschichte, vol vii part 2, p 757 sqq The true original is the copy

cessors of St. Peter and Constantine ascended their thrones; the two nations assembled in the cathedral of Florence; their representatives, Cardinal Julian, and Bessarion, Archbishop of Nice, appeared in the pulpit, and, after reading, in their respective tongues, the act of union, they mutually embraced, in the name and the presence of their applauding brethren. The pope and his ministers then officiated according to the Roman liturgy; the creed was chanted with the addition of *filioque;* the acquiescence of the Greeks was poorly excused by their ignorance of the harmonious, but inarticulate, sounds;[75] and the more scrupulous Latins refused any public celebration of the Byzantine rite. Yet the emperor and his clergy were not totally unmindful of national honour. The treaty was ratified by their consent: it was tacitly agreed that no innovation should be attempted in their creed or ceremonies; they spared, and secretly respected, the generous firmness of Mark of Ephesus; and, on the decease of the patriarch, they refused to elect his successor, except in the cathedral of St. Sophia. In the distribution of public and private rewards, the liberal pontiff exceeded their hopes and his promises; the Greeks, with less pomp and pride, returned by the same road of Ferrara and Venice; and their reception at Constantinople was such as will be described in the following chapter.[76] The success of the first trial encouraged Eugenius to repeat the same edifying scenes; and the deputies of the Armenians, the Maronites, the Jacobites of Syria and Egypt, the Nestorians, and the Ethiopians were successively introduced, to kiss the feet of the Roman pontiff, and to announce the obedience and the orthodoxy of the East. These Oriental

which is kept under glass in the Laurentian Library at Florence. The text of the Union decree — in Greek, in Latin, and a German translation — is given in Hefele, *ib.* p. 742-753.]

[75] Ἡμῖν δὲ ὡς ἄσημοι ἐδόκουν φῶναι (Syropul. p. 297).

[76] In their return, the Greeks conversed at Bologna with the ambassadors of England; and, after some questions and answers, these impartial strangers laughed at the pretended union of Florence (Syropul. p. 307).

embassies, unknown in the countries which they presumed to represent,[77] diffused over the West the fame of Eugenius; and a clamour was artfully propagated against the remnant of a schism in Switzerland and Savoy, which alone impeded the harmony of the Christian world. The vigour of opposition was succeeded by the lassitude of despair the council of Basil was silently dissolved; and Felix, renouncing the tiara, again withdrew to the devout or delicious hermitage of Ripaille.[78] A general peace was secured by mutual acts of oblivion and indemnity; all ideas of reformation subsided; the popes continued to exercise and abuse their ecclesiastical despotism; nor has Rome been since disturbed by the mischiefs of a contested election.[79]

The journeys of three emperors were unavailing for their temporal, or perhaps their spiritual, salvation, but they were productive of a beneficial consequence, the revival of the Greek learning in Italy, from whence it was propagated to the

[77] So nugatory, or rather so fabulous, are these reunions of the Nestorians, Jacobites, &c that I have turned over, without success, the Bibliotheca Orientalis of Assemanus, a faithful slave of the Vatican

[78] Ripaille is situate near Thonon in Savoy, on the southern side of the lake of Geneva. It is now a Carthusian abbey, and Mr Addison (Travels into Italy, vol. ii p. 147, 148, of Baskerville's edition of his works) has celebrated the place and the founder Æneas Sylvius, and the fathers of Basil, applaud the austere life of the ducal hermit, but the French and Italian proverbs most unluckily attest the popular opinion of his luxury

[79] In this account of the councils of Basil, Ferrara, and Florence, I have consulted the original acts, which fill the xviith and xviiith tomes of the edition of Venice, and are closed by the perspicuous, though partial, history of Augustin Patricius, an Italian of the xvth century They are digested and abridged by Dupin (Bibliothèque Ecclés tom xii), and the continuator of Fleury (tom. xxii), and the respect of the Gallican church for the adverse parties confines their members to an awkward moderation [An English translation of Gorski's (Russian) History of the Council of Florence appeared in 1861 (ed by Neale) Kalligas wrote an important essay on it, which is published in his Μελέται καὶ λόγοι (1882), p 1-181 See also Draseke Zum Kircheneinigungsversuch des Jahres 1439, in Byz Zeitsch v p 572 sqq , Frommann, Kritische Beitrage zur Geschichte der florentinischen Kircheneinigung, 1862 The full story of the Councils of Constance, Basil, Ferrara, and Florence is contained in vol. vii , parts i and ii , of Hefele's Conciliengeschichte]

last nations of the West and North. In their lowest servitude
and depression, the subjects of the Byzantine throne were
still possessed of a golden key that could unlock the treasures
of antiquity, of a musical and prolific language, that gives a
soul to the objects of sense and a body to the abstractions of
philosophy. Since the barriers of the monarchy, and even
of the capital, had been trampled under foot, the various
Barbarians had doubtless corrupted the form and substance
of the national dialect; and ample glossaries have been composed, to interpret a multitude of words of Arabic, Turkish,
Sclavonian, Latin, or French origin.[80] But a purer idiom
was spoken in the court and taught in the college; and the
flourishing state of the language is described, and perhaps
embellished, by a learned Italian,[81] who, by a long residence
and noble marriage,[82] was naturalised at Constantinople about

[80] In the first attempt, Meursius collected 3600 Græco-Barbarous words, to
which, in a second edition, he subjoined 1800 more: yet what plenteous
gleanings did he leave to Portius, Ducange, Fabrotti, the Bollandists, &c
(Fabric Bibliot Græc tom x p 101, &c) *Some* Persic words may be
found in Xenophon, and some Latin ones in Plutarch, and such is the
inevitable effect of war and commerce, but the form and substance of the
language were not affected by this slight alloy [On foreign words in Greek
see. G Meyer, Neugriechische Studien, ii. (Slavonic, Albanian, and Rou-
manian loanwords), in the Sitzungsberichte of the Vienna Academy, vol cxxx , 1894,
and vol cxxxii , 1895 Also F Miklosich, Die slavischen Elemente im
Neugriechischen, *ib* vol lxiii , 1870, and Die turkischen Elemente in den
sudosteuropaischen Sprachen, in the Denkschriften of the Vienna Acad ,
vols xxxiv , xxxv , xxxviii (1884, 1886, 1890).]

[81] The life of Francis Philelphus, a sophist, proud, restless, and rapacious,
has been diligently composed by Lancelot (Mémoires de l'Académie des
Inscriptions, tom x p 691–751), and Tiraboschi (Istoria della Letteratura
Italiana, tom. vii p 282–294), for the most part from his own letters His
elaborate writings, and those of his contemporaries, are forgotten, but their
familiar epistles still describe the men and the times [G Voigt, Die Wie-
derbelebung des klassischen Alterthums, 3rd ed , 1893, T Klette, Beitrage
zur Geschichte und Litteratur der italienischen Gelehrtenrenaissance, 1890
(part iii contains Greek Letters of Philelphus) Legrand, Centdix lettres
grecques de François Filelfe, 1892]

[82] He married, and had perhaps debauched, the daughter of John, and the
grand-daughter of Manuel, Chrysoloras She was young, beautiful, and

thirty years before the Turkish conquest. "The vulgar speech," says Philelphus,[83] "has been depraved by the people, and infected by the multitude of strangers and merchants, who every day flock to the city and mingle with the inhabitants It is from the disciples of such a school that the Latin language received the versions of Aristotle and Plato, so obscure in sense, and in spirit so poor. But the Greeks who have escaped the contagion are those whom *we* follow; and they alone are worthy of our imitation. In familiar discourse, they still speak the tongue of Aristophanes and Euripides, of the historians and philosophers of Athens; and the style of their writings are still more elaborate and correct. The persons who, by their birth and offices, are attached to the Byzantine court are those who maintain, with the least alloy, the ancient standard of elegance and purity; and the native graces of language most conspicuously shine among the noble matrons, who are excluded from all intercourse with foreigners. With foreigners do I say? They live retired and sequestered from the eyes of their fellow-citizens. Seldom are they seen in the streets; and, when they leave their houses, it is in the dusk of evening, on visits to the churches and their nearest kindred On these occasions, they are on horseback, covered with a veil, and encompassed by their parents, their husbands, or their servants " [84]

Among the Greeks, a numerous and opulent clergy was

wealthy, and her noble family was allied to the Dorias of Genoa and the emperors of Constantinople

[83] Græci quibus lingua depravata non sit   ita loquuntur vulgo hâc etiam tempestate ut Aristophanes comicus, aut Euripides tragicus, ut oratores omnes, ut historiographi, ut philosophi   literati autem homines et doctius et emendatius . . . Nam viri aulici veterum sermonis dignitatem atque elegantiam retinebant in primisque ipsæ nobiles mulieres, quibus cum nullum esset omnino cum viris peregrinis commercium, merus ille ac purus Græcorum sermo servabatur intactus (Philelph Epist ad ann 1451, apud Hodium, p 188, 189) He observes in another passage, uxor illa mea Theodora locutione erat admodum moderatâ et suavi et maxime Attici

[84] Philelphus, absurdly enough, derives this Greek or Oriental jealousy from the manners of ancient Rome.

dedicated to the service of religion; their monks and bishops
have ever been distinguished by the gravity and austerity of
their manners, nor were they diverted, like the Latin priests,
by the pursuits and pleasures of a secular and even military
life.   After a large deduction for the time and talents that
were lost in the devotion, the laziness, and the discord of the
church and cloister, the more inquisitive and ambitious
minds would explore the sacred and profane erudition of their
native language   The ecclesiastics presided over the education of youth; the schools of philosophy and eloquence were
perpetuated till the fall of the empire, and it may be affirmed
that more books and more knowledge were included within
the walls of Constantinople than could be dispersed over the
extensive countries of the West.[85]   But an important distinction has been already noticed · the Greeks were stationary
or retrograde, while the Latins were advancing with a rapid
and progressive motion   The nations were excited by the
spirit of independence and emulation; and even the little
world of the Italian states contained more people and industry
than the decreasing circle of the Byzantine empire.   In
Europe, the lower ranks of society were relieved from the yoke
of feudal servitude, and freedom is the first step to curiosity
and knowledge.   The use, however rude and corrupt, of the
Latin tongue had been preserved by superstition, the universities, from Bologna to Oxford,[86] were peopled with thou-

[85] See the state of learning in the xiiith and xivth centuries, in the learned
and judicious Mosheim (Institut Hist Eccles p 434-440, 490-494)

[86] At the end of the xvth century, there existed in Europe about fifty universities, and of these the foundation of ten or twelve is prior to the year 1300
They were crowded in proportion to their scarcity   Bologna contained
10,000 students, chiefly of the civil law   In the year 1357, the number at
Oxford had decreased from 30,000 to 6000 scholars (Henry's History of
Great Britain, vol iv p 478)   Yet even this decrease is much superior to the
present list of the members of the university [These numbers are grossly
exaggerated   See Mr H Rashdall, Universities of Europe in the Middle
Ages, vol ii , pt ii , where a short chapter (xiii) is devoted to the subject.
He concludes (p 589) that "the maximum number at Oxford was something
between 1500 and 3000 By about 1438 the numbers had fallen to under

sands of scholars; and their misguided ardour might be directed to more liberal and manly studies. In the resurrection of science, Italy was the first that cast away her shroud, and the eloquent Petrarch, by his lessons and his example, may justly be applauded as the first harbinger of day. A purer style of composition, a more generous and rational strain of sentiment, flowed from the study and imitation of the writers of ancient Rome; and the disciples of Cicero and Virgil approached, with reverence and love, the sanctuary of their Grecian masters. In the sack of Constantinople, the French, and even the Venetians, had despised and destroyed the works of Lysippus and Homer; the monuments of art may be annihilated by a single blow; but the immortal mind is renewed and multiplied by the copies of the pen, and such copies it was the ambition of Petrarch and his friends to possess and understand. The arms of the Turks undoubtedly pressed the flight of the Muses; yet we may tremble at the thought that Greece might have been overwhelmed, with her schools and libraries, before Europe had emerged from the deluge of Barbarism, that the seeds of science might have been scattered by the winds, before the Italian soil was prepared for their cultivation.

The most learned Italians of the fifteenth century have confessed and applauded the restoration of Greek literature, after a long oblivion of many hundred years.[87] Yet in that

1000 " He thinks it improbable that the number at Bologna or at Paris ever went beyond about 6000 or 7000]

[87] Of those writers, who professedly treat of the restoration of the Greek learning in Italy, the two principal are Hodius, Dr Humphrey Hody (de Græcis Illustribus, Linguæ Græcæ Literarumque humaniorum Instauratoribus, Londini, 1742, in large octavo), and Tiraboschi (Istoria della Letteratura Italiana, tom v p 364–377, tom vii p 112–143) The Oxford professor is a laborious scholar, but the librarian of Modena enjoys the superiority of a modern and national historian [Cp above note 81 Legrand, Biographie hellénique, vol 1, 1885 J A Symonds, The Renaissance in Italy, ii, The Revival of Learning, 1877 Thereanos, in the first volume of his biography of Koraês (Ἀδαμάντιος Κοραῆς, 1889), gives a good summary of the movement G Fioretto, Gli umanisti, o lo studio del Latino

country, and beyond the Alps, some names are quoted · some
profound scholars, who, in the darker ages, were honourably
distinguished by their knowledge of the Greek tongue; and
national vanity has been loud in the praise of such rare
examples of erudition   Without scrutinising the merit of
individuals, truth must observe that their science is without a
cause and without an effect; that it was easy for them to satisfy themselves and their more ignorant contemporaries; and
that the idiom, which they had so marvellously acquired, was
transcribed in few manuscripts, and was not taught in any
university of the West.   In a corner of Italy it faintly existed
as the popular, or at least as the ecclesiastical, dialect.[88]   The
first impression of the Doric and Ionic colonies has never been
completely erased; the Calabrian churches were long attached to the throne of Constantinople; and the monks of St.
Basil pursued their studies in Mount Athos and the schools of
the East.   Calabria was the native country of Barlaam, who
has already appeared as a sectary and an ambassador; and
Barlaam was the first who revived, beyond the Alps, the memory, or at least the writings, of Homer.[89]   He is described, by

e del Greco nel secolo xv in Italia, 1881.   See also the excellent monograph
on Vittorino da Feltre, dealing with the education of the Humanist teachers
in Italy, by W H Woodward, 1897]

[88] In Calabriâ quæ olim magna Græcia dicebatur, coloniis Græcis repletâ
remansit quædam linguæ veteris cognitio (Hodius, p 2)   If it were eradicated by the Romans, it was revived and perpetuated by the monks of St
Basil, who possessed seven convents at Rossano alone (Giannone, Istoria di
Napoli, tom 1 p 520)   [Greek is still spoken by a population of about
20,000 in both the heel and the toe of Italy — in the land of Otranto and in
the territory of Bova, these two dialects differ considerably   Comparetti,
Saggi dei dialetti greci dell' Italia meridionale, 1866, Morosi, Studi sui
dialetti greci della Terra d'Otranto, 1870, and Dialetti romaici del manda-
mento di Bova in Calabria, 1874, Pellegrini, Il dialetto greco-calabro di
Bova, 1880, H F Tozer, The Greek-speaking Population of Southern
Italy, in Journal of Hellenic Studies, x p 11 *sqq*]

[89] Ii Barbari (says Petrarch, the French and Germans) vix non dicam
libros sed nomen Homeri audiverunt   Perhaps, in that respect, the xiiith
century was less happy than the age of Charlemagne   [Barlaam was a native
of Seminaria in Calabria   His work (against the Roman church) περὶ τῆς

Petrarch and Boccace,[90] as a man of a diminutive stature, though truly great in the measure of learning and genius; of a piercing discernment, though of a slow and painful elocution. For many ages (as they affirm) Greece had not produced his equal in the knowledge of history, grammar, and philosophy; and his merit was celebrated in the attestations of the princes and doctors of Constantinople One of these attestations is still extant; and the emperor Cantacuzene, the protector of his adversaries, is forced to allow that Euclid, Aristotle, and Plato were familiar to that profound and subtle logician [91] In the court of Avignon, he formed an intimate connection with Petrarch,[92] the first of the Latin scholars; and the desire of mutual instruction was the principle of their literary commerce. The Tuscan applied himself with eager curiosity and assiduous diligence to the study of the Greek language; and, in a laborious struggle with the dryness and difficulty of the first rudiments, he began to reach the sense, and to feel the spirit, of poets and philosophers whose minds were congenial to his own. But he was soon deprived of the society and lessons of this useful assistant. Barlaam relinquished his fruitless embassy; and, on his return to Greece, he rashly provoked the swarms of fanatic monks by attempting to substitute the light of reason to that of their navel. After a separation of three years, the two friends again met in the court of Naples; but the generous pupil renounced the fairest occasion of improvement; and by his recommendation Barlaam

---

ἀρχῆς τοῦ πάπα is published in Migne, P G 151, p 1256 sqq There is an account of Barlaam's work in T Uspenski's essay, Philosophskoe i bogoslovskoe dvizhenie v xiv viekie, printed in his Ocherki, p 246–364 (1892)]

[90] See the character of Barlaam in Boccace de Genealog Deorum, l xv. c 6

[91] Cantacuzen l ii c 36

[92] For the connection of Petrarch and Barlaam, and the two interviews at Avignon in 1339, and at Naples in 1342, see the excellent Mémoires sur la Vie de Pétrarque, tom i p 406–410, tom ii p 75–77. [G Mandolori, Fra Barlaamo Calabrese, maestro del Petrarca, 1888, P de Nolhac, Pétrarque et l'humanisme, 1892 On Petrarch see further below chap lxx ad init]

was finally settled in a small bishopric of his native Calabria [93] The manifold avocations of Petrarch, love and friendship, his various correspondence and frequent journeys, the Roman laurel, and his elaborate compositions in prose and verse, in Latin and Italian, diverted him from a foreign idiom; and, as he advanced in life, the attainment of the Greek language was the object of his wishes rather than of his hopes. When he was about fifty years of age, a Byzantine ambassador, his friend, and a master of both tongues, presented him with a copy of Homer; and the answer of Petrarch is at once expressive of his eloquence, gratitude, and regret. After celebrating the generosity of the donor, and the value of a gift more precious in his estimation than gold or rubies, he thus proceeds: "Your present of the genuine and original text of the divine poet, the fountain of all invention, is worthy of yourself and of me; you have fulfilled your promise and satisfied my desires. Yet your liberality is still imperfect · with Homer you should have given me yourself a guide, who could lead me into the fields of light, and disclose to my wondering eyes the specious miracles of the Iliad and Odyssey. But, alas! Homer is dumb, or I am deaf; nor is it in my power to enjoy the beauty which I possess. I have seated him by the side of Plato, the prince of poets near the prince of philosophers; and I glory in the sight of my illustrious guests. Of their immortal writings, whatever had been translated into the Latin idiom, I had already acquired; but, if there be no profit, there is some pleasure in beholding these venerable Greeks in their proper and national habit. I am delighted with the aspect of Homer; and, as often as I embrace the silent volume, I exclaim, with a sigh, Illustrious bard! with what pleasure should I listen to thy song, if my sense of hearing were not obstructed and lost

[93] The bishopric to which Barlaam retired was the old Locri, in the middle ages Scta Cyriaca, and by corruption Hieracium, Gerace (Dissert Chorographica Italiæ medii Ævi, p 312) The dives opum of the Norman times soon lapsed into poverty, since even the church was poor, yet the town still contains 3000 inhabitants (Swinburne, p 340)

by the death of one friend, and in the much lamented absence of another! Nor do I yet despair; and the example of Cato suggests some comfort and hope, since it was in the last period of age that he attained the knowledge of the Greek letters."[94]

The prize which eluded the efforts of Petrarch was obtained by the fortune and industry of his friend Boccace,[95] the father of the Tuscan prose. That popular writer, who derives his reputation from the Decameron, an hundred novels of pleasantry and love, may aspire to the more serious praise of restoring in Italy the study of the Greek language. In the year one thousand three hundred and sixty, a disciple of Barlaam, whose name was Leo or Leontius Pilatus, was detained in his way to Avignon by the advice and hospitality of Boccace, who lodged the stranger in his house, prevailed on the republic of Florence to allow him an annual stipend, and devoted his leisure to the first Greek professor who taught the language in the Western countries of Europe. The appearance of Leo might disgust the most eager disciple he was clothed in the mantle of a philosopher, or a mendicant; his countenance was hideous, his face was overshadowed with black hair; his beard long and uncombed, his deportment rustic; his temper gloomy and inconstant; nor could he grace his discourse with the ornaments or even the perspicuity of Latin elocution. But his mind was stored with a treasure of Greek learning; history and fable, philosophy and grammar, were alike at his

[94] I will transcribe a passage from this epistle of Petrarch (Famil iv 2). Donasti Homerum non in alienum sermonem violento alveo derivatum, sed ex ipsis Græci eloqui scatebris, et qualis divino illi profluxit ingenio
Sine tuâ voce Homerus tuus apud me mutus, immo, vero ego apud illum surdus sum Gaudeo tamen vel adspectu solo, ac sæpe illum amplexus atque suspirans dico, O magne vir! &c
[95] For the life and writings of Boccace, who was born in 1313, and died in 1375, Fabricius (Bibliot Latin medii Ævi, tom i p 248, &c) and Tiraboschi (tom v p 83, 439-451) may be consulted The editions, versions, imitations of his novels are innumerable Yet he was ashamed to communicate that trifling and perhaps scandalous work to Petrarch his respectable friend, in whose letters and memoirs he conspicuously appears.

command; and he read the poems of Homer in the schools of Florence. It was from his explanation that Boccace composed and transcribed a literal prose version of the Iliad and Odyssey, which satisfied the thirst of his friend Petrarch, and which perhaps, in the succeeding century, was clandestinely used by Laurentius Valla, the Latin interpreter. It was from his narratives that the same Boccace collected the materials for his treatise on the genealogy of the heathen gods; a work, in that age, of stupendous erudition, and which he ostentatiously sprinkled with Greek characters and passages, to excite the wonder and applause of his more ignorant readers.[96] The first steps of learning are slow and laborious: no more than ten votaries of Homer could be enumerated in all Italy; and neither Rome nor Venice nor Naples could add a single name to this studious catalogue. But their numbers would have multiplied, their progress would have been accelerated, if the inconstant Leo, at the end of three years, had not relinquished an honourable and beneficial station. In his passage, Petrarch entertained him at Padua a short time : he enjoyed the scholar, but was justly offended with the gloomy and unsocial temper of the man. Discontented with the world and with himself, Leo depreciated his present enjoyments, while absent persons and objects were dear to his imagination. In Italy, he was a Thessalian, in Greece, a native of Calabria; in the company of the Latins, he disdained their language, religion, and manner: no sooner was he landed at Constantinople, than he again sighed for the wealth of Venice and the elegance of Florence. His Italian friends were deaf to his importunity; he depended on their curiosity and indulgence, and embarked on a second voyage; but, on his entrance into the Adriatic, the

[96] Boccace indulges an honest vanity: Ostentationis causâ Græca carmina adscripsi . . . jure utor meo; meum est hoc decus, mea gloria scilicet inter Etruscos Græcis uti carminibus. Nonne ego fui qui Leontium Pilatum, &c. (de Genealogiâ Deorum, l. xv. c. 7, a work which, though now forgotten, has run through thirteen or fourteen editions). [It was Leontius Pilatus himself who translated Homer.]

ship was assailed by a tempest, and the unfortunate teacher, who, like Ulysses, had fastened himself to the mast, was struck dead by a flash of lightning. The humane Petrarch dropped a tear on his disaster; but he was most anxious to learn whether some copy of Euripides or Sophocles might not be saved from the hands of the mariners.[97]

But the faint rudiments of Greek learning, which Petrarch had encouraged and Boccace had planted, soon withered and expired. The succeeding generation was content for a while with the improvement of Latin eloquence; nor was it before the end of the fourteenth century that a new and perpetual flame was rekindled in Italy [98] Previous to his own journey, the emperor Manuel despatched his envoys and orators to implore the compassion of the Western princes. Of these envoys, the most conspicuous or the most learned was Manuel Chrysoloras,[99] of noble birth, and whose Roman ancestors are supposed to have migrated with the great Constantine. After visiting the courts of France and England, where he obtained some contributions and more promises, the envoy was invited to assume the office of a professor; and Florence had again the honour of this second invitation. By his knowledge, not only of the Greek but of the Latin tongue, Chrysoloras deserved the stipend and surpassed the expectation of the republic;

[97] Leontius, or Leo Pilatus, is sufficiently made known by Hody (p 2-11), and the Abbé de Sade (Vie de Pétrarque, tom iii p 625-634, 670-673), who has very happily caught the lively and dramatic manner of his original

[98] Dr Hody (p 54) is angry with Leonard Aretin, Guarinus, Paulus Jovius, &c for affirming that the Greek letters were restored in Italy *post septingentos annos*, as if, says he, they had flourished till the end of the viith century These writers most probably reckoned from the last period of the exarchate, and the presence of the Greek magistrates and troops at Ravenna and Rome must have preserved, in some degree, the use of their native tongue

[99] See the article of Emanuel, or Manuel Chrysoloras, in Hody (p 12-54), and Tiraboschi (tom. vii p 113-118) The precise date of his arrival floats between the years 1390 and 1400, and is only confined by the reign of Boniface IX [The Greek grammar of Chrysoloras was printed in Venice in 1484. For the chronology of his life cp Klette, *op. cit* part 1]

his school was frequented by a crowd of disciples of every rank and age; and one of these, in a general history, has described his motives and his success. "At that time," says Leonard Aretin,[100] "I was a student of the civil law; but my soul was inflamed with the love of letters; and I bestowed some application on the sciences of logic and rhetoric.   On the arrival of Manuel, I hesitated whether I should desert my legal studies or relinquish this golden opportunity; and thus, in the ardour of youth, I communed with my own mind — Wilt thou be wanting to thyself and thy fortune?   Wilt thou refuse to be introduced to a familiar converse with Homer, Plato, and Demosthenes? with those poets, philosophers, and orators, of whom such wonders are related, and who are celebrated by every age as the great masters of human science?   Of professors and scholars in civil law, a sufficient supply will always be found in our universities; but a teacher, and such a teacher, of the Greek language, if he once be suffered to escape, may never afterwards be retrieved.   Convinced by these reasons, I gave myself to Chrysoloras; and so strong was my passion that the lessons which I had imbibed in the day were the constant subject of my nightly dreams."[101] At the same time and place the Latin classics were explained by John of Ravenna, the domestic pupil of Petrarch;[102] the Italians, who illustrated their age and country, were formed in this double school; and Florence became the fruitful

[100] The name of *Aretinus* has been assumed by five or six natives of *Arezzo* in Tuscany, of whom the most famous and the most worthless lived in the xvith century.   Leonardus Brunus Aretinus, the disciple of Chrysoloras, was a linguist, an orator, and an historian, the secretary of four successive popes, and the chancellor of the republic of Florence, where he died, A.D. 1444, at the age of seventy-five (Fabric. Bibliot. medii Ævi, tom. i. p. 190, &c.; Tiraboschi, tom. vii. p. 33–38).

[101] See the passage in Aretin. Commentario Rerum suo Tempore in Italiâ gestarum, apud Hodium, p. 28–30.

[102] In this domestic discipline, Petrarch, who loved the youth, often complains of the eager curiosity, restless temper, and proud feelings, which announce the genius and glory of a riper age (Mémoires sur Pétrarque, tom. iii. p. 700–709).

seminary of Greek and Roman erudition [103] The presence
of the emperor recalled Chrysoloras from the college to the
court, but he afterwards taught at Pavia and Rome with equal
industry and applause. The remainder of his life, about
fifteen years, was divided between Italy and Constantinople,
between embassies and lessons. In the noble office of en-
lightening a foreign nation, the grammarian was not unmindful of a more sacred duty to his prince and country; and
Emanuel Chrysoloras died at Constance, on a public mission
from the emperor to the council.

After his example, the restoration of the Greek letters in
Italy was prosecuted by a series of emigrants, who were destitute of fortune, and endowed with learning, or at least with
language. From the terror or oppression of the Turkish arms
the natives of Thessalonica and Constantinople escaped to a
land of freedom, curiosity, and wealth The synod introduced into Florence the lights of the Greek church and the
oracles of the Platonic philosophy; and the fugitives who
adhered to the union had the double merit of renouncing their
country not only for the Christian but for the Catholic cause.
A patriot who sacrifices his party and conscience to the allure-
ments of favour may be possessed, however, of the private
and social virtues; he no longer hears the reproachful epithets
of slave and apostate, and the consideration which he ac-
quires among his new associates will restore in his own eyes
the dignity of his character. The prudent conformity of
Bessarion was rewarded with the Roman purple, he fixed
his residence in Italy; and the Greek cardinal, the titular

---

[103] Hinc Græcæ Latinæque scholæ exortæ sunt, Guarino Philelpho,
Leonardo Aretino, Caroloque, ac plerisque aliis tanquam ex equo Trojano
prodeuntibus, quorum emulatione multa ingenia deinceps ad laudem excitata
sunt (Platina in Bonifacio IX) Another Italian writer adds the names of
Paulus Petrus Vergerius, Omnibonus [Ognibene da Lonigo], Vincentius,
Poggius, Franciscus Barbarus, &c But I question whether a rigid chronology would allow Chrysoloras *all* these eminent scholars (Hodius, p 25-
27, &c). [Vergerius (who *was* one of his pupils) wrote the epitaph on
Chrysoloras which is to be seen in the kitchen of the Hôtel Insel at Constance]

patriarch of Constantinople, was respected as the chief and protector of his nation.[104] His abilities were exercised in the legations of Bologna, Venice, Germany, and France; and his election to the chair of St. Peter floated for a moment on the uncertain breath of a conclave.[105] His ecclesiastical honours diffused a splendour and pre-eminence over his literary merit and service: his palace was a school; as often as the cardinal visited the Vatican, he was attended by a learned train of both nations;[106] of men applauded by themselves and the public; and whose writings, now overspread with dust, were popular and useful in their own times. I shall not attempt to enumerate the restorers of Grecian literature in the fifteenth century; and it may be sufficient to mention with gratitude the names of Theodore Gaza, of George of Trebizond, of John Argyropulus, and Demetrius Chalcondyles, who taught their native language in the schools of Florence and Rome. Their labours were not inferior to those of Bessarion, whose purple they revered, and whose fortune was the secret object of their envy. But the lives of these grammarians were humble and obscure; they had declined the lucrative paths of the church; their dress and manners secluded them from the commerce of the world; and, since they were confined to the merit, they might be content with the rewards, of learning. From this character Janus Lascaris[107]

[104] See in Hody the article of Bessarion (p. 136-177). Theodore Gaza [of Thessalonica], George of Trebizond, and the rest of the Greeks whom I have named or omitted, are inserted in their proper chapters of his learned work. See likewise Tiraboschi, in the 1st and 2d parts of the vith tome. [See Legrand's work quoted above, note 87.]

[105] The cardinals knocked at his door, but his conclavist refused to interrupt the studies of Bessarion: "Nicholas," said he, "thy respect hath cost thee an hat, and me the tiara."

[106] Such as George of Trebizond, Theodore Gaza, Argyropulus, Andronicus of Thessalonica, Philelphus, Poggius, Blondus, Nicholas Perrot, Valla, Campanus, Platina, &c. Viri (says Hody, with the pious zeal of a scholar) nullo ævo perituri (p. 156).

[107] He was born before the taking of Constantinople, but his honourable life was stretched far into the xvith century (A.D. 1535). Leo X. and Francis I.

will deserve an exception. His eloquence, politeness, and Imperial descent recommended him to the French monarchs, and in the same cities he was alternately employed to teach and to negotiate. Duty and interest prompted them to cultivate the study of the Latin language; and the most successful attained the faculty of writing and speaking with fluency and elegance in a foreign idiom But they ever retained the inveterate vanity of their country: their praise, or at least their esteem, was reserved for the national writers, to whom they owed their fame and subsistence; and they sometimes betrayed their contempt in licentious criticism or satire on Virgil's poetry and the oratory of Tully.[108] The superiority of these masters arose from the familiar use of a living language; and their first disciples were incapable of discerning how far they had degenerated from the knowledge, and even the practice, of their ancestors. A vicious pronunciation,[109] which they introduced, was banished from

were his noblest patrons, under whose auspices he founded the Greek colleges of Rome and Paris (Hody, p 247-275) He left posterity in France, but the counts de Vintimille, and their numerous branches, derive the name of Lascaris from a doubtful marriage, in the xiiith century, with the daughter of a Greek emperor (Ducange, Fam Byzant p 224-230)

[108] Two of his epigrams against Virgil, and three against Tully, are preserved and refuted by Franciscus Floridus, who can find no better names than Græculus ineptus et impudens (Hody, p 274) In our own times, an English critic has accused the Æneid of containing multa languida, nugatoria, spiritu et majestate carminis heroici defecta; many such verses as he, the said Jeremiah Markland, would have been ashamed of owning (præfat. ad Statii Sylvas, p 21, 22).

[109] Emanuel Chrysoloras, and his colleagues, are accused of ignorance, envy, or avarice (Sylloge, &c. tom. ii. p 235). The modern Greek pronounces the B as a V consonant, and confound three vowels (η ι υ) and several diphthongs [$\epsilon\iota$, $o\iota$, $\upsilon\iota$] Such was the vulgar pronunciation which the stern Gardiner maintained by penal statutes in the University of Cambridge, but the monosyllable $\beta\eta$ represented to an Attic ear the bleating of sheep, and a bell-wether is better evidence than a bishop or a chancellor. The treatises of those scholars, particularly Erasmus, who asserted a more classical pronunciation, are collected in the Sylloge of Havercamp (2 vols in octavo, Lugd Bat 1736, 1740), but it is difficult to paint sounds by words, and in their reference to modern use they can be understood only by their respective

the schools by the reason of the succeeding age. Of the
power of the Greek accents they were ignorant; and those
musical notes, which, from an Attic tongue and to an Attic
ear, must have been the secret soul of harmony, were to their
eyes, as to our own, no more than mute or unmeaning marks,
in prose superfluous and troublesome in verse.[109a] The art
of grammar they truly possessed; the valuable fragments of
Apollonius and Herodian were transfused into their lessons;
and their treatises of syntax and etymology, though devoid of
philosophic spirit, are still useful to the Greek student. In the
shipwreck of the Byzantine libraries, each fugitive seized a
fragment of treasure, a copy of some author, who, without
his industry, might have perished; the transcripts were multiplied by an assiduous, and sometimes an elegant, pen; and
the text was corrected and explained by their own comments
or those of the elder scholiasts. The sense, though not the
spirit, of the Greek classics was interpreted to the Latin
world; the beauties of style evaporate in a version; but the
judgment of Theodore Gaza selected the more solid works
of Aristotle and Theophrastus, and their natural histories
of animals and plants opened a rich fund of genuine and
experimental science.[110]

Yet the fleeting shadows of metaphysics were pursued with
more curiosity and ardour. After a long oblivion, Plato was
revived in Italy by a venerable Greek,[111] who taught in the

countrymen. We may observe that our peculiar pronunciation of the
θ to *th* is approved by Erasmus (tom. ii. p. 130) [θ is so pronounced in modern Greek].

[109a] [It is to be observed however that the system of accent-notation was
first introduced by the Alexandrines. Gibbon assumes that the meaning of
the accents was in ancient times entirely different from their meaning in
modern Greek. This is improbable. But it is still a problem how the Greeks
conciliated their accentuation with the rhythms of their verses.]

[110] [On Theodore Gaza see the biographical essay of L. Stein in the Archiv
für Geschichte der Philosophie, ii. p. 426 *sqq.*, 1889.]

[111] George Gemistus Pletho, a various and voluminous writer, the master
of Bessarion and all the Platonists of the times. He visited Italy in his old
age, and soon returned to end his days in Peloponnesus. See the curious

house of Cosmo of Medicis. While the synod of Florence was involved in theological debate, some beneficial consequences might flow from the study of his elegant philosophy; his style is the purest standard of the Attic dialect, and his sublime thoughts are sometimes adapted to familiar conversation, and sometimes adorned with the richest colours of poetry and eloquence. The dialogues of Plato are a dramatic picture of the life and death of a sage, and, as often as he descends from the clouds, his moral system inculcates the love of truth, of our country, and of mankind. The precept and example of Socrates recommended a modest doubt and liberal inquiry; and, if the Platonists, with blind devotion, adored the visions and errors of their divine master, their enthusiasm might correct the dry dogmatic method of the Peripatetic school. So equal, yet so opposite, are the merits of Plato and Aristotle that they may be balanced in endless controversy, but some spark of freedom may be produced by the collision of adverse servitude. The modern Greeks were divided between the two sects; with more fury than skill they fought under the banner of their leaders; and the field of battle was removed in their flight from Constantinople to Rome. But this philosophic debate soon degenerated into an angry and personal quarrel of grammarians; and Bessarion, though an advocate for Plato, protected the national honour, by interposing the advice and authority of a mediator. In the gardens of the Medici, the academical doctrine was enjoyed by the polite and

Diatribe of Leo Allatius de Georgiis, in Fabricius (Bibliot. Græc. tom x. p 739-756) [The study of Plato was revived in the 11th century by Michael Psellus For Plethon see H F Tozer, A Byzantine Reformer, in the Journal of Hellenic Studies, vii p 353 *sqq*, 1886, and F Schultze, Geschichte der Philosophie der Renaissance, vol 1, 1874 The Memoir on the state of the Peloponnesus, which he addressed to the emperor Manuel, is edited by Ellissen in his Analekten der mittel- und neugriechischen Litteratur, vol iv, part ii, with a German translation Plethon's works are collected in Migne's P G vol clx On the theological side of his works see W Gass, Gennadius und Pletho, Aristotelismus und Platonismus in der griechischen Kirche, 1844.]

learned; but their philosophic society was quickly dissolved; and, if the writings of the Attic sage were perused in the closet, the more powerful Stagirite continued to reign the oracle of the church and school [112]

I have fairly represented the literary merits of the Greeks; yet it must be confessed that they were seconded and sur- passed by the ardour of the Latins. Italy was divided into many independent states, and at that time it was the ambi- tion of princes and republics to vie with each other in the en- couragement and reward of literature. The fame of Nicholas the Fifth [113] has not been adequate to his merits. From a plebeian origin he raised himself by his virtue and learning· the character of the man prevailed over the interest of the pope; and he sharpened those weapons which were soon pointed against the Roman church. [114] He had been the friend of the most eminent scholars of the age; he became their patron, and such was the humility of his manners that the change was scarcely discernible either to them or to himself. If he pressed the acceptance of a liberal gift, it was not as the measure of desert, but as the proof of benevolence; and, when modest merit declined his bounty, "Accept it," would he say with a consciousness of his own worth, "you will not always have a Nicholas among ye" The influence of the holy see pervaded Christendom; and he exerted that influence in the search, not of benefices, but of books. From the ruins of the Byzantine libraries, from the darkest monasteries of Germany

[112] The state of the Platonic philosophy in Italy is illustrated by Boivin (Mém de l'Acad des Inscriptions, tom. ii p 715-729) and Tiraboschi (tom. vi p 1 p 259-288)

[113] See the life of Nicholas V by two contemporary authors, Janottus Manettus (tom. iii p ii p. 905-962), and Vespasian of Florence (tom xxv p 267-290), in the collection of Muratori, and consult Tiraboschi (tom. vi p 1 p 46-52, 109), and Hody in the articles of Theodore Gaza, George of Trebizond, &c

[114] Lord Bolingbroke observes, with truth and spirit, that the popes, in this instance, were worse politicians than the muftis, and that the charm which had bound mankind for so many ages was broken by the magicians themselves (Letters on the Study of History, l vi p 165, 166, octavo edition,

and Britain, he collected the dusty manuscripts of the writers of antiquity; and, wherever the original could not be removed, a faithful copy was transcribed and transmitted for his use The Vatican, the old repository for bulls and legends, for superstition and forgery, was daily replenished with more precious furniture, and such was the industry of Nicholas that in a reign of eight years he formed a library of five thousand volumes. To his munificence the Latin world was indebted for the versions of Xenophon, Diodorus, Polybius, Thucydides, Herodotus, and Appian; of Strabo's Geography, of the Iliad, of the most valuable works of Plato and Aristotle, of Ptolemy and Theophrastus, and of the fathers of the Greek church. The example of the Roman pontiff was preceded or imitated by a Florentine merchant, who governed the republic without arms and without a title. Cosmo of Medicis [115] was a father of a line of princes, whose name and age are almost synonymous with the restoration of learning; his credit was ennobled into fame; his riches were dedicated to the service of mankind; he corresponded at once with Cairo and London, and a cargo of Indian spices and Greek books was often imported in the same vessel. The genius and education of his grandson Lorenzo rendered him, not only a patron, but a judge and candidate, in the literary race. In his palace, distress was entitled to relief, and merit to reward; his leisure-hours were delightfully spent in the Platonic academy; he encouraged the emulation of Demetrius Chalcondyles and Angelo Politian; and his active missionary, Janus Lascaris, returned from the East with a treasure of two hundred manuscripts, fourscore of which were as yet unknown in the libraries of Europe.[116] The rest of

[115] See the literary history of Cosmo and Lorenzo of Medicis, in Tiraboschi (tom vi p 1 l 1 c 2), who bestows a due measure of praise on Alphonso of Arragon, king of Naples, the dukes of Milan, Ferrara, Urbino, &c The republic of Venice has deserved the least from the gratitude of scholars

[116] Tiraboschi (tom vi p 1 p 104), from the preface of Janus Lascaris to the Greek Anthology, printed at Florence, 1494 Latebant (says Aldus in

Italy was animated by a similar spirit, and the progress of the
nation repaid the liberality of her princes   The Latins held
the exclusive property of their own literature; and these
disciples of Greece were soon capable of transmitting and
improving the lessons which they had imbibed.   After a
short succession of foreign teachers, the tide of emigration
subsided, but the language of Constantinople was spread
beyond the Alps, and the natives of France, Germany, and
England [117] imparted to their country the sacred fire which
they had kindled in the schools of Florence and Rome.[118]
In the productions of the mind, as in those of the soil, the
gifts of nature are excelled by industry and skill; the Greek
authors, forgotten on the banks of the Ilissus, have been illustrated on those of the Elbe and the Thames, and Bessarion or Gaza might have envied the superior science of the
Barbarians: the accuracy of Budæus, the taste of Erasmus,
the copiousness of Stephens, the erudition of Scaliger, the
discernment of Reiske or of Bentley.   On the side of the
Latins, the discovery of printing was a casual advantage;
but this useful art has been applied by Aldus, and his innumerable successors, to perpetuate and multiply the works
of antiquity.[119]   A single manuscript imported from Greece

his preface to the Greek Orators, apud Hodium, p 249) in Atho Thraciæ
monte.   Eas Lascaris   . . in Italiam reportavit.   Miserat enim ipsum
Laurentius ille Medices in Græciam ad inquirendos simul et quantovis
emendos pretio bonos libros   It is remarkable enough that the research was
facilitated by Sultan Bajazet II

[117] The Greek language was introduced into the University of Oxford in
the last years of the xvth century, by Grocyn, Linacer, and Latimer, who had
all studied at Florence under Demetrius Chalcondyles.   See Dr Knight's
curious Life of Erasmus   Although a stout academical patriot, he is forced
to acknowledge that Erasmus learned Greek at Oxford and taught it at
Cambridge

[118] The jealous Italians were desirous of keeping a monopoly of Greek
learning   When Aldus was about to publish the Greek scholiasts on Sophocles and Euripides, Cave (say they), cave hoc facias, ne *Barbari* istis adjuti
domi maneant, et pauciores in Italiam ventitent (Dr Knight, in his Life of
Erasmus, p 365, from Beatus Rhenanus)

[119] The press of Aldus Manutius, a Roman, was established at Venice

is revived in ten thousand copies; and each copy is fairer than
the original. In this form, Homer and Plato would peruse
with more satisfaction their own writings; and their scholiasts
must resign the prize to the labours of our Western editors.

Before the revival of classic literature, the Barbarians in
Europe were immersed in ignorance; and their vulgar
tongues were marked with the rudeness and poverty of their
manners. The students of the more perfect idioms of
Rome and Greece were introduced to a new world of light
and science; to the society of the free and polished nations
of antiquity; and to a familiar converse with those immortal
men who spoke the sublime language of eloquence and reason.
Such an intercourse must tend to refine the taste, and to
elevate the genius, of the moderns; and yet, from the first
experiments, it might appear that the study of the ancients
had given fetters, rather than wings, to the human mind.
However laudable, the spirit of imitation is of a servile cast;
and the first disciples of the Greeks and Romans were a colony of strangers in the midst of their age and country. The
minute and laborious diligence which explored the antiquities of remote times might have improved or adorned the
present state of society: the critic and metaphysician were the
slaves of Aristotle; the poets, historians, and orators were
proud to repeat the thoughts and words of the Augustan age;
the works of nature were observed with the eyes of Pliny and
Theophrastus; and some pagan votaries professed a secret
devotion to the gods of Homer and Plato.[120] The Italians

about the year 1494. He printed above sixty considerable works of Greek
literature, almost all for the first time; several containing different treatises
and authors, and of several authors two, three, or four editions (Fabric.
Bibliot. Græc. tom. xiii. p. 605, &c.). Yet his glory must not tempt us to
forget that the first Greek book, the Grammar of Constantine Lascaris, was
printed at Milan in 1476; and that the Florence Homer of 1488 displays all
the luxury of the typographical art. See the Annales Typographici of
Mattaire and the Bibliographie Instructive of De Bure, a knowing bookseller
of Paris. [A. F. Didot, Alde Manuce et l'hellénisme à Venise, 1875.]

[120] I will select three singular examples of this classic enthusiasm. 1. At

were oppressed by the strength and number of their ancient auxiliaries: the century after the deaths of Petrarch and Boccace was filled with a crowd of Latin imitators, who decently repose on our shelves, but in that era of learning it will not be easy to discern a real discovery of science, a work of invention or eloquence, in the popular language of the country.[121] But, as soon as it had been deeply saturated with the celestial dew, the soil was quickened into vegetation and life; the modern idioms were refined; the classics of Athens and Rome inspired a pure taste and a generous emulation; and in Italy, as afterwards in France and England, the pleasing reign of poetry and fiction was succeeded by the light of speculative and experimental philosophy. Genius may anticipate the season of maturity; but in the education of a people, as in that of an individual, memory must be exercised, before the powers of reason and fancy can be expanded; nor may the artist hope to equal or surpass, till he has learned to imitate, the works of his predecessors.

the synod of Florence, Gemistus Pletho said in familiar conversation to George of Trebizond, that in a short time mankind would unanimously renounce the Gospel and the Koran for a religion similar to that of the Gentiles (Leo Allatius, apud Fabricium, tom v p 751)   2 Paul II persecuted the Roman academy which had been founded by Pomponius Lætus; and the principal members were accused of heresy, impiety, and *paganism* (Tiraboschi, tom vi p i p 81,82)   [Cp Burckhardt, Die Cultur der Renaissance in Italien, ii 252]   3 In the next century, some scholars and poets in France celebrated the success of Jodelle's tragedy of Cleopatra by a festival of Bacchus, and, it is said, by the sacrifice of a goat (Bayle, Dictionnaire, JODELLE, Fontenelle, tom iii p 56-61)   Yet the spirit of bigotry might often discern a serious impiety in the sportive play of fancy and learning

[121] The survivor of Boccace died in the year 1375, and we cannot place before 1480 the composition of the Morgante Maggiore of Pulci, and the Orlando Inamorato of Boyardo (Tiraboschi, tom. vi. p. ii p 174-177)

CHAPTER LXVII

Schism of the Greeks and Latins — Reign and Character of Amurath the Second — Crusade of Ladislaus, King of Hungary — His Defeat and Death — John Huniades — Scanderbeg — Constantine Palæologus, last Emperor of the East

THE respective merits of Rome and Constantinople are compared and celebrated by an eloquent Greek, the father of the Italian schools [1] The view of the ancient capital, the seat of his ancestors, surpassed the most sanguine expectations of Emanuel Chrysoloras, and he no longer blamed the exclamation of an old sophist, that Rome was the habitation, not of men, but of gods. Those gods and those men had long since vanished, but, to the eye of liberal enthusiasm, the majesty of ruin restored the image of her ancient prosperity. The monuments of the consuls and Cæsars, of the martyrs and apostles, engaged on all sides the curiosity of the philosopher and the Christian; and he confessed that in every age the arms and religion of Rome were destined to reign over the earth. While Chrysoloras admired the venerable beauties of the mother, he was not forgetful of his native country, her fairest daughter, her Imperial colony, and the Byzantine patriot expatiates with zeal and truth on the eternal advantages of nature and the more transitory glories of art and

---

[1] The epistle of Emanuel Chrysoloras to the emperor John Palæologus will not offend the eye or ear of a classical student (ad calcem Codini de Antiquitatibus C P. p 107-126) The superscription suggests a chronological remark that John Palæologus II was associated in the empire before the year 414, the date of Chrysoloras's death A still earlier date, at least 1408, is deduced from the age of his youngest sons Demetrius and Thomas, who were both *Porphyrogeniti* (Ducange, Fam Byzant p 244, 247).

dominion, which adorned, or had adorned, the city of Constantine. Yet the perfection of the copy still redounds (as he modestly observes) to the honour of the original; and parents are delighted to be renewed, and even excelled, by the superior merit of their children "Constantinople," says the orator, "is situate on a commanding point, between Europe and Asia, between the Archipelago and the Euxine. By her interposition, the two seas and the two continents are united for the common benefit of nations; and the gates of commerce may be shut or opened at her command. The harbour, encompassed on all sides by the sea and the continent, is the most secure and capacious in the world. The walls and gates of Constantinople may be compared with those of Babylon; the towers are many; each tower is a solid and lofty structure, and the second wall, the outer fortification, would be sufficient for the defence and dignity of an ordinary capital. A broad and rapid stream may be introduced into the ditches, and the artificial island may be encompassed, like Athens,[2] by land or water." Two strong and natural causes are alleged for the perfection of the model of new Rome. The royal founder reigned over the most illustrious nations of the globe, and, in the accomplishment of his designs, the power of the Romans was combined with the art and science of the Greeks Other cities have been reared to maturity by accident and time, their beauties are mingled with disorder and deformity, and the inhabitants, unwilling to remove from their natal spot, are incapable of correcting the errors of their ancestors and the original vices of situation or climate. But the free idea of Constantinople was formed and executed by a single mind; and the primitive model was improved by the obedient zeal of the subjects and successors of the first

---

[2] Somebody observed, that the city of Athens might be circumnavigated (τις εἶπεν τὴν πόλιν τῶν Ἀθηναίων δύνασθαι καὶ παραπλεῖν καὶ περιπλεῖν). But what may be true in a rhetorical sense of Constantinople cannot be applied to the situation of Athens, five miles from the sea, and not intersected or surrounded by any navigable streams

monarch   The adjacent isles were stored with an inexhaustible supply of marble; but the various materials were
transported from the most remote shores of Europe and Asia;
and the public and private buildings, the palaces, churches,
aqueducts, cisterns, porticoes, columns, baths, and hippo-
dromes, were adapted to the greatness of the capital of the
East.   The superfluity of wealth was spread along the shores
of Europe and Asia, and the Byzantine territory, as far as
the Euxine, the Hellespont, and the long wall, might be considered as a populous suburb and a perpetual garden.   In this
flattering picture, the past and the present, the times of prosperity and decay, are artfully confounded, but a sigh and a
confession escape from the orator, that his wretched country
was the shadow and sepulchre of its former self   The works
of ancient sculpture had been defaced by Christian zeal or
Barbaric violence, the fairest structures were demolished,
and the marbles of Paros or Numidia were burnt for lime or
applied to the meanest uses.   Of many a statue, the place was
marked by an empty pedestal; of many a column, the size
was determined by a broken capital, the tombs of the emperors were scattered on the ground, the stroke of time was
accelerated by storms and earthquakes; and the vacant space
was adorned, by vulgar tradition, with fabulous monuments
of gold and silver.   From these wonders, which lived only
in memory or belief, he distinguishes, however, the porphyry
pillar, the column and colossus of Justinian,[3] and the church,

[3] Nicephorus Gregoras has described the colossus of Justinian (l vii 12),
but his measures are false and inconsistent.   The editor, Boivin, consulted
his friend Girardon, and the sculptor gave him the true proportions of an
equestrian statue   That of Justinian was still visible to Peter Gyllius, not
on the column, but in the outward court of the seraglio, and he was at Constantinople when it was melted down and cast into a brass cannon (de
Topograph C P. l ii c 17)   [The equestrian statue of Justinian was in the
Augusteum.   What seems to be the base of the statue has been found near
the Church of SS Sergius and Bacchus (the Kutchuk Aya Sophia) with
an inscription beginning Ἐπιβίσι (sic) ἐπὶ τοὺς ἵππους σου καὶ ἡ ἱππασία
σου σωτηρία (from Habakkuk, iii 8).   See Mordtmann, Esquisse topo-
graphique, § 97 (p. 55)]

more especially the dome, of St. Sophia: the best conclusion, since it could not be described according to its merits, and after it no other object could deserve to be mentioned. But he forgets that a century before the trembling fabrics of the colossus and the church had been saved and supported by the timely care of Andronicus the Elder. Thirty years after the emperor had fortified St. Sophia with two new buttresses, or pyramids, the eastern hemisphere suddenly gave way; and the images, the altars, and the sanctuary were crushed by the falling ruin. The mischief indeed was speedily repaired; the rubbish was cleared by the incessant labour of every rank and age; and the poor remains of riches and industry were consecrated by the Greeks to the most stately and venerable temple of the East.[4]

The last hope of the falling city and empire was placed in the harmony of the mother and daughter, in the maternal tenderness of Rome and the filial obedience of Constantinople. In the synod of Florence, the Greeks and Latins had embraced, and subscribed, and promised; but these signs of friendship were perfidious or fruitless;[5] and the baseless fabric of the union vanished like a dream.[6] The emperor and his prelates returned in the Venetian galleys; but, as they touched at the Morea and the isles of Corfu and Lesbos, the subjects of the

[4] See the decay and repairs of St. Sophia, in Nicephorus Gregoras (l. vii. 12; l. xv. 2). The building was propped by Andronicus in 1317, the eastern hemisphere fell in 1345. The Greeks, in their pompous rhetoric, exalt the beauty and holiness of the church, an earthly heaven, the abode of angels, and of God himself, &c. [Cp. Cantacuzenus, i. p. 30, ed. Bonn. See Lethaby and Swainson, Sancta Sophia, p. 124 and p. 152.]

[5] The genuine and original narrative of Syropulus (p. 312-351) opens the schism from the first *office* of the Greeks at Venice to the general opposition at Constantinople of the clergy and people.

[6] On the schism of Constantinople, see Phranza (l. ii. c. 17), Laonicus Chalcondyles (l. vi. p. 155, 156 [pp. 292 *sqq.* ed. B.]), and Ducas (c. 31); the last of whom writes with truth and freedom. Among the moderns we may distinguish the continuator of Fleury (tom. xxii. p. 338, &c., 401, 420, &c.) and Spondanus (A.D. 1440-80). The sense of the latter is drowned in prejudice and passion, as soon as Rome and religion are concerned.

Latins complained that the pretended union would be an instrument of oppression   No sooner did they land on the Byzantine shore than they were saluted, or rather assailed, with a general murmur of zeal and discontent   During their absence, above two years, the capital had been deprived of its civil and ecclesiastical rulers; fanaticism fermented in anarchy; the most furious monks reigned over the conscience of women and bigots, and the hatred of the Latin name was the first principle of nature and religion.   Before his departure for Italy, the emperor had flattered the city with the assurance of a prompt relief and a powerful succour, and the clergy, confident in their orthodoxy and science, had promised themselves and their flocks an easy victory over the blind shepherds of the West.   The double disappointment exasperated the Greeks; the conscience of the subscribing prelates was awakened; the hour of temptation was past, and they had more to dread from the public resentment than they could hope from the favour of the emperor or the pope.   Instead of justifying their conduct, they deplored their weakness, professed their contrition, and cast themselves on the mercy of God and of their brethren.   To the reproachful question, What had been the event or use of their Italian synod? they answered, with sighs and tears, "Alas ! we have made a new faith; we have exchanged piety for impiety, we have betrayed the immaculate sacrifice; and we are become *Azymites.*"   (The Azymites were those who celebrated the communion with unleavened bread; and I must retract or qualify the praise which I have bestowed on the growing philosophy of the times.)   "Alas ! we have been seduced by distress, by fraud, and by the hopes and fears of a transitory life. The hand that has signed the union should be cut off; and the tongue that has pronounced the Latin creed deserves to be torn from the root "   The best proof of their repentance was an increase of zeal for the most trivial rites and the most incomprehensible doctrines, and an absolute separation from all, without excepting their prince, who preserved some

regard for honour and consistency. After the decease of the
patriarch Joseph, the archbishops of Heraclea and Trebizond
had courage to refuse the vacant office; and Cardinal Bessarion preferred the warm and comfortable shelter of the
Vatican. The choice of the emperor and his clergy was confined to Metrophanes of Cyzicus: he was consecrated in St.
Sophia, but the temple was vacant; the cross-bearers abdicated their service; the infection spread from the city to the
villages; and Metrophanes discharged, without effect, some
ecclesiastical thunders against a nation of schismatics. The
eyes of the Greeks were directed to Mark of Ephesus, the
champion of his country; and the sufferings of the holy confessor were repaid with a tribute of admiration and applause.
His example and writings propagated the flame of religious
discord; age and infirmity soon removed him from the world;
but the gospel of Mark was not a law of forgiveness; and he
requested with his dying breath that none of the adherents of
Rome might attend his obsequies or pray for his soul.[7]

The schism was not confined to the narrow limits of the

[7] [Since the publication of the De Ecclesiae occidentalis atque Orientalis
perpetuâ consensione of Leo Allatius, it has been generally supposed that
a Synod, held at St. Sophia in A.D. 1450, under the auspices of the Emperor
Constantine, repudiated the Acts of the Council of Florence. Allatius (c.
1380) gave an account of the "Acts" of this Synod, and condemned them as
spurious, on account of some obvious blunders which appeared in their Title.
An edition of these Acts was shortly afterwards published by Dositheus,
Patriarch of Jerusalem, in his Τόμος καταλλαγῆς, p. 454 sqq.; but in the
Title, in his edition, the blunders were corrected, and he defended the
genuineness of the document. But, quite apart from the title, the document
is marked by anachronisms and blunders which have been recently exposed
by Ch. Papaioannu. This Russian scholar has submitted the Acts to a
thorough-going criticism (Akty tak nazyvaemago posliedniago Sophiiskago
Sobora (1450 g.) i ich istoricheskoe dostoinstvo, in Vizantiiskii Vremennik,
ii. p. 394 sqq., 1895), and has shown convincingly not only that the Acts are
spurious but that no such Synod was ever held. The first Synod that rejected the decrees of Florence was that of A.D. 1484. The Synod of 1450
was invented and the Acts forged probably not later than the beginning of the
17th century. One of the anachronisms which the unknown forger com-
mitted was making Marcus of Ephesus take part in the Synod. But Marcus
had died before 1448; probably (as Papaioannu shows, p. 398–399) in 1447.]

Byzantine empire. Secure under the Mamaluke sceptre, the three patriarchs of Alexandria, Antioch, and Jerusalem assembled a numerous synod; disowned their representatives at Ferrara and Florence; condemned the creed and council of the Latins; and threatened the emperor of Constantinople with the censures of the Eastern church. Of the sectaries of the Greek communion, the Russians were the most powerful, ignorant, and superstitious. Their primate, the cardinal Isidore, hastened from Florence to Moscow,[8] to reduce the independent nation under the Roman yoke. But the Russian bishops had been educated at Mount Athos; and the prince and people embraced the theology of their priests. They were scandalised by the title, the pomp, the Latin cross, of the legate, the friend of those impious men who shaved their beards and performed the divine office with gloves on their hands and rings on their fingers. Isidore was condemned by a synod; his person was imprisoned in a monastery; and it was with extreme difficulty that the cardinal could escape from the hands of a fierce and fanatic people.[9] The Russians refused a passage to the missionaries of Rome, who aspired to convert the pagans beyond the Tanais;[10] and their refusal

[8] Isidore was metropolitan of Kiow, but the Greeks subject to Poland have removed that see from the ruins of Kiow to Lemberg or Leopold [Lvov] (Herbestein, in Ramusio, tom. ii. p. 127). On the other hand, the Russians transferred their spiritual obedience to the archbishop, who became, in 1588, the patriarch of Moscow (Levesque, Hist. de Russie, tom. iii. p. 188, 190, from a Greek MS. at Turin, Iter et labores Archiepiscopi Arsenii).

[9] The curious narrative of Levesque (Hist. de Russie, tom. ii. p. 242-247) is extracted from the patriarchal archives. The scenes of Ferrara and Florence are described by ignorance and passion; but the Russians are credible in the account of their own prejudices.

[10] The Shamanism, the ancient religion of the Samanæans and Gymnosophists, has been driven by the more popular Bramins from India into the northern deserts; the naked philosophers were compelled to wrap themselves in fur; but they insensibly sunk into wizards and physicians. The Mordvans and Tcheremisses, in the European Russia, adhere to this religion, which is formed on the earthly model of one King or God, his ministers or angels, and the rebellious spirits who oppose his government. As these tribes of the Volga have no images, they might more justly retort on the Latin missionaries

was justified by the maxim that the guilt of idolatry is less damnable than that of schism. The errors of the Bohemians were excused by their abhorrence for the pope; and a deputation of the Greek clergy solicited the friendship of those sanguinary enthusiasts.[11] While Eugenius triumphed in the union and orthodoxy of the Greeks, his party was contracted to the walls, or rather to the palace, of Constantinople. The zeal of Palæologus had been excited by interest; it was soon cooled by opposition: an attempt to violate the national belief might endanger his life and crown; nor could the pious rebels be destitute of foreign and domestic aid. The sword of his brother Demetrius, who, in Italy, had maintained a prudent and popular silence, was half unsheathed in the cause of religion; and Amurath, the Turkish sultan, was displeased and alarmed by the seeming friendship of the Greeks and Latins.

"Sultan Murad, or Amurath, lived forty-nine, and reigned thirty years, six months, and eight days. He was a just and valiant prince, of a great soul, patient of labours, learned, merciful, religious, charitable; a lover and encourager of the studious, and of all who excelled in any art or science; a good emperor, and a great general. No man obtained more or greater victories than Amurath; Belgrade alone withstood his attacks. Under his reign, the soldier was ever victorious, the citizen rich and secure. If he subdued any country, his first care was to build moschs and caravanseras, hospitals, and colleges. Every year he gave a thousand pieces of gold to the sons of the Prophet; and sent two thousand five hundred to the religious persons of Mecca, Medina, and Jerusalem."[12] This portrait is transcribed from the historian of the

---

the name of Idolaters (Levesque, Hist. des Peuples soumis à la Domination des Russes, tom. i. p. 194-237; 423-460).

[11] Spondanus, Annal. Eccles. tom. ii. A.D. 1451, No. 13. The epistle of the Greeks, with a Latin version, is extant in the college library at Prague.

[12] See Cantemir, History of the Othman Empire, p. 94. Murad, or Morad, may be correct; but I have preferred the popular name to that

Othman empire, but the applause of a servile and superstitious people has been lavished on the worst of tyrants;
and the virtues of a sultan are often the vices most useful to
himself, or most agreeable to his subjects. A nation ignorant
of the equal benefits of liberty and law must be awed by the
flashes of arbitrary power the cruelty of a despot will assume the character of justice, his profusion, of liberality;
his obstinacy, of firmness If the most reasonable excuse be
rejected, few acts of obedience will be found impossible,
and guilt must tremble where innocence cannot always be
secure. The tranquillity of the people and the discipline
of the troops were best maintained by perpetual action in the
field; war was the trade of the Janizaries, and those who
survived the peril and divided the spoil applauded the generous ambition of their sovereign. To propagate the true
religion was the duty of a faithful Musulman the unbe-
lievers were *his* enemies, and those of the Prophet; and, in
the hands of the Turks, the scymetar was the only instrument
of conversion. Under these circumstances, however, the
justice and moderation of Amurath are attested by his conduct and acknowledged by the Christians themselves; who
consider a prosperous reign and a peaceful death as the reward of his singular merits In the vigour of his age and
military power, he seldom engaged in a war till he was justified by a previous and adequate provocation; the victorious
sultan was disarmed by submission; and in the observance of

obscure diligence which is rarely successful in translating an Oriental into the
Roman alphabet [A Burgundian knight, Bertrandon de la Brocquière
(see below p 326, note 62) gives the following description of Murad —
  "He is a little short thick man, with the physiognomy of a Tartar He has
a broad and brown face, high cheek bones, a round beard, a great and
crooked nose, with little eyes, but they say he is kind, good, generous, and
willingly gives away lands and money He is thought not to love war,
and this seems to be well founded . He loves liquor and those who drink
hard" He threw a Moor into prison who ventured to admonish him
against indulgence in wine (T. Wright's Early Travels in Palestine, p 346–
347)]

treaties his word was inviolate and sacred.[13]　The Hungarians
were commonly the aggressors; he was provoked by the
revolt of Scanderbeg, and the perfidious Caramanian was
twice vanquished and twice pardoned by the Ottoman monarch　Before he invaded the Morea, Thebes had been surprised by the despot; in the conquest of Thessalonica,[14]
the grandson of Bajazet might dispute the recent purchase of
the Venetians; and, after the first siege of Constantinople,
the sultan was never tempted, by the distress, the absence,
or the injuries of Palæologus to extinguish the dying light of
the Byzantine empire.

But the most striking feature in the life and character of
Amurath is the double abdication of the Turkish throne;
and, were not his motives debased by an alloy of superstition,
we must praise the royal philosopher,[15] who, at the age of
forty, could discern the vanity of human greatness.　Resigning the sceptre to his son, he retired to the pleasant residence
of Magnesia, but he retired to the society of saints and her-
mits.　It was not till the fourth century of the Hegira that
the religion of Mahomet had been corrupted by an institution
so adverse to his genius; but in the age of the crusades the
various orders of Dervishes were multiplied by the example

[13] See Chalcondyles (l vii p. 186, 198), Ducas (c. 33), and Marinus
Barletius (in Vit Scanderbeg, p 145, 146)　In his good faith towards the
garrison of Sfetigrade he was a lesson and example to his son Mahomet
[14] [There is an account of Murad's conquest of Thessalonica, A D. 1430,
by John Anagnostes (publ at the end of the Bonn edition of Phrantzes, p
484 *sqq*), written in imitation of the account of the Saracen siege in A D 904
by Cameniates　Two popular Greek ballads on the capture are given in
Passow's Popularia Carmina Graeciae recentioris, cxciv cxcv (cp Miss
F M'Pherson, Journal of Hellenic Studies, x p 86, 87).　The lines occur —

πῆραν τὴν πόλι, πῆραν τὴν, πῆραν τὴν Σαλονίκη,
πῆραν καὶ τὴν ἁγιὰ Σοφιὰ, τὸ μέγα μοναστῆρι]

[15] Voltaire (Essai sur l'Histoire Générale, c 89, p 283, 284) admires
le Philosophe Turc, would he have bestowed the same praise on a Christian
prince for retiring to a monastery?　In his way, Voltaire was a bigot, an
intolerant bigot.

of the Christian, and even the Latin, monks.[16] The lord of nations submitted to fast, and pray, and turn round in endless rotation with the fanatics who mistook the giddiness of the head for the illumination of the spirit.[17] But he was soon awakened from this dream of enthusiasm by the Hungarian invasion; and his obedient son was the foremost to urge the public danger and the wishes of the people. Under the banner of their veteran leader, the Janizaries fought and conquered, but he withdrew from the field of Varna, again to pray, to fast, and to turn round with his Magnesian brethren. These pious occupations were again interrupted by the danger of the state. A victorious army disdained the inexperience of their youthful ruler; the city of Hadrianople was abandoned to rapine and slaughter; and the unanimous divan implored his presence to appease the tumult, and prevent the rebellion, of the Janizaries. At the well-known voice of their master, they trembled and obeyed, and the reluctant sultan was compelled to support his splendid servitude, till, at the end of four years, he was relieved by the angel of death. Age or disease, misfortune or caprice, have tempted several princes to descend from the throne; and they have had leisure to repent of their irretrievable step. But Amurath alone, in the full liberty of choice, after the trial of empire and solitude, has *repeated* his preference of a private life.

After the departure of his Greek brethren, Eugenius had not been unmindful of their temporal interest; and his tender regard for the Byzantine empire was animated by a just ap-

[16] See the articles *Dervische, Fakir, Nasser, Rohbaniat*, in d'Herbelot's Bibliothèque Orientale. Yet the subject is superficially treated from the Persian and Arabian writers. It is among the Turks that these orders have principally flourished

[17] Rycaut (in the Present State of the Ottoman Empire, p 242-268) affords much information, which he drew from his personal conversation with the heads of the dervishes, most of whom ascribed their origin to the time of Orchan. He does not mention the *Zichidæ* of Chalcondyles (l. vii p 286), among whom Amurath retired, the *Seids* of that author are the descendants of Mahomet

prehension of the Turks, who approached, and might soon
invade, the borders of Italy. But the spirit of the crusades
had expired; and the coldness of the Franks was not less
unreasonable than their headlong passion In the eleventh
century, a fanatic monk could precipitate Europe on Asia for
the recovery of the holy sepulchre, but, in the fifteenth, the
most pressing motives of religion and policy were insufficient
to unite the Latins in the defence of Christendom. Germany was an inexhaustible storehouse of men and arms,[18]
but that complex and languid body required the impulse of
a vigorous hand, and Frederic the Third was alike impotent
in his personal character and his Imperial dignity. A long
war had impaired the strength, without satiating the animosity, of France and England;[19] but Philip, duke of Burgundy, was a vain and magnificent prince; and he enjoyed,
without danger or expense, the adventurous piety of his subjects, who sailed, in a gallant fleet, from the coast of Flanders
to the Hellespont. The maritime republics of Venice and
Genoa were less remote from the scene of action; and their
hostile fleets were associated under the standard of St. Peter.
The kingdoms of Hungary and Poland, which covered, as it
were, the interior pale of the Latin church, were the most
nearly concerned to oppose the progress of the Turks. Arms
were the patrimony of the Scythians and Sarmatians, and
these nations might appear equal to the contest, could they

[18] In the year 1431, Germany raised 40,000 horse, men at arms, against
the Hussites of Bohemia (Lenfant, Hist du Concile de Basle, tom 1 p 318).
At the siege of Nuys [Neuss] on the Rhine, in 1474, the princes, prelates, and
cities sent their respective quotas, and the bishop of Munster (qui n'est pas
des plus grands) furnished 1400 horse, 6000 foot, all in green, with 1200 waggons The united armies of the king of England and the duke of Burgundy scarcely equalled one third of this German host (Mémoires de
Philippe de Comines, l iv c 2) At present, six or seven hundred thousand
men are maintained in constant pay and admirable discipline by the powers
of Germany.

[19] It was not till the year 1444, that France and England could agree on a
truce of some months (see Rymer's Fœdera, and the chronicles of both
nations)

point, against the common foe, those swords that were so
wantonly drawn in bloody and domestic quarrels. But the
same spirit was adverse to concord and obedience; a poor
country and a limited monarch are incapable of maintaining
a standing force, and the loose bodies of Polish and Hungarian horse were not armed with the sentiments and weapons
which, on some occasions, have given irresistible weight to the
French chivalry Yet, on this side, the designs of the Roman
pontiff and the eloquence of Cardinal Julian, his legate, were
promoted by the circumstances of the times, [20] by the union
of the two crowns on the head of Ladislaus,[21] a young and
ambitious soldier, by the valour of an hero, whose name, the
name of John Huniades, was already popular among
the Christians and formidable to the Turks. An endless
treasure of pardons and indulgences were scattered by the
legate; many private warriors of France and Germany
enlisted under the holy banner, and the crusade derived
some strength, or at least some reputation, from the new allies,
both of Europe and Asia A fugitive despot of Servia exaggerated the distress and ardour of the Christians beyond
the Danube, who would unanimously rise to vindicate their
religion and liberty. The Greek emperor,[22] with a spirit
unknown to his fathers, engaged to guard the Bosphorus, and
to sally from Constantinople at the head of his national and

[20] In the Hungarian crusade, Spondanus (Annal Eccles A D 1443, 1444)
has been my leading guide He has diligently read, and critically compared,
the Greek and Turkish materials, the historians of Hungary, Poland, and
the West His narrative is perspicuous, and, where he can be free from a
religious bias, the judgment of Spondanus is not contemptible

[21] I have curtailed the harsh letter (Wladislaus) which most writers affix
to his name, either in compliance with the Polish pronunciation, or to
distinguish him from his rival the infant Ladislaus of Austria Their competition for the crown of Hungary is described by Callimachus (l 1 11 p 447-
486), Bonfinius (Decad 111 l 1v), Spondanus, and Lenfant

[22] The Greek historians, Phranza, Chalcondyles, and Ducas, do not
ascribe to their prince a very active part in this crusade, which he seems to
have promoted by his wishes and injured by his fears

VOL XI 20

mercenary troops. The sultan of Caramania [23] announced the retreat of Amurath and a powerful diversion in the heart of Anatolia; and, if the fleets of the West could occupy at the same moment the straits of the Hellespont, the Ottoman monarchy would be dissevered and destroyed   Heaven and earth must rejoice in the perdition of the miscreants; and the legate, with prudent ambiguity, instilled the opinion of the invisible, perhaps the visible, aid of the Son of God and his divine mother.

Of the Polish and Hungarian diets, a religious war was the unanimous cry; and Ladislaus, after passing the Danube, led an army of his confederate subjects as far as Sophia, the capital of the Bulgarian kingdom.[24] In this expedition they obtained two signal victories, which were justly ascribed to the valour and conduct of Huniades   In the first, with a vanguard of ten thousand men, he surprised the Turkish camp; in the second, he vanquished and made prisoner the most renowned of their generals, who possessed the double advantage of ground and numbers.   The approach of winter and the natural and artificial obstacles of Mount Hæmus arrested the progress of the hero, who measured a narrow interval of six days' march from the foot of the mountains to the hostile towers of Hadrianople and the friendly capital of the Greek empire.   The retreat was undisturbed; and the entrance into Buda was at once a military and religious triumph.   An ecclesiastical procession was followed by the king and his warriors on foot; he nicely balanced the merits and rewards of the two nations; and the pride of conquest

[23] Cantemir (p 88) ascribes to his policy the original plan, and transcribes his animating epistle to the king of Hungary   But the Mahometan powers are seldom informed of the state of Christendom, and the situation and correspondence of the knights of Rhodes must connect them with the sultan of Caramania

[24] [For this expedition see Katona, Histor crit reg Hung Stirpis mixtae, vi p. 245 *sqq* , Nesri (in Thúry's Torok torténetírók, vol 1), p 58, the Anonymous of 1486, *ib* p 18, 19, Sad ad-Din, *ib* p 136 *sqq* , Zinkeisen, Gesch. des osmanischen Reiches, 1 611 *sqq*]

was blended with the humble temper of Christianity. Thirteen bashaws, nine standards, and four thousand captives were unquestionable trophies; and, as all were willing to believe and none were present to contradict, the crusaders multiplied, with unblushing confidence, the myriads of Turks whom they had left on the field of battle.[25] The most solid proof and the most salutary consequence of victory was a deputation from the divan to solicit peace, to restore Servia, to ransom the prisoners, and to evacuate the Hungarian frontier. By this treaty, the rational objects of the war were obtained the king, the despot, and Huniades himself, in the diet of Segedin, were satisfied with public and private emolument, a truce of ten years was concluded, and the followers of Jesus and Mahomet, who swore on the Gospel and the Koran, attested the word of God as the guardian of truth and the avenger of perfidy. In the place of the Gospel, the Turkish ministers had proposed to substitute the Eucharist, the real presence of the Catholic deity; but the Christians refused to profane their holy mysteries; and a superstitious conscience is less forcibly bound by the spiritual energy, than by the outward and visible symbols, of an oath [26]

During the whole transaction the cardinal-legate had observed a sullen silence, unwilling to approve, and unable to oppose, the consent of the king and people. But the diet was not dissolved before Julian was fortified by the welcome intelligence that Anatolia was invaded by the Caramanian, and Thrace by the Greek emperor, that the fleets of Genoa, Venice, and Burgundy were masters of the Hellespont, and

[25] In their letters to the emperor Frederic III the Hungarians slay 30,000 Turks in one battle, but the modest Julian reduces the slaughter to 6000 or even 2000 infidels (Æneas Sylvius in Europ c 5, and epist 44, 81, apud Spondanum)

[26] See the origin of the Turkish war, and the first expedition of Ladislaus, in the vth and vith books of the iiid Decad of Bonfinius, who, in his division and style, copies Livy with tolerable success Callimachus (l ii p 487-196) is still more pure and authentic.

that the allies, informed of the victory, and ignorant of the
treaty, of Ladislaus, impatiently waited for the return of his
victorious army. "And is it thus," exclaimed the cardinal,[27]
"that you will desert their expectations and your own fortune?
It is to them, to your God, and your fellow-Christians, that
you have pledged your faith; and that prior obligation anni-
hilates a rash and sacrilegious oath to the enemies of Christ.
His vicar on earth is the Roman pontiff; without whose sanction you can neither promise nor perform. In his name I
absolve your perjury and sanctify your arms; follow my footsteps in the paths of glory and salvation; and, if still ye have
scruples, devolve on my head the punishment and the sin."
This mischievous casuistry was seconded by his respectable
character and the levity of popular assemblies. War was
resolved on the same spot where peace had so lately been
sworn; and, in the execution of the treaty, the Turks were
assaulted by the Christians; to whom, with some reason,
they might apply the epithet of Infidels. The falsehood of
Ladislaus to his word and oath was palliated by the religion
of the times; the most perfect, or at least the most popular,
excuse would have been the success of his arms and the deliverance of the Eastern church. But the same treaty which
should have bound his conscience had diminished his strength.
On the proclamation of the peace, the French and German
volunteers departed with indignant murmurs; the Poles
were exhausted by distant warfare, and perhaps disgusted
with foreign command; and their palatines accepted the first
licence and hastily retired to their provinces and castles.
Even Hungary was divided by faction or restrained by a

[27] I do not pretend to warrant the literal accuracy of Julian's speech,
which is variously worded by Callimachus (l. iii. p. 505-507), Bonfinius
(Dec. iii. l. vi. p. 457, 458), and other historians, who might indulge their
own eloquence, while they represent one of the orators of the age. But they
all agree in the advice and arguments for perjury, which in the field of controversy are fiercely attacked by the Protestants and feebly defended by the
Catholics. The latter are discouraged by the misfortune of Varna.

laudable scruple; and the relics of the crusade that marched in the second expedition were reduced to an inadequate force of twenty thousand men. A Walachian chief, who joined the royal standard with his vassals, presumed to remark that their numbers did not exceed the hunting retinue that sometimes attended the sultan; and the gift of two horses of matchless speed might admonish Ladislaus of his secret foresight of the event. But the despot of Servia, after the restoration of his country and children, was tempted by the promise of new realms; and the inexperience of the king, the enthusiasm of the legate, and the martial presumption of Huniades himself were persuaded that every obstacle must yield to the invincible virtue of the sword and the cross. After the passage of the Danube, two roads might lead to Constantinople and the Hellespont: the one direct, abrupt, and difficult, through the mountains of Hæmus; the other more tedious and secure, over a level country, and along the shores of the Euxine; in which their flanks, according to the Scythian discipline, might always be covered by a moveable fortification of waggons. The latter was judiciously preferred · the Catholics marched through the plains of Bulgaria, burning, with wanton cruelty, the churches and villages of the Christian natives; and their last station was at Warna, near the seashore, on which the defeat and death of Ladislaus have bestowed a memorable name.[28]

It was on this fatal spot that, instead of finding a confederate fleet to second their operations, they were alarmed by the approach of Amurath himself, who had issued from his Magnesian solitude and transported the forces of Asia to the

---

[28] Warna, under the Grecian name of Odessus, was a colony of the Milesians which they denominated from the hero Ulysses (Cellarius, tom i p 374; d'Anville, tom i p 312) According to Arrian's Periplus of the Euxine (p 24, 25, in the first volume of Hudson's Geographers), it was situate 1740 stadia, or furlongs, from the mouth of the Danube, 2140 from Byzantium, and 360 to the north of a ridge or promontory of Mount Hæmus, which advances into the sea

defence of Europe. According to some writers, the Greek emperor had been awed, or seduced, to grant the passage of the Bosphorus; and an indelible stain of corruption is fixed on the Genoese, or the pope's nephew, the Catholic admiral, whose mercenary connivance betrayed the guard of the Hellespont.[29] From Hadrianople, the sultan advanced, by hasty marches, at the head of sixty thousand men; and, when the cardinal and Huniades had taken a nearer survey of the numbers and order of the Turks, these ardent warriors proposed the tardy and impracticable measure of a retreat. The king alone was resolved to conquer or die; and his resolution had almost been crowned with a glorious and salutary victory. The princes were opposite to each other in the centre; and the Beglerbegs, or generals of Anatolia and Romania, commanded on the right and left against the adverse divisions of the despot and Huniades. The Turkish wings were broken on the first onset, but the advantage was fatal; and the rash victors, in the heat of the pursuit, were carried away far from the annoyance of the enemy or the support of their friends When Amurath beheld the flight of his squadrons, he despaired of his fortune and that of the empire. a veteran Janizary seized his horse's bridle; and he had magnanimity to pardon and reward the soldier who dared to perceive the terror, and arrest the flight, of his sovereign. A copy of the treaty, the monument of Christian perfidy, had been displayed in the front of battle; and it is said that the sultan in his distress, lifting his eyes and his hands to heaven, implored the protection of the God of truth; and called on the prophet Jesus himself to avenge the impious mockery of his name and religion.[30] With inferior numbers

[29] [It is difficult to understand what the Papal fleet was doing The place where Murad crossed is uncertain The Turkish sources differ, they agree only that he did not cross at Gallipoli Cp Thúry's note, *op cit* p 21]

[30] Some Christian writers affirm that he drew from his bosom the host or wafer on which the treaty had *not* been sworn The Moslems suppose, with

and disordered ranks, the king of Hungary rushed forwards in the confidence of victory, till his career was stopped by the impenetrable phalanx of the Janizaries. If we may credit the Ottoman annals, his horse was pierced by the javelin of Amurath,[31] he fell among the spears of the infantry, and a Turkish soldier proclaimed with a loud voice, "Hungarians, behold the head of your king!" The death of Ladislaus was the signal of their defeat On his return from an intemperate pursuit, Huniades deplored his error and the public loss, he strove to rescue the royal body, till he was overwhelmed by the tumultuous crowd of the victors and vanquished; and the last efforts of his courage and conduct were exerted to save the remnant of his Walachian cavalry. Ten thousand Christians were slain in the disastrous battle of Warna The loss of the Turks, more considerable in numbers, bore a smaller proportion to their total strength, yet the philosophic sultan was not ashamed to confess that his ruin must be the consequence of a second and similar victory. At his command, a column was erected on the spot where Ladislaus had fallen, but the modest inscription, instead of accusing the rashness, recorded the valour, and bewailed the misfortune, of the Hungarian youth.[32]

more simplicity, an appeal to God and his prophet Jesus, which is likewise insinuated by Callimachus (l iii p 516, Spondan A D 1444, No 8).

[31] A critic will always distrust these *spolia opima* of a victorious general, so difficult for valour to obtain, so easy for flattery to invent (Cantemir, p 90, 91) Callimachus (l iii p 517) more simply and probably affirms, supervenientibus Janizaris, telorum multitudine non tam confossus est quam obrutus

[32] Besides some valuable hints from Æneas Sylvius, which are diligently collected by Spondanus, our best authorities are three historians of the xvth century, Philippus Callimachus (de rebus a Vladislao Polonorum atque Hungarorum Rege gestis, libri iii in Bel [= Schwandtner] Script Rerum Hungaricarum, tom i p 433–518), Bonfinius (decad iii l v p 460–467), and Chalcondyles (l vii p 165–179) The two first were Italians, but they passed their lives in Poland and Hungary (Fabric Bibliot Latin med et infimæ Ætatis, tom i p 324, Vossius de Hist Latin l iii c. 8, 11, Bayle, Dictionnaire, BONFINIUS) A small tract of Fælix Petancius, chancellor of Segnia (ad calcem Cuspinian de Cæsaribus, p 716–722), represents the

Before I lose sight of the field of Warna, I am tempted to pause on the character and story of two principal actors, the cardinal Julian, and John Huniades. Julian [33] Cæsarini was born of a noble family of Rome; his studies had embraced both the Latin and Greek learning, both the sciences of divinity and law; and his versatile genius was equally adapted to the schools, the camp, and the court. No sooner had he been invested with the Roman purple than he was sent into Germany to arm the empire against the rebels and heretics of Bohemia. The spirit of persecution is unworthy of a Christian; the military profession ill becomes a priest; but the former is excused by the times; and the latter was ennobled by the courage of Julian, who stood dauntless and alone in the disgraceful flight of the German host. As the pope's legate, he opened the council of Basil; but the president soon appeared the most strenuous champion of ecclesiastical freedom; and an opposition of seven years was conducted by his ability and zeal. After promoting the strongest measures against the authority and person of Eugenius, some secret motive of interest or conscience engaged him to desert, on a sudden, the popular party. The cardinal withdrew himself from Basil to Ferrara; and, in the debates of the Greeks and Latins, the two nations admired the dexterity of his arguments and the depth of his theological erudition. [34] In his

theatre of the war in the xvth century [The story of the Varna campaign by Callimachus or Philip Buonaccorsi has recently been edited by Kwiatkovski in vol vi of the Monum Polon Hist (1893) See also the authorities cited in Katóna, *op cit* vol vi , and the Turkish writers cited above, note 24 A full description of the battle will be found in Hammer, i p 355-357, and in Zinkeisen, i p 689 *sqq* There is a description of the battle in Greek verse by Paraspondylus Zoticus, who professes to have been an eye-witness It has been edited (with Hungarian notes) by W Pecz, 1894, and it was included in Legrand's Collection de Monuments, Nouvelle série, v p 51 *sqq*]

[33] M Lenfant has described the origin (Hist du Concile de Basle, tom i p 247, &c), and Bohemian campaign (p 315, &c), of Cardinal Julian His services at Basil and Ferrara, and his unfortunate end, are occasionally related by Spondanus and the continuator of Fleury

[34] Syropulus honourably praises the talents of an enemy (p 117) : τοιαῦτά

Hungarian embassy we have already seen the mischievous effects of his sophistry and eloquence, of which Julian himself was the first victim. The cardinal, who performed the duties of a priest and a soldier, was lost in the defeat of Warna The circumstances of his death are variously related; but it is believed that a weighty incumbrance of gold impeded his flight, and tempted the cruel avarice of some Christian fugitives.

From an humble or at least a doubtful origin, the merit of John Huniades promoted him to the command of the Hungarian armies His father was a Walachian, his mother a Greek: her unknown race might possibly ascend to the emperors of Constantinople, and the claims of the Walachians, with the surname of Corvinus, from the place of his nativity, might suggest a thin pretence for mingling his blood with the patricians of ancient Rome.[35] In his youth, he served in the wars of Italy, and was retained, with twelve horsemen, by the bishop of Zagrab, the valour of the *white knight*[36] was soon conspicuous; he increased his fortunes by a noble and wealthy marriage; and in the defence of the Hungarian borders he won, in the same year, three battles against the Turks. By his influence, Ladislaus of Poland obtained the crown of Hungary; and the important service was rewarded by the title and office of Waivod of Transylvania The

τινα εἶπεν ὁ Ἰουλιανός, πεπλατυσμένως ἄγαν καὶ λογικῶς, καὶ μετ' ἐπιστήμης καὶ δεινότητος ῥητορικῆς.

[35] See Bonfinius, decad iii 1 iv p. 423 Could the Italian historian pronounce, or the king of Hungary hear, without a blush, the absurd flattery which confounded the name of a Walachian village with the casual though glorious epithet of a single branch of the Valerian family at Rome? [For the Walachian origin of Hunyady, cp Xénopol, Histoire des Roumains, 1 p 264]

[36] Philip de Comines (Mémoires, 1 vi c 13), from the tradition of the times, mentions him with high encomiums, but under the whimsical name of the Chevalier Blanc de Valaigne (Valachia) The Greek Chalcondyles, and the Turkish Annals of Leunclavius, presume to accuse his fidelity or valour [Teleki, A Hunyadiak kora Magyarországon (The Age of the Hunyadys in Hungary), vols 1-5, 1852-7]

first of Julian's crusades added two Turkish laurels on his brow; and in the public distress the fatal errors of Warna were forgotten. During the absence and minority of Ladislaus of Austria, the titular king, Huniades was elected supreme captain and governor of Hungary; and, if envy at first was silenced by terror, a reign of twelve years supposes the arts of policy as well as of war. Yet the idea of a consummate general is not delineated in his campaigns; the white knight fought with the hand rather than the head, as the chief of desultory Barbarians, who attack without fear and fly without shame; and his military life is composed of a romantic alternative of victories and escapes. By the Turks, who employed his name to frighten their perverse children, he was corruptly denominated *Jancus Lain*, or the Wicked; their hatred is the proof of their esteem; the kingdom which he guarded was inaccessible to their arms; and they felt him most daring and formidable, when they fondly believed the captain of his country irrecoverably lost. Instead of confining himself to a defensive war, four years after the defeat of Warna he again penetrated into the heart of Bulgaria; and in the plain of Cossova sustained, till the third day, the shock of the Ottoman army, four times more numerous than his own. As he fled alone through the woods of Walachia, the hero was surprised by two robbers; but, while they disputed a gold chain that hung at his neck, he recovered his sword, slew the one, terrified the other; and, after new perils of captivity or death, consoled by his presence an afflicted kingdom. But the last and most glorious action of his life was the defence of Belgrade against the powers of Mahomet the Second in person. After a siege of forty days, the Turks, who had already entered the town, were compelled to retreat; and the joyful nations celebrated Huniades and Belgrade as the bulwarks of Christendom.[37] About a month

---

[37] See Bonfinius (decad iii. l. viii. p. 492) and Spondanus (A.D. 1456, No. 1–7). Huniades shared the glory of the defence of Belgrade with Capis-

after this great deliverance, the champion expired; and his most splendid epitaph is the regret of the Ottoman prince, who sighed that he could no longer hope for revenge against the single antagonist who had triumphed over his arms.   On the first vacancy of the throne, Matthias Corvinus, a youth of eighteen years of age, was elected and crowned by the grateful Hungarians.   His reign was prosperous and long. Matthias aspired to the glory of a conqueror and a saint; but his purest merit is the encouragement of learning; and the Latin orators and historians, who were invited from Italy by the son, have shed the lustre of their eloquence on the father's character [38]

In the list of heroes, John Huniades and Scanderbeg are commonly associated; [39] and they are both entitled to our notice, since their occupation of the Ottoman arms delayed the ruin of the Greek empire.   John Castriot, the father of

tran, a Franciscan friar, and in their respective narratives neither the saint nor the hero condescends to take notice of his rival's merit   [On John Capistrano see Hermann, Capistranus triumphans seu historia fundamentalis de S Joanne Cap , 1700, Cataneo, Vita di S Giovanni da Capistrano, 1691, Guérard, S Jean de Capistran et son temps, 1865   The last campaign of Hunyady is the subject of a monograph by Kiss (Hunyadi János utolsó hadjárata, 1857)   The siege of Belgrade has been treated fully by Mr R N Bain in the Eng Historical Review for July, 1892]

[38] See Bonfinius, decad iii l viii –decad iv l viii   The observations of Spondanus on the life and character of Matthias Corvinus are curious and critical (A D 1464, No 1, 1475, No 6, 1476, No 14-16, 1490, No 4, 5) Italian fame was the object of his vanity   His actions are celebrated in the Epitome Rerum Hungaricarum (p 322-412) of Peter Ranzanus, a Sicilian His wise and facetious sayings are registered by Galeotus Martius of Narni (528-568), and we have a particular narrative of his wedding and coronation These three tracts are all contained in the first vol of Bel's Scriptores Rerum Hungaricarum   [The best monograph on Matthias Corvinus is that of W Fraknói which has appeared in a German translation (from the Hungarian) in 1891   It is furnished with interesting illustrations]

[39] They are ranked by Sir William Temple, in his pleasing Essay on Heroic Virtue (Works, vol iii p 385), among the seven chiefs who have deserved, without wearing, a royal crown; Belisares, Narses, Gonsalvo of Cordova, William first prince of Orange, Alexander duke of Parma, John Huniades, and George Castriot, or Scanderbeg

Scanderbeg,[40] was the hereditary prince of a small district of
Epirus or Albania, between the mountains and the Adriatic
Sea.   Unable to contend with the sultan's power, Castriot
submitted to the hard conditions of peace and tribute; he
delivered his four sons as the pledges of his fidelity; and the
Christian youths, after receiving the mark of circumcision,
were instructed in the Mahometan religion, and trained in
the arms and arts of Turkish policy.[41]   The three elder
brothers were confounded in the crowd of slaves; and the
poison to which their deaths are ascribed cannot be verified
or disproved by any positive evidence.   Yet the suspicion is
in a great measure removed by the kind and paternal treatment of George Castriot, the fourth brother, who, from his
tender youth, displayed the strength and spirit of a soldier.
The successive overthrow of a Tartar and two Persians, who
carried a proud defiance to the Turkish court, recommended
him to the favour of Amurath, and his Turkish appellation
of Scanderbeg (*Iskender beg*), or the lord Alexander, is an
indelible memorial of his glory and servitude.   His father's
principality was reduced into a province; but the loss was
compensated by the rank and title of Sanjiak, a command of
five thousand horse, and the prospect of the first dignities of

[40] I could wish for some simple authentic memoirs of a friend of Scanderbeg, which would introduce me to the man, the time, and the place.   In the
old and national history of Marinus Barletius, a priest of Scodra (de Vitâ,
Moribus, et Rebus gestis Georgii Castrioti, &c. libri xiii. p. 367, Argentorat.
1537, in fol.), his gaudy and cumbersome robes are stuck with many false
jewels.   See likewise Chalcondyles, l. vii. p. 185 [p. 350, ed. B.]; l. viii.
p. 229 [p. 432].   [Besides the contemporary authority, Barletius, we know
indirectly of another contemporary source written by an anonymous man of
Antivari.   This work (Historia Scanderbegi edita per quendam Albanensem)
was printed at Venice in 1480, but is now lost.   But it is known to us through
Giammaria Bienami, who used it for his Istoria di Giorgio Castriota, detto
Scander Begh, 1742.   The best modern work on the life and exploits of
Scanderbeg is that of Julius Pisko: Skanderbeg, 1894; a number of new
documents are printed in an appendix.]

[41] His circumcision, education, &c. are marked by Marinus with brevity
and reluctance (l. i. p. 6, 7).

the empire He served with honour in the wars of Europe
and Asia, and we may smile at the art or credulity of the
historian, who supposes that in every encounter he spared
the Christians, while he fell with a thundering arm on his
Musulman foes The glory of Huniades is without reproach he fought in the defence of his religion and country;
but the enemies who applaud the patriot have branded his
rival with the name of traitor and apostate. In the eyes of
the Christians the rebellion of Scanderbeg is justified by his
father's wrongs, the ambiguous death of his three brothers,
his own degradation, and the slavery of his country, and
they adore the generous though tardy zeal with which he
asserted the faith and independence of his ancestors. But
he had imbibed from his ninth year the doctrines of the
Koran; he was ignorant of the Gospel, the religion of a
soldier is determined by authority and habit, nor is it easy
to conceive what new illumination at the age of forty [42] could
be poured into his soul. His motives would be less exposed
to the suspicion of interest or revenge, had he broken his chain
from the moment that he was sensible of its weight; but a
long oblivion had surely impaired his original right; and every
year of obedience and reward had cemented the mutual bond
of the sultan and his subject. If Scanderbeg had long har-
boured the belief of Christianity and the intention of revolt,
a worthy mind must condemn the base dissimulation, that
could only serve to betray, that could promise only to be for-
sworn, that could actively join in the temporal and spiritual
perdition of so many thousands of his unhappy brethren.
Shall we praise a secret correspondence with Huniades, while
he commanded the vanguard of the Turkish army? shall we

[42] Since Scanderbeg died, A D 1466, in the 63d year of his age (Marinus,
l xiii p 370), he was born in 1403 [1404], since he was torn from his parents
by the Turks when he was *novennis* (Marinus, l i. p 1, 6), that event must
have happened in 1412 [or 1413], nine years before the accession of Amurath
II, who must have inherited, not acquired, the Albanian slave. Spondanus
has remarked this inconsistency, A D 1431, No 31, 1443, No 14.

excuse the desertion of his standard, a treacherous desertion, which abandoned the victory to the enemies of his benefactor? In the confusion of a defeat, the eye of Scanderbeg was fixed on the Reis Effendi, or principal secretary; with a dagger at his breast, he extorted a firman or patent for the government of Albania; and the murder of the guiltless scribe and his train prevented the consequences of an immediate discovery. With some bold companions, to whom he had revealed his design, he escaped in the night, by rapid marches, from the field of battle to his paternal mountains. The gates of Croya were opened to the royal mandate; and no sooner did he command the fortress than George Castriot dropped the mask of dissimulation, abjured the Prophet and the sultan, and proclaimed himself the avenger of his family and country. The names of religion and liberty provoked a general revolt: the Albanians, a martial race, were unanimous to live and die with their hereditary prince; and the Ottoman garrisons were indulged in the choice of martyrdom or baptism. In the assembly of the states of Epirus, Scanderbeg was elected general of the Turkish war; and each of the allies engaged to furnish his respective proportion of men and money. From these contributions, from his patrimonial estate, and from the valuable salt-pits of Selina, he drew an annual revenue of two hundred thousand ducats; [43] and the entire sum, exempt from the demands of luxury, was strictly appropriated to the public use. His manners were popular; but his discipline was severe; and every superfluous vice was banished from his camp; his example strengthened his command; and under his conduct the Albanians were invincible in their own opinion and that of their enemies. The bravest adventurers of France and Germany were allured by his fame and retained in his service; his standing militia consisted of eight thousand horse and seven thousand foot; the horses were small, the men were active; but he viewed with

---

[43] His revenue and forces are luckily given by Marinus (l. ii. p. 44).

a discerning eye the difficulties and resources of the mountains; and, at the blaze of the beacons, the whole nation was
distributed in the strongest posts   With such unequal arms,
Scanderbeg resisted twenty-three years the powers of the
Ottoman empire, and two conquerors, Amurath the Second
and his greater son, were repeatedly baffled by a rebel whom
they pursued with seeming contempt and implacable resentment   At the head of sixty thousand horse and forty thousand Janizaries,[44] Amurath entered Albania · he might
ravage the open country, occupy the defenceless towns,
convert the churches into moschs, circumcise the Christian
youths, and punish with death his adult and obstinate captives, but the conquests of the sultan were confined to the
petty fortress of Sfetigrade; and the garrison, invincible to
his arms, was oppressed by a paltry artifice and a superstitious
scruple.[45] Amurath retired with shame and loss from the
walls of Croya, the castle and residence of the Castriots;
the march, the siege, the retreat, were harassed by a vexatious
and almost invisible adversary;[46] and the disappointment
might tend to embitter, perhaps to shorten, the last days of
the sultan.[47] In the fulness of conquest, Mahomet the Second
still felt at his bosom this domestic thorn; his lieutenants

[44][Biemmi says that the total number of fighting men did not exceed
70,000, see Pisko, p 47]

[45]There were two Dibras, the upper and lower, the Bulgarian and Albanian: the former, 70 miles from Croya (l 1 p 17), was contiguous to the
fortress of Sfetigrade, whose inhabitants refused to drink from a well into
which a dead dog had traitorously been cast (l. v p. 139, 140)   We want a
good map of Epirus [The site of Sfetigrad is uncertain   It was in the
Upper Dibre, and perhaps near Trebište See Pisko, p 18 note, and for
the mode of its capture, p 50, 51]

[46]Compare the Turkish narrative of Cantemir (p 92) with the pompous
and prolix declamation in the ivth, vth, and vith books of the Albanian priest,
who has been copied by the tribe of strangers and moderns

[47]In honour of his hero, Barletius (l vi p 188–192) kills the sultan, by
disease indeed, under the walls of Croya But this audacious fiction is disproved by the Greeks and Turks, who agree in the time and manner of
Amurath's death at Hadrianople

were permitted to negotiate a truce, and the Albanian prince
may justly be praised as a firm and able champion of his
national independence. The enthusiasm of chivalry and
religion has ranked him with the names of Alexander and
Pyrrhus, nor would they blush to acknowledge their intrepid
countryman; but his narrow dominion and slender powers
must leave him at an humble distance below the heroes of
antiquity, who triumphed over the East and the Roman
legions. His splendid achievements, the bashaws whom he
encountered, the armies that he discomfited, and the three
thousand Turks who were slain by his single hand, must be
weighed in the scales of suspicious criticism. Against an
illiterate enemy, and in the dark solitude of Epirus, his partial
biographers may safely indulge the latitude of romance; but
their fictions are exposed by the light of Italian history; and
they afford a strong presumption against their own truth by
a fabulous tale of his exploits, when he passed the Adriatic
with eight hundred horse to the succour of the king of Naples.[48]
Without disparagement to his fame, they might have owned
that he was finally oppressed by the Ottoman powers; in his
extreme danger, he applied to Pope Pius the Second for a
refuge in the ecclesiastical state; and his resources were
almost exhausted, since Scanderbeg died a fugitive at Lissus,
on the Venetian territory.[49] His sepulchre was soon violated

[48] See the marvels of his Calabrian expedition in the ixth and xth books of
Marinus Barletius, which may be rectified by the testimony or silence of
Muratori (Annali d'Italia, tom xiii p 291), and his original authors (Joh
Simonetta de Rebus Francisci Sfortiæ, in Muratori, Script Rerum Ital
tom xxi p 728, et alios). The Albanian cavalry, under the name of *Stradiots*,
soon became famous in the wars of Italy (Mémoires de Comines, l viii
c 5). [The date of Scanderbeg's expedition to Italy is fixed by Pisko (p 86–
88) by means of new documents According to Antonius Guidobonus, the
ambassador of Milan at Venice, the troops which Scanderbeg took with
him numbered 2000 foot and 1000 horse]

[49] Spondanus, from the best evidence and the most rational criticism, has
reduced the giant Scanderbeg to the human size (A D 1461, No 20, 1463,
No 9; 1465, No 12, 13, 1467, No 1) His own letter to the pope, and the
testimony of Phranza (l in c. 28), a refugee in the neighbouring isle of Corfu,

by the Turkish conquerors, but the Janizaries, who wore
his bones enchased in a bracelet, declared by this superstitious amulet their involuntary reverence for his valour. The
instant ruin of his country may redound to the hero's glory;
yet, had he balanced the consequences of submission and
resistance, a patriot, perhaps, would have declined the unequal contest which must depend on the life and genius of
one man. Scanderbeg might indeed be supported by the
rational though fallacious hope that the pope, the king of
Naples, and the Venetian republic would join in the defence
of a free and Christian people, who guarded the sea-coast of
the Adriatic and the narrow passage from Greece to Italy.
His infant son was saved from the national shipwreck; the
Castriots [50] were invested with a Neapolitan dukedom, and
their blood continues to flow in the noblest families of the
realm A colony of Albanian fugitives obtained a settlement
in Calabria, and they preserve at this day the language and
manners of their ancestors [51]

In the long career of the decline and fall of the Roman
empire, I have reached at length the last reign of the princes
of Constantinople, who so feebly sustained the name and
majesty of the Cæsars.[52] On the decease of John Palæologus,
who survived about four years the Hungarian crusade,[53] the

demonstrate his last distress, which is awkwardly concealed by Marinus
Barletius (l. x)

[50] See the family of the Castriots in Ducange (Fam Dalmaticæ, &c
xviii p. 348-350).

[51] This colony of Albanese is mentioned by Mr. Swinburne (Travels into
the Two Sicilies, vol i p 350-354)

[52] [Constantine is generally numbered as Constantine XI , but Gibbon
(who counts Constantine, son of Romanus I , as Constantine VIII , see
above, vol viii p 265) makes him Constantine XII He was distinguished by
the surname Dragases, derived through his mother Irene, who was daughter
of Constantine Dragases, a Servian prince]

[53] The chronology of Phranza is clear and authentic , but, instead of four
years and seven months, Spondanus (A D 1445, No 7) assigns seven or eight
years to the reign of the last Constantine, which he deduces from a spurious
epistle of Eugenius IV to the king of Ethiopia.

royal family, by the death of Andronicus and the monastic profession of Isidore, was reduced to three princes, Constantine, Demetrius, and Thomas, the surviving sons of the emperor Manuel. Of these the first and the last were far distant in the Morea; but Demetrius, who possessed the domain of Selybria, was in the suburbs, at the head of a party; his ambition was not chilled by the public distress; and his conspiracy with the Turks and the schismatics had already disturbed the peace of his country. The funeral of the late emperor was accelerated with singular and even suspicious haste, the claim of Demetrius to the vacant throne was justified by a trite and flimsy sophism, that he was born in the purple, the eldest son of his father's reign. But the empress-mother, the senate and soldiers, the clergy and people, were unanimous in the cause of the lawful successor; and the despot Thomas, who, ignorant of the change, accidentally returned to the capital, asserted with becoming zeal the interest of his absent brother. An ambassador, the historian Phranza, was immediately despatched to the court of Hadrianople. Amurath received him with honour, and dismissed him with gifts; but the gracious approbation of the Turkish sultan announced his supremacy, and the approaching downfall of the Eastern empire. By the hands of two illustrious deputies, the Imperial crown was placed at Sparta on the head of Constantine.[54] In the spring, he sailed from the Morea, escaped the encounter of a Turkish squadron, enjoyed the acclamations of his subjects, celebrated the festival of a new reign, and exhausted by his donatives the treasure, or rather the indigence, of the state   The emperor immediately resigned to his brothers the possession of the Morea, and the brittle friendship of the two princes, Demetrius and Thomas, was confirmed in their mother's presence

[54] [The ceremony was not renewed at Constantinople   The emperor desired to avoid any occasion for quarrels between the Unionists and anti-Unionists]

by the frail security of oaths and embraces. His next occupation was the choice of a consort. A daughter of the doge of Venice had been proposed; but the Byzantine nobles objected the distance between an hereditary monarch and an elective magistrate; and in their subsequent distress the chief of that powerful republic was not unmindful of the affront. Constantine afterwards hesitated between the royal families of Trebizond and Georgia; and the embassy of Phranza represents in his public and private life the last days of the Byzantine empire.[55]

The *protovestiare*, or great chamberlain, Phranza, sailed from Constantinople as minister of a bridegroom; and the relics of wealth and luxury were applied to his pompous appearance. His numerous retinue consisted of nobles and guards, of physicians and monks; he was attended by a band of music; and the term of his costly embassy was protracted above two years. On his arrival in Georgia or Iberia, the natives from the towns and villages flocked around the strangers; and such was their simplicity that they were delighted with the effects, without understanding the cause, of musical harmony. Among the crowd was an old man, above an hundred years of age, who had formerly been carried away a captive by the Barbarians,[56] and who amused his hearers with a tale of the wonders of India,[57] from whence he had returned to Portugal by an unknown sea.[58] From

[55] Phranza (l. iii. c. 1-6) deserves credit and esteem.

[56] Suppose him to have been captured in 1394, in Timour's first war in Georgia (Sherefeddin, l. iii. c. 50), he might follow his Tartar master into Hindostan in 1398, and from thence sail to the spice-islands.

[57] The happy and pious Indians lived 150 years, and enjoyed the most perfect productions of the vegetable and mineral kingdoms. The animals were on a large scale: dragons seventy cubits, ants (the *formica Indica*) nine inches long, sheep like elephants, elephants like sheep. Quidlibet audendi, &c.

[58] He sailed in a country vessel from the spice-islands to one of the ports of the exterior India; invenitque navem grandem *Ibericam*, quâ in *Portugalliam* est delatus. This passage, composed in 1477 (Phranza, l. iii. c. 30), twenty years before the discovery of the Cape of Good Hope, is spurious or

this hospitable land Phranza proceeded to the court of Trebizond, where he was informed by the Greek prince of the recent decease of Amurath. Instead of rejoicing in the deliverance, the experienced statesman expressed his apprehension that an ambitious youth would not long adhere to the sage and pacific system of his father. After the sultan's decease, his Christian wife Maria,[59] the daughter of the Servian despot, had been honourably restored to her parents. on the fame of her beauty and merit, she was recommended by the ambassador as the most worthy object of the royal choice; and Phranza recapitulates and refutes the specious objections that might be raised against the proposal. The majesty of the purple would ennoble an unequal alliance; the bar of affinity might be removed by liberal alms and the dispensation of the church; the disgrace of Turkish nuptials had been repeatedly overlooked; and, though the fair Maria was near fifty years of age, she might yet hope to give an heir to the empire. Constantine listened to the advice, which was transmitted in the first ship that sailed from Trebizond; but the factions of the court opposed his marriage; and it was finally prevented by the pious vow of the sultana, who ended her days in the monastic profession. Reduced to the first alternative, the choice of Phranza was decided in favour of a Georgian princess; and the vanity of her father was dazzled by the glorious alliance. Instead of demanding, according to the primitive and national custom, a price for his daughter,[60] he offered a portion of fifty-six thousand, with an annual pension of five thousand, ducats; and the services of the

wonderful   But this new geography is sullied by the old and incompatible error which places the source of the Nile in India

[59] Cantemir (p 83), who styles her the daughter of Lazarus Ogli, and the Helen of the Servians, places her marriage with Amurath in the year 1424. It will not easily be believed that in six and twenty years' cohabitation the sultan corpus ejus non tetigit   After the taking of Constantinople, she fled to Mahomet II (Phranza, l iii c 22).

[60] The classical reader will recollect the offers of Agamemnon (Iliad I v 144) and the general practice of antiquity.

ambassador were repaid by an assurance that, as his son had
been adopted in baptism by the emperor, the establishment
of his daughter should be the peculiar care of the empress of
Constantinople. On the return of Phranza, the treaty was
ratified by the Greek monarch, who with his own hand impressed three vermilion crosses on the Golden Bull, and
assured the Georgian envoy that in the spring his galleys
should conduct the bride to her Imperial palace. But Constantine embraced his faithful servant, not with the cold
approbation of a sovereign, but with the warm confidence of
a friend, who, after a long absence, is impatient to pour his
secrets into the bosom of his friend. "Since the death of
my mother and of Cantacuzene, who alone advised me without interest or passion,[61] I am surrounded," said the emperor,
"by men whom I can neither love nor trust nor esteem. You
are not a stranger to Lucas Notaras, the great admiral:
obstinately attached to his own sentiments, he declares, both
in private and public, that his sentiments are the absolute
measure of my thoughts and actions   The rest of the courtiers
are swayed by their personal or factious views; and how can
I consult the monks on questions of policy and marriage?
I have yet much employment for your diligence and fidelity
In the spring you shall engage one of my brothers to solicit
the succour of the Western powers; from the Morea you
shall sail to Cyprus on a particular commission; and from
thence proceed to Georgia to receive and conduct the future
empress." "Your commands," replied Phranza, "are irresistible; but deign, great Sir," he added, with a serious smile,
"to consider that, if I am thus perpetually absent from my
family, my wife may be tempted either to seek another husband or to throw herself into a monastery." After laughing
at his apprehensions, the emperor more gravely consoled him

---

[61] Cantacuzene (I am ignorant of his relation to the emperor of that name)
was a great domestic, a firm assertor of the Greek creed, and a brother of
the queen of Servia, whom he visited with the character of ambassador
(Syropulus, p 37, 38, 45).

by the pleasing assurance that *this* should be his last service abroad, and that he destined for his son a wealthy and noble heiress; for himself, the important office of great logothete, or principal minister of state. The marriage was immediately stipulated; but the office, however incompatible with his own, had been usurped by the ambition of the admiral. Some delay was requisite to negotiate a consent and an equivalent; and the nomination of Phranza was half declared and half suppressed, lest it might be displeasing to an insolent and powerful favourite. The winter was spent in the preparations of his embassy; and Phranza had resolved that the youth his son should embrace this opportunity of foreign travel, and be left, on the appearance of danger, with his maternal kindred of the Morea Such were the private and public designs, which were interrupted by a Turkish war, and finally buried in the ruins of the empire.[62]

[62] [A Burgundian knight, Bertrandon de la Brocquière, returning from a pilgrimage to Jerusalem, visited Constantinople in 1432, and has left us a very interesting description of life in that city, and also of Murad's court at Hadrianople Legrand D'Aussy published this work (Voyage d'Outremer et Retour de Jérusalem en France) in 1804, and it has been re-edited by C. Schefer, 1892 An English edition appeared in T Wright's Early Travels in Palestine (ed Bohn, 1848, p 283-382).

Finlay writes (Hist of Greece, iii p 492) "Court processions, religious ceremonies, and national vanity amused and consoled the Greeks as they hastened along the path of degradation and ruin Dramatic representations of sacred subjects were performed in the Church of St Sophia, as musical exhibitions had been celebrated in earlier days Exercises of archery and imitations of Turkish horsemanship replaced the military pageants and the games of the hippodrome which had been the delight of the Byzantine populace in better days."]

APPENDIX

ADDITIONAL NOTES BY THE EDITOR

1 AUTHORITIES

LAONICUS CHALCONDYLES[1] belonged to a good Athenian family. He went twice as an ambassador to the Sultan Murad, and was on both occasions imprisoned His History in 10 books covers the period 1298–1463 and thus includes the fall of the Empire of Trebizond He was a man of great ability, and, though we may wish that he had not set it before himself to imitate Herodotus and Thucydides, we must recognise the talent which he displayed in handling a most intractable period of history It is very interesting to pass from his predecessors in the series of the Byzantine historians to this writer We no longer watch events from the single and simple standpoint of Constantinople The true theme of Chalcondyles is not the decline of the diminished empire, but the growth and development of the Ottoman State[2] The centre of events shifts with the movements of the sultan. The weakest point of Chalcondyles is his chronology (Ed Baumbach (Geneva), 1615, ed Bekker (Bonn), 1843)

DUCAS was a grandson of Michael Ducas (a scion of the imperial family of that name), who is mentioned as having taken part in the struggle between Cantacuzenus and John Palaeologus in the 14th century He was secretary of the Genoese podestà at Phocaea, before the siege of Constantinople, and afterwards he was employed by the Gattilusi of Lesbos as an ambassador to the sultan His connection with the Genoese helped, probably, to determine his ecclesiastical views, he was a hearty supporter of union with the Latin Church, as the great safeguard against the Turks His History covers the period 1341–1462, he is more accurate than Chalcondyles In language he is not a purist; his work is full of foreign words (Ed Bullialdus (Paris), 1649, ed Bekker (Bonn), 1834, with a 15th cent Italian translation, which fills up some gaps in the Greek)

GEORGE PHRANTZES (cp above, p 250, note 33), born 1401, was secretary of the Emperor Manuel, whose son Constantine he rescued at Patias in 1429 In 1432 Protovestiarios, he was made Prefect of Sparta in 1448, and then elevated to the post of Great Logothete See further above, p 250 and p 322 *sqq* Taken prisoner on the capture of Constantinople (cp vol VII p 47), he fled to the Peloponnesus, visited Italy, and ended his life as Brother Gregory in a monastery of Corfu where he composed his Chronicle This work, when Gibbon wrote, was accessible only in the Latin translation of Pontanus (1604) The Greek original was first published by F K Alter (Vienna, 1796), from an inferior MS An improved text was issued by Bek-

---

[1] Chalcondyles, for Chalc<oc>ondyles, is explained by Krumbacher as meaning the man with the bronze handle (Gesch der byz Litt , p 305)
[2] This has been excellently brought out by Krumbacher, *op. cit* p 302

ker in the Bonn series, 1838 [3] The history covers a longer period than that of Chalcondyles, beginning A D 1258, it comes down to A D. 1476, the year before the work was completed   Bk 1 comes down to the death of Manuel, Bk 2, to the death of John, Bk 3 treats of the reign of Constantine and the capture of the city, Bk 4 the events of the following twenty-three years. The high position which he held in the State and his opportunities of knowledge render Bks 2 and 3 especially valuable   He is naturally a good hater of the Turks, from whom he had suffered so much.   His style is not pedantic like that of Chalcondyles   (Biographical Monograph by G Destunis in the Zhurnal Ministerstva narodn prosv, vol 287, p. 427 *sqq*, 1893)

CRITOBULUS of Imbros wrote a history of the deeds of Mohammad II from A D 1451 to 1467   Although he is not out of sympathy with his countrymen, he has thrown his lot in with the conquerors, and he writes from the Turkish point of view. This is the interesting feature of his work, which is thus sharply contrasted with the histories of Chalcondyles and Ducas   He inscribes the book, in a dedicatory epistle, to Mohammad himself, whom he compares to Alexander the Great   Like Ducas and Chalcondyles, he describes the siege of Constantinople at second hand, but like theirs his very full description is a most valuable source for comparison with the accounts of the eyewitnesses.   He can indeed be convicted of many small inaccuracies For example, he states that Giustiniani was wounded in the chest, and that Constantine was slain near the Cercoporta; and in other parts of his work, his chronology is at fault   He was an imitator of Thucydides, and puts Thucydidean speeches into the mouth of Mohammad. But he does not scruple to use a "modern" foreign word like τούφακες, "guns" (from the Turkish; cp modern Greek τουφέκι, a gun)   The history of Critobulus is extant in an MS at Constantinople, and it was first published by C. Muller, in the 2nd part of vol v of Fragmenta Historicorum Graecorum, p 40 *sqq*, 1870, with very useful notes

The description of Murad's siege of Constantinople by JOHN CANANUS is mentioned above, p 224, note 93, and that of the siege of Thessalonica in 1430, by JOHN ANAGNOSTES, on p 302, note 14

The chronicle of the last years of the empire is briefly told in the anonymous EKTHESIS CHRONIKΓ, a work of the 16th century, published by C. Sathas in Bibl. Graec Med Aev. vii p 556 *sqq* (1894)   A new edition of this little work by Prof Lampros is in preparation

It remains to mention the Anonymous Dirge concerning Tamurlane, Θρῆνος περὶ Ταμυρλάγγου, written during the campaign of Timur into Asia Minor   It is published by Papadimitriu in the Lietopis 1st-phil obschestva of Odessa (Vizant Otdiel), ii p. 173 *sqq* (Older, bad ed in Wagner's Medieval Greek Texts, p 105 *sqq*)   Timur's name also appears in this poem as Ταμυρλάνης (l 47) and Τεμύρης (l 41)

RASHID AD-DIN, born 1247 at Hamadān was originally a physician, but became Vizir of Persia, 1298   He was executed by Abū Said in 1318   In the preface to his Jāmi at-Tawārīkh he acknowledges his obligations to a minister of Mongol birth and name, who was versed in Turkish and Mongolian history   He refers to the *Altan depter*, a book of Mongol annals which was in the Khan's treasury, text and Russian translation by J. N. Berezin, 1858 *sqq*

[3] There is also extant an abbreviated version of the Chronicle in colloquial Greek, and it seems to have been prepared by Phrantzes himself. Cp Krumbacher, *op cit* p 308   It has been edited in Mai's Class Auct ix p 594 *sqq*, 1837, and reprinted in Migne, P G 156.

Alā ad-Dīn Ata-mulk JUVAINĪ composed a work entitled Jahān Kushāi (a history of the Conqueror of the World) on the last ten years of Chingiz, and coming down as far as A D 1257 Born in Khorāsān in A D 1227-8, he visited the court of Mangū Khān c. A D. 1249 His work (of which there is a MS in the British Museum) has never been printed, though he is one of the best authorities on the history of his time But it has been largely used by D'Ohsson and others. For his biography see Fundgruben des Orients, i 220-34

Minhāj-i-Sirāj JŪZJĀNĪ, son of a cadi of the army of Mohammad Ghōrī, lived c A D 1200-70, and wrote his history, the Tabākāt-i-Nāsirī, about the middle of the century, at the court of Nāsir ad-Dīn Mahmūd, King of Delhi Beginning with the Patriarchs, he brought his history down to his own day, and Bk 23 is occupied with the incursions of the Turks and Mongols, — the Karā-Khitāy Chingiz and his successors, to A D 1259 The author writes in a clear straightforward style, and supports his narrative by references to sources The work was translated by Major Raverty in the Bibliotheca Indica (1848, etc), and there are large extracts in Elliot and Dowson, History of India as told by its own historians, ii 266 sqq

The second and third Books of the Memoirs of TĪMŪR are the Institutions and Designs which were translated by Major Davy (1783) and used by Gibbon Book iv coming down to 1375 A D has since been translated by Major Charles Stewart, 1830 (The Mulfuzāt Tīmūry, or autobiographical Memoirs of the Moghul Emperor Tīmūr) The original memoirs were written in Turkish (in the "Jagtay Tūrky language") and were rendered into Persian by Abū Tālib Husaini The English translations are made from the Persian version

Mirza HAIDAR lived in the 16th century and was a cousin of the famous Bābar His Tarīkh-i-Rashīdī (transl. by Elias and Ross, see above p 133, note 12, with learned apparatus of introduction and notes) is "the history of that branch of the Moghul Khans who separated themselves, about the year 1321, from the main stem of the Chaghatai, which was then the ruling dynasty in Transoxiana, and it is the only history known to exist of this branch of the Moghuls" (Elias, ib p. 7) There are two parts of the work, the second contains memoirs of the author's life, etc , which do not concern any events touched upon by Gibbon In the first part, written in 1544-6 in Cashmir, the author follows the history of two dynasties the Khans of Moghulistān, beginning with Tughluk Tīmūr, and their vassals the Dughlāt amīrs of Eastern Turkestan, from one of whom Haidar was descended This part of the work is based largely on oral traditions, but the author also made use of the work of Sharaf ad-Dīn. Mr Elias criticises "the weakness of the chronology and the looseness with which numbers and measurements are made "

Of Chinese authorities for the history of the Mongols, the most important is the annals entitled YUAN SHI, of which Bretschneider (Mediaeval Researches for Eastern Asiatic Sources, 1888) gives the following account (vol i p 180 sqq) In 1369 "the detailed records of the reigns of the thirteen Yuan emperors were procured, and the emperor (Hungwu) gave orders to compile the history of the Yuan [Mongols], under the direction of Sung Lien and Wang Wei The work, which occupied sixteen scholars, was begun in the second month of 1369 and finished in the eighth month of the same year But as at that time the record of the reign of Shun ti (the last Mongol emperor in China) was not yet received, the scholar Ou yang Iu and others were sent to Pei p'ing to obtain the required information In the sixth month of 1370 the Yuan Shi was complete." There were various subsequent editions. "The Yüan Shi has been compiled from official documents. Perhaps we must except the biographies, for which the information was probably often derived from private sources. It seems that the greater part of the documents on which the Chinese history of the Mongols is based had been drawn up in the Chinese language; but in some cases they appear to have been translated from the Mongol. I conclude this from the fact that in the Yüan Shi places are often mentioned, not, as usually, by their Chinese names, but by their Mongol names represented in Chinese characters" (p. 183). The Yüan Shi (p. 185 *sqq.*) is divided into four sections: (1) consists of the lives of the 13 Mongol Khans in Mongolia and China, and the annals of their reigns from Chingiz to Shun ti (1368); (2) memoirs (geographical, astronomical, politico-economical notices; regulations on dress, rites, public appointments, etc.; military ordinances, etc.); (3) genealogical tables and lists; (4) about a thousand biographies of eminent men of the period [Bretschneider observes that these biographies "bear evidence to the liberal views of the Mongol emperors as to the acknowledgment of merit. They seem never to have been influenced by national considerations"]; and notices of foreign lands and nations south and east of China (*e.g.*, Korea, Japan, Burma, Sumatra).

An abstract of the annals of the Yüan shi is contained in the first ten chapters of the YÜAN SHI LEI PIEN (an abbreviated History of the Mongols) which were translated by Gaubil in his Histoire de Gentchiscan (see above p. 133, note 11). From this abstract, and the Yüan shi and another work entitled the Shi Wei (Woof of History), Mr. R. K. Douglas compiled his Life of Jinghiz Khān, 1877.

The YÜAN CH'AO PI SHI, Secret History of the Mongol dynasty, is a Chinese translation of a Mongol work, which was completed before 1240. It contains the early history of the Mongols, the reign of Chingiz, and part of the reign of Ogotai; and it was translated into Chinese in the early period of the Ming dynasty. An abridgment of this work was translated into Russian by Palladius, and published in 1866 in the Records of the Russian Ecclesiastical Mission at Peking, vol. 4. It was only six years later that Palladius found that the work was extant in a fuller form. Bretschneider says: This document "corroborates generally Rashid-eddin's records, and occasionally we find passages in it which sound like a literal translation of the statements of the Persian historiographer. This proves that Rashid had made use of the same source of information as the unknown author of the Yüan ch'ao pi shi. As to the dates in the latter work, they are generally in accordance with the dates given by the Mohammadan authors; but in a few cases the Yüan ch'ao pi shi commits great chronological blunders and misplacements of events, as, for instance, with respect to the war in the west."

In his work cited above Bretschneider has rendered accessible other Chinese documents bearing on Mongol history, especially some relations of Chinese travellers and envoys; for example, an extract (i. p. 9 *sqq.*) from the Si Yu Lu (Description of Journey to the West) of Ye-lü Ch'u ts'ai, a minister of Chingiz who attended him to Persia, 1219-24. (There is a biography of this Ye-lü in the Yüan Shi.) Bretschneider makes valuable contributions to the difficult subject of geographical identifications, and discusses among other documents the account of the Armenian prince Haithon's visit to Mongolia, written by Guiragos Gandsaketsi. This Haithon I. must not be confounded with Haithon, the monk of Prémontré, mentioned by Gibbon (above p. 133, note 13). The account of Guiragos was translated into French by Klaproth (Nouv. Journ. Asiat., p. 273 *sqq.*, 1833) from a Russian version by Argutinski, but the history of Guiragos has since been translated by Brosset

SSANANG SSETSEN, a prince of the tribe of Ordus and a descendant of Chingiz, born A.D. 1604, wrote in Turkish a history of the eastern Mongols which he finished in 1662 It was thus written after the Manchus had conquered China and overthrown the Mongols The earlier part of the book is practically a history of Tibet The account of the origin of the Mongols is translated from Chinese sources The author is a zealous Buddhist and dwells at great length on all that concerned the interests of his religion, other matters are often dismissed far too briefly The relation of the career of Chingiz is marked by many anachronisms and inaccuracies The work was made accessible by the German translation of I J Schmidt, under the title Geschichte der Ostmongolen und ihres Furstenhauses, 1829

MODERN WORKS Finlay, History of Greece, vol III J von Hammer, Geschichte des osmanischen Reiches, vol i 1834 J W Zinkeisen, Geschichte des osmanischen Reiches in Europa, vol i, 1840 Sir H H Howorth, History of the Mongols (see above, p 133, note 12) Gregorovius, History of the City of Rome in the Middle Ages (see vol vii p 66, note 2)

For a sketch of the history of the Ottoman Turks S Lane-Poole, Turkey (Story of the Nations), La Jonquière, Histoire de l'empire Ottoman

For the laws, constitution, etc, of the Ottoman empire, the chief work is Mouradja d'Ohsson's Tableau général de l'empire Ottoman, 7 vols 1788–1824

2 THE ACCIAJOLI — (P 92)

If Gibbon had been more fully acquainted with the history of the family of the Acciajoli, he would have probably devoted some pages to the rise of their fortunes They rose to such power and influence in Greece in the 14th century that the subjoined account, taken from Finlay (vol iv p 157 sqq) — with a few additions in square brackets — will not be out of place

"Several members of the family of Acciajoli, which formed a distinguished commercial company at Florence in the thirteenth century, settled in the Peloponnesus about the middle of the fourteenth, under the protection of Robert, king of Naples Nicholas Acciajoli was invested, in the year 334, with the administration of the lands which the company had acquired in payment or in security of the loans it had made to the royal House of Anjou, and he acquired additional possessions in the principality of Achaia, both by purchase and grant, from Catherine of Valois, titular empress of Romania and regent of Achaia for her son prince Robert   [It is disputed whether he was her lover] The encroachments of the mercantile spirit on the feudal system are displayed in the concessions obtained by Nicholas Acciajoli in the grants he received from Catherine of Valois   He was invested with the power of mortgaging, exchanging, and selling his fiefs, without any previous authorisation from his suzerain   Nicholas acted as principal minister of Catherine during a residence of three years in the Morea, and he made use of his position, like a prudent banker, to obtain considerable grants of territory. He returned to Italy in 1341 and never again visited Greece; but his estates in Achaia were administered by his relations and other members of the banking house at Florence, many of whom obtained considerable fiefs for themselves through his influence

"Nicholas Acciajoli was appointed hereditary grand seneschal of the kingdom of Naples by Queen Jeanne, whom he accompanied in her flight to Provence when she was driven from her kingdom by Louis of Hungary.

On her return he received the rich country of Amalfi, as a reward for his fidelity, and subsequently Malta was added to his possessions. He was an able statesman and a keen political intriguer; and he was almost the first example of the superior position the purse of the moneyed citizen was destined to assume over the sword of the feudal baron and the learning of the politic churchman. Nicholas Acciajoli was the first of that banking aristocracy which has since held an important position in European history. He was the type of a class destined at times to decide the fate of kingdoms and at times to arrest the progress of armies. He certainly deserved to have his life written by a man of genius, but his superciliousness and assumption of princely state, even in his intercourse with the friends of his youth, disgusted Boccaccio, who alone of Florentine contemporaries could have left a vivid sketch of the career which raised him from the partner of a banking-house to the rank of a great feudal baron and to live in the companionship of kings. Boccaccio, offended by his insolence, seems not to have appreciated his true importance as the type of a coming age and a new state of society; and the indignant and satirical record he has left of the pride and presumption of the mercantile noble is by no means a correct portrait of the Neapolitan minister. Yet even Boccaccio records in his usual truthful manner that Nicholas had dispersed powerful armies, though he unjustly depreciates the merit of the success, because the victory was gained by combinations effected by gold, and not by the headlong charge of a line of lances. [Boccaccio dedicated his *Donne illustri* to Niccolo's sister Andrea, the countess of Monte Oderisio.]

"Nicholas Acciajoli obtained a grant of the barony and hereditary governorship of the fortress of Corinth in the year 1358. He was already in possession of the castles of Vulcano [at Ithome], Piadha near Epidauros, and large estates in other parts of the Peloponnesus. He died in 1365;[1] and his sons Angelo and Robert succeeded in turn to the barony and government of Corinth. Angelo mortgaged Corinth to his relative [second cousin], Nerio Acciajoli, who already possessed fiefs in Achaia, and who took up his residence at Corinth on account of the political and military importance of the fortress as well as to enable him to administer the revenues of the barony in the most profitable manner.

"Nerio Acciajoli, though he held the governorship of Corinth only as the deputy of his relation, and the barony only in security of a debt, was nevertheless, from his ability, enterprising character, great wealth, and extensive connections, one of the most influential barons of Achaia; and, from the disorderly state of the principality he was enabled to act as an independent prince."

"The Catalans were the constant rivals of the Franks of Achaia, and Nerio Acciajoli, as governor of Corinth, was the guardian of the principality against their hostile projects. The marriage of the young countess of Salona [whose father Count Lewis died 1382] involved the two parties in war. The mother of the bride was a Greek lady; she betrothed her daughter to Simeon [Stephen Ducas], son of the prince of Vallachian Thessaly; and the Catalans, with the two Laurias at their head, supported this arrangement. But the barons of Achaia, headed by Nerio Acciajoli, pretended that the Prince of Achaia as feudal suzerain of Athens was entitled to dispose of the hand of the countess. Nerio was determined to bestow the young countess, with all

[1] [There is a great memorial of Niccolo at Florence, the Gothic Certosa San Lorenzo. Gregorovius calls it "the first monument of historical relations between Florence and Greece"; for just as Pisa used her revenue from Constantinople to build her cathedral, Niccolo devoted moneys from Greece to build San Lorenzo. His tomb is to be seen in a subterranean chapel.]

her immense possessions, on a relative of the Acciajoli family, named Peter Sarrasin[2] The war concerning the countess of Salona and her heritage appears to have commenced about the year 1386 [1385]. The Catalans were defeated, and Nerio gained possession of Athens, Thebes, and Livadea "

"About the commencement of the year 1394 Ladislas, king of Naples, conferred on him by patent the title of Duke of Athens — Athens forming, as the king pretended, part of the principality of Achaia "

Nerio died in 1394 His illegitimate son Antonio inherited Thebes and Livadia, and wrested to himself the government of Athens, which Nerio's will had placed under the protection of Venice on behalf of his daughter (the wife of Count Tocco of Cephalonia) Under Antonio "Athens enjoyed uninterrupted tranquillity for forty years The republic of Florence deemed it an object worthy of its especial attention to obtain a commercial treaty with the duchy, for the purpose of securing to the citizens of the republic all the privileges enjoyed by the Venetians, Catalans, and Genoese " The conclusion of this treaty is almost the only event recorded concerning the external relations of Athens during the long reign of Antonio The Athenians appear to have lived happily under his government, and he himself seems to have spent his time in a joyous manner, inviting his Florentine relations to Greece, and entertaining them with festivals and hunting parties Yet he was neither a spendthrift nor a tyrant, for Chalcocondylas, whose father lived at his court, records that, while he accumulated great wealth with prudent economy, he at the same time adorned the city of Athens with many new buildings He died in 1435, and was succeeded by Nerio II, grandson of Donato, the brother of Nerio I

[Buchon, Nouvelles Recherches, vols i and ii ; L Tanfani, Niccolo Acciajoli, 1863, Hopf, Hist Duc Att Fontes, Gregorovius, Geschichte der Stadt Athen im Mittelalter, vol ii]

3 THE ISLAND DYNASTIES AFTER THE LATIN CONQUEST — (P 89)

The facts about the history of the Greek islands during the 13th, 14th and 15th centuries were enveloped in obscurity, and fictions and false hypotheses were current, until the industry of Professor C Hopf drew the material from the archives of Vienna and Venice His publications rendered the work of Buchon and Finlay obsolete so far as the islands are concerned He won the right of referring with contempt to Buchon's schonrednerische Fabeleien und Finlays geistreich-unkritischer Hypothesenwust The following list of the island-lordships is taken from his Urkunden und Zusatze zur Geschichte der Insel Andros und ihrer Beherrscher in dem Zeitraume von 1207 to 1566, published in the Sitzungsberichte of the Vienna Academy, 1856, vol 21, p 221 sqq.

Corfu	Venetian 1207–c 1214, to Despotate of Epirus c 1214–1259; King Manfred and Filippo Chinardo 1259–1267, Neapolitan 1267–1386, Venetian 1386–1797.
Cefalonia, Zante, Ithaca.	Despotate of Epirus 1205–1337, Greek Empire 1337–1357, the Tocchi 1357–1482

[2] [His own brother-in-law, for he was married to Agnes Saraceno]

Santa Maura.

Despotate of Epirus 1205–1331; Giorgi 1331–1362; the Tocchi 1362–1482.

Paxo.

With Cefalonia 1205–1357; St. Ippolyto 1357–1484; Ugoth (Gotti) 1484–1527. With Cerigotto 1527–1797.

Cerigo (Cythera).

The Venieri 1207–1269; the Mono-janni 1267–1309; the Venieri 1309–1797.

Cerigotto.

The Viari 1207–1655; the Foscarini and Giustiniani 1655–1797.

Salamis.

With Athens.

Aegina.

With Carystos 1205–1317; Aragonese 1317–c. 1400; Cavopena c. 1400–1451; Venetian 1451–1537.

Delos, Gyaros, Cythnos (Patmos).

With Naxos. [Sanudo allowed Pat-mos, the apostle's island, to pre-serve its independence.]

Tinos and Miconos.

The Ghisi 1207–1390; Venetian 1390–1718. (Held in fief by Venetian counts belonging to the houses of Bembo, Quirini, and Fabieri 1407–1429.)

Andros.

The Dandoli 1207–1233; the Ghisi 1233–c. 1250; the Sanudi c. 1250–1384; the Zeni 1384–1437; the Sommaripa 1437–1566.

Syra.

With Naxos.

Zia (Ceos).[1]

$\frac{3}{4}$: The Giustiniani 1207–1366; the da Coronia 1366–1464; the Gozza-dini 1464–1537.

$\frac{1}{4}$: The Michieli 1207–1355; the Premarini 1355 forward.

$\frac{1}{2}$: The Ghisi 1207–1328; the Pre-marini 1328–1375.

$\frac{9}{16}$: The Premarini 1375–1537.

$\frac{3}{16}$: The Sanudi 1375–1405; the Gozzadini 1405–1537.

Serfene (Seriphos).[1]

$\frac{1}{2}$: the Michieli 1207–1537;

$\frac{1}{4}$: the Giustiniani 1207–c. 1412; the Adoldi 1412 forward.

$\frac{1}{4}$: the Ghisi 1207–1334; the Bragadini 1334–1354; the Minotti 1354–1373; the Adoldi 1373–1432; the Michieli 1432–1537.

Thermia (Cythnos).

The Sanudi 1207–c. 1320; the Castelli c. 1322–1331; the Gozzadini 1331–1537.

Sifanto (Siphnos), Sikino, Polycandro (Pholegandros).

The Sanudi 1207–1269 (titular, 1341; the Grimani titular 1341–1537); Greek Empire 1269–1307; the da Coronia 1307–1464; the Gozza-dini 1464–1617.

[1] Ceos and Seriphos were under the Greek Empire from 1269 to 1296.

Milos and Cimolos	The Sanudi 1207–1376, the Crispi 1376–1566
Santorin (Thera) and Therasia.	The Barozzi 1207–1335, with Naxos 1335–1477, the Pisani 1477–1487; with Naxos 1487–1537
Namfio (Anaphe).	The Foscoli 1207–1269, Greek Empire 1269–1307, the Gozzadini 1307–1420, the Crispi 1420–1469, the Barbari 1469–1528, the Pisani 1528–1537
Nio (Anaea).	The Sanudi 1207–1269, Greek Empire 1269–1292, the Schiavi 1292–c 1320, with Naxos c 1320–1420, collateral branch of the Crispi 1420–1508, the Pisani 1508–1537
Paros and Nausa.	With Naxos 1207–1389, the Sommaripa 1389–1516; the Venieri 1516–1531, the Sagredi 1531–1537.
Antiparos	With Paros 1207–1439, the Loredani 1439–c 1490, the Pisani 1490–1537.
Naxos	The Sanudi 1207–1362, the Dalle Carceri 1362–1383; the Crispi 1383–1566
Scyros, Sciathos, Chelidromi.	The Ghisi 1207–1269, Greek Empire 1269–1455, Venetian 1455–1537
Scopelos.	The Ghisi 1207–1262; the Tiepoli 1262–1310, the Greek Empire 1310–1454, Venetian 1454–1538
Negroponte	$\frac{1}{3}$· the dalle Carceri 1205–1254, the da Verona 1254–1383, the Sommaripa 1383–1470 $\frac{1}{3}$ the Peccorari 1205–1214, the dalle Carceri 1214–c 1300, the Ghisi c. 1300–1390, Venetian 1390–1470 $\frac{1}{3}$ The da Verona 1205–1383, the da Noyer 1383–1470.
Carystos (in Negroponte).	The dalle Carceri 1205–c 1254, the Cicons c 1254–1292, the da Verona, 1292–1317, Aragonese 1317–1365, Venetian 1365–1386, the Giustiniani 1386–1404, Venetian 1404–1406, the Giorgi 1406–1470
Lemnos.	The Navigajosi (with these, subsequently, the Gradenighi and Foscari) 1207–1269, Greek Empire 1269–1453, the Gattilusj 1453–1462
Lesbos.	The Greek Empire 1205–1355, the Gattilusj 1355–1462.
Chios, Samos.	With Constantinople (Empire of Romania) 1205–1247, with Lesbos 1247–1303; the Zaccaria 1303–1333, Greek Empire 1333–1346,

	the joint stock company of the Giustiniani, in 14 and more branches, 1346–1566.
Nikaria (Icaria).	The Beazzani 1205–1333; with Chios 1333–1481; the knights of St. John 1309–1521.
Stampali (Astypalaea).	The Quirini 1207–1269; Greek Empire 1260–1310; the Quirini and Grimani 1310–1537.
Amorgos.	The Ghisi 1207–1269; Greek Empire 1269–1296 [? 1303]; the Ghisi 1296–1368; ½: the Quirini 1368–1537; ½: the Grimani 1368–1446; the Quirini 1446–1537.
Nisyros, Piscopia, Calchi.	With Rhodes 1205–1306; the Assanti 1306–1385; with Rhodes 1385–1521.
Rhodes.	Gavalas 1204–1246; Greek Empire 1246–1283; the Aidonoghlii 1283–1309; the Knights of St. John 1309–1521.
Scarpanto (Carpathos).	With Rhodes 1204–1306; the Moreschi 1306–1309; the Cornari 1309–1522.
Candia.	Montferrat 1203–1204; Venetian 1204–1669.

[See further Hopf's Griechische Geschichte (cited above, vol. xi. App. 1. *ad fin.*); on Carystos, his art. in the Sitzungsber. of the Vienna Acad., 11, p. 555 *sqq.* (1853); on Andros, *ib.*, 16, p. 23 *sqq.* (1855); on Chios, his article on the Giustiniani in Ersch and Gruber's Enzyklopädie, vol. 68, p. 290 *sqq.*, 1859 (and see T. Bent, The Lords of Chios, Eng. Hist. Rev. 4, p. 467 *sqq.*, 1889); on the Archipelago his Veneto-byzantinische Analekten, 1860, and his article on the Ghisi in Ersch and Gruber, vol. 64, p. 336 *sqq.*, 1857; on Negroponte, see J. B. Bury, The Lombards and Venetians in Euboea, in Journal of Hellenic Studies, 7, p. 309 *sqq.*, 8, p. 194 *sqq.*, 9, p. 91 *sqq.* (1886–8); and L. de Mas Latrie in the Rev. de l'Orient Latin, 1, p. 413 *sqq.* (1893).]

4. MONGOL INVASION OF EUROPE, A.D. 1241 — (P. 146, 147)

It is only recently that European history has begun to understand that the successes of the Mongol army which overran Poland and occupied Hungary in the spring of A.D. 1241 were won by consummate strategy and were not due to a mere overwhelming superiority of numbers. But this fact has not yet become a matter of common knowledge; the vulgar opinion which represents the Tartars as a wild horde carrying all before them solely by their multitude, and galloping through Eastern Europe without a strategic plan, rushing at all obstacles and overcoming them by mere weight, still prevails. It will therefore not be amiss to explain very briefly the plan and execution of the Mongol campaign. The nominal commander-in-chief was Batu, but there is no doubt that the management of the expedition was in the hands of Subutai.

The objective of Subutai was Hungary, — the occupation of Hungary and the capture of Gran (Strigonium), which was then not only the ecclesiastical capital but the most important town in the country. In advancing on Hungary, his right flank was exposed to an attack from the princes of Poland, behind whom were the forces of Bohemia and North Germany. To meet this danger, Subutai divided his host into two parts, which we may call the northern and the southern army. The duty of the northern army was to sweep over Poland, advance to Bohemia, and effectually prevent the princes of the north from interfering with the operations of the southern army in Hungary. Thus strategically the invasion of Poland was subsidiary to the invasion of Hungary, and the northern army, when its work was done, was to meet the southern or main army on the Danube.

The northern army advanced in three divisions. The main force under Baidar marched through the dominions of Boleslaw the Chaste, and took Cracow, then bearing north-westward it reached Oppeln on the Oder, where it defeated Prince Mieczyslaw, and descended the Oder to Breslau. At the same time Kaidu advanced by a more northerly route through the land of Conrad, prince of Mosovia and Cujavia, while on the extreme right a force under Ordu terrified the Lithuanians and Prussians and crossed the Lower Vistula. The three divisions reunited punctually at Breslau, the capital of Henry II of Lower Silesia, and all took part in the battle of Liegnitz (April 9), for which King Wenzel of Bohemia arrived too late. Just one day too late: the Mongol generals had skilfully managed to force Prince Henry to fight before his arrival. Wenzel discreetly withdrew beyond the mountains into Bohemia, all he could hope to do was to defend his own kingdom. Saxony now lived in dread that its turn had come. But it was no part of the plan of Subutai to launch his troops into Northern Germany. They had annihilated the forces of Poland, it was now time for them to approach the main army in Hungary. The Mongols therefore turned their back upon the north, and marched through Upper Silesia and Moravia, capturing town after town as they went. Upon Wenzel who watched them with a large army, expecting them to invade Bohemia, they played a trick. He was posted near the defile of Glatz and the Mongols were at Ottmachau. They were too wary to attack him in such a position; it was necessary to remove him. Accordingly they marched back as if they purposed to invade Bohemia by the pass of the Konigstein in the north. Wenzel marched to the threatened point, and when the Mongols saw him safely there, they rapidly retraced their steps and reached Moravia (end of April, beginning of May.)

Meanwhile the main army advanced into Hungary in three columns converging on the Upper Theiss. The right wing was led by Shaiban, a younger brother of Batu, and seems to have advanced on the Porta Hungariae — the north-western entrance to Hungary, in the Little Carpathians. The central column under Subutai himself, with Batu, marched on the Porta Rusciae, the defile which leads from Galicia into the valley of the Theiss. The left column, under Kadan and Buri, moved through Transylvania towards the Koros.

The Porta Rusciae was carried, its defenders annihilated, on March 15; and a flying column of Tartars shot across Hungary, in advance of the main army. On March 15 they were half a day's journey from Pest, having ridden about 180 miles in less than three days. On the 17th they fought and defeated an Hungarian force, and on the same day Shaiban's right column captured Waitzen, a fort near the angle where the Danube bends southward. The object of Subutai in sending the advance squadron Pest-ward was doubtless to multiply difficulties for the Hungarians in organising their preparations. These preparations were already hampered by the conflicts and jealousies between the king and his nobles; and then towards the end of March befell the murder of Kutan, the chief of the Cumans, and the consequent revolt of the Cumans, — mentioned by Gibbon, — which demolished the defence of Eastern Hungary. Meanwhile Kadan's left column had advanced through Transylvania and passed the Körös and Theiss; in the first days of April it advanced to the Danube, in the neighbourhood of Pest. Subutai had in the meantime arrived himself with the main central column, and the three columns of the central army were now together in position on the left bank of the Danube from Waitzen to Pest. But the Hungarian army with its German allies and Slavonic contingents had united at Pest, about 100,000 strong; and it was impossible for the Mongols to cross in the face of such a host. Accordingly Subutai began a retreat, drawing the enemy after him. He retired behind the Sajó, not far from the confluence of that river with the Theiss, — a central position on the route from Pest to Galicia, where he was in touch with his own base of operations near Unghvar and the Porta Rusciae. The Hungarians took up their position on the opposite bank in the plain of Mohi. By skilful tactics the Mongols surrounded their camp and cut them to pieces on April 11, two days after the northern army had gained the battle of Liegnitz.

It was wonderful how punctually and effectually the arrangements of the commander were carried out in operations extending from the Lower Vistula to Transylvania. Such a campaign was quite beyond the power of any European army of the time; and it was beyond the vision of any European commander. There was no general in Europe, from Frederick II. downward, who was not a tiro in strategy compared to Subutai. It should also be noticed that the Mongols embarked upon the enterprise, with full knowledge of the political situation of Hungary and the condition of Poland; they had taken care to inform themselves by a well-organised system of spies: on the other hand, the Hungarians and Christian powers, like childish Barbarians, knew hardly anything about their enemies.

The foregoing summary is founded on the excellent study of G. Strakosch-Grassmann, Der Einfall der Mongolen, in Mitteleuropa in den Jahren 1241 und 1242, 1893, and the vivid account of L. Cahun, in his Introduction à l'Histoire de l'Asie, p. 352 sqq. The chief defect in Strakosch-Grassmann's book is that he does not give to Subutai his proper place. The important Chinese biography of Subutai is translated in the first vol. of Bretschneider's Mediæval Researches from Eastern Asiatic Sources, 1888. All the western authorities have been carefully studied and analysed by Strakosch-Grassmann. (The account of the Mongol campaigns in Köhler's Die Entwicklung des Kriegswesens und der Kriegführung in der Ritterzeit, vol. 3, pt. 3, 1889, may also be compared.)